SEXTANT CONFERENCE

November-December 1943

PAPERS

AND

MINUTES OF MEETINGS
SEXTANT AND EUREKA CONFERENCES

EDITED AND PUBLISHED BY THE

OFFICE, U. S. SECRETARY
OFFICE OF THE COMBINED CHIEFS OF STAFF

1943

Published by Books Express Publishing
Copyright © Books Express, 2011
ISBN 978-1-78039-486-2

Books Express publications are available from all good retail
and online booksellers. For publishing proposals and direct
ordering please contact us at: info@books-express.com

TABLE OF CONTENTS

PAPERS

TABLE OF CONTENTS

PAPERS

TABLE OF CONTENTS

PAPERS

TABLE OF CONTENTS

PAPERS

TABLE OF CONTENTS

MINUTES

PAGE

TABLE OF CONTENTS

MINUTES

TABLE OF CONTENTS

MINUTES

TABLE OF CONTENTS

MINUTES

TABLE OF CONTENTS

MINUTES

C.C.S. 270/13 and 270/14

USE OF FACILITIES IN THE AZORES BY U.S. AIRCRAFT

Reference:

CCS 138th Meeting, Item 6

In reply to a memorandum from the British Chiefs of Staff (C.C.S. 270/12) which outlined a formula for operational control in the Azores, the United States Chiefs of Staff (C.C.S. 270/13, 6 December 1943) noted that consideration is being deferred. They suggested steps to expedite an early completion of Lagens Field. The British Chiefs of Staff (C.C.S. 270/14, 6 December 1943) outlined formulae for the development of facilities in the Azores.

C.C.S. 270/13 and C.C.S. 270/14 were considered by the Combined Chiefs of Staff in their 138th Meeting. They approved C.C.S. 270/14 with the elimination of the last sentence of paragraph 4 and agreed that details regarding the use of the Azores facilities by United States Army Air Forces should be settled directly between General Arnold and Air Chief Marshal Portal.

C.C.S. 270/13   6 December 1943

COMBINED CHIEFS OF STAFF

USE OF FACILITIES IN THE AZORES BY U.S. AIRCRAFT

Memorandum by the United States Chiefs of Staff

1. Although the United States Chiefs of Staff have noted the memorandum from the British Chiefs of Staff (C.C.S. 270/12), dated 3 December 1943, it is considered necessary to defer its consideration until more detailed reports and recommendations are available from such sources as the U.S. Army-Navy Reconnaissance Party in the Azores, the Air Ministry Officers now at Lagens Field, Terceira, the Air Transport Command, A.A.F., and the Transport Command, R.A.F.

2. Whatever decisions may be reached concerning the future extent, nature, and control of U.S. and British anti-submarine and in transit aircraft operations in the Azores, it is apparent that the expansion, completion, and maximum possible use of Lagens Field are matters of urgency. In order to render all possible assistance in the early completion of Lagens Field and to maintain U.S. anti-submarine, ferried, and transport aircraft operations, it is proposed to send appropriate U.S. construction, communications, meteorological and maintenance material and equipment, supplies, and personnel to Terceira on the first possible convoy. The United States Chiefs of Staff have been advised by representatives of the United States in Lisbon that Dr. Antonio Salazar, Premier of the Portuguese Government, has replied favorably to questions regarding this procedure.

C.C.S. 270/14   6 December 1943

COMBINED CHIEFS OF STAFF

DEVELOPMENT OF FACILITIES IN THE AZORES

Memorandum by the British Chiefs of Staff

1. Reports from Lisbon indicate that, provided the U.S. are prepared to work under British cover, they will be able to obtain all the essential facilities in the Azores they require for the prosecution of the war.

2. As regards U. S. operational facilities at Lagens, we would suggest that a formula on the following lines might be acceptable to the Portuguese Government. They might be informed that American operational units in the Azores would be on loan to H.M.G. operating under the command of a British officer from a base under British control.

3. As regards transit facilities, we recommend that we should await the outcome of Dr. Salazar's consideration of the American proposal that the U.S. should construct an aerodrome on Santa Maria on behalf of the Portuguese Government. If this is unfavorable, as it may be in view of Dr. Salazar's insistence on retaining the framework and principles of the British agreement, the British should then ask for authority to construct an aerodrome and should use American material and assistance under British cover.

4. The formula we would suggest for American transit aircraft would be that aircraft in transit through the Azores are controlled by British Air Transport Command. The second airfield, when constructed, would be under British Command, and aircraft using it would fulfill the same conditions as those using Lagens.

5. In any case the first step would be a survey of Santa Maria which could be done ostensibly by the British, but with the assistance of the four American officers who remained behind in Terceira, pending further instructions, after completion of work by American survey party recently in that island.

6. We do not foresee any requirements for two B-24 squadrons in the Azores, or, in fact, for two American squadrons of any type. Our requirement is a total of three squadrons of which two should be British squadrons, and we prefer to retain the two Fortress squadrons now at Terceira. We recommend that the third squadron should be an American B-24 squadron, which would replace the Hudsons now in the Azores. If this is agreed, we could also make the point to Dr. Salazar that the majority of operational units would be British and all under British command.

C.C.S. 300/2

ESTIMATE OF ENEMY SITUATION, 1944—PACIFIC-FAR EAST

Reference:

CCS 128th Meeting, Item 3

C.C.S. 300/2 was circulated for the information of the Combined Chiefs of Staff and as a basis of discussion at *SEXTANT*.

C.C.S. 300/2   18 November 1943

COMBINED CHIEFS OF STAFF

ESTIMATE OF ENEMY SITUATION, 1944—PACIFIC-FAR EAST

Memorandum by the United States Chiefs of Staff

The United States Chiefs of Staff submit herewith an estimate of the enemy situation, 1943-44, Pacific-Far East area for information of the Combined Chiefs of Staff at the *SEXTANT* Conference.

ENCLOSURE

ESTIMATE OF ENEMY SITUATION, 1944—PACIFIC-FAR EAST
(As of 1 November 1943)

THE PROBLEM

1. To estimate the enemy situation in the Pacific-Far East, 1944, with due regard to Soviet and Chinese capabilities and intentions.

DISCUSSION AND CONCLUSIONS

2. We do not feel it practicable to attempt a summarization of the enemy situation in the Pacific-Far East as projected through 1944. Such a condensation, in our opinion, would inevitably result in incomplete treatment of factors essential to the over-all picture. Our view of the situation, 1944, is therefore attached as Appendix "A," to which reference is hereby made.

3. As of 1 November 1943, we estimate Japanese intentions in the Far East, 1944, as follows:

a. General. Japan will probably remain on the strategic defensive unless convinced that the U.S.S.R. has decided to attack her or to grant to the other United Nations the use of Siberian air bases. In such an event Japan would attack the Soviet Union. It is probable, however, that Japan will assume the tactical offensive whenever she considers it necessary, and it may be expected that Japan will initiate local offensive actions to forestall operations by the United Nations in Burma and to prevent the establishment of air bases by the United Nations in China. Japan will take full advantage of any breathing spell permitted her by Allied inactivity to strengthen her defensive cordon with installations of all types in order to make Allied advance most costly in time and casualties.

b. North Pacific. We believe that Japan will continue to strengthen her defenses in the Kuriles and Hokkaido, but is not likely to depart from the defensive except in case of war with the Soviet Union.

c. Manchuria. We believe that Japan will continue to seek to avoid war with the U.S.S.R. in all circumstances except as already mentioned above.

She will continue to balance Soviet strength in Siberia, reducing her forces in Manchuria only in case of necessity.

d. China (including Yunnan). Although Japan will continue to seek a satisfactory solution in China by political means, chances of success have deteriorated since the Moscow conference. We believe that she will undertake decisive military operations only to prevent the United Nations from establishing offensive air bases for action against her vital installations.

e. Burma and Southeast Asia. We believe that Japan will seek to maintain her present position in Burma and Southeast Asia, devoting especial attention to Burma, while extending her efforts when necessary to prevent large scale reinforcements and supplies reaching China.

f. Southwest and Central Pacific. We believe that Japan will remain on the strategic defensive, continuing her efforts to build up her local defensive forces and facilities and her naval striking force.

4. Our estimate of Japanese intentions, as set out in paragraph 3 above, is in part based upon our beliefs as to Soviet and Chinese capabilities and intentions, which are attached as Appendix "B" and Appendix "C."

APPENDIX "A"

ESTIMATE OF ENEMY SITUATION, 1944—PACIFIC-FAR EAST
(As of 1 November 1943)

1. *BASIC FACTORS IN THE JAPANESE SITUATION*

a. Objectives. Japan's basic objective is to establish undisputed control of an area in East Asia and the Western Pacific which shall be militarily secure and as nearly self-sufficient economically as possible. The area now occupied by her approximates the territorial requirements of this objective but is deficient in three respects, as follows: (1) the possession of eastern *Siberia* by a latently hostile power; (2) the existence in *China* of unoccupied areas within bombing range of Japan and of important Japanese lines of communication; and (3) the presence of United Nations forces in the Japanese defensive perimeter in the *Melanesia* area. Other territories beyond the limits of present occupation may be objects of ultimate Japanese aspiration, but only those specified are essential to the immediate basic objective.

b. Relationship to the Axis. Japan's connection with the Axis is a matter of expediency only. Her action will be coordinated with that of Germany only in so far as she estimates that such coordination will contribute to the realization of her basic objective.

c. Relations with the U.S.S.R. There exists between the U.S.S.R. and Japan a basic conflict of interest. Japan cannot enjoy complete strategic security without gaining control of the eastern region of Siberia. The U.S.S.R. is determined to hold that region, the strategic security of which requires the ultimate expulsion of Japan from the mainland of Asia and from southern Sakhalin. For the present, however, both the U.S.S.R. and Japan desire to avoid war with each other in order to be free to direct their efforts against their respective enemies.

d. Relations with subject peoples. Wherever circumstances allow, Japan's policy is to establish nominally independent, but actually controlled, national governments. This policy fits in with two powerful propaganda themes: (1) "Asia for the Asiatics"; (2) the "Co-Prosperity Sphere," ostensibly a cooperative project.

Appendix "A"

Japan has recognized the "independence" of *China*, as represented by the Nanking puppet government, and has sought to enlist Chinese nationalism in support of that regime by surrendering to it various foreign concessions, notably those at Shanghai. She has granted "independence" to *Burma* and the *Philippines*, thereby seeking to enlist the relatively developed nationalism of those countries in her favor. She has hinted that other occupied areas, e.g., *Java*, may receive similar grants of independence. *Thailand* has been rewarded for cooperation by the cession of bits of neighboring territory to which she had some pretensions. By such policies, Japan hopes to strengthen somewhat her position among the subject peoples.

e. Strategic and economic position. Although the strategic initiative has passed from Japan to the United Nations, a far-flung perimeter of defense positions must be penetrated before areas of great strategic or economic importance to Japan are subject to attack. Within this empire, Japan is practically self-sufficient except for textiles. Furthermore, Japan, by stockpiling materials from the Outer Zone and by pursuing a policy of developing resources within the Inner Zone wherever possible, has obtained within the Inner Zone a high degree of short range self-sufficiency in most of the essential materials of war. However, the loss of Sumatra and Borneo would seriously impair Japan's oil position, and loss of the Philippines would seriously impair her ferro-alloys position. Her manufacturing facilities, located mainly in Japan proper and in Manchuria, are accessible only to air attack. Meanwhile, the expansion of war production capacity undertaken in recent years will bear fruit in growing rates of output. For certain critical items, however, growing output is unlikely to offset attrition (ships) or to do more than keep pace with losses (planes). Japan should expect that ultimately greatly superior forces can be directed against her, but she will continue to hope that the United Nations will hesitate to face the tremendous logistical problems, or pay the price in lives, involved in an invasion of Japan proper.

f. Psychology and morale. The Japanese, traditionally, are a close-knit family whose broad characteristics are a toughness of fibre and a fatalistic singleness of purpose. They have been taught that they are of divine origin and that the Emperor is directly descended from the god-founder of the nation. They are taught that the Japanese are divinely and infallibly guided towards the establishment of a new world order dominated by Japan.

To attain this goal the Japanese soldier is taught to give blind obedience and to regard death in the service of the Emperor as an honor.

Appendix "A"

10

He is told that he is invincible and that to show weakness or to surrender is to accept disgrace.

As a result of these teachings, the morale of the Japanese populace, and especially of the armed forces, remains high in spite of recent reverses. As much of popular morale is, however, based upon the theory of invincibility, a series of sharp defeats when and if brought home to them will tend to confuse and bewilder the people as a whole.

In contrast with the broad mass of the people, real power in Japan rests in the hands of small groups of leaders capable of manipulating the symbols of emperor-worship for their own self-interest. An early collapse of Germany would have a tremendously depressing effect upon such leaders. This, combined with ever increasing United Nations pressure and approach to the homeland, might conceivably bring about a re-shuffle of the ruling cliques followed by an attempt to secure a negotiated peace.

g. Propaganda. Official propaganda on the home front has shifted from that of the self-assured offensive to propaganda of the defensive, and determination to fight for existence is replacing exaltation in victory. The potential of the United Nations is admitted to be high, and the government has announced its intention to prepare for the defense of the capital and the production centers of the homeland. The government is also preparing the Japanese people for more serious German reverses in Europe. Japanese withdrawals are admitted, and it is implied that the Japanese have finished winning independence for other Asiatic countries and now must prepare to defend their own islands from frontal attack.

2. *THE EXISTING OVER-ALL SITUATION*

a. Military strength. We estimate the present strength of her armed forces to be as follows: (1) *Naval,* 11 battleships, 7 aircraft carriers, 5 auxiliary aircraft carriers, 14 heavy cruisers, 18 light cruisers, 78 destroyers, 89 submarines. (2) *Air,* 1,660 fighters, 1,770 bombers, 490 float planes and 300 other types. Of the total, 110 fighters and 130 bombers, and 185 float planes are ship-based. In addition to the above total of 4,220 U.E. combat aircraft there are some 1,375 combat type aircraft engaged in advanced operational training. (3) *Ground,* a total ground strength of 2,500,000 representing approximately 110 equivalent divisions, which include 65 infantry divisions, 18 independent mixed brigades, 1 infantry brigade, 3 cavalry brigades, 20 tank regiments, 13 border garrisons, 17 independent garrisons and other independent units. (4) *Totaling* in round numbers 3,500,000 men (exclusive of Puppet Troops).

Puppet Troops. There are some 330,000 Manchurian troops and more than 420,000 Nanking puppet troops. For the most part, both forces are organized into small garrison units lacking in automatic weapons and artillery. Some Manchurian combat divisions exist, and similar Nanking divisions are said to be forming (strength about 6,000 per division), but it is doubtful whether Japan can provide for them normal equipment in heavier weapons in view of her own shortages in those categories. Japan has found Nanking troops particularly unreliable in the past.

Burmese and other puppet forces are so small as to be inconsequential.

b. Positional strength. Japan is now on the strategic defensive. Her control of Burma, Malaya, the Netherlands Indies, Pacific islands and parts of China keeps United Nations forces at a distance too great for delivery of effective blows against Japan itself and prevents effective development and use of the Chinese war potential. Thus Japan's position, facing United Nations forces from the North Pacific around to India, is one of great natural strength. At this time, her position in China is secure because of the present inability of either China or the other United Nations to mount large-scale operations there. Soviet commitments in Europe and Japanese strength in Manchuria insure for the time being the security of Japan's northern flank, Japan is able at present to direct her maximum effort toward building up her economic and military strength.

c. Limitations on Japanese Power

(1) *Shipping.* Japan's defensive position requires secure and adequate ocean transport over long lines of communication. The Japanese shipping situation has become acute, with her total tonnage being further reduced by sinkings in excess of total new construction. We estimate that 50-60% of her total tonnage is committed to maintaining her military forces outside the homeland and that the remainder is used primarily to maintain the essential part of her war economy. From this latter bracket some tonnage might still be found for new operations by diverting it from trade, and, provided such diversions were temporary, this would not necessarily have serious effects on Japan's capacity to wage war. Since, however, Japan's rate of building, though on the increase, cannot keep pace even with the present rate of sinkings, she

Appendix "A"

would be reluctant to risk adding further to her shipping commitments. Although attempts are being made to improve the position by building a large number of small and medium-size wooden ships, the general shipping position is becoming increasingly difficult and may well become precarious in 1944. The situation in regard to tankers is also acute. Japan is attempting to meet a deficiency in this respect by continuing to fit out dry-cargo ships for use as oil carriers.

(2) *Air requirements.* Until recently Japan has not only been able to maintain her over-all air strength at approximately the same total figure but has kept her allocated air strength along the perimeter in reasonable balance with her requirements. At present, however, indications point to such a rapid attrition in the Melanesian area that she is having difficulty in replacing losses. We believe that as United Nations pressure increases along the outer defense frontier, she will be unable to maintain sufficient strength to offer effective resistance at all points under attack. Assuming that the United Nations carry out the agreed program for 1944, we are of the opinion that Japan's defensive air requirements will preclude the possibility of her engaging in any offensive operation requiring heavy air support.

(3) *Naval requirements.* Japan cannot afford to risk large commitments of naval strength except for the defense of vital areas. Her extended lines of communication already entail a large commitment of naval strength for the protection of essential shipping. Their further extension, or indecisive action entailing heavy attrition, might well be unacceptable.

(4) *Military requirements.* A large proportion of Japanese ground forces is required for occupational duties and for concentration in Manchuria to balance Soviet forces in Siberia. Japan, however, has ample ground forces for any probable combat requirements, inasmuch as the insular character of much of the occupied area and the topography of New Guinea, the Indo-Burmese frontier and China limit the scale of ground operations in those areas. Developments of the last few months indicate the necessity of using her superiority in ground forces to compensate for her relative inferiority in naval and air forces. Her ability to move her strategic reserve is restricted by availability of shipping.

Appendix "A"

13

3. *THE EXISTING LOCAL SITUATION*

a. North Pacific. Japan is strengthening the fortifications and garrisons on her "Northern Fortress" (Shimushu and Paramushiru), and we believe that preparations are being made for a determined defense in the Kuriles.

b. Manchuria. Japanese ground forces in Manchuria probably balance the Soviet ground forces in Eastern Siberia-Outer Mongolia, but Japanese air strength is believed to be relatively inferior. Japan has the advantage in strategic position, equipment, and supply but is deterred from aggression by respect for Soviet armed forces and reluctance to commit herself further while her army is actively engaged in other areas. Japan is also apprehensive of vulnerability to bombing and submarine attack and fears the probability that in the event of war between Japan and the U.S.S.R., the United States would utilize air bases in Siberia for direct attacks on Japan.

c. China (except Yunnan). The front has been largely stabilized for years, with the Japanese in possession of the country's principal productive areas and communications lines. The Japanese are deterred from further expansion primarily by logistical difficulties and secondarily by Chinese resistance. On occasion the Japanese engage in minor offensive operations to season inexperienced troops and accomplish limited objectives such as the temporary denial of facilities to the Chinese. Although nominally in overwhelming numerical strength, the Chinese forces are at present so poorly equipped, supplied, fed, and trained that they are unable to prevent these forays or to undertake other than local action. This Chinese military weakness springs in large part from China's generally anemic condition, which has resulted from loss of productive areas, disruption of internal communications, isolation from outside support, and war-weariness.

d. Yunnan. Active operations have recently been launched by the Japanese along the Salween River. We believe these operations are to strengthen the Japanese position along the Burma frontier in anticipation of a United Nations increase in activity in that area.

e. Burma. The wet monsoon very greatly hinders major operations from May to October. Recently the Japanese have been increasing their ground and air forces in Burma. It may be that the supply to these forces overland via Indochina and Thailand may be increased considerably in the near future.

Appendix "A"

14

f. Southwest Pacific. The ground and air strength in the Timor-Inner Seas area and New Guinea-Bismarcks area appears to be defensive in character. Because of recent United Nations successes in this area, Japan, in order to maintain her defensive position has been forced to increase her strength by one division over and above replacements for her combat losses. Due to extreme losses in this area, it now appears that she is having difficulty in maintaining the air strength disposed heretofore.

g. Central Pacific. At present Japan bases 50-60% of her naval strength at Truk. The total air strength of this area has been increasing, particularly in the Marshalls and Gilberts.

4. *STRATEGIC RESERVES*

a. Air. We believe no strategic reserve exists as such. Although Japan's staging facilities are sufficiently developed to enable her to fly even fighter planes to practically any part of her position, theoretically allowing the quick reinforcement of any threatened front, there are indications that simultaneous pressure on several fronts would prevent substantial reinforcements being sent to more than one area.

b. Naval. Normally Japan maintains her battleship and carrier strength in home waters and at Truk, shifting the center of gravity according to circumstances. A formidable striking force, which can reach any threatened point of the defensive perimeter in from 6-9 days, can be quickly assembled in either of these central areas. However, destroyer shortage is becoming critical.

c. Ground. Surplus ground strength in Central China constitutes Japan's initial reserve. If hard pressed, she can also draw surplus strength from Japan and North China and in extremity from Manchuria.

5. *PROSPECTIVE DEVELOPMENTS THROUGH 1944*

a. Air strength. Although Japanese aircraft production is expected to continue to increase gradually during the remainder of 1943 and during 1944, attrition will probably keep pace with and may even exceed this increased production.

b. Naval strength. Disregarding attrition, we estimate that Japanese naval strength should increase as a result of new construction to the following totals:

Appendix "A"

	Battle-ships	Air-craft Car.	Aux. Air-craft Car.	Heavy Cruis-ers	Light Cruis-ers	Des-troy-ers	Subma-rines
1 Nov. 43	11	7	5	14	18	78	89
1 Jan. 44	12	8	5	14	18	85	97
1 June 44	12	10	6	15	19	95	113
1 Jan. 45	13	14	7	16	20	105	130

c. *Ground strength.* We expect that by the end of 1944 the strength of the Japanese army will have increased to 2,750,000, comprising approximately 120 equivalent divisions (including 73 infantry divisions and 14 independent mixed brigades, 3 cavalry brigades, and 24 tank regiments, 20 independent garrisons, and 13 border garrisons).

d. *Shipping.* Despite Japan's strenuous shipbuilding efforts, estimates of the rate of loss and rate of construction of steel ships indicate that the Japanese may suffer a net loss of 1,500,000 gross registered tons of steel operating tonnage from 1 November 1943 to the end of 1944. However, construction of wooden vessels and further substitution of land transport may offset a part of the estimated net loss of steel ships.

e. *War production.* Assuming that Japan retains control of the productive areas now under occupation, that shipments by sea can be maintained, and that there be no effective bombing of Japanese industry or land transportation, Japan's production of critical *finished war goods* may increase materially in 1944 as compared with 1943. *Heavy industrial production as a whole*, however, is not expected to show great gains in 1944, chiefly because steel output seems unlikely to rise by more than a few percent. The steady development of economically unprofitable but strategically important resources of Japan proper and immediately adjacent areas and the use of stock piles will make it possible for Japan's war industry to continue for about two years at approximately its present rate of consumption of raw materials (except for oil, chromite, and possibly lead and zinc), even if cut off from access to resources south of the Yangtze River.

Appendix "A"

APPENDIX "B"

U.S.S.R. CAPABILITIES AND INTENTIONS IN THE FAR EAST

1. *STRENGTH*

We estimate that total Soviet air strength east of Lake Baikal consists of some 2,000 tactical aircraft. Of these, some 1,200 are believed to be organized into operational squadrons. This force is apparently disposed on the southern border of Soviet-controlled territory from Ulan Bator to Vladivostok. Existing airfields are believed adequate for flexible operation.

Naval strength is estimated to consist of one light cruiser, 9 destroyers, 6 torpedo boats, 60 submarines, 60 motor torpedo boats, and a number of assorted small craft of no combatant value. There are believed to be sufficient bases available for this force.

The ground strength east of Lake Baikal is estimated to total some 660,000 men divided into units as follows:

> 20 infantry divisions (15,000 men each)
>
> 11 cavalry divisions (6,600 men each)
>
> 1 mountain division (9,000 men)
>
> 2 motorized divisions (7,000 men each)
>
> 13 tank brigades (2,000 men each)
>
> 5 motorized brigades (4,000 men each)
>
> 9 infantry brigades (4,000 men each)
>
> 1 composite brigade (5,000 men)
>
> Corps, army, line of communication, and other troops (180,000 men)

Pending the defeat of Germany, reinforcement is unlikely. Although these forces in the Far East are supposed to be self-sufficient, their local sources of supply are actually both limited and vulnerable. Support, in any case, would have to be delivered via a long, and in part exposed, line of communication.

Appendix "B"

2. CAPABILITIES

Offensively, the U.S.S.R. could scarcely hope for any success until her forces in the west have been released by the defeat of Germany or until after the other United Nations have gained access from the Pacific to the Sea of Okhotsk. Defensively the U.S.S.R. would probably be unable to prevent the isolation of the Maritime Provinces by the cutting of, or at least demolitions on, the Trans-Siberian Railroad. Holding operations, however, should be possible on present stored reserves for at least six months. Subsequent developments in the whole area would depend largely on the effectiveness of the assistance of the other United Nations.

3. INTENTIONS

Pending further information as to the results of the Moscow Conference, we estimate Soviet intentions as follows:

The U.S.S.R. is likely to intervene in the war against Japan at some stage, but not before the German menace to her has been removed. After that, she would be likely to intervene only when she reckoned that Japan could be defeated at small cost to her. It is unlikely that any arguments that we might bring forward, except substantial progress in our war against Japan, would greatly affect the timing of Soviet intervention. On the other hand, we believe that large-scale hostilities between the United States and Japan in the Northwest Pacific would make the Soviet Union's present neutrality in the Far East increasingly difficult to maintain.

Appendix "B"

APPENDIX "C"

CHINESE CAPABILITIES AND INTENTIONS

1. *STRENGTH*

The Chinese active army has a nominal strength of 320 infantry and 16 cavalry divisions, plus 30 independent infantry brigades. Infantry divisions average 7,000 each; cavalry divisions and infantry brigades average 3,000 each. The combat efficiency of the bulk of the force never was very high and it has deteriorated considerably since 1938. At the present time malnutrition and lack of medical attention are prevalent and have reduced the combat potential of many units to a very low point. Armament consists almost wholly of infantry weapons. Such heavy material as is available is inadequate and is largely obsolete. The augmentation of this armament to any appreciable degree by the United Nations will not be possible until capacity of transport into China is greatly increased. We feel that, at most, not more than one-fifth of the Chinese Army is currently capable of sustained defensive operations and then only with effective air support; we believe that with the possible exception of the American-trained Chinese divisions, no large number of troops can be expected to undertake more than very limited objective offensive operations, at the present time.

Chinese guerrillas, whose strength is estimated to be 600,000 part-time troops, have proved of value. In recent months, they have done the bulk of the fighting against the Japanese. They share with the regular divisions credit for retaining substantial Japanese occupational forces in China.

2. *CAPABILITIES*

If given adequate United Nations air support, China might be able to defend her major strategic areas against a Japanese offensive and might be able to execute a very limited objective offensive.

3. *INTENTIONS*

The Chinese probably intend to remain generally on the defensive, pending the re-equipping and training of their army for offensive action at a later date.

Appendix "C"

C.C.S. 300/3

ESTIMATE OF ENEMY SITUATION, 1944—EUROPE

Reference:

CCS 131st Meeting, Item 4A

C.C.S. 300/3 was circulated for the information of the Combined Chiefs of Staff and as a basis for discussion at *SEXTANT*.

C.C.S. 300/3   18 November 1943

COMBINED CHIEFS OF STAFF

ESTIMATE OF ENEMY SITUATION, 1944—EUROPE

Memorandum by the United States Chiefs of Staff

The United States Chiefs of Staff submit herewith an estimate of the enemy situation, 1944—Europe, for information of the Combined Chiefs of Staff at the *SEXTANT* Conference.

E N C L O S U R E

ESTIMATE OF ENEMY SITUATION, 1944—EUROPE
(As of 1 November 1943)

THE PROBLEM

1. To prepare an estimate of the enemy situation, 1944 — Europe.

SUMMARY OF THE EXISTING SITUATION (1 November 1943)

2. Germany is now under severe strain, and her general situation is deteriorating. Her strength remains formidable, however, and, granted relief from pressure, she still has the power of recuperation.

Germany is now on the defensive on all fronts. She has no decisive offensive capabilities. Her military resources are inadequate to meet all of her defensive requirements. The German Air Force is unable to ward off destructive Allied strategic bombing. Its concentration to resist such bombing leaves Germany's land fronts in the east and south inadequately supported. On both of these fronts the German Army has been compelled to yield considerable ground, at the sacrifice of military, economic, political, and psychological interests, in order to conserve its strength for a final decisive conflict. The German

Navy has been unable to prevent the build-up of Allied offensive forces within striking distance of the Continent.

The bomber offensive is increasingly destructive of German air strength, industrial capacity, and morale. Reserves of fit German manpower being now exhausted, continued heavy casualties must cause either a decrease in strength or a decline in quality in the German Army. The prospect is such as to cause her allies to seek means of escape, to encourage renewed resistance in occupied areas, and to impair her own morale. Signs of deterioration in her political structure are beginning to be discernible.

Nevertheless, Germany's armed forces are still strong, experienced, and willing to fight hard. By reason of past conquests, she is still able to fight well in advance of her vital areas (except in the air). Her political structure is designed to withstand internal strain. Given any relief from pressure, she has the power of recovery.

GERMANY'S MOST PROBABLE COURSES OF ACTION

3. We conclude that Germany's most probable courses of action (*a* and *b* to be followed concurrently) are:

   a. To stand on the strategic defensive. This includes:

   (1) Continuation of the war against shipping.

   (2) Continued direction of her primary air effort to defense against the bomber offensive.

   (3) An intention to counterattack to destroy or expel any hostile force entering her defensive perimeter.

   (4) A probable intention to yield outlying occupied territory only under pressure and with maximum practicable delaying action.

   b. To seek a negotiated peace by psychological and political means. This includes continuation of her efforts to divide her principal enemies.

   c. To sue for peace only after it has been proved impossible to achieve either a negotiated peace or a stalemate.

FORECAST FOR 1944

4. Our forecast for 1944, so far as we are now able to make one, is that:

a. The German war against shipping will continue, but probably with diminishing effect.

b. The bomber offensive against Germany will have cumulative effect destructive of the German fighter force, industrial capacity, and morale. It will create conditions within Germany conducive to complete military defeat.

c. The final German defensive line in the east appears to be marked by the rivers Dniester-(Polish) Bug-Niemen. There they must stand and give decisive battle since further withdrawal would uncover vital areas.

d. Germany will continue to resist as long as hope persists that thereby she may gain a stalemate or negotiated peace. When that hope fails, the High Command may assume control in order to halt destruction prejudicial to Germany's eventual recovery. Unmistakable signs of German collapse will not become apparent until the end of resistance is close at hand; when that point has been reached, disintegration will proceed with startling rapidity.

e. Germany's allies (Hungary, Rumania, Bulgaria, Finland) will come come to terms whenever forced to bear the brunt of direct and sustained attack or whenever relieved of fear of Germany or of the U.S.S.R.

APPENDIX

ESTIMATE OF ENEMY SITUATION, 1944—EUROPE

(As of 1 November 1943)

1. *BASIC FACTORS IN THE EUROPEAN SITUATION*

a. Predominance of Germany. The enemy situation in Europe must be estimated in terms of the German situation. Hungary, Rumania, Bulgaria, and Finland are merely satellites of Germany and, to a considerable degree, prisoners of circumstance. None of them could offer prolonged resistance without effective German support; any of them would now disassociate itself from Germany if it could do so without fear of Germany or of the U.S.S.R.

b. Germany's Basic Task is now to defend "Festung Europa,"* with such assistance as she can extort from satellite and occupied countries. We believe that her leaders now realize that they cannot win the military victory, but that they still hope that they may be able to avert complete defeat by making the operations of the United Nations to that end so costly as to induce one or more of them to conclude some type of negotiated peace. These hopes provide a basis for continued resistance.

*c. "Festung Europa."** Germany now controls, directly or indirectly, all of continental Europe west of the Soviet front, except part of Italy and the territories of five neutral states (Sweden, Switzerland, Spain, Portugal, and Turkey). This control extends to include the Baltic and Aegean Seas and the Mediterranean islands of Crete and Rhodes. This whole area is encircled by blockade but contains within itself the essentials of a military self-sufficiency.

The western and southern faces of this position are now subject to invasion only by difficult amphibious attack or through mountainous terrain. The eastern face is, however, without clear natural definition. For that reason, and because of the immense forces deployed by the U.S.S.R., the Eastern Front must continue to be Germany's chief preoccupation in land operations.

---

* As herein conceived, "Festung Europa" consists of an essential core (roughly Germany itself, most of Poland, Hungary, and Rumania), surrounded by outer defensive and auxiliary areas.

Despite the best efforts of German propaganda and the employment of large occupational forces, resistance (active or passive) by the subject peoples within "Festung Europa" continues to increase.

2. *THE EXISTING OVER-ALL SITUATION*

a. Ground Forces. European Axis armies now (1 November 1943) comprise 433 combat divisions—315 German, 29 Rumanian, 37 Hungarian, 21 Bulgarian, 15 Finnish, 8 Croat, 6 Slovak, and the equivalent of 2 Italian divisions. Only 258 German divisions and the 7 depleted Rumanian divisions in the Crimea could, however, be counted on for front line service.

The German Army has been brought to such strength only by lowering the physical standards, combing out industrial personnel hitherto deferred, and enlisting considerable numbers of non-Germans. In consequence, the average quality of German divisions has declined. Assuming a continuation of losses at current rates, Germany must either permit the size of her armed forces to decrease or see their quality deteriorate further.

Morale among the German ground forces until lately has been generally excellent, but among the satellite forces it has been only good to fair. Further reverses may produce a lowering of morale during 1944.

b. Air Forces. The total first-line strength of the German Air Force (29 October 1943) is approximately 5,325 U.E. aircraft. The high proportion of fighters (2,550) to bombers (2,300) and other types (475) is indicative of the continued emphasis upon defensive capabilities at the expense of offensive. The rate of production has recently declined as a result principally of bombing attacks, bringing it into approximate balance with the rate of attrition. If the attrition rate can be maintained and further reduction in the rate of production can be effected by increased bombing attacks, a downward trend in over-all strength would promptly result, for no substantial stored reserves of aircraft exist to serve as a cushion.

Owing largely to the shortage of trained crews, the efficiency of the long-range bomber force continues to be low. In equipment, some improvement in present types continues, but no important production of radically new types is expected. In defense against daylight bombing attacks and in offensive operations against shipping, some tactical and technical improvements have been made, particularly in the use of rocket projectiles and radio-controlled bombs, and further improvement may probably be expected. Little, if any, deterioration of air force morale is apparent.

We believe that the remnants of the Italian Air Force in German hands have little, if any, present or potential value. Satellite air strength is negligible except for that of Rumania, which has about 200 aircraft of modern type, half of which are on the southern section of the Eastern Front. Dependent as the satellite air forces are upon German production, they are unlikely to receive any substantial increase in first-line equipment.

c. Naval Forces

(1) *Submarines.* Germany now (1 November 1943) possesses around 400 German-built submarines, of which about 200 are attached to the operating forces. Of the ex-Italian submarines a few in use as supply vessels or blockade runners may be operational but probably no others. None of the ex-French submarines are believed to be operational.

The rate of completion of new submarines (all German-built) may be expected to continue at approximately 20 a month.

Germany is encountering great difficulty in manning submarines. The quality and morale of the personnel have on the average declined and in some instances are very low, but there are no reliable indications that any general breakdown of morale is imminent.

(2) *Surface Vessels (effective combatant types — 1 November 1943).* The major units are 2 battleships, 2 pocket battleships, 2 heavy cruisers, and 4 light cruisers. Of these, the battleships *TIRPITZ* (damaged to an unknown extent) and *SCHARNHORST* are in northern Norwegian waters; the rest are in the Baltic with their effectiveness probably much reduced by the transfer of experienced personnel to submarines. (The aircraft carrier *GRAF ZEPPELIN* is not operational.) Some 30 destroyers and 40 torpedo boats are in waters from the Bay of Biscay northward (including the Baltic). In service in Mediterranean waters are perhaps 2 destroyers and 3 torpedo boats in the Western Basin and perhaps 5 destroyers and torpedo boats in the Aegean (all ex-French or ex-Italian); as many as 40 more of such light units might be placed in service but no major units.

New construction in progress consists of about 18 destroyers and possibly two ex-Netherlands light cruisers.

We believe that morale is low in the major units but is reasonably high in the light forces.

d. Manpower. German reserves of combat manpower (physically fit German men aged 17-37) are by now exhausted. Future losses in that category can be replaced only from boys attaining age 17 and from recruitment of foreigners and over-age German men.

In contrast to the position in German combat manpower, large reserves of German men in the limited service categories and of foreign manpower still are available.

During the past year the civilian labor force in Germany has actually increased slightly in numbers, mainly as a result of compulsory recruitment of foreigners. It is, however, still 3,000,000 (8%) below the figure for May, 1939. It has been kept up, despite drafts of men for the armed services, by recruitment of foreigners, women, and substandard men. This change in composition has caused a decline of about 5 percent in per capita productivity, additional to the numerical decline previously noted.

e. War Economy

(1) *General.* The general level of German industrial production has declined probably 10 percent in recent months, principally because of Allied bombing. Other factors are the blockade, sabotage, and the general strain of war. The deterioration would have been greater had the Germans not achieved improvements in industrial efficiency and obtained additions to the labor force.

(2) *War Production.* Aircraft production and submarine construction facilities have been particular objects of air attack. Single-engine fighter production has been so reduced that it no longer exceeds attrition; submarine construction has fallen below attrition. Motor vehicle production also has failed to equal recent wastage rates. The production of anti-friction bearings has been so seriously interrupted that it is now believed to be inadequate to sustain the required flow of military equipment. With the exception of fighter aircraft, however, these losses may not be felt immediately on fighting fronts.

With respect to synthetic rubber, aircraft tires, and petroleum products, the protective cushion afforded by excess capacity has already been dangerously thinned or eliminated.

The production of anti-aircraft equipment has probably increased.

The German retreat in the east has brought a saving in rail transport of the order of 3 percent of total ton-miles. This eases the entire German rail situation and permits reallocations of materials and labor as between rail equipment and other products. There is also a saving of the several hundred thousand tons of steel required for repairs of Soviet railroads in 1942.

(3) *Civilian Economy.* Civilian economy in Germany is seriously strained. On top of the pre-war shortage, 15 percent of all dwellings in 43 cities subjected to Allied air attacks have been rendered uninhabitable, and three times that number have suffered damage requiring some emergency repair. Four and one-half million persons have been transferred from danger areas. This, in addition to the social dislocations involved, has placed a heavy burden on transportation. There is a severe shortage of most civilian goods, and services such as electric power and transportation have been greatly curtailed. The food situation is, however, reasonably satisfactory; and, except in heavily bombed areas, civilian living standards have been maintained at a tolerable level.

f. German Civilian Morale and Internal Political Situation. A popular feeling of intense war-weariness and discouragement exists in Germany as a result of the vanishing prospects of victory, the heavy damage and casualties inflicted by the Anglo-American bomber offensive, the heavy casualties on the Eastern Front, the reverses on that front and in North Africa and Italy, the defection of Italy, the comparative failure of the submarine campaign, the feeling that all the victories to date have accomplished nothing decisive while their achievement has drained Germany's strength, the long hours of work, and the uncomfortable, though not generally intolerable, living conditions. But the popular acceptance of the war's continuation is supported by deep fear of the consequences of surrender, which has been zealously fostered by propaganda.

Because of the ruthless and thorough methods employed to prevent the existence in Germany of any free political parties or other voluntary organizations except the churches, almost no opportunities exist for low popular morale to find effective expression in concerted action. The only change of leadership which therefore appears possible at an early date is one which might be engineered by army officers, supported by big industrialists and landowners. Such a change might, however, lead to a weakening or relaxation of the system of control and thereby make it less difficult for low popular morale to express itself in effective action.

Lacking channels of effective expression, low popular morale appears generally to be taking the form of numbness and apathy. For this reason the internal political situation appears today less precarious than it was, say, in August 1918.

Unmistakable signs of German collapse will probably not become apparent until the end of resistance is close at hand. We believe that the cumulative effect of the factors listed above will then cause disintegration to proceed with startling rapidity.

3. *THE SITUATION BY FRONTS—1 NOVEMBER 1943*

a. The War Against Shipping. Germany's war against ocean shipping has fallen far short of achieving its objective of preventing effective support from overseas of United Nations operations. It has, however, succeeded in delaying such support and limiting its scale, and its effects are still felt in such ways. Moreover, the Germans realize that as long as they continue their submarine attacks, or threaten them, on a serious scale, they will force the United Nations to devote to anti-submarine activities large amounts of manpower, energy, and materials which could advantageously be used for other war purposes and will prevent them from making the most efficient use of available shipping. We believe that the effectiveness of the war against shipping will not increase.

b. Strategic Air Operations. The current primary commitment of the German Air Force is defense against Allied strategic bombing. To this end, out of an over-all fighter strength of 2,422 in operational units, 1,686 are concentrated in Germany, the Low Countries, and France. In addition to established dispositions and installations for defense against bombing attacks from Great Britain, it has now become necessary to set up in southern Germany and Austria similar defenses against such attacks from Mediterranean bases. In order to meet these requirements, German air support of the Eastern and Mediterranean land fronts has been seriously curtailed.

Despite these efforts and sacrifices, the Germans have not succeeded in warding off the Allied air offensive, which continues to develop in weight of attack, range of penetration, and technical effectiveness. In addition to general destruction of German industrial capacity and dislocation of civilian life,* the German Air Force itself has suffered direct and indirect damage which tends to impair its ability to maintain the present scale of defense. Heavy combat losses have been inflicted on it, single-engine fighter production has been substantially reduced, the percentage of serviceability has been lowered, and the flow of replacements has been seriously interrupted. The growth of the German fighter force has been checked; attrition and production are now approximately in balance; and, if the attack is pressed, and resisted at current intensity, a decline in strength may be expected, opening the way to further progress in the effectiveness of the attack.

Assuming continued growth in the strength of the Allied air offensive, the results achieved may be expected to increase progressively. The cumulative effects may so weaken Germany's capacity for armed resistance as to accelerate greatly the collapse of her will to continue the conflict.

c. *Eastern Front (from Leningrad southward)*. During 1943 approximately two-thirds of Germany's ground strength has been committed to this front. The proportion of Germany's air strength so committed has been significantly less and has been steadily reduced to meet the increasing requirements of the Western and Mediterranean Fronts, thus facilitating the Soviet advance. German ground strength on the Eastern Front consists of 205 German and 14 satellite divisions of varying strength. Numerically, Soviet ground strength is to the German approximately as 3 to 2. Present air strengths may be compared as follows:

	Fighters	Bombers	Others
Germany	393	1,062†	237
U.S.S.R.	1,700	2,450	250

† Includes 90 Rumanian.

During 1943 Germany has surrendered the initiative to the U.S.S.R. and has accepted the necessity of yielding space under pressure in order to minimize losses. The Germans may have hoped that eventually the extension of Red communications and the shortening of their own would bring them to a position which could be held with reduced forces against weakened Red pressure. Thus they might gain greater freedom of action in meeting the requirements of 1944. However, the pressure developed and

---

* See paragraphs 2 *e* and 2 *f*, Appendix to C.C.S. 300/3.

maintained by the Red Army has exceeded German expectations; and German losses of men, material, and ground have been greater than were anticipated.

At present (1 November 1943) Red penetrations of the Dnieper Bend and the Nogai Steppe have rendered those areas untenable and German withdrawal from them is apparently in progress. The Crimea has been isolated, and may not be tenable for long.* In the Ukraine the Germans may well attempt delay in successive positions (e.g., Kremenchug-Krivoi Rog-lower Dnieper, and Cherkassy-Nikolaev), but no position suitable for a determined stand is apparent east of the general line Dniester River-Zhitomir-Pripet Marshes.

Between the Pripet Marshes and the Dvina River, the Germans will apparently seek to hold on the general line Dnieper River-Orsha-Vitebsk. Further north they may withdraw from the Leningrad-Novgorod area to the general line Vitebsk-Pskov-Narva.

The final German defensive line in the east appears to be marked by the rivers Dniester-(Polish) Bug-Niemen. There they must stand and give decisive battle, since further withdrawal would uncover vital areas.

d. Finland and Adjacent Norway. This front has long been quiet. Finnish strength is equivalent to 15 divisions, with 7 German divisions in northern Finland and adjacent Norway. The Soviet numerical superiority is as 3 to 2. Air strengths in the area may be compared as follows:

	Fighters	Bombers	Others
Germany	66	63	27
U.S.S.R.	100	50	50

A German withdrawal from before Leningrad would have psychological repercussions in Finland, but would not affect basically the military situation so long as the Germans remained in Estonia.

e. Norway and Denmark. In Norway (less the area adjacent to Finland) there are 11 German divisions; in Denmark, 5. Of these 16, only 6, in Norway,

---

* Axis naval forces in the Black Sea consist principally of 4 Rumanian destroyers, a few submarines, and some motor torpedo boats.

are offensive in type. German air strength in the area consists of 126 fighters, 42 bombers, and 45 other types. Two German battleships, one of which is damaged, and their accompanying light forces remain in north Norwegian waters.

f. Western Front. The coast from Brest to Den Helder has been well fortified in depth. Although various interior installations have been locally fortified, it is now believed that no prepared defensive line exists between the coast and the West Wall.

In France and the Low Countries there are 42 German divisions (including 10 training divisions). Seventeen of them are offensive in type, but only 11 of these are now fully effective. German air strength in the same area, less southern France, consists of 796 fighters, 267 bombers, and 30 other types.

g. Italy. We believe that from 22 to 25 German divisions are in Italy, all of them offensive in type. Twenty have been identified, of which 10 are panzer or panzer grenadier. Ten are at Rome or southward (3 panzer, 3 panzer grenadier, 2 infantry, 2 parachute). Five (2 panzer, 3 infantry) are engaged against Partisans in Venezia Julia, and a sixth (panzer grenadier) may be en route thither. The remaining identified divisions (4 infantry) are in the Po Valley and Tuscany and are considered as equivalent to the minimum occupational requirement for that area. In Italy elements of 4 Italian divisions are cooperating with the Germans, of which only one is actively engaged (against the Partisans in Venezia Julia).

German air strength in Italy and southern France consists of 132 fighters, 362 bombers, and 27 other types. It is, for the most part, held back in the north, German air support in central Italy having been relatively slight.

Since the topography in central Italy is well suited to defense against frontal attack, the Germans are now principally concerned lest their flanks be turned by amphibious operations. Their intention appears to be to engage in strong delaying actions in successive positions as long as possible and eventually to hold when equilibrium is established, probably north of Rome but south of the Po watershed. A counter offensive capability exists, however, and may be promptly exploited if a good opportunity is offered. For such a purpose ground strength could be drawn, not only from northern Italy, but also from France. The principal deterrent factor would be Allied air superiority.

h. Adriatic-Aegean Area. Axis ground strength in Yugoslavia, Albania, Greece, and the Aegean islands consists of 20 German, 8 Croat, 1 Serb, and 9 Bulgar divisions. Of these, only 14 German divisions are offensive in type. German air strength consists of 65 fighters, 199 bombers, and 63 other types. Naval strength in the Aegean consists only of few ex-Italian destroyers and torpedo boats and some motor torpedo boats.

Germany's vigorous reaction to Italian defection in this area indicates a determination to maintain her position there. The prompt seizure of the Adriatic ports and the islands of Corfu, Cephalonia, Rhodes, and Cos, has practically restored the front. The British still hold Leros and Samos. The Germans are sensitive to this penetration and attacks to recapture these islands are anticipated.

Axis occupational forces are stretched thin to make up for the disappearance of 30 Italian divisions. They are still able to hold important localities and routes of communication, but they are inadequate to suppress guerrilla activity and probably inadequate to hold the interior and resist invasion simultaneously.

i. Strategic Reserves. No strategic reserves exist as such. Relief and reinforcement are accomplished by transfer of units from one front to another according to circumstances. Since air strength is inadequate on all fronts, reinforcement of one is possible only at the sacrifice of less important interests on another. With respect to ground forces, it still remains possible to withdraw one or two divisions from any one front (except the Balkans) without undue risk, and several such withdrawals in combination may constitute an appreciable reinforcement at the point where they are needed, but it is no longer possible to withdraw any considerable number of divisions from any one front.

In France an apparent surplus of divisions over minimum defensive requirements exists. France is a notable training and reforming area, however, and consequently a number of the divisions there are not fully effective. They could nevertheless be of some use in extreme emergency. France is thus the principal source of possible reinforcements for other fronts.

4. *THE SITUATIONS IN THE SATELLITE COUNTRIES*

a. Hungary and Rumania. Because of the vital importance to her of Rumanian oil and of Hungarian lines of communication and oil, Germany will maintain a firm grip on both countries as long as possible. Each wishes to escape that grip but is prevented from surrendering or terminating its resistance principally by fear of German occupation. Each also fears the U.S.S.R. and the other, and Hungary also has reason to fear Yugoslavia and Czechoslovakia.

b. Bulgaria. The death of King Boris has as yet brought no significant political change, though future governments will find it harder to sustain a pro-German policy. The people of Bulgaria look to the U.S.S.R. for support, and the widespread pro-Soviet sentiment forces the government to maintain diplomatic relations with that country. Bulgaria has achieved her territorial aspirations at the expense of Yugoslavia and Greece and might not relinquish them easily.

c. Finland. Overwhelming fear of the U.S.S.R. is by far the greatest factor binding Finland to Germany. Less important factors are Finland's dependence on Germany for essential supplies and the presence of German troops in northern Finland. If a satisfactory territorial adjustment with the U.S.S.R. could be made, the less important factors probably could be overcome and Finland would willingly withdraw from the war.

5. *THE SITUATIONS IN OCCUPIED COUNTRIES*

a. Norway. Strong underground resistance continues to increase. Some rifts between the underground and the Government in exile are appearing. There is also some evidence, not yet fully evaluated, of Communist influence in the underground.

b. Denmark. As a result of German demands arising out of increased Danish resistance and sabotage the Danish Government tendered its resignation to the King. Although their resignations were not formally accepted, Denmark has since been without a Government and is ruled directly by the Germans.

c. The Low Countries. A general increase in sabotage and civilian resistance, somewhat more advanced in the Netherlands than in Belgium, has been accompanied by a disintegration of native pro-Nazi parties in both countries. Both countries are compelled to contribute substantial industrial manpower to Germany. Belgian industry, though below capacity, is important.

d. France. Resistance to German control has greatly increased and is seriously affecting production for the Axis. Recruitment of labor for Germany has nearly stopped. The underground movement, increasingly unified and confident, has now reached a stage of considerable political effectiveness. French underground leaders show great irritation over attempts to exclude France from major political decisions. The present Vichy Government is likely to give way soon to a more pro-German regime, and even Laval and Petain are making overtures to the United Nations.

e. Italy. The Germans appear to have the situation behind their lines in Italy reasonably well in hand, although some Italian units continue to resist in the Alpine area, particularly on the French and Yugoslav frontiers, and some sabotage continues. The Mussolini Government appears to have acquired relatively few supporters.

f. Yugoslavia. The surrender of Italy and the disintegration of the Italian forces of occupation touched off more active campaigns by guerrilla forces. In spite of extensive operations by German forces, these activities, strengthened by the adherence of certain Italian units, the acquisition of Italian arms, the increased scale of Allied material support, and the psychological effect of the surrender of Italy, have now reached considerable proportions, especially in the western half of the country. The internal conflict between the Partisans and the Chetniks has, however, reduced guerrilla effectiveness.

g. Albania. There is some guerrilla activity but on a much smaller scale than in Yugoslavia.

h. Greece (Including Crete). Despite the exhaustion of the country there is considerable and increasing underground and guerrilla activity, but on a much smaller scale than in Yugoslavia. Greek guerrilla forces are divided politically and have clashed. There is general opposition to a restoration of King George II.

i. Poland. Considerable underground activity is carried on, but the situation is complicated by a boundary dispute with the U.S.S.R. and the presence of Soviet guerrillas and various Soviet fostered organizations independent of the Polish Government in London. Poland contributes manpower, and coal, food, and some oil to Germany.

j. Occupied U.S.S.R. Considerable guerrilla activity continues behind the German lines. German efforts to organize anti-Communists forces have had virtually no success. The Germans have obtained manpower and some food and raw materials from Occupied U.S.S.R. The food dividend for this crop year is at least partly safe against Soviet recapture.

6. *THE ATTITUDES OF EUROPEAN NEUTRALS*

a. Sweden. Sweden is determined to maintain her neutrality and is now taking a firm attitude in her relations with Germany. Public expression of sympathy with the United Nations and with German occupied countries, especially Norway and Denmark, is greatly increasing. Swedish fear of ultimate Soviet intentions in the Baltic area continues, however, to be a factor in the Swedish attitude toward the developing war situation.

b. Switzerland. Despite their isolation, the Swiss have succeeded in maintaining a firmly neutral attitude. However, Switzerland depends heavily upon trade with Germany and continues to make economic contributions of value to that country.

c. Spain. The Franco regime is apparently torn between the dictates of sympathy and of discretion, with Spain's internal situation unstable but held in delicate balance. Since November 1942 Spanish policy has been progressively readjusted away from non-belligerent adherence to the Axis to one of "vigilant neutrality" in accordance with the increase of United Nations power in the Mediterranean. The fall of Mussolini, the capitulation of Italy, and its declaration of war against Germany have made a profound impression on Franco. It is possible that, in order to hold his position, he may seek British and American support and even acquiesce in a return of the monarchy, in which he might retain a favorable post.

d. Portugal. The Government of Portugal desires above all to remain neutral on the Continent. Owing to the need for outside economic aid and to popular sympathy toward the United Nations, Portugal has shown increased leanings towards them by granting to Britain the use of the Azores as bases. Further concessions cannot, however, be expected in the near future.

e. Turkey. Turkey's fear of Soviet domination of the Balkans or Dardanelles will probably lead her to active participation in the war in order to obtain a voice in the peace settlement. But such participation will not take place until it can be done at minimum cost.

7. *SUMMARY OF THE EXISTING SITUATION—SEE PARAGRAPH 2.*

8. *COURSES OF ACTION OPEN TO GERMANY IN 1944*

a. To Stand on the Strategic Defensive. In view of Germany's lack of decisive offensive capabilities and the prospect of having to meet attack on three fronts, this is the only general course of military action open to her. It is a negative course, which cannot bring victory but which might serve to avert defeat. Although her military resources are inadequate to meet all of her defensive requirements, Germany may yet hope that a prolongation of resistance may lead to a favorable stroke of fortune or at least to a stalemate.

Within this general course are several subordinate courses of action, as follows:

(1) *To Continue the War Against Shipping.* Germany will follow this course to the end in order to impede support of Allied operations in Europe.

(2) *To Continue to Direct Her Air Effort Primarily to Defense Against Strategic Bombing.* Germany is compelled to adopt this course, regardless of its effect upon air support of her land fronts and upon her offensive air capabilities.

(3) *To Counterattack to Destroy or Expel any Hostile Force Entering Her Defensive Perimeter.* Germany's last military hope is by exploiting interior lines to concentrate against her enemies in detail and to inflict on at least one of them a repulse severe enough to induce a willingness to negotiate.

(4) *To Abandon Outlying Territory (e.g., Norway, France, Italy, Greece, Occupied Russia, Finland).* This course is responsive to Germany's need to conserve and concentrate strength. However, the consequent impairment of her military, economic, political, or psychological situations will not permit her to adopt it voluntarily.

b. Contingent Courses of Action. Within the concept of the strategic defensive are certain contingent courses of offensive action. Since all involve dispersion of force, she will adopt none of them except under imperative necessity to forestall or counteract certain unfavorable developments.

(1) *To Invade Sweden.* Certain intelligence that United Nations bombers were to be permitted to operate against her from Swedish bases would compel Germany to adopt this course. German forces now surrounding Sweden cannot undertake the operation and at the same time

maintain their outward fronts against the United Nations. Their reinforcement would be required.

(2) *To Invade Spain.* In present circumstances this course could be adopted only as a diversion. A counter-offensive in Italy would probably be regarded as more effective for that purpose, at less cost in increased commitments.

(3) *To Invade Turkey.* Germany's present strength in the Balkans-Aegean area is barely adequate to occupy and defend it. She is apparently determined, however, to maintain her position there, and, if compelled by a threat to it from Turkey, could divert sufficient strength from other fronts to advance at least to the Straits for defensive purposes.

(4) *To Occupy Hungary, Rumania, or Bulgaria.* Germany would occupy any one of them if it were absolutely necessary to prevent or counteract its defection.

c. To Seek a Negotiated Peace. Germany will continue, by means of propaganda warfare, to seek to persuade her principal enemies that her defeat is impossible or is possible only at prohibitive cost, in hope of inducing them to accept a negotiated peace advantageous to her. Included in this will be continued efforts to divide her principal enemies so as at least to impede their operations and at best to secure a negotiated peace with one which would enable her to concentrate against the others.

d. To Surrender. Actual or virtual surrender will remain unacceptable so long as there is hope of achieving a stalemate or a negotiated peace. It will, presumably, never be acceptable to the Nazi leaders. The only possibility of political change presently apparent in Germany is an assumption of control by the High Command. If Germany cannot conduct a successful defense on all fronts and cannot divide her enemies, making peace with one in order to concentrate against the others, the High Command may elect to sue for peace in order to avert further destruction prejudicial to Germany's eventual recovery .

C.C.S. 308/7

BOUNDARIES OF THE SOUTHEAST ASIA COMMAND

Reference:

CCS 129th Meeting, Item 6

C.C.S. 308/7 was circulated by the United States Chiefs of Staff 24 November 1943. The Combined Chiefs of Staff considered this paper in their 129th Meeting and agreed to defer action.

C.C.S. 308/7   24 November 1943

COMBINED CHIEFS OF STAFF

BOUNDARIES OF THE SOUTHEAST ASIA COMMAND

Memorandum by the United States Chiefs of Staff

1. The Generalissimo has indicated his objection to the boundaries of the Southeast Asia Command proposed at *QUADRANT* and in lieu thereof, after conferences with Admiral Mountbatten and Lieutenant General Somervell, has indicated his views as follows:

The Generalissimo approves wholeheartedly unity of command under Mountbatten for the Burma campaign. Under existing circumstances he feels that the inclusion of Thailand and Indochina in the Southeast Asia Theater would not be practicable and would deter rather than further the success of any project designed to defeat Japan. He cites as his reasons for this belief the effect which a change of boundary would have on the Chinese people, on Chinese troops, on the people of Thailand and Indochina and on the Japanese. The Chinese people and army are aware that those countries were included in the China Theater of War and that now to make the change would strike a blow at their morale which would affect the conduct of the coming operations and attitude of the people and troops towards the war. This is borne out by the effect of the announcement in the British press that such a change was contemplated. This caused repercussions involving necessity for the Chinese news agency to deny the statements. Japanese propaganda has been directed to convincing people of Indochina and Thailand that the British intended to hold those countries after the war. A change in boundaries at this time would tend to convince people that Japanese were correct and thus incur hostility to our cause and lastly the change would permit Japanese propaganda in China to be more successful in creating a breach in present happy British, American, and Chinese relations.

The China Theater comprises Thailand, Indochina, and the whole of China. As the war develops, the scope of operations of the United Nations' Supreme Commander of the Southeast Asia Theater newly created, besides Burma and Malaya, may involve Thailand and Indochina. In order to enable

42

the two theaters to cooperate closely and satisfactorily, the Generalissimo deems advisable to reach the following arrangements in advance:

a. When the time comes for two theaters to launch assaults upon the enemy in Thailand and Indochina, the Chinese troops will attack from the north, and the troops under the command of the Southeast Asia Theater, Mountbatten, are expected to make full use of facilities afforded by the ports and air bases under its control and attack from the south. If the troops are landed in those countries, the boundaries between the two theaters are to be decided at the time in accordance with the progress of advances the respective forces made.

b. All matters of political nature that arise during operations will be dealt with at a Chinese-British-American committee which is to be located in the headquarters of the Supreme Commander of the China Theater.

2. Admiral Mountbatten has accepted the suggestions of the Generalissimo insofar as the boundaries are concerned but objects to the political commission.

3. The United States Chiefs of Staff and the President have approved the proposal of the Generalissimo as it stands and recommend British acceptance of his proposals.

C.C.S. 320/4 (Revised)

OPERATION "RANKIN"

References:

CCS 134th Meeting, Items 5, 6, and 7

5th Plenary Meeting

C.C.S. 320/4 was circulated by the United States Chiefs of Staff 4 December 1943. The Combined Chiefs of Staff in their 134th Meeting agreed to accept C.C.S. 320/4 as modified (subsequently circulated as C.C.S. 320/4 (Revised)).

C.C.S. 320/4 (Revised)   4 December 1943

COMBINED CHIEFS OF STAFF

OPERATION "RANKIN"

Reference: CCS 320 Series

Memorandum by the United States Chiefs of Staff

1. In developing his plans for *RANKIN*, *COSSAC* has submitted a recommendation (paragraph 11, C.C.S. 320/2) that under the general direction of the Supreme Allied Commander the territories to be occupied should be divided into two spheres, the British sphere, including northwest Germany, Belgium, Luxembourg, Holland and Denmark, and the U.S. sphere, generally southern Germany and France, with Austria a U.S. sphere, initially under the Mediterranean command. It is understood that planning by *COSSAC* is now proceeding on this basis.

2. The United States Chiefs of Staff now propose that these spheres be changed as follows:

   a. U.S. sphere. The general area Netherlands, Northern Germany as far east as the line Berlin-Stettin, Denmark, Norway and Sweden. The boundary of this area is to be as follows: Southern boundary of the Netherlands; thence to Duesseldorf on the Rhine; down the east bank of the Rhine to Mains; thence due east to Beyreuth; thence north to Leipzig; thence northeast to Cottbus; thence north to Berlin (exclusive); thence to Stettin (inclusive).

   b. British sphere. Generally the territory to the west and south of the American western boundary.

3. The United States Chiefs of Staff further propose that *COSSAC* be directed to examine and report on the implications of revising his planning on the basis of the new allocation of spheres of occupation.

C.C.S. 379/7

RETENTION OF LST'S IN THE MEDITERRANEAN

References:

CCS 132d Meeting

2d Plenary Meeting

C.C.S. 379/7 circulated a memorandum by the Commander in Chief, Allied Force Headquarters, 27 November 1943. The Combined Chiefs of Staff resolved this matter in their 132d Meeting and informed General Eisenhower (FAN 281) that the 68 LST's which are due to be sent from the Mediterranean to the United Kingdom for *OVERLORD* be retained in the Mediterranean until 15 January.

C.C.S. 379/7   27 November 1943

COMBINED CHIEFS OF STAFF

RETENTION OF LST'S IN THE MEDITERRANEAN

Memorandum by the Commander in Chief, Allied Force Headquarters

22 November 1943

1. In my NAF 486 and 505 I outlined my plans for the capture of Rome and explained the great part which an amphibious operation might play should the opportunity arise.

2. This operation is now being planned to take place south of Rome, but it cannot be launched until we are ready to advance from the Frosinone area. The reason is that the assault force, unable to depend on maintenance over beaches owing to the unreliability of weather on the Italian coast in winter, must be joined by the overland force within 48 hours in order to insure maintenance and withstand the estimated scale of enemy counter action.

3. We estimate that we will not be able to advance from the Frosinone area and launch the amphibious assault before mid-December.

4. If circumstances prevent our launching the amphibious assault, we will be faced with continued frontal assaults and there will be compelling demands for more infantry divisions and, therefore, for all available landing craft. I would remind you that our divisions will have been engaged in bitter fighting under very exacting conditions for many weeks with little or no relief, and I am concerned about the possibility of a low state of battle efficiency in January.

5. These requirements have not taken into account the possibility that the Combined Chiefs of Staff may order accelerated operations north of Rome. In any event, it is essential that these LST's remain in this area.

48

C.C.S. 380/2

BASIC POLICIES FOR THE NEXT UNITED STATES-
BRITISH STAFF CONFERENCE

Reference:

CCS 127th Meeting, Item 5

The Combined Chiefs of Staff, in their 127th Meeting, accepted the over-all strategic concept and basic undertakings as set out in C.C.S. 380/2.

C.C.S. 380/2   6 November 1943

COMBINED CHIEFS OF STAFF

BASIC POLICIES FOR THE NEXT
UNITED STATES-BRITISH STAFF CONFERENCE

Note by the Secretaries

The enclosure, approved by the Combined Chiefs of Staff in their 126th Meeting, is circulated for the information of the Combined Chiefs of Staff.

H. REDMAN,

F. B. ROYAL,

Combined Secretariat.

ENCLOSURE

COMBINED CHIEFS OF STAFF

BASIC POLICIES FOR THE NEXT
UNITED STATES-BRITISH STAFF CONFERENCE

1. The Combined Chiefs of Staff agree that the following statement of basic stategy and policies will be used as a basis for the next United States-British Staff Conference, it being understood that such agreement does not exclude from consideration courses of action which might appear likely to facilitate or accelerate the attainment of the over-all objectives.

I. OVER-ALL OBJECTIVE

2. In conjuction with Russia and other Allies to bring about at the earliest possible date the unconditional surrender of the Axis Powers.

II. OVER-ALL STRATEGIC CONCEPT FOR THE PROSECUTION OF THE WAR

3. In cooperation with Russia and other Allies to bring about at the earliest possible date the unconditional surrender of the Axis in Europe.

4. Simultaneously, in cooperation with other Pacific Powers concerned to maintain and extend unremitting pressure against Japan with the purpose of continually reducing her military power and attaining positions from which her ultimate surrender can be forced. The effect of any such extension on the over-all objective to be given consideration by the Combined Chiefs of Staff before action is taken.

5. Upon the defeat of the Axis in Europe, in cooperation with other Pacific Powers and, if possible, with Russia, to direct the full resources of the United States and Great Britain to bring about at the earliest possible date the unconditional surrender of Japan.

III. BASIC UNDERTAKINGS IN SUPPORT OF OVER-ALL STRATEGIC CONCEPT

6. Whatever operations are decided on in support of the over-all strategic concept, the following established undertakings will be a first charge against our resources, subject to review by the Combined Chiefs of Staff in keeping with the changing situation.

   a. Maintain the security and war-making capacity of the Western Hemisphere and the British Isles.

   b. Support the war-making capacity of our forces in all areas.

   c. Maintain vital overseas lines of communication, with particular emphasis on the defeat of the U-boat menace.

   d. Continue the disruption of Axis sea communications.

   e. Intensify the air offensive against the Axis Powers in Europe.

   f. Concentrate maximum resources in a selected area as early as practicable for the purpose of conducting a decisive invasion of the Axis citadel.

   g. Undertake such measures as may be necessary and practicable to aid the war effort of Russia.

   h. Undertake such measures as may be necessary and practicable in order to aid the war effort of China as an effective Ally and as a base for operations against Japan.

   i. Undertake such action to exploit the entry of Turkey into the war as is considered most likely to facilitate or accelerate the attainment of the over-all objectives.

   j. Continue assistance to the French and Italian forces to enable them to fulfill an active role in the war against the Axis Powers.

   k. Prepare to reorient forces from the European Theater to the Pacific and Far East as soon as the German situation allows.

C.C.S. 387 and 387/3

MEDITERRANEAN COMMAND ARRANGEMENTS

References:

CCS 131st Meeting, Item 4B

CCS 134th Meeting, Item 3

CCS 135th Meeting, Item 4

C.C.S. 387 circulated a memorandum by the Representatives of the British Chiefs of Staff 3 November 1943. This paper was considered by the Combined Chiefs of Staff in their 131st Meeting, wherein they agreed to the unification of command in the Mediterranean as outlined in C.C.S. 387. C.C.S. 387/1 circulated a directive to the Commander in Chief, Allied Forces proposed by the United States Chiefs of Staff, and C.C.S. 387/2 circulated a directive proposed by the British Chiefs of Staff.

The Combined Chiefs of Staff in their 135th Meeting amended and accepted C.C.S. 387/2. The approved directive was subsequently circulated as C.C.S. 387/3.

C.C.S. 387   3 November 1943

COMBINED CHIEFS OF STAFF

MEDITERRANEAN COMMAND ARRANGEMENTS

Memorandum by the Representatives of the British Chiefs of Staff

1. The British Chiefs of Staff have been considering the present system of command in the Mediterranean under which General Eisenhower is responsible for operations in the Central Mediterranean and the Commander in Chief, Middle East, for operations in the Eastern Mediterranean and the Balkans.

2. They point out that the success or failure in one Mediterranean theater has an immediate effect upon the other theater. The present system whereby all transfers of even small forces have to be referred to the Combined Chiefs of Staff, involves delays which are likely to lead to failure to take advantage of fleeting opportunities as has been illustrated by recent events in the Aegean. The restoration of our control of the Mediterranean has removed the necessity for two naval commands.

3. The British Chiefs of Staff therefore consider that the time has come for one Commander to be made responsible for all operations in the Mediterranean and suggest that the Commander in Chief, Allied Forces, should now assume responsibility for operations in the following areas in addition to those already in his command, Greece, Albania, Yugoslavia, Bulgaria, Rumania, Hungary, Crete, Aegean Islands and Turkey. The three Commanders in Cairo would be under his orders for these operations, but would remain responsible to the British Chiefs of Staff for operation of the Middle East base and for all matters pertaining to those parts of the present Middle East Commands situated in Africa, Asia and Levant (except Turkey) and should continue to receive political guidance from the Minister of State resident in the Middle East in respect of these responsibilities.

4. Such reorganization would insure that operations in the Mediterranean are regarded as a whole and would empower the Commander in Chief to

transfer forces from one part of the area to another in order to take advantage of fleeting opportunities. The British Chiefs of Staff consider this particularly desirable in view of possible opportunities in the Balkans and the effect that operations in that theater might have on the main operations in Italy.

5. On Air Marshal Tedder's recommendation the British Chiefs of Staff would like to suggest that the Mediterranean Air Command should be renamed Mediterranean Allied Air Forces.

6. The views of the United States Chiefs of Staff on these proposals are requested. A diagram of the proposals is attached as an enclosure.

E N C L O S U R E

PROPOSED SYSTEM OF COMMAND IN THE MEDITERRANEAN

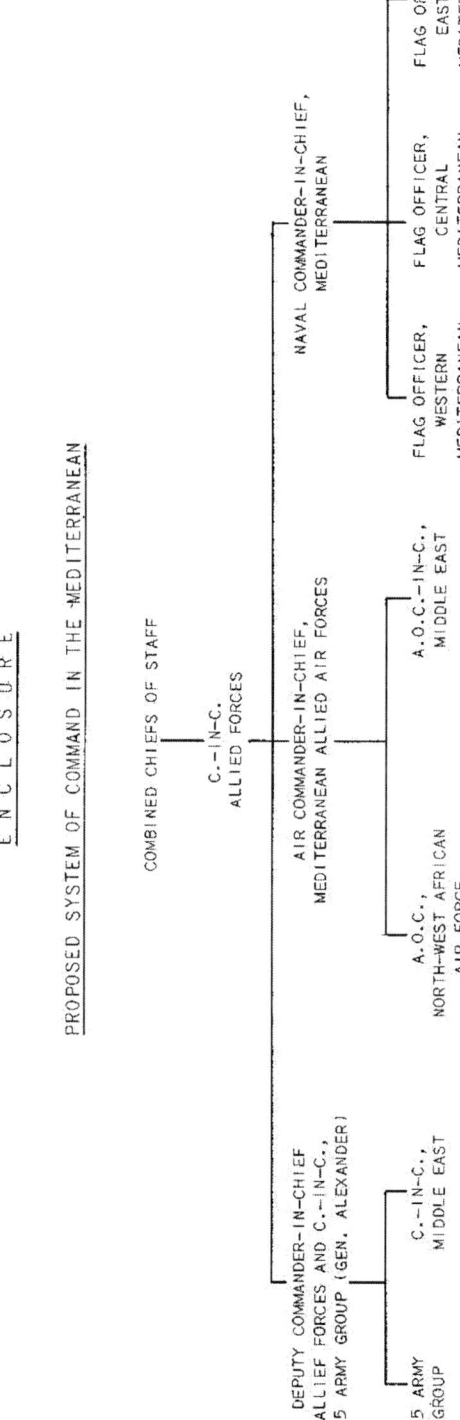

RESERVATIONS.

The above system is subject to the reservations that the three Commanders in Cairo (Flag Officer Levant, C.-in-C., Middle East, and A.O.C.-in-C., Middle East) should remain responsible to the British Chiefs of Staff for:-

(i) All matters pertaining to those parts of the present Middle East Commands situated in Africa, Asia or the Levant except Turkey, and

(ii) The operation of the Middle East Base;

and that in respect of these responsibilities they will continue to receive political guidance from the Minister of State Resident in the Middle East.

C.C.S. 387/3   5 December 1943

COMBINED CHIEFS OF STAFF

DIRECTIVE FOR UNIFICATION OF COMMAND IN
THE MEDITERRANEAN

Note by the Secretaries

The attached directive for unification of command in the Mediterranean was approved by the Combined Chiefs of Staff at their 135th Meeting.

H. REDMAN,

F. B. ROYAL,

Combined Secretariat.

ENCLOSURE

DIRECTIVE TO COMMANDER IN CHIEF, ALLIED FORCES

NORTH AFRICA

1. We have decided to set up a unified command in the Mediterranean Theater on account of its geographical unity and its dependence on all bases in the area.

2. We have no intention of changing existing organization and arrangements any more than is necessary to give effect to our main intention. You should assume, therefore, that all present arrangements continue with the exceptions outlined below but you should report as necessary whether you consider any further changes are required in the light of experience.

3. To your present responsibilities you will add responsibility for operations in Greece, Albania, Yugoslavia, Bulgaria, Rumania, Hungary, Crete and Aegean Islands and Turkey. The British and American forces allocated to you from Middle East will be determined by the British and United States Chiefs of Staff, respectively. You will have full liberty to transfer forces from one part of your Command to another for the purposes of conducting operations which we have agreed. The Commanders in Chief, Middle East, will be under your orders for operations in these areas.

4. You will provide U.S. Strategic Air Forces under separate command, but operating in your area, with the necessary logistical and adminstrative support in performance of Operation *POINTBLANK* as the air operation of first priority. Should a strategic or tactical emergency arise, you may, at your discretion, utilize the 15th U.S. Strategic Air Force for purposes other than its primary mission, informing the Combined Chiefs of Staff and the Commanding General, U.S. Strategic Air Forces in Europe, if and when that command is organized.

5. You will in addition, assume responsibility for the conduct of guerrilla and subversive action in all the territories in your command and for setting up the necessary organization for the dispatch of supplies to resistance groups in occupied territories.

6. The Commanders in Chief, Middle East, will remain directly responsible to the British Chiefs of Staff for all the territories at present in Middle East Command situated in Africa, Palestine, Syria and the Lebanon, and for the operation and security of the Middle East base with such forces as the British Chiefs of Staff may allot for this purpose from time to time.

7. You will be notified later of any adjustments which are thought necessary to the machinery by which you receive political guidance. In the meantime, in respect of the new territories in your command you should obtain any necessary political advice from C-in-C Middle East through the channels he at present uses.

8. The system of Command is shown on the attached diagram (Appendix "A"). You will note that the Mediterranean Air Command will now be known as Mediterranean Allied Air Forces.

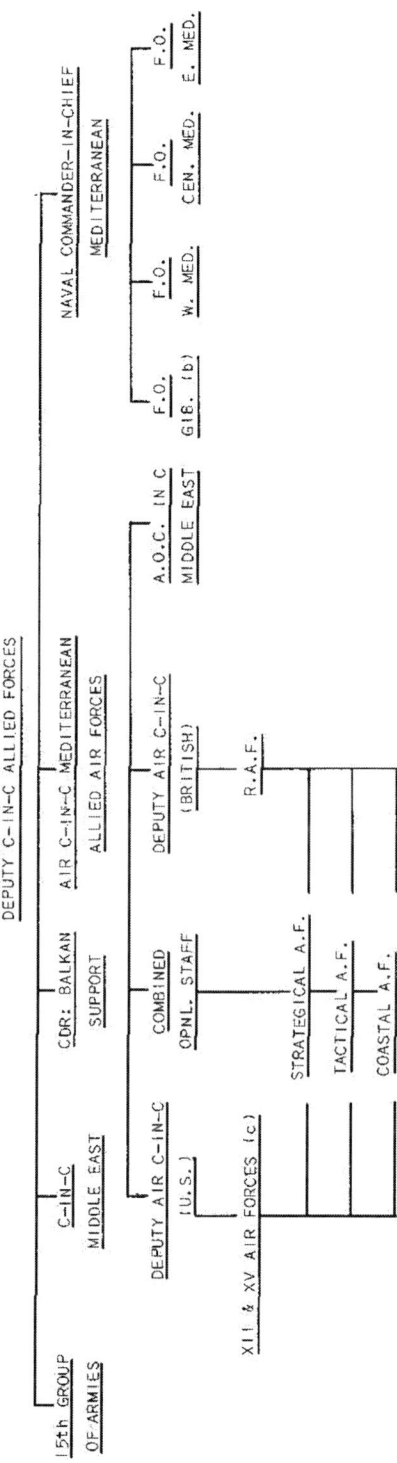

A P P E N D I X "A"

PROPOSED SYSTEM OF COMMAND IN THE MEDITERRANEAN

RESERVATIONS

The above system is subject to the reservations that the three Commanders in Cairo (Flag Officer Levant, C-in-C, Middle East, and A.O.C.-in-C., Middle East) should remain responsible to the British Chiefs of Staff for:-

(i) All matters pertaining to territories of the present Middle East Command situated in Africa, Palestine, Syria and the Lebanon, and

(ii) The operations of the Middle East Base:

and that in respect of these responsibilities they will continue to receive political guidance from the Minister of State Resident in the Middle East.

NOTES: (a) At present acts only as C-in-C 15 Group of Armies.

(b) Flag Officer Gibraltar is responsible to Naval C-in-C Mediterranean for area between the longitude of Cape St. Vincent and longitude 3W. For the remainder of the Gibraltar Command he is responsible direct to Admiralty.

(c) As from 1 January 1944 Fifteenth Air Force will be placed under command of USSAFE for assignment of missions and for technique and tactics employed in their execution. (See also Directive to Commanding Generals NATO, ETOUSA, and USSAFE dated _____.)

Appendix "A"

APPENDIX "B"

BALKAN SUPPORT

It was agreed at the *EUREKA* Conference that our support of the Patriots in the Balkans, which now falls within the area in which you are responsible for Allied operations, should be intensified in order to increase their effectiveness.

You will be responsible for supporting them to the greatest practicable extent by increasing the supply of arms and equipment, clothing, medical stores, food and such other supplies as they may require. You should also support them by commando operations and by furnishing such air support as you may consider advisable in the light of the general situation.

You should examine the possibility of continuing to supply the Patriots with Italian equipment, in the use of which they are already experienced, making good deficiencies in Italian formations to such extent as may be necessary with available British or American equipment.

We consider that this mission is of such importance that it would best be controlled on a regular basis by a special commander and joint staff.

Appendix "B"

C.C.S. 390/1

FUTURE OPERATIONS IN THE SOUTHEAST ASIA COMMAND

References:

CCS 128th Meeting, Item 4

1st Plenary Meeting

2d Plenary Meeting

3d Plenary Meeting

4th Plenary Meeting

CCS 397 (Revised)

CCS 427 and 427/1

C.C.S. 390/1 circulated a memorandum by the United States Chiefs of Staff. The Combined Chiefs of Staff, in their 128th Meeting, approved C.C.S. 390/1 but agreed to suspend final decision regarding Operation *BUCCANEER* until later in the *SEXTANT* Conference. The decision relative to Operation *BUCCANEER* was resolved in the consideration of C.C.S. 427 (Operations in the Southeast Asia Command).

C.C.S. 390/1   18 November 1943

COMBINED CHIEFS OF STAFF

FUTURE OPERATIONS IN THE SOUTHEAST ASIA COMMAND

Reference:

CCS 390

Memorandum by the United States Chiefs of Staff

1. The United States Chiefs of Staff realize that it is undesirable for the Combined Chiefs of Staff to enter into the details of various operations, but do not agree, however, that only matters of grand strategy should be considered by the Combined Chiefs of Staff.

2. The *QUADRANT* decisions (C.C.S. 319/5, paragraph 58) state that the Combined Chiefs of Staff would exercise a general jurisdiction over strategy for the Southeast Asia Theater. This is construed as requiring decision by the Combined Chiefs of Staff as to which of several courses of action are to be undertaken, and their sequence and timing.

3. Since the United States cannot furnish the required assistance for *FIRST CULVERIN*, it is agreed that Operation *BUCCANEER* should be mounted as early as practicable. However, we believe it may prove possible to conduct additional land, sea, and air operations in order to pin down Japanese forces in South Burma. We therefore recommend that the CinC, Southeast Asia, be directed to explore this subject, and to submit recommendations thereon to the Combined Chiefs of Staff.

C.C.S. 397 (Revised)

SPECIFIC OPERATIONS FOR THE DEFEAT OF JAPAN, 1944

References:

CCS 137th Meeting, Item 5

1st Plenary Meeting

2d Plenary Meeting

C.C.S. 397 (Revised) circulated a memorandum by the United States Chiefs of Staff, 3 December 1943. The Combined Chiefs of Staff, in their 137th Meeting, approved the specific operations against Japan, 1944, set out in C.C.S. 397 (Revised) with the exception of the references contained therein to Operation *BUCCANEER*.

C.C.S. 397 (Revised)   3 December 1943

COMBINED CHIEFS OF STAFF

SPECIFIC OPERATIONS FOR THE DEFEAT OF JAPAN, 1944

References: a. CCS 242/6
b. CCS 319/5
c. CCS 417

Memorandum by the United States Chiefs of Staff

1. We are agreed that every effort should be exerted to bring the U.S.S.R. into the war against Japan at the earliest practicable date, and that plans should be prepared in that event.

2. We are agreed that plans should be prepared for operations in the event that Germany is defeated earlier than the fall of 1944.

3. A schedule of proposed operations and projected target dates for planning purposes is given in the appendix to the enclosure (pages 70 and 71). The operations envisaged are based on a concept of obtaining strategic objectives and bases from which to conduct further operations to force the unconditional surrender of Japan at the earliest practicable date. The operations are in consonance with the over-all objective and over-all strategic concept agreed upon at *QUADRANT* and reaffirmed by the Combined Chiefs of Staff in C.C.S. 380/2, and with the provisions of C.C.S. 417 (Over-all Plan for the Defeat of Japan).

4. *General.* In addition to the specific objectives hereinafter indicated, supporting operations should be conducted. Both the specific and supporting operations will be designed to destroy the Japanese Fleet at an early date; to secure maximum attrition of enemy air forces; to intensify air, submarine, and mining operations against enemy shipping and lines of communication; to establish air and sea blockade of the main Japanese islands; to continue efforts to keep China in the war; and to enable us to launch land and carrier-based air operations against Japan.

5. *North Pacific*. Plans for the North Pacific involve the augmentation of base facilities and defensive installations in the Aleutians in preparation for entry into the Kuriles and Soviet territory in the event of Russian collaboration. Naval surface and submarine action, including raids on the Japanese fishing fleet will be carried out. Preparations will be made for executing very long range strategic bombing against the Kuriles and northern Japan.

6. *Central, South and Southwest Pacific*. The advance along the New Guinea-N.E.I.-Philippine axis will proceed concurrently with operations for the capture of the Mandated Islands. A strategic bombing force will be established in Guam, Tinian, and Saipan for strategic bombing of Japan proper. Air bombardment of targets in the N.E.I.-Philippine Area and the aerial neutralization of Rabaul will be intensified.

7. *China*. Our efforts in the China area should have as their objective the intensification of land and air operations in and from China and the build-up of the U.S.A.A.F. and the Chinese army and air forces. It shall include also the establishing, without materially affecting other approved operations, of a very long range strategic bombing force at Calcutta, with advanced bases at Chengtu to attack vital targets in the Japanese "inner zone."*

8. *Southeast Asia*. Operations for the capture of Upper Burma in the spring of 1944 in order to improve the air route and establish overland communications with China, and an amphibious operation at approximately the same time. Continuance of operations during the autumn of 1944 within the limits of the forces available (see paragraph 14, C.C.S. 417) to extend the position held in upper Burma.

Should the means be available, additional ground, sea and air offensive operations, including carrier-borne raids, with the object of maintaining pressure on the enemy, forcing dispersion of his forces, and attaining the maximum attrition practicable on his air and naval forces and shipping.

9. As more carriers become available, the operations set forth should be supplemented, between scheduled operational dates as practicable, with massed carrier task force strikes against selected vital targets.

* Includes: Japan proper, Manchuria, Korea, North China, Karafuto (Japanese Sakhalin) and Formosa.

10. The completion of these operations will place the United Nations in positions from which to use most advantageously the great air, ground, and naval resources which will be at our disposal after Germany is defeated.

ENCLOSURE

A schedule of operations for 1944 is set forth in the appendix. Target dates which have been determined after careful consideration of prospective means and of time and space factors, are presented for planning purposes only. We are convinced that the sequence of operations must be flexible; we must be prepared to take all manner of short cuts made possible by developments in the situation. The four primary developments which may permit short cuts are:

a. Early defeat of the Japanese Fleet.

b. Sudden withdrawal of Japanese forces from areas (as from Kiska).

c. Increase in our means such as by acceleration of the assault ship-building program and by an earlier defeat of Germany than 1 October 1944.

d. The early collaboration of the U.S.S.R. in the war against Japan.

We have directed that further study be conducted and plans made and kept up to date for the conditions assumed in *c* and *d.*

We have directed that special attention be given to the optimum employment of the enormous air forces which will be released upon the defeat of Germany.

We have directed that a study be made for the optimum use, timing, and deployment in the war against Japan of very long range bombers.

APPENDIX

SCHEDULE FOR PLANNING PURPOSES OF OPERATIONS FOR
OBTAINING THE FOLLOWING SPECIFIC OBJECTIVES IN 1944

Target Dates	*Central Pacific*	*Southwest Pacific*	*Southeast Asia Command and China*
1-31 Jan. 1944	Seizure of the Marshalls, including Eniwetok and Kusaie.	Complete the seizure of Western New Britain; continue neutralization of Rabaul.	
15 Jan.-15 March 1944			Operations in Upper Burma, Arakan Region and China. Amphibious operations in Southeast Asia. *(BUCCANEER)*
1 Feb. 1944		Seizure of Hansa Bay area.	
20 March 1944		Capture of Kavieng.	
20 April 1944		Seizure of Manus.	
1 May 1944	Seizure of Ponape.		Initiate V.L.R. bombing of vital targets in Japanese "Inner Zone" from bases in China.
1 June 1944		Seizure of Hollandia. (Humboldt Bay)	

(Table Continued on Following Page)

Target Dates	Central Pacific	Southwest Pacific	Southeast Asia Command and China
20 July 1944	Seizure of Eastern Carolines (Truk Area).	Initiate V.L.R. bombing of vital targets in the Netherlands East Indies.	
15 Aug. 1944		Advance to westward along north coast of New Guinea to include Vogelkop.	
1 Oct. 1944	Seizure of Guam and Japanese Marianas.		
1 Nov. 1944 (end of monsoon)			Intensification of offensive operations in the Southeast Asia Command.
31 Dec. 1944	Initiate V.L.R. bombing of vital targets in Japanese "Inner Zone" from bases in the Marianas.		

C.C.S. 398

SPECIFIC OPERATIONS FOR THE DEFEAT OF GERMANY AND HER SATELLITES, 1943-44

C.C.S. 398 circulated a memorandum by the United States Chiefs of Staff. This memorandum was noted informally by the British Chiefs of Staff.

C.C.S. 398   18 November 1943

COMBINED CHIEFS OF STAFF

SPECIFIC OPERATIONS FOR THE DEFEAT OF GERMANY AND HER

SATELLITES, 1943-44

Memorandum by the United States Chiefs of Staff

The United States Chiefs of Staff propose the following specific operations for the defeat of Germany and her satellites in 1943-44.

1. *Facilities in the Azores Islands.* The facilities of the Azores Islands will be used for (1) intensified sea and air operations against the U-boat, and (2) air ferry operations. The British Chiefs of Staff reaffirm the assurance given by them in *QUADRANT* that everything will be done by the British as soon as possible to assist in making arrangements for facilities in the Azores for U.S. naval participation in the anti-U-boat campaign and for the operational and transit use by U.S. aircraft.

2. *The Combined Bomber Offensive.* The progressive destruction and dislocation of the German military, industrial and economic system, the disruption of vital elements of lines of communication and the material reduction of German air combat strength by the successful prosecution of the Combined Bomber Offensive from all convenient bases is a prerequisite to *OVERLORD*. The Combined Bomber Offensive continues to have highest strategic priority. We have directed that studies be made of the use of bases in the U.S.S.R. for shuttle bombing operations.

3. *Operation OVERLORD*

    a. This operation will be the primary U.S.-British ground and air effort against Germany. (Target date 1 May 1944.) In the preparatory phase immediately preceding the invasion, the whole of the available air power in the U.K., tactical and strategic, will be employed in a concentrated effort to create the conditions essential to the success of the assault. After adequate channel ports have been secured, exploitation will be directed toward securing areas that will facilitate both ground and air operations against

74

the enemy. Following the establishment of strong Allied Air Forces in France, an intensive air attack on Germany and her military forces, communications and installations will be launched, designed to precipitate the collapse of enemy resistance prior to a general assault on the hostile ground forces in the advance into the heart of Germany.

b. There will be a balanced ground and air force build-up for *OVERLORD*, and continuous planning for and maintenance of those forces available in the United Kingdom in readiness to take advantage of any situation permitting an opportunistic cross-Channel move into France.

c. As between Operation *OVERLORD* and operations in the Mediterranean, where there is a shortage of resources, available resources will be distributed and employed with the main object of insuring the success of *OVERLORD*. Operations in the Mediterranean Theater will be carried out with the forces allotted except in so far as these may be varied by decision of the Combined Chiefs of Staff.

d. The Supreme Allied Commander for Operation *OVERLORD*, when appointed, will establish contact with the Commander in Chief, North African Theater of Operations, and the Commanders in Chief, Middle East, or with the Allied Commander in Chief, Mediterranean, if and when appointed, and recommend to the Combined Chiefs of Staff their general missions and objectives, and the timing of their operations, so as best to support *OVERLORD*.

4. *Planning for OVERLORD.* Pending the appointment of the Supreme Allied Commander, *COSSAC* will continue with the detailed planning and with full preparations for operations *OVERLORD* and *RANKIN*.

5. *Operations in Scandinavia*

a. Strong carrier-based raids on German combatant ships in northern Norway should be undertaken in order to relieve naval units from the eastern Atlantic for operations in other theaters.

b. Plans should be developed for operations in the Scandinavian area in the event that circumstances should render the execution of *OVERLORD* impossible. Such plans should envisage collaboration with the U.S.S.R., with particular reference to opening communications to Sweden and developing a situation favorable for Sweden to enter the war. In the event Sweden enters the war, we should make use of her air bases to establish an air task force of suitable composition to aid in the strategic bombing of Germany.

6. *Operations in Italy.* The maximum possible pressure will be maintained, with the forces allocated, on German forces in Italy, in order to assist in the creation of the conditions required for *OVERLORD*, and of a situation favorable for the eventual entry of our forces, including the bulk of the re-equipped French Army and Air Force into Southern France. The Allied Commander, North Africa, (or the Allied Commander in Chief, Mediterranean, if and when appointed) will, in the light of the changing strategic situation, make recommendations from time to time to the Supreme Allied Commander for Operation *OVERLORD* concerning the operations in the Mediterranean that will, in his judgment, make the greatest contribution towards insuring the success of Operation *OVERLORD*. Pending the appointment of the Supreme Allied Commander, these recommendations will be made, after coordination with *COSSAC*, to the Combined Chiefs of Staff.

7. *Operations in the Balkan-Eastern Mediterranean Region*

a. Recognizing that (1) the Balkan-Eastern Mediterranean approach to the European Fortress is unsuitable, due to terrain and communication difficulties, for large-scale military operations, (2) the implementation of our agreed strategy for the defeat of Germany will require all available military means, and (3) our experience shows that the acceptance of limited objective operations, however attractive in themselves, invariably requires resources beyond those initially anticipated, we are agreed that our strategy will be best served by causing Germany to dissipate her defensive strength in maintaining her position in the Balkan-Aegean area. So long, therefore, as the present strategic situation in this area remains substantially unchanged, operations in the Balkan-Eastern Mediterranean region will be limited to:

(1) The supply of Balkan guerrillas by sea and air transport.

(2) Minor action by Commando forces.

(3) The bombing of vital strategic targets.

b. We agree that it is desirable to bring Turkey into the war at this time but this must be brought about without diversion of resources that would prejudice the success of our commitments elsewhere. To this end, in full collaboration with the U.S.S.R., we should bring pressure to bear on Turkey to enter the war and conduct offensive operations in the Balkans to the extent possible with the resources presently available to her. It must be made clear that military assistance to be furnished Turkey by the United States and Great Britain is limited to such supplies and equipment as can be furnished without prejudice to the successful accomplishment of our commitments elsewhere.

8. *Garrison Requirements and Security of Lines of Communication in the Mediterranean.* Defensive garrison commitments in the Mediterranean area will be reviewed from time to time, with a view to effecting economy of force. The security of our lines of communication through the Straits of Gibraltar will be assured by appropriate dispositions of our forces in Northwest Africa, so long as there remains even a remote possibility of the Germans' invading the Iberian Peninsula.

9. *Coordinated U.S.-British-U.S.S.R. Operations.* We are now examining, and shall continue to seek out, methods and means whereby the defeat of Germany and her satellites can be expedited through maximum coordination of United States, British, and U.S.S.R. operations.

10. *Emergency Entry into Europe.* We have directed that an extended *RANKIN* plan be prepared in collaboration with the U.S.S.R., in order that available Allied forces may take prompt action in the event an opportunistic entry into Europe becomes possible. The extended plan will provide for emergency entry into Europe in collaboration with the U.S.S.R. of United Nations forces from the United Kingdom, the North African Theater of Operations, Middle East, and, if required, directly from the United States.

11. *German Satellites.* We are agreed that, in so far as means can be made available without prejudice to the over-all strategy agreed hereto, effort should be made to separate the satellite powers from Germany.

12. *Relations With Patriot Forces in Europe.* Within the limits of available means and without prejudice to major operations, patriot forces everywhere within enemy occupied territory in Europe, should be furnished supplies to enable them to conduct sabotage, propaganda, intelligence and guerrilla warfare.

C.C.S. 399

REPORT ON RECENT AND PROSPECTIVE DEVELOPMENTS

IN ANTI-SUBMARINE OPERATIONS SINCE "QUADRANT"

Reference:

CCS 133d Meeting, Item 5

C.C.S. 399 circulated a report from the Commander in Chief, United States Fleet and Chief of Naval Operations. The Combined Chiefs of Staff took note of this report.

C.C.S. 399   18 November 1943

COMBINED CHIEFS OF STAFF

REPORT ON RECENT AND PROSPECTIVE DEVELOPMENTS
IN ANTI-SUBMARINE OPERATIONS SINCE "QUADRANT"

Memorandum by the United States Chiefs of Staff

The enclosed memorandum from the Commander in Chief, United States Fleet and Chief of Naval Operations is presented herewith for the consideration of the Combined Chiefs of Staff.

E N C L O S U R E

REPORT ON RECENT AND PROSPECTIVE DEVELOPMENTS
IN ANTI-SUBMARINE OPERATIONS SINCE "QUADRANT"

Memorandum from Commander in Chief, United States Fleet
and Chief of Naval Operations

8 November 1943

Subject: Report on Recent and Prospective Developments in Anti-Submarine Operations Since *QUADRANT*.

Enclosure: (A) Surface craft chart.
           (B) Aircraft chart.
           (C) Prospective Deployments of Anti-Submarine Aircraft.

1. *OPERATIONS — AVAILABILITY AND EMPLOYMENT OF SURFACE CRAFT AND AIRCRAFT*

a. In September, 17 merchant M/Vs were sunk; in October, 15. In September, 11 U-boats were sunk; in October, 32. For 1942, 1 submarine was sunk or probably sunk for every 9.3 M/Vs lost. For 1943 to date this figure is 2.1 M/Vs; for the past 5 months —.5.

b. Enclosure (A) indicates the status of Atlantic Fleet and Sea Frontier escorts as of 1 August and 1 November. Significant are:

(1) The increase of 51 DEs in the Atlantic Fleet;

(2) From 1 August to 1 November the reduction in DDs temporarily assigned ComNavNaw from 28 to 13;

(3) There were still 16 Pacific Fleet DDs on temporary duty with CinCLant on 1 November.

c. Matters of prospective interest in the escort situation are:

(1) Commencing with UGS 22 (about 25 October) a minimum escort strength of 1 DE Division plus 1 DD Division (10 ships) was established

81

for these convoys. This will be raised to 12 as a standard and CinCLant plans to gradually increase this to 16 when more slow DEs become available.

(2) The number of escort groups for CU convoys is being increased from 1 to 4 because of reduced sailing interval.

(3) DesDiv 57 (ODDs) now with Fourth Fleet will be replaced by CortDiv18. The 4 ODDs in CaribSeaFron and 1 ODD in PaSeaFron will also be replaced by 327 ft. Coast Guard Cutters.

(4) 18 acquired craft 100 ft.-150 ft. category in Sea Frontiers and LantFlt will be replaced by standard service designed craft, and 4 have been decommissioned without relief.

d. Enclosure (B) indicates the status of anti-submarine aircraft as of 1 August and 1 November.

(1) The anti-submarine aircraft available are adequate to cope with the anti-submarine situation present and prospective. It should be noted, however, that the availability of PVs and B-24s until 1944 will not permit those squadrons to be built up to 15 planes as planned and that there is some question as to whether the 8 B-24 Squadrons can be maintained at the strength of 12 planes, unless B-24s not now in the program for the Atlantic are obtained. This plane shortage may adversely affect our ability to meet emergencies.

(2) The present CVE situation will remain unchanged until the end of the year when *MISSION BAY* is scheduled to arrive in the Atlantic. Six additional CVEs are scheduled to arrive on the east coast during the first quarter of the calendar year 1944. The CVEs have continued their effective offensive operations against U-boats and only 1 ship has been sunk in convoys in the Atlantic that have been covered by a U.S. CVE Support Group.

(3) All Army aircraft in our Frontiers were relieved from anti-submarine duties with the Navy by 1 October except 1 squadron of B-25s in the Caribbean Sea Frontier equipped with 75 mm. cannon which were loaned to the Navy for anti-submarine evaluation of that weapon. The 4 Army B-24 Squadrons on anti-submarine operations in U.K. were relieved by Navy squadrons in October. The 2 remaining

Army B-24 squadrons in anti-submarine operations in Morocco are in process of being relieved by Navy B-24 squadrons.

2. MATERIEL

a. Surface Craft

(1) A single towed parallel rod noisemaker is now issued to all U.S. escorts to counter enemy acoustic torpedo. Expendable devices actuated by explosives or air are under test and give promise of being superior to FXR.

(2) A surface craft division of the Anti-Submarine Development Detachment has been established, and in addition to conducting experiments will further develop coordinated air and surface anti-submarine tactics.

(3) Mark 9 Depth Charges with faster sinking rate now replacing Mark 6 Ash Can type depth charge.

(4) Mark 8 Depth Charge with proximity pistol now being produced with quantity production commencing 1 December.

(5) Bearing Deviation Indicators to improve echo-ranging sound equipment is in quantity production.

(6) Bathyothermograph giving a water temperature depth curve is now being issued to escorts to obtain more accurate information on the sound conditions.

(7) 100 in. Dome being installed in new construction DDs will give improved echo-ranging performance at higher speeds — over 20 kts.

(8) Shipboard Anti-Submarine Attack Teacher is being issued to assist in shipboard training.

(9) Prospective developments to be accomplished within the next six months are:

(a) Mark 9 Mod 2 Depth Charge with Doppler Acoustic Proximity Fuse and improved sinking rate.

(b) Scatter Depth Charge to be projected from the usual projector.

(c) Mark 12 Depth Charge — small fast sinking stern dropped depth charges.

(d) The net result to be expected from improvements in depth charges is that effectiveness of patterns will be improved about 6 times.

b. *Aircraft*

(1) Rocket Projectile equipment is being introduced into service in both the Atlantic and Pacific Fleets; in the Atlantic as an anti-submarine weapon.

(2) Intercept receivers for enemy radar without direction finder and homing features are being installed in many Atlantic Fleet aircraft. A special test plane (B-24) is now in Moroccan Sea Frontier for purposes of obtaining data on German Radar wave lengths, etc. and when this is determined installed detectors will be made directional.

(3) Sono-radio Buoys and associated receivers are being installed in the Atlantic Fleet aircraft in limited numbers.

(4) Aircraft tactics to counter radar and use of intercept receivers by the enemy are being revised as new information is received.

(5) Increased forward firing power, additional armor and leak-proof tanks are being provided for all A/S aircraft to offset the fighting back tactics of U-boats.

STATUS OF ATLANTIC FLEET AND SEA FRONTIER ESCORTS

1 AUGUST ~ 1 NOVEMBER 1943

STATUS OF ANTI-SUBMARINE AIRCRAFT

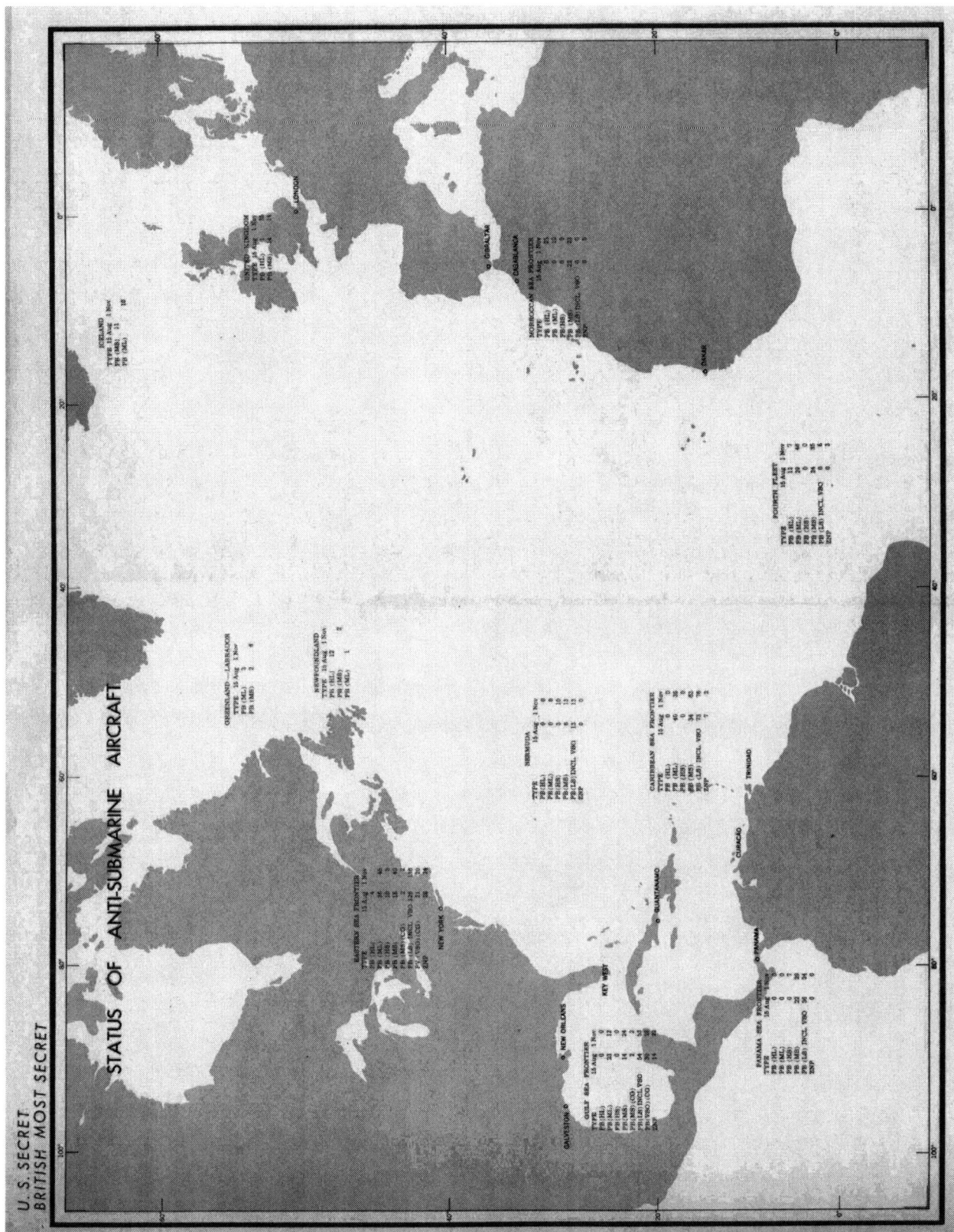

PROSPECTIVE DEPLOYMENTS OF ANTI-SUBMARINE AIRCRAFT

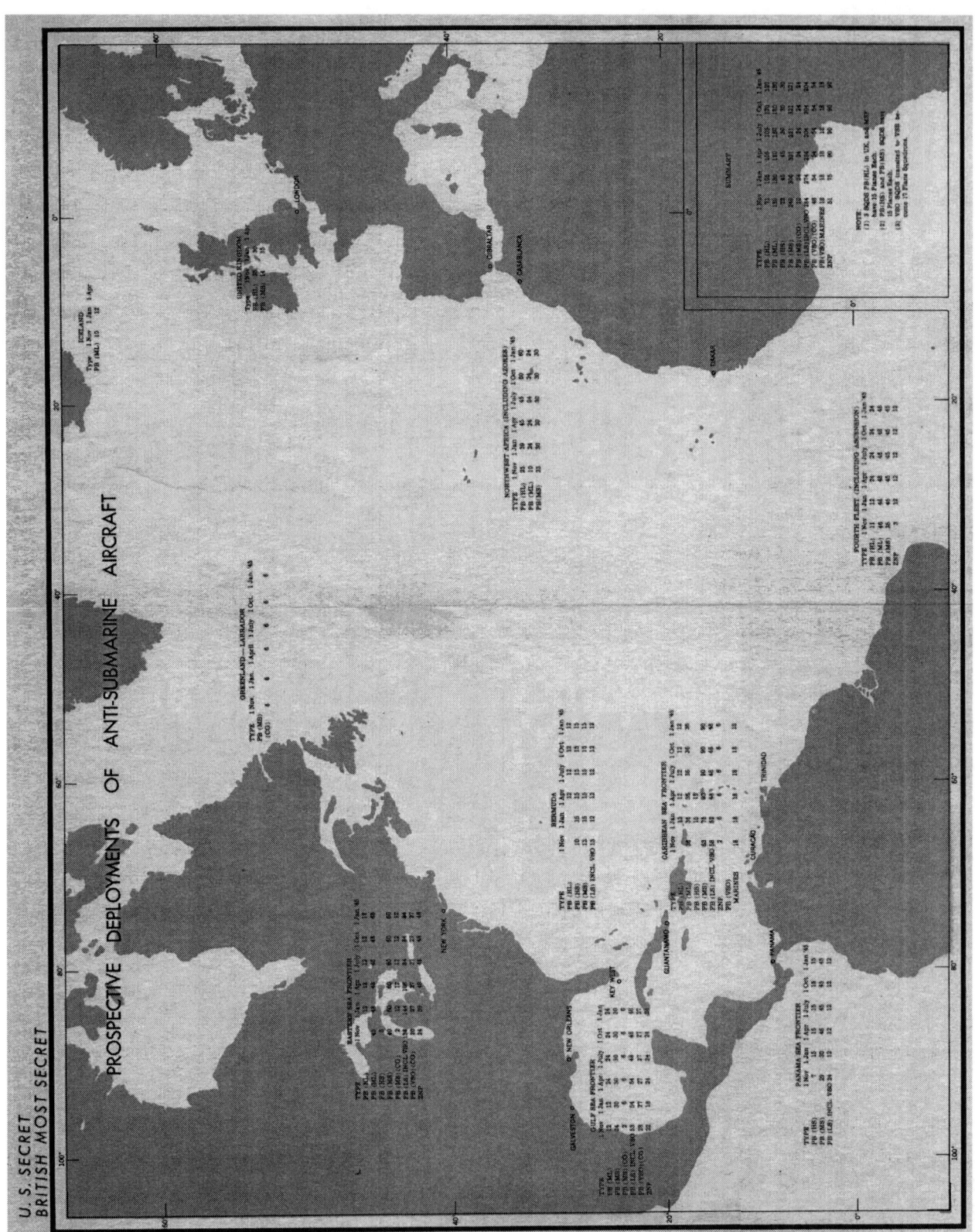

C.C.S. 399/1

PROGRESS REPORT ON THE U-BOAT WAR— SEPTEMBER-OCTOBER 1943

Reference:

CCS 133d Meeting, Item 5

C.C.S. 399/1 circulated a report from the British Chiefs of Staff. The Combined Chiefs of Staff took note of this report.

C.C.S. 399/1   23 November 1943

COMBINED CHIEFS OF STAFF

PROGRESS REPORT ON THE U-BOAT WAR— SEPTEMBER-OCTOBER 1943

Memorandum by the British Chiefs of Staff

7 November 1943

U-BOAT TREND

1. After an absence since May, 1943, U-boats again formed a pack of more than 15 in the North Atlantic and broke the lull on the 19th of September. Since that date this pack has been maintained, refuelling as necessary from supply boats and the pack being moved to intercept convoys.

2. U-boats have only operated on other stations in a sporadic fashion. A group of U-boats has carried out a campaign in the Indian Ocean in the approaches to convoy assembly ports, but this appears to be on the wane; one or two U-boats have operated off the Brazilian Coast, the West African Coast, in the Caribbean, off the U.S. Coast, and off the Canadian Coast.

3. Recent successes against fuel supply U-boats must be causing the enemy much inconvenience and seriously restricting the length of patrols in the N. Atlantic and the number of 500-ton U-boats that can operate in distant areas.

4. One attempt was made during September to reinforce the 14 U-boats at present in the Mediterranean. To the best of our belief, only one or two passed Gibraltar and the remainder turned back. Recent attacks in the Cape St. Vincent area indicate that this attempt at reinforcement continues, and two U-boats have been sunk in the Straits of Gibraltar.

OPERATIONS BY AREAS

North Atlantic

5. When the enemy reopened his attack on North Atlantic convoys his U-boats were armed with a new weapon—the acoustic homing torpedo—and there is some evidence that experts in listening to our H/F D/F R/T wave were also carried in a few U-boats. The first two convoys intercepted (O.N.S. 18 and O.N. 202) were joined together in order to get the full benefit of the 17 A/S vessels escorting them. The enemy succeeded in torpedoing six merchant vessels, their new weapon sank three escorts and damaged one for a probable loss of three U-boats sunk.

6. This pack failed to intercept a convoy again until 7 October owing to the success of our evasive routing. On this date they commenced an operation against S.C. 143 but only succeeded in torpedoing one merchant vessel and one escort for the loss of three U-boats.

7. Two further convoys were shadowed and attacked ineffectively during October (O.N. 206 and O.N.S. 20). One merchant vessel sunk for the loss of six U-boats.

Air cooperation with the above convoys was very satisfactory and the U-boats suffered severely on each attempt to attack.

8. Three British Escort Carriers are now operating with the support groups. U.S. Carriers operating in the North Atlantic have been most successful.

Gibraltar Convoys

9. Most of the convoys between Gibraltar and the United Kingdom and vice versa have been shadowed by enemy long-range aircraft, probably with the object of homing U-boats onto them. It appears that a small pack of U-boats was concentrated on S.L. 138/M.K.S. 28 on the last day of October, one ship being torpedoed. Weather prevented air cooperation but effective counter-attack by surface escorts appears to have prevented the assembly of the pack and probably resulted in sinking at least one U-boat.

Azores Area

10. There has been no U-boat activity in connection with our occupation of the Azores, although it is probable that a few U-boats did reconnoiter the area, and then left again owing to lack of profitable targets. Two Fortress squadrons are now based in the Azores and will afford A/S protection to U.K.-U.S.A. convoys on the southern route and to the U.K.-Gibraltar-Freetown convoys.

Caribbean Area

11. There has been only slight evidence of U-boat activity in the Caribbean, but it is suspected that mines may have been laid in the approaches to ports.

West African and Brazilian Areas

12. During September a German U-boat sank two ships off Brazil and was attacked by aircraft. Towards the end of October two or three U-boats operating between Freetown and Pointe Noire have sunk a single merchant vessel and her trawler escort. The small degree of success achieved off Brazil suggests that at least one of the U-boats operating there may have been sunk or driven off.

Indian Ocean

13. In the Indian Ocean, one U-boat was sunk by aircraft near Muscat and it appears that the campaign is now coming to a close. Japanese U-boats have also been taking part in this campaign. Twelve ships have been torpedoed and sunk in this area during the two months.

OPERATIONS AGAINST U-BOATS IN TRANSIT AREAS

14. U-boats in the transit areas are no longer remaining on the surface and fighting aircraft by day. They surface only to charge batteries for a minimum period by night, accepting the long time to pass through the danger area. The formation of a pack in the Atlantic forced us to withdraw escort vessels cooperating with Coastal Command aircraft in the Bay of Biscay.

15. The number of aircraft sightings in the Bay has dropped severely as we have insufficient aircraft fitted with Leigh searchlights; the Wellingtons so fitted are of insufficient range and bad weather has interfered with flying. Flying was cancelled on 13 nights in September. A comparison between the figures for sightings and attacks by aircraft taking part in the Bay offensive including sorties from Gibraltar and North Afrfica, and those by aircraft in the remainder of the North Atlantic, is as follows:

| | BAY OFFENSIVE | | NORTH ATLANTIC | |
	Sightings	*Attacks*	*Sightings*	*Attacks*
September	24	12	9	5
October	13	10	31	26

16. Similarly, the sightings in the Northern transit area have been very disappointing. We have inadequate air and surface forces for this task.

TACTICS

17. The use of an acoustic homing torpedo by a U-boat has increased the risk to an escort vessel chasing and attacking a contact. Measures have been introduced to enable an escort to avoid the probable danger area when these torpedos are suspected of having been fired (known as the "step aside" approach). They are apparently proving effective and, while delaying attack on the U-boat, enable an escort to continue the hunt as soon as clear of danger.

18. Otherwise there appears to have been little change in either the U-boat's method of attack or the escort's hunting tactics, although possibly the former are showing a greater timidity in closing to effective range when firing torpedoes.

NOISE-MAKING DEVICES TO COUNTER THE ACOUSTIC TORPEDO

19. The noise-maker known as the "Foxer," two of which are towed astern of each escort vessel, is now in sufficient production for all slower escorts to be fitted before sailing for convoy duty. Its operation is proving unsatisfactory owing to structural weakness of design which prevents it standing up to heavy weather, and to the interference that it causes with Asdic detection results. It is hoped that some of these difficulties may be overcome.

20. The development of other noise-making devices is proceeding under first priority. Generally speaking, the acoustic torpedo has not yet given the

enemy the advantage they must have hoped for, and it is worth noting that the Germans claimed they had sunk fifteen destroyers when, in fact, they had only sunk three and damaged one.

RADAR DECOYS

21. U-boats have been employing a Radar decoy balloon, a device which carries a length of line secured to a small wooden float with metal foil reflectors suspended on the line. U-boats are believed to carry about 50 of these decoys with apparatus for inflating the balloons on deck. The best counter-measure to this device is for the ship to start a plot of the suspicious echo immediately it is detected. The fact that echoes travelling in a direction other than down-wind cannot be due to decoys will be a means of differentiating between decoys and U-boats.

FUTURE POLICY

22. There is no doubt that the U-boats have returned to the North Atlantic convoy routes in considerable force and will endeavor to remain there until their losses become unacceptably high. They have been roughly handled by both aircraft and escorts and, from the number of attacks they have made on the latter, it can be assumed that they are endeavoring to torpedo escorts, using their acoustic homing torpedo, before concentrating on the convoy. In other respects the normal pack tactics are apparently still being employed. It is appreciated that enemy losses are already approaching the breaking limit and we must be prepared for yet another change on the part of the enemy.

23. When the aircraft in the Azores come into operation we may have great scope for evasive routing between the Azores zone and that of Iceland, and it may well be found that we can successfully secure the Atlantic trade routes by means of evasion.

24. This added scope will enable us to concentrate our striking forces in threatened areas and so develop the offensive against the U-boat. Coordination of the offensive with U.S.A. striking forces is satisfactory.

25. The above policy may not produce decisive results and we must take further measures to ensure making contact with U-boat concentrations and completing their destruction.

26. We have had opportunity to review the morale of the U-boat personnel in this new campaign and to assess their degree of determination or timidity. It is apparent from this examination that the U-boats are not pressing home their attacks and that they are more concerned with their own safety than heretofore.

27. It is considered, therefore, that we are now in a position to sail selected convoys on the most favorable route for air cover and efficient surface and air escort, prepared to accept battle with the U-boats in the confidence that we shall be masters of the situation whatever circumstances arise. This course of action has frequently been considered in the past, but the time has only just arrived when it is considered reasonable to accept the increased risk of encountering U-boats.

28. It is hoped that the above measures will inflict such heavy casualties on the enemy that he will be forced once again to withdraw from the North Atlantic and concentrate on attacks in dispersed areas.

29. This will be the moment to reinforce the Bay offensive to the maximum extent. Surface and air escorts to the convoys will have to be cut to a minimum in order to produce the necessary forces.

30. Preparations are now well in hand to provide increased numbers of Leigh Light-fitted aircraft, particularly to those of the V.L.R. and L.R. category. The enemy may be expected to strive for early warning of approaching aircraft by the use of listening devices against our A.S.V. and also by means of his own Radar. Measures have been taken to provide an alternative A.S.V. for our aircraft, also a device by which we can listen to enemy Radar and so home onto the U-boat. As expected from the outset of the Bay offensive in its present form, the only full answer to successful "early warning" of U-boats is the provision of sufficient aircraft for "flooding," i.e., such vigorous and continuous flying that will force the U-boat commander to exhaust his batteries if he dives on every occasion an aircraft threatens him. This technique would necessitate reinforcing the air forces operating in the Bay.

31. It is by these means we hope finally to break the morale of the U-boat service, and encompass its destruction. If successful, it may well prove a decisive factor in the defeat of the German High Command and the armed forces of the Reich.

APPENDIX

U-BOAT SINKINGS

U-boats sunk and probably sunk are:-

September	8
October	26
	34

SHIPPING LOSSES (By U-boat) (September and October)

A. *According to Areas*

	Number	Tonnage
Atlantic North of Equator	11	63,600
Atlantic South of Equator	4	20,500
Mediterranean	4	27,000
Indian Ocean	12	65,300
	31	176,400

B. *According to Duty*

	Number	Tonnage
Convoy and Escorted Groups	15	87,600
Independents	16	88,800
	31	176,400

C.C.S. 400, 400/1 and 400/2

INTEGRATED COMMAND OF U.S. STRATEGIC AIR FORCES IN THE EUROPEAN-MEDITERRANEAN AREA

References:

CCS 134th Meeting, Item 2
CCS 135th Meeting, Item 3
CCS 137th Meeting, Item 3
CCS 138th Meeting, Item 2

C.C.S. 400 circulated a memorandum by the United States Chiefs of Staff dated 18 November 1943. The British Chiefs of Staff circulated their reply (C.C.S. 400/1) on 26 November. The conclusions of the United States Chiefs of Staff relative to the alternate proposal suggested by the British Chiefs of Staff in C.C.S. 400/1 were circulated as C.C.S. 400/2, 4 December 1943.

The Combined Chiefs of Staff, in their 138th Meeting, agreed to accept C.C.S. 400/2.

C.C.S. 400   18 November 1943

COMBINED CHIEFS OF STAFF

INTEGRATED COMMAND OF U.S. STRATEGIC AIR FORCES

IN THE EUROPEAN-MEDITERRANEAN AREA

Memorandum by the United States Chiefs of Staff

THE PROBLEM

1. The provision of a directive to insure the most effective utilization of the U.S. Army Air Forces strategic bombing capabilities from all available European-Mediterranean bases in the accomplishment of the objectives of *POINTBLANK*.

DISCUSSION

(See Enclosure)

CONCLUSIONS

2. *a.* That control of all U.S. Strategic Air Forces in the European-Mediterranean area, including the control of movement of forces from one area to another, should be vested in a single command in order to exploit U.S. heavy bomber aircraft capabilities most effectively; and that these forces should be employed primarily against *POINTBLANK* objectives, or such other objectives as the Combined Chiefs of Staff may from time to time direct.

b. That such a command should likewise be charged with the coordination of these operations with those of the R.A.F. Bomber Command.

c. That the responsibility for over-all base service and administrative control of these Strategic Air Forces should remain in the appropriate Commanders of U.S. Army forces in the United Kingdom and in the Mediterranean area.

d. That provision should be made to assure the assignment of resources, supplies and other services between tactical and strategic operations so as

94

to bring the required support to *POINTBLANK* as the air operation of first priority.

e. That the headquarters of such U.S. Strategic Air Forces should be established in the United Kingdom because of the facilities available, the existing weight of the respective bomber forces, and the necessity for continuous integration of operations with the R.A.F.

RECOMMENDATIONS

3. It is recommended that:

a. There be established a U.S. Strategic Air Force Command with Headquarters in the United Kingdom, charged with the direction and coordination of all U. S. Strategic Air Force operations in the European-Mediterranean area.

b. A directive to implement the above, attached as Appendix, be issued to the following:

> Supreme Allied Commander,
>
> Commanding General, ETOUSA
>
> Allied Commander in Chief, NATO
>
> Commanding General, U. S. Strategic
>   Air Forces in Europe.

ENCLOSURE

DISCUSSION

1. There are at present in the Mediterranean Theater the 12th U.S. Army Air Force (Tactical) and the 15th U.S. Army Air Force (Strategic), as approved by the Combined Chiefs of Staff in a directive issued to General Eisenhower (C.C.S. 217/1, Appendix "C"), under which directive the Allied Commander in Chief, NATO, is charged with employing the 15th U.S. Air Force primarily against the selected targets of *POINTBLANK*. It is additionally directed that the operations of the 15th U.S. Air Force will be closely coordinated by direct liaison with the 8th U.S. Air Force.

2. The division of heavy bomber units between the 8th and the 15th U.S. Air Forces is likewise set forth in the above directive, upon a quarterly basis, resulting in the deployment of 41 heavy bomber groups in the U.K., and 21 heavy bomber groups in the Mediterranean, by 30 June 1944. This directive provides that those units of the current 12th U.S. Air Force, assigned to the newly organized 15th U.S. Air Force, may continue to be employed primarily against objectives other than *POINTBLANK* until such time as the air base objective area, north and east of Rome, is secured, and further that, should a tactical or strategical emergency arise, requiring such action, the U.S. Theater Commander is authorized, at his decision, to employ the 15th U.S. Air Force for purposes other than its primary mission, informing the Combined Chiefs of Staff of the action taken.

3. *Strategic bombing operations from bases other than the United Kingdom which compel German forces to spread in breadth and depth for the defense of other areas, or cause parallel destruction of selected POINTBLANK objectives, and particularly to the German fighter aircraft and aircraft industry, will contribute heavily to the success of POINTBLANK*, hasten the deterioration of the enemy over-all position and decrease losses.

4. Timing and coordination of the mutually supporting operations of the two Strategic Air Forces from the various bases is essential to achieve the most effective exploitation of U.S. heavy bomber aircraft capabilities. Forces should be moved promptly from one area to another to take immediate advantage of varying weather conditions, dispositions of enemy forces, current tactical operations or other circumstances of opportunity. The present command arrangement with the 8th Air Force under CG, ETOUSA and the 15th Air Force under CG, NATO requires decisions to be reached on a mutually cooperative basis in

which both commanders must agree. The integration of timing and services, to capitalize fully upon the mobility of aircraft and the need for prompt command decision not possible under the existing situation require a cohesive over-all control, not existent under present command directives.

5. The Joint Chiefs of Staff consider that the air war in Europe has reached a stage where the necessity for command direction over the components of the Strategic Air Forces is imperative. Unified command is necessary in order to achieve effective results from the concerted efforts of the bomber forces, and to reach the vital targets with minimum losses from the formidable defenses established by the enemy. Base facilities in the United Kingdom and the Mediterranean provide a potential flexibility which must be exploited to confuse, saturate and disperse the enemy defenses and reduce our losses. We feel that it is most urgent that we adopt every means known to us to save the lives of our men and sustain the impetus of their offensive. The one effective method is to insure the rapid, coordinated employment of the two components of our daylight striking force on a day-to-day basis, in order to obtain the maximum dispersion of enemy defenses and to take advantage of weather conditions in the United Kingdom and in the Mediterranean. Unified command over the Eighth and Fifteenth U.S. Air Forces must, therefore, be established without delay.

APPENDIX

DRAFT OF A PROPOSED DIRECTIVE

To: The Supreme Allied Commander
The Commanding General ETOUSA
Allied Commander in Chief NATO
Commanding General U.S. Strategic Air Forces in Europe

1. Effective 1 January 1944 there will be established an air command designated "The U.S. Strategic Air Forces in Europe," for the purpose of directing and coordinating the operations of the U.S. Strategic Air Forces in the European and Mediterranean areas. Headquarters for this air command will be established in the United Kingdom.

2. Lieut. General Carl Spaatz is designated "Commanding General, U.S. Strategic Air Forces in Europe."

3. The U.S. Strategic Air Forces in Europe will come directly under the command of the Supreme Allied Commander at a date to be announced later by the Combined Chiefs of Staff. In the interim the commander of the U.S. Strategic Air Forces in Europe will be directly under the Combined Chiefs of Staff.

4. The U.S. Strategic Air Forces in Europe will consist initially of the Eighth and Fifteenth U.S. Army Air Forces.

5. The U.S. Strategic Air Forces in Europe will be employed initially to achieve the objectives of the Combined Bomber Offensive, as directed by the Combined Chiefs of Staff. The Commanding General, USSAFE, will be charged with the strategic direction of the U.S. Strategic Air Forces, and he will assign missions to them, keeping the appropriate theater commanders informed. In carrying out his strategic objectives, the Commanding General, U.S. Strategic Air Forces in Europe is authorized to allocate, reallocate, or move any or all of the air force units placed under his command.

6. The Commanding General, U.S. Strategic Air Forces in Europe, will be charged with the coordination of the operations of the U.S. Strategic Air Forces with those of the R.A.F. Bomber Command, through the Chief of the Air Staff R.A.F.

7. The commanders of the U.S. Army Forces in the United Kingdom and in the Mediterranean area will continue to be responsible for administrative control of the U.S. Army air units in their respective areas, including the provision of base services. They will exercise a judicious allocation of resources and supplies and other services between tactical and strategic air forces in such manner as to provide the necessary support to *POINTBLANK* as the air operation of first priority.

8. Should a strategical or tactical emergency arise requiring such action, theater commanders may, at their discretion, utilize the strategic air forces, which are based within their respective theaters, for purposes other than their primary mission, informing the Combined Chiefs of Staff and the Commanding General, USSAFE, of the action taken.

9. The Commanding General, USSAFE, will employ six heavy bombardment groups and two long-range fighter groups of the Fifteenth Air Force to meet the requirements of the Commanding General, NATO, in operations against objectives other than those prescribed for *POINTBLANK*, until such time as the air base objective area, north and east of Rome, is secured, in accordance with the provision of the directive issued by the Combined Chiefs of Staff on 22 October (FAN 254).

CC.S. 400/1 26 November 1943

COMBINED CHIEFS OF STAFF

CONTROL OF STRATEGIC AIR FORCES IN NORTHWEST

EUROPE AND THE MEDITERRANEAN

Memorandum by the British Chiefs of Staff

1. In C.C.S. 400 the United States Chiefs of Staff have proposed that the U.S. Strategic Air Forces operating from the United Kingdom and from Mediterranean bases, the 8th and 15th Air Forces respectively, should be placed under a single Command—the U.S. Strategic Air Forces in Europe—with a Headquarters in the United Kingdom. The object of this proposal is to achieve the more effective exploitation of U.S. heavy bomber capabilities which, it is hoped, the new Headquarters will secure in two ways:

   a. By organizing mutually supporting operations of the two Strategic Air Forces in order to obtain the maximum dispersal of enemy defenses;

   b. By enabling advantage to be taken of changing weather and tactical conditions by switching heavy bomber forces quickly from one theater to another.

2. This proposal affects directly only U.S. heavy bomber forces, and we recognize the ultimate right of the United States Chiefs of Staff to decide the organization of U.S. forces in any theater of operations. We feel bound, however, to record our view that the adoption of this proposal would entail serious disadvantages far outweighing any advantages to be derived from it.

3. To deal first with the advantages which are expected from the present proposal:

   a. Great operational benefit would undoubtedly result if an effective combination of operations in the two theaters could be achieved. The operation of a large force of heavy day bombers is however a considerable undertaking and a period of up to 24 hours is required for the preparation and loading of aircraft and the briefing of crews. Unfortunately, the weather in the European theater is so uncertain that the decision to dispatch heavy bomber forces can only be taken a few hours before the time of take-off and it is then too late to make changes in targets and the timing of attacks. The conduct of operations in accordance with a settled policy in either theater is therefore a matter of great difficulty and frequently much effort is wasted, both in abortive operations and in standing by for operations which have to be canceled. A fortiori, the detailed coordination of attacks from two bases so far apart as the U.K. and Italy would be still more difficult and would in fact prove impossible. A commander set up to control the two forces would find in practice that he could do no more than insure that the subordinate commanders in each theater worked to a general plan and kept him and each other closely informed of the situation on their own front so that the general plan could be altered as necessary. Coordination of this type can be secured with the present organization without the introduction of a new headquarters.

b. The possibility of switching heavy bomber forces from one theater to another is at first sight an attractive one. In order to obtain full benefit from the plan, it would however be necessary to build up a margin of facilities in the two theaters involving the preparation of heavy bomber airfields, runways, and maintenance depots over and above what is required for the forces already based in the theater, and the locking up of additional maintenance personnel. If these additional facilities were not provided, the serviceability and effectiveness of the heavy bombers would fall considerably as soon as they were transferred and the operations carried out would be on a smaller scale and less effective than if the forces had to remain at their normal bases. The Air Ministry have, in the past, given very careful consideration to this plan but they have been forced to the conclusion that, except on rare occasions, the results would not justify the effort involved. Such occasional transfers of forces as are likely to be profitable can be secured by the present machinery.

c. The provision of the necessary margin of facilities which, if a large transfer of force is envisaged, may be considerable, must of necessity conflict in the U.K. with other service and governmental requirements. In Italy or other active theaters of war they can only be provided at the expense of other service requirements.

There is therefore a potential conflict of interest between the commander of the Strategic Air Force on the one hand and the U.K. Government and theater commanders on the other.

4. Our conclusion is that the setting up of a new higher headquarters would not achieve the advantages which are claimed from it and would not in fact

be any improvement over the existing machinery. It would, moreover, entail certain disadvantages which we consider to be serious, namely the following:

a. The most serious disadvantage is that it would destroy the present arrangements for the close coordination of the 8th Air Force and the R.A.F. including the 2nd Tactical Air Force. This depends for its effectiveness on the fact that general direction over their operations is exercised by the Chief of the Air Staff, R.A.F. The latter, with his headquarters in London, possesses not only a complete operational staff but is also served by the central Intelligence Staff of the three Services, the Ministry of Economic Warfare, and the Secret Intelligence Service, and is in the closest touch with the Admiralty, Foreign Office, Ministry of Home Security, and other Government departments. The Air Staff is also in constant touch with the Mediterranean Air Command on matters concerned with operations and Intelligence, and very close liaison arrangements have been made between the different commanders in the Mediterranean theater and in the United Kingdom.

The interposition of a new link in the chain of control would, we are convinced, cause a reduction in the efficiency of these arrangements, and the reduction would be even more serious if, as indicated in paragraph 3 of the directive proposed to C.C.S. 400, the Commanding General of U.S. Strategic Air Forces in Europe is placed as an interim measure directly under the Combined Chiefs of Staff. This latter proposal would mean the termination of the arrangement agreed to at Casablanca whereby the C.A.S. exercises general direction over the operations of the 8th Air Force in furtherance of the combined bomber offensive and would, in our opinion, be a retrograde step. It would in fact mean that the ultimate control required for the direction of the bomber offensive would have to be effected in Washington rather than as at present in London. Since all the Intelligence and administrative services which are essential for the efficiency of the bomber offensive are centralized in London, there could not fail to be a grave reduction in efficiency from this change.

The final arrangement proposed is that the new Commander should come directly under the Command of the Supreme Allied Commander for Operations in N.W. Europe. In our opinion, it would be fundamentally wrong in principle that the direction of a large part of the strategic bomber offensive which affects operations on all fronts in the European theater should be exercised by the Theater Commander of any single theater.

b. The new Commander would presumably require a large staff of all kinds in order to exercise operational and the necessary administrative control. We cannot help thinking that the provision of the large numbers of specialized and skilled staff officers needed must be a matter of considerable difficulty at the present time and, since the benefits expected from this proposal are in fact attainable under the present organization, that it would be highly wasteful in skilled manpower.

c. The proposal would also cause serious difficulties in the Mediterranean Air Command not only by a division of operational from administrative responsibility but also because it would mean that the night bomber component of the Mediterranean Strategical Air Force would be served by a different chain of information and would be under a different authority from the day bombing component though operated by the same headquarters staff in the Mediterranean theater. This could only make for confusion.

5. To summarize, we consider that the present proposal:

a. Would not secure any advantage over the present system of control;

b. Would mean breaking up the present highly integrated system of control, which has achieved considerable success, and the replacement of it by a less closely integrated and less effective system;

c. Would be wasteful in skilled staff.

We recognize however that there is much to be gained by having a single authority charged with the general direction of the heavy bomber offensive against Germany—someone who can interpret the Combined Chiefs of Staff directives by issuing detailed instructions from time to time according to the changing situation and who can exercise a general supervision over all bomber operations against Germany and the administrative support that they require, and over the provision of Intelligence and Tactical information so as to secure the most effective use of the heavy bomber forces engaged in the Combined Bomber Offensive. We do not see how such an authority can be on a lower level than a Chief of Staff since only on this level can the supervising authority keep in touch with all the strategical political and administrative factors which affect the bombing programme. Our conclusion is that the authority best able to exercise this general control is the Chief of the Air Staff. The latter, acting as the agent of the Combined Chiefs of Staff, is already charged with the coordination of the operations of the 8th Air Force and the R.A.F. This coordination has been of the closest and, in our opinion, has enabled the best possible use to be made of the available forces. It would not be difficult to extend this system to the 15th Air Force by giving the C.A.S. authority to regulate, in conformity with the plans of the Commanders of R.A.F. Bomber Command and the 8th Air Force in this country, the priority of objectives to be attacked by the 15th Air Force. The C.A.S. would also be in a position, subject to the Theater Commander's assessment of his administrative capacity, to transfer strategical forces from the United Kingdom to the Mediterranean and back if this seemed profitable.

6. The United States Chiefs of Staff may wish to consider this alternative arrangement to secure the advantages which they have in mind in putting forward their present proposal.

C.C.S. 400/2   4 December 1943

COMBINED CHIEFS OF STAFF

CONTROL OF STRATEGIC AIR FORCES IN NORTHWEST
EUROPE AND IN THE MEDITERRANEAN

Memorandum by the United States Chiefs of Staff

1. The United States Chiefs of Staff have considered the subject matter presented in the memorandum from the British Chiefs of Staff, C.C.S. 400/1, and concluded that the advantages to be gained by a more effective exploitation of U.S. daylight precision bombing capabilities, through unification of the command of U.S. Strategic Air Forces, outweigh the disadvantages anticipated by the British Chiefs of Staff.

2. We do not consider that the occasional transfer of aircraft from one theater to another will occasion any significant wastage of manpower or facilities, as each A.A.F. group station is organized to take care of the needs of two groups for brief periods.

3. Neither do we consider that there should be any slackening in the existing close coordination of operations between the U.S. Strategic Air Forces and the R.A.F., as the headquarters of the former will remain in the U.K. in unaltered contact with the intelligence and other services provided by the latter. In fact, this coordination should be broadened by drawing the 15th Strategic Air Force into a unified command.

4. The U.S. Joint Chiefs of Staff, after giving careful consideration to the alternative arrangement suggested by the British Chiefs of Staff, have concluded:

   a. That control of all U.S. Strategic Air Forces in the European-Mediterranean area, including the control of movement of forces from one area to another, should be vested in a single command in order to exploit the flexibility of U.S. heavy bomber capabilities most effectively and that these forces should be employed primarily against *POINTBLANK* objectives or such other objectives as the Combined Chiefs of Staff may from time to time direct.

b. That such a command should likewise be charged with the coordination of these operations with those of the R.A.F. Bomber Command.

c. That the responsibility for over-all base services and administrative control of these Strategic Air Forces should remain with the appropriate commanders of U.S. Army Forces in the United Kingdom and in the Mediterranean area.

d. That provision should be made to assure the assignment of resources, supplies, and other services between tactical and strategic operations so as to bring the required support to *POINTBLANK* as the air operation of first priority.

e. That the headquarters of such U.S. Strategic Air Forces should be established in the United Kingdom because of the facilities available, the existing weight of the respective bomber forces, and the necessity for continuous integration of operations with the R.A.F.

f. That the Commanding General, U.S. Army Air Forces, should continue to have direct channels of approach to the U.S. Strategic Air Force Commander in order to provide direct technical control and insure that operational and training technique and uniformity of U.S. tactical doctrine are maintained.

5. A directive to implement the above, attached as Enclosure, is therefore being issued to the following:

> Commanding General, USSAFE
> Commanding General, ETOUSA
> Commanding General, NATO

E N C L O S U R E

DRAFT OF A DIRECTIVE

To be Issued by the United States Chiefs of Staff

TO: Commanding General, U.S. Strategic Air Forces in Europe.
The Commanding General, ETOUSA.
The Commanding General, NATO.

1. Effective 1 January 1944 there will be established an air command designated "The U.S. Strategic Air Forces in Europe," consisting initially of the Eighth and Fifteenth U.S. Army Air Forces. Headquarters for this air command will be established in the United Kingdom. An officer of the U.S. Army Air Forces will be designated Commanding General, U.S. Strategic Air Forces in Europe.

2. The U.S. Strategic Air Forces in Europe will come directly under the command of the Supreme Allied Commander at a date to be announced later by the Combined Chiefs of Staff. In the interim the Chief of the Air Staff, R.A.F. will continue to act as the agent of the Combined Chiefs of Staff, pending transfer of the USSAFE to the command of the S.A.C., and will be responsible under the Combined Chiefs of Staff for coordination of all *POINT-BLANK* operations. Under his direction, the Commanding General, U.S. Strategic Air Forces in Europe will be responsible for the determination of priorities of *POINTBLANK* targets to be attacked by the Eighth and Fifteenth Air Forces and for the technique and tactics employed and is authorized to move the units of the Eighth and Fifteenth Air Forces between theaters within the limits of base area facilities and available for his forces.

3. The Commanding General USSAFE will keep the Allied Commander in Chief in the Mediterranean Theater informed of his general intentions and requirements. As far as possible, consistent with the performance of his primary mission, the Commanding General USSAFE will coordinate his operations with those of the Allied Commander in Chief in the Mediterranean.

4. The Commanding General, U.S. Army Forces in the European and North African Theaters of operations will continue to be responsible for the administrative control of the U.S. Army air units in their respective area, including

the provision of base services. The Commander in Chief, Allied Forces in the Mediterranean will provide the necessary logistical support to the Fifteenth Air Force in performance of operation *POINTBLANK* as the air operation of first priority.

5. Should a strategical or tactical emergency arise requiring such action, theater commanders may, at their discretion utilize the strategic air forces, which are based within their respective theaters, for purposes other than their primary mission, informing the Combined Chiefs of Staff and the Commanding General, USSAFE of the action taken.

6. The Commanding General, USSAFE, will employ six heavy bombardment groups and two long-range fighter groups of the Fifteenth Air Force to meet the requirements of the Commanding General, NATO, in operations against objectives other than those prescribed for *POINTBLANK*, until such time as the air base objective area, north and east of Rome, is secured, in accordance with the provisions of the directive issued by the Combined Chiefs of Staff on 22 October (FAN 254).

C.C.S. 401, 401/1, and 401/2

V.L.R. AIRFIELDS (B-29) IN THE CHINA-BURMA-INDIA AREA

C.C.S. 401 circulated a memorandum by the United States Chiefs of Staff. The reply from the British Chiefs of Staff was circulated as C.C.S. 401/1.

Informal agreement on interpretation of paragraph 3, C.C.S. 401/1 is noted by the Combined Chiefs of Staff in C.C.S. 401/2, circulated 6 December 1943.

C.C.S. 401   18 November 1943

COMBINED CHIEFS OF STAFF

V.L.R. AIRFIELDS (B-29) IN THE CHINA-BURMA-INDIA AREA

References: a. CCS 323
b. CCS 319/5

Memorandum by the United States Chiefs of Staff

1. In the final *QUADRANT* Report, C.C.S. 319/5, the following decisions were made:

"6. *h.* Undertake such measures as may be necessary and practicable in order to aid the war effort of China as an effective ally and as a base for operations against Japan."

"40. To continue to build up and increase the air routes and air supplies of China, and the development of air facilities, with a view to:

a. Keeping China in the war.

b. Intensifying operations against the Japanese.

c. Maintaining increased U.S. and Chinese Air Forces in China.

d. Equipping Chinese ground forces."

2. It now appears possible that B-29 aircraft will be available early in 1944 and that offensive operations from India and China against Japan might be intensified earlier than contemplated at *QUADRANT* if suitable airfields could be constructed in India and the Chengtu area of China.

3. Current studies indicate that a minimum of four such airfields in the Calcutta area and five in the Chengtu area would probably be required for the employment of these aircraft.

4. The airfields in the Calcutta area would be constructed in coordination with British authorities in India.

5. The airfields at Chengtu would be constructed in coordination with the Chinese Government.

6. It is believed that operations against the Japanese from China can be intensified in the spring of 1944 by the use of B-29 bombers if airfields are made available in the Calcutta and Chengtu areas.

RECOMMENDATIONS

7. It is recommended:

   a. That the Combined Chiefs of Staff impress the proper authoritites to make available in the Calcutta area the facilities which are necessary for the construction of four V.L.R. airfields.

   b. That the proper U.S. authorties initiate necessary measures to construct five V.L.R. airfields in the Chengtu area of China.

   c. That these airfields be completed not later than May 1944 insofar as consistent with the commitments already placed on the Allied Commanders in those areas.

C.C.S 401/1   23 November 1943

COMBINED CHIEFS OF STAFF

V.L.R. AIRFIELDS (B-29) IN THE CHINA-BURMA-INDIA AREA

Memorandum by the British Chiefs of Staff

1. As the United States Chiefs of Staff will be aware, the President has already telegraphed to the Prime Minister with regard to the provision of suitable airdromes in India and China for the operation of B-29 aircraft against Japan in the spring of 1944. The Prime Minister has instructed the Commander in Chief, India, to render every possible assistance in the construction of the four air bases in India and has so informed the President. An examination of the project has been undertaken and we are satisfied that the difficulties involved, including the movement of the extra tonnage required through the port of Calcutta, can be overcome.

2. We therefore accept the recommendations of the United States Chiefs of Staff contained in paragraph 7 of C.C.S. 401 and are issuing the necessary instructions to the British authorities concerned.

3. If the necessary work in India is to be completed in time, it is essential that the United States units and equipment required should arrive in Calcutta by 15 Janaury; otherwise the work will not be completed by 1 April and in fact would have to be stopped to allow resources temporarily diverted owing to airfield construction to be sent through to Ledo.

C.C.S. 401/2 6 December 1943

COMBINED CHIEFS OF STAFF

V.L.R. AIRFIELDS (B-29) IN THE CHINA-BURMA-INDIA AREA

Note by the Secretaries

The Combined Chiefs of Staff have agreed to the following interpretation of paragraph 3 of C.C.S. 401/1:

"If the necessary work in India is to be completed by the desired date of April first, it is essential that the United States units and equipment required should arrive in Calcutta by the 15th of January and, in addition, that certain resources be diverted from Ledo, which would result in delaying progress of road construction for a period of six weeks to two months.

"Certain preparatory work in advance of arrival of American units and equipment can be done without interfering with S.E.A.C. projects which, with arrival of necessary resources from the U.S. by January 15th, will permit completion of the airfields by May 15th."

H. REDMAN,

F. B. ROYAL,

Combined Secretariat.

C.C.S. 403 and 403/1

PROGRESS REPORT, COMBINED BOMBER OFFENSIVE

References:

CCS 133d Meeting, Items 5 and 6

C.C.S. 403 circulated a progress report on the Combined Bomber Offensive prepared by the Chief of the Air Staff and the Commanding General, U.S. Eighth Air Force. C.C.S. 403/1 presented comments by the British Chief of Air Staff which were circulated for information.

The Combined Chiefs of Staff in their 133d Meeting considered the Combined Bomber Offensive plan and agreed:

a. That the present plan for the Combined Bomber Offensive should remain unchanged.

b. That General Eaker should not be urged to catch up the three months of arrears.

c. That General Eaker should be told to expand his operations to the extent possible with the aircraft and crews available.

C.C.S. 403   21 November 1943

COMBINED CHIEFS OF STAFF

PROGRESS REPORT, COMBINED BOMBER OFFENSIVE

Note by the Secretaries

The attached message, on the program of the Combined Bomber Offensive, has been received from the Chief of the Air Staff and the Commanding General, U.S. Eighth Air Force, and is submitted for the consideration of the Combined Chiefs of Staff.

H. REDMAN,

F. B. ROYAL,

Combined Secretariat.

116

INDEX

ENCLOSURE

PROGRESS MADE BY THE R.A.F. AND UNITED STATES EIGHTH AIR FORCE IN THE COMBINED BOMBER OFFENSIVE

PERIOD COVERED

1. This report covers the period from 4 February to 31 October 1943. The former is the date of issue to Bomber Command and the Eighth Air Force of the Combined Chiefs of Staff directive C.C.S. 166/1/D, approved by the Combined Chiefs of Staff on 21 January 1943. This directive is attached as Appendix "A," C.C.S. 403/1.

METHOD OF EMPLOYMENT OF THE FORCES

2. The forces concerned have operated in accordance with that directive and a supplementary directive issued on 10 June 1943 by the Chief of the Air Staff, in order to implement the Combined Bomber Offensive Plan as approved by the Combined Chiefs of Staff. This directive is attached as Appendix "B," C.C.S. 403/1.

3. The primary object of the bomber offensive from the United Kingdom as stated in the earlier directive was:

> "The progressive destruction and dislocation of the German military, industrial, and economic system and the undermining of the morale of the German people to a point where their capacity for armed resistance is fatally weakened."

The primary object of the subsequent directive remained as set out above. In view, however, of the increasing strength of the German fighter forces, and in order to check their growth and reduce their strength, it was decided that first priority should be accorded to the attack of these forces and the industry on which they depended.

4. At the beginning of the period covered by this report the Eighth Bomber Command, while in process of developing their offensive power, were employed mainly in the attack of submarine construction yards and operating bases. From the beginning of April, with the formulation of the Combined Bomber Offensive Plan, their effort was directed increasingly to the destruction of the

G.A.F. fighter forces. In the summer months the R.A.F. Bomber Command, being limited in radius of action by the available hours of darkness, concentrated upon the destruction of the Ruhr-Rhineland industries and the undermining of the morale of the workers of that area. With the incidence of longer nights they have been able to make a more direct contribution to the reduction of the German Air Force, and vastly to extend their effects on the enemy's military industrial and economic systems as well as on enemy morale generally, by the destruction of a number of towns and cities of critical importance in the enemy's war economy.

5. The British and United States medium bombers and British fighter-bombers have been used mainly against enemy airfields in diversionary attacks, so timed and directed as to reduce the concentration of fighters which could oppose the passage of the heavy formations.

6. British and United States fighters have been used increasingly to cover the bomber formations, both on the outward and return passage, to the limits of their range. By the use of long-range tanks, American fighters have been able to give effective fighter cover to targets as far afield as Bremen and the Ruhr.

FORCES EMPLOYED

7. The strategic bomber forces available during the period under review are shown in Plates I and II. The effort of the medium and light bomber and fighter aircraft in support of the Combined Bomber Offensive is shown in Plates III, IV, V, and VI.

ASSESSMENT OF RESULTS ACHIEVED

8. In assessing the results of the Combined Bomber Offensive it will be appreciated that our sources of information are necessarily limited; a complete and accurate picture of results achieved is not possible. We are dependent to a large extent on air photography, but much damage sustained in air bombardment is not revealed by air photography. Assessments of results based on photographs, even when interpreted in the light of known effects produced by the enemy attacks on objectives in the United Kingdom, are liable to large discrepancies. Comparison is the more difficult since the scale of enemy attack on this country, even when the enemy was making his heaviest raids in 1940 and 1941, was far smaller than we are now delivering on objectives in Germany.

Moreover, his general economic structure is far weaker and less resilient than was that of the United Kingdom at that time. Viewed as a whole, however, all evidence points to the fact that conditions in Germany are resolving themselves into an ever more acute conflict of priorities, and a marked deterioration in morale.

GENERAL RESULTS ON TOWNS AND CITIES

9. With photographic cover as the basis of calculation, it is estimated that of the towns of outstanding importance in the enemy's war economy 19 have been virtually destroyed, 19 seriously damaged, and 9 damaged. The term "destroyed" can be taken as expressing devastation to a degree which makes the objective a liability to the total German war effort in excess of any remaining assets; "serious damage" implies urban destruction greater than the most serious damage experienced in the United Kingdom.

10. This degree of devastation of industry and urban areas is illustrated by the following figures of acreage devastated by our own attacks on Germany and by enemy attacks on the United Kingdom:

> *Coventry:* 120 out of 1,922 acres devastated.
> *Hamburg:* 6,200 out of 8,382 acres devastated.
> *Cologne:* 1,785 out of 3,320 acres devastated.
> *Essen:* 1,030 out of 2,630 acres devastated.
> *Elberfeld:* 825 out of 1,068 acres devastated.

GENERAL RESULTS OF PRECISE DAY ATTACKS

11. VIII Bomber Command have concentrated their attacks upon individual targets, as well as individual industries, selected in the light of their critical importance to the German war effort. Damage to such targets must, therefore, have proportionately greater effect upon the German military machine as a whole than damage achieved in the course of area attack, which normally embraces a wide range of unrelated industries. Thus the attacks on the ball-bearing industry at Schweinfurt and the synthetic rubber plant at Huls have undoubtedly produced far-reaching effects throughout the range of German war industry.

12. Similarly the ability to concentrate a series of daylight attacks on a single vital system, as in the case of the attacks made upon the fighter

factories at Regensburg, Kassel, Oschersleben, Marienburg, Anklam, Warnemunde and Wiener Neustadt are likely to have produced effects within that industry far in excess of the sum of the visible damage. Thus by means of precise and selective attack it may well be possible to reduce below a critical level an individual industry without which Germany cannot continue her military resistance.

EFFECTS ON ENEMY'S WAR ECONOMY GENERALLY

13. The general effects of our bomber offensive against Germany are indicated briefly in the following extracts from a Joint Report by the Ministry of Economic Warfare and the Air Ministry Intelligence Branch:

Over-all Effects

(i) (a) "It is difficult to estimate the over-all effect in quantitative terms, but it is considered to be now in the region of 10 percent of the total war potential. A total decline of 20 percent in over-all effort may well be fatal."

(b) "The effects of bombing do not fall evenly on the various parts of the enemy's war potential, and, to some extent, they are redistributed according to the immediate requirements of the consumers of war material having the highest priority in Germany."

(c) "There is the very much greater decline in some individual industries (e.g., ball-bearings and rubber), which may be near the point where they could cause the collapse of the whole war machine."

Effects on manpower

(ii) "The employment of a considerable and increasing number of full-time adult personnel in anti-aircraft and civil defense, factory repair and reconstruction, and first-aid to housing, represents a serious drain on Germany's industrial manpower that might otherwise have been employed on production."

Effects on Fighter Aircraft Production

(iii) "Damage to assembly factories alone . . . . has resulted in the production loss of 880 single-engined fighter aircraft, and production in October was between 600 and 700 against an estimated planned production of 1,000."

"Single-engined fighter production in the months of September and October was on a lower level than in the month of July, notwithstanding the high degree of priority accorded to single-engined fighter production and the considerable planned expansion in output."

Effects on Morale

(iv)   "The maintenance of morale is the greatest single problem confronting the home authorities. The full effects of air attack since the devastation of Hamburg have become known in all parts of the country. The increasing death roll is the important factor and, coupled with military failures, the general attitude is approaching one of 'peace at any price' and the avoidance of the wholesale destruction of further cities in Germany."

"Damage to housing, combined with evacuation, has resulted in the final saturation of all suitable accommodation in Germany. In the coming winter the problem of housing evacuees, many of whom have hitherto been in temporary dwellings unsuitable to winter conditions, will put upon the home administration a burden that it may not be able to support."

". . . . The housing situation and the general morale are both so bad that either might cause a collapse before industry became unable to sustain the war effort.

EFFECTS ON THE GENERAL MILITARY SITUATION

14. The bomber offensive has made a significant contribution to the success of the Allied military operations on the Mediterranean and Russian Fronts. The enemy has been compelled to withdraw fighters from the support of his armies to counter the threat from the West. A year ago 38 percent of his fighter strength was deployed on the Western Front. With the growth of the bomber offensive the proportion had risen to 45 percent in April and is now 63 percent. The changes in this situation are outlined in Plate VII. The repercussions upon the armies in the field of this denial of the essential minimum of air support have been far reaching in their general effect on the conduct of enemy military operations, particularly on the Russian Front, where our Allies have now achieved outstanding air superiority as a direct result of our efforts on the Western Front. The very fact of these changes which have been imposed on the enemy is an indication that he is forced to defend his home front even at the cost of serious military reverses.

15. The reduction of supplies of weapons, technical equipment and transport vehicles consequent upon our sustained and damaging air offensive has doubtless played a great part in further restricting the enemy's military capabilities.

EFFECTS ON U-BOAT WAR

16. The attacks by the VIII Bomber Command on submarine construction yards and operating bases, coupled with the area attacks upon industrial centres by the R.A.F. Bomber Command, have reduced the scale of U-boat activity. It is estimated that attacks on U-boat construction and components manufacture have in 1943 caused a direct loss of at least 22 U-boats out of a total of about 200 that would have been launched by the end of October. The delayed action of attacks on areas producing materials and components appears now to be having an effect on the average rate of completion. See Appendix "C", C.C.S. 403/1.

DETAILED ESTIMATES OF THE TOTAL EFFECTS
OF THE BOMBER OFFENSIVE

17. Estimates of the total effects of the Bomber Offensive are given in the following reports:

   (i) Joint report by the Ministry of Economic Warfare and the Air Ministry Intelligence Branch dated 4 November 1943. Appendix "C", C.C.S. 403/1.

   (ii) Summary of conclusions on effects of bombing offensive on German war effort in 1943 up to July by the British War Cabinet Joint Intelligence Subcommittee. Appendix "D", C.C.S. 403/1.

   (iii) Summary of conclusions on effects of bombing offensive on German war effort for the period July to October 1943 by the British War Cabinet Joint Intelligence Subcommittee. Appendix "E", C.C.S. 403/1.

   (iv) Joint Report by the Air Ministry Intelligence Branch and the Political Warfare Executive on Allied Air Attacks and German Morale. Appendix "F", C.C.S. 403/1.

SCALE OF EFFORT

18. The effort of the combined strategic bomber forces during the period under review totalled 61,690 sorties. They consisted of:

Night sorties	45,844
Day sorties	15,846
Total	61,690

19. The detailed statistics of scale of effort are given in Plates VIII, IX, X, and XI.

CASUALTIES INVOLVED

20. The number of strategic bombers missing during the period under review was:

R.A.F. (averaging 198 a month with a cumulative rate of 3.9 percent)	1,784
VIIIth Bomber Command (averaging 78 a month with a cumulative rate of 4.4 percent)	698
Total (cumulative rate, 4 percent)	2,482

21. Notwithstanding these casualties, and the higher rate incurred in deep daylight penetrations into Germany, the morale of crews remains high. It appears to be governed only by the degree of success achieved.

22. The casualties for heavy, medium and light bombers and fighters are given in Plates VIII, X, XII, and XIII.

ENEMY EFFORTS TO COUNTER THE BOMBER OFFENSIVE

23. The enemy has been unsuccessful in his attempt to counter effectively the bomber offensive, and there is as yet no indication that he can develop new methods which will defeat our offensive. His efforts have taken the form of:

(i) Increased production of fighters at the expense of bombers.

(ii) Redistribution of fighter and other defense resources to meet the threat.

(iii) New tactics and weapons.

24. The increasing effort devoted to fighter production continues. This is shown graphically in Plate XIV. Single-engined fighter production, on which our attacks have so far been concentrated, has been reduced materially, but production of twin-engined fighters has increased. Bomber production continues on a reduced scale. The first-line strengths of the German fighter and bomber forces are shown in Plate XV.

25. The German fighter force has been increasingly concentrated on the Western Front until it has now reached a figure of 1,800. The redistribution of fighter forces following on our bomber offensive is shown in Plate VII.

26. The deep daylight penetrations into Germany of the United States bombers have forced the enemy to deploy his defenses in depth. Although he has disposed on the Western Front the maximum possible number of fighters, this in itself does not meet his needs, and he has been forced to increase their mobility and to employ increasing numbers of twin-engined fighters. He can now concentrate against bomber formations penetrating deep into Germany, fighters from an area extending from the West of Paris to the Baltic. The main counter to this mobility continues to be feints and diversionary attacks.

27. At night the use of "Window" and other radio counter-measures has largely neutralized his controlled night fighter system. He has been forced to adopt a new system of concentrating large forces of single-engined and twin-engined fighters which "free-lance" over what he assumes will be the target. This opens up exceptional opportunities for feint attacks, and these have already been exploited with success; the enemy night defense system has frequently been thrown into great confusion.

28. Flak and searchlights have equally been disorganized by "Window," the use of which, coupled with the expected presence of night fighters over the target, has restricted flak activity to barrage fire below the level of the bomber stream. This has increased the reliance and hence the strain on the fighter defenses. Our new tactics have substantially reduced the percentage success of the enemy's night fighter sorties, and up to date he has found no method of meeting the situation, except to increase continuously the number of fighters available for the purpose.

29. The day and night fighters responsible for the defense of Germany have now been placed under a single command, and are required to deal with both the United States attacks by day and the R.A.F. attacks by night. This system of employment in a dual role may produce weaknesses during the periods of sustained day and night attack.

30. The principal new weapon developed for day use by the enemy is the rocket, mounted mainly on twin-engined fighters. This weapon has been used effectively in massed attacks delivered from the rear of the bomber formations and from beyond the range of the .50 calibre tail guns. Such attacks have been coordinated with single-engined fighter attacks from other quarters. Rocket-equipped aircraft are extremely vulnerable to our fighters, and although their employment is increasing, the most dangerous enemy of the day bomber remains the single-engined cannon fighter.

31. In the face of these new tactics and new weapons the bombers have continued to operate successfully and have every expectation of being able so to continue.

RECOMMENDATION

32. All evidence indicates that the Combined Bomber Offensive is achieving a profound effect upon Germany's war economy and upon the morale of her people. In the continuation of the offensive toward a decision, time is a vital factor. The offensive should be pressed on, in accordance with the existing directives, with all vigor, and its intensity increased.

7 November 1943

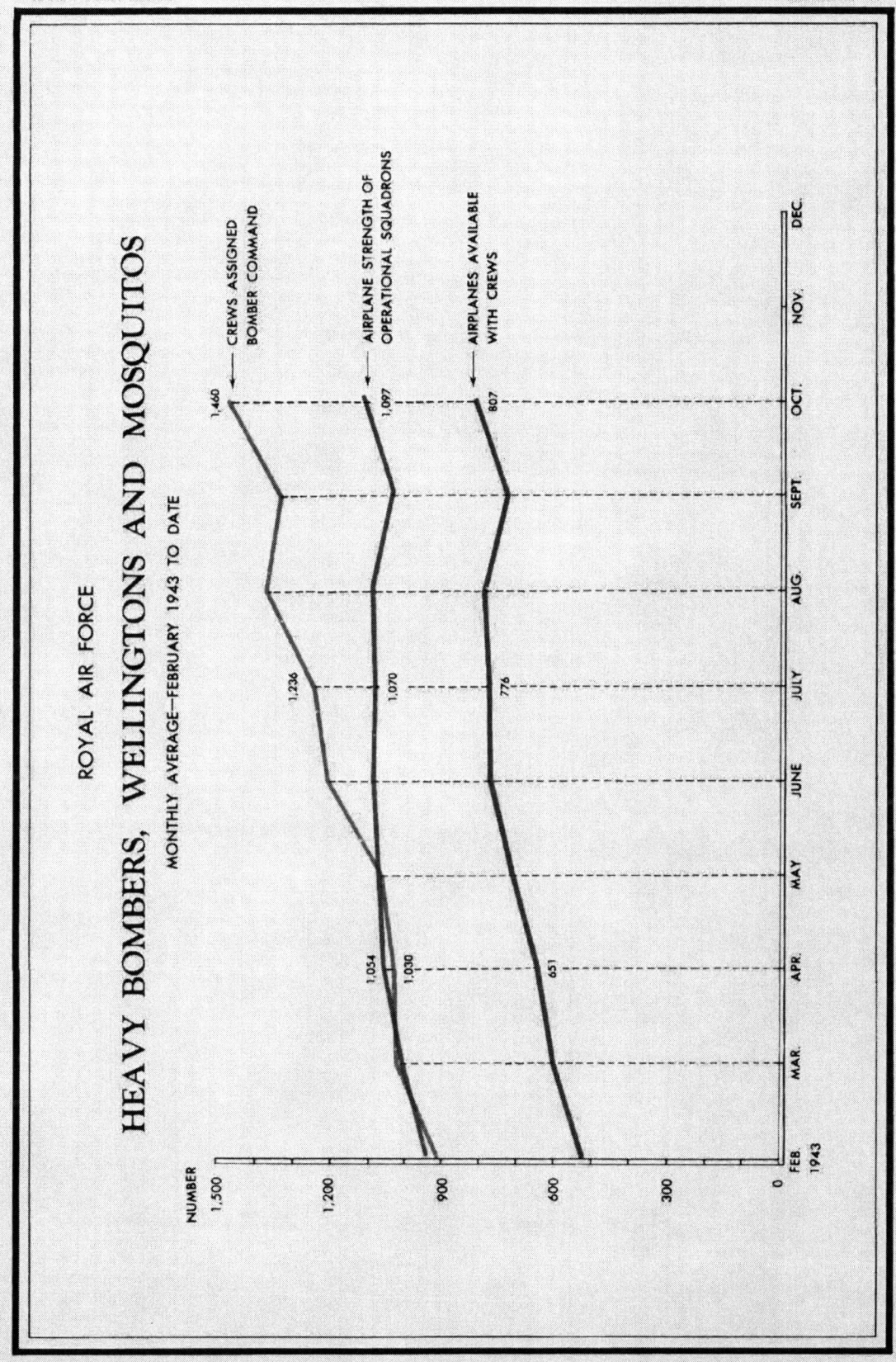

ROYAL AIR FORCE

HEAVY BOMBERS, WELLINGTONS AND MOSQUITOS

MONTHLY AVERAGE—FEBRUARY 1943 TO DATE

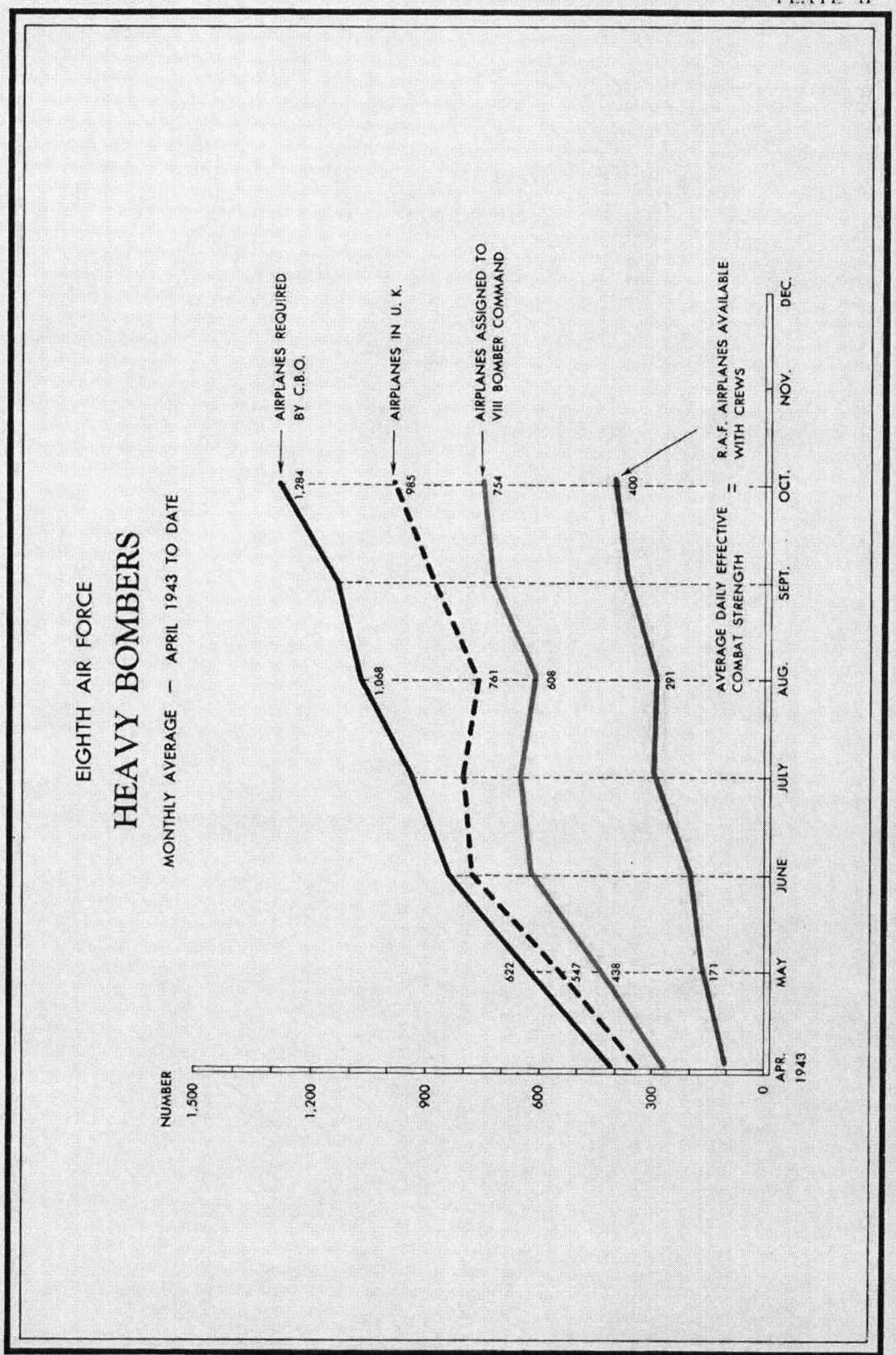

EIGHTH AIR FORCE

HEAVY BOMBERS

MONTHLY AVERAGE — APRIL 1943 TO DATE

AIRPLANES REQUIRED BY C.B.O.

AIRPLANES IN U. K.

AIRPLANES ASSIGNED TO VIII BOMBER COMMAND

R.A.F. AIRPLANES AVAILABLE WITH CREWS

AVERAGE DAILY EFFECTIVE COMBAT STRENGTH =

129

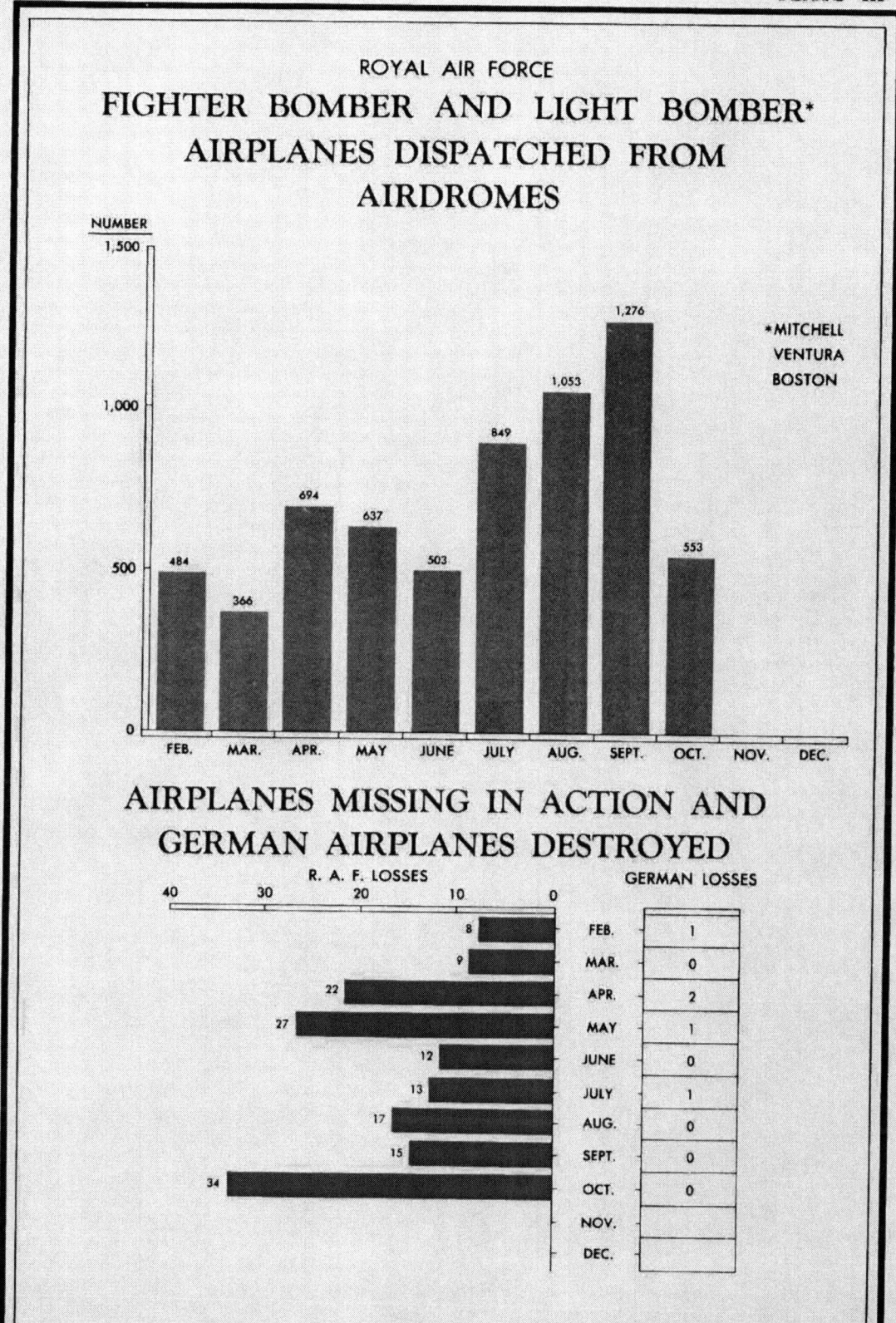

ROYAL AIR FORCE

FIGHTER BOMBER AND LIGHT BOMBER* AIRPLANES DISPATCHED FROM AIRDROMES

*MITCHELL
VENTURA
BOSTON

AIRPLANES MISSING IN ACTION AND GERMAN AIRPLANES DESTROYED

131

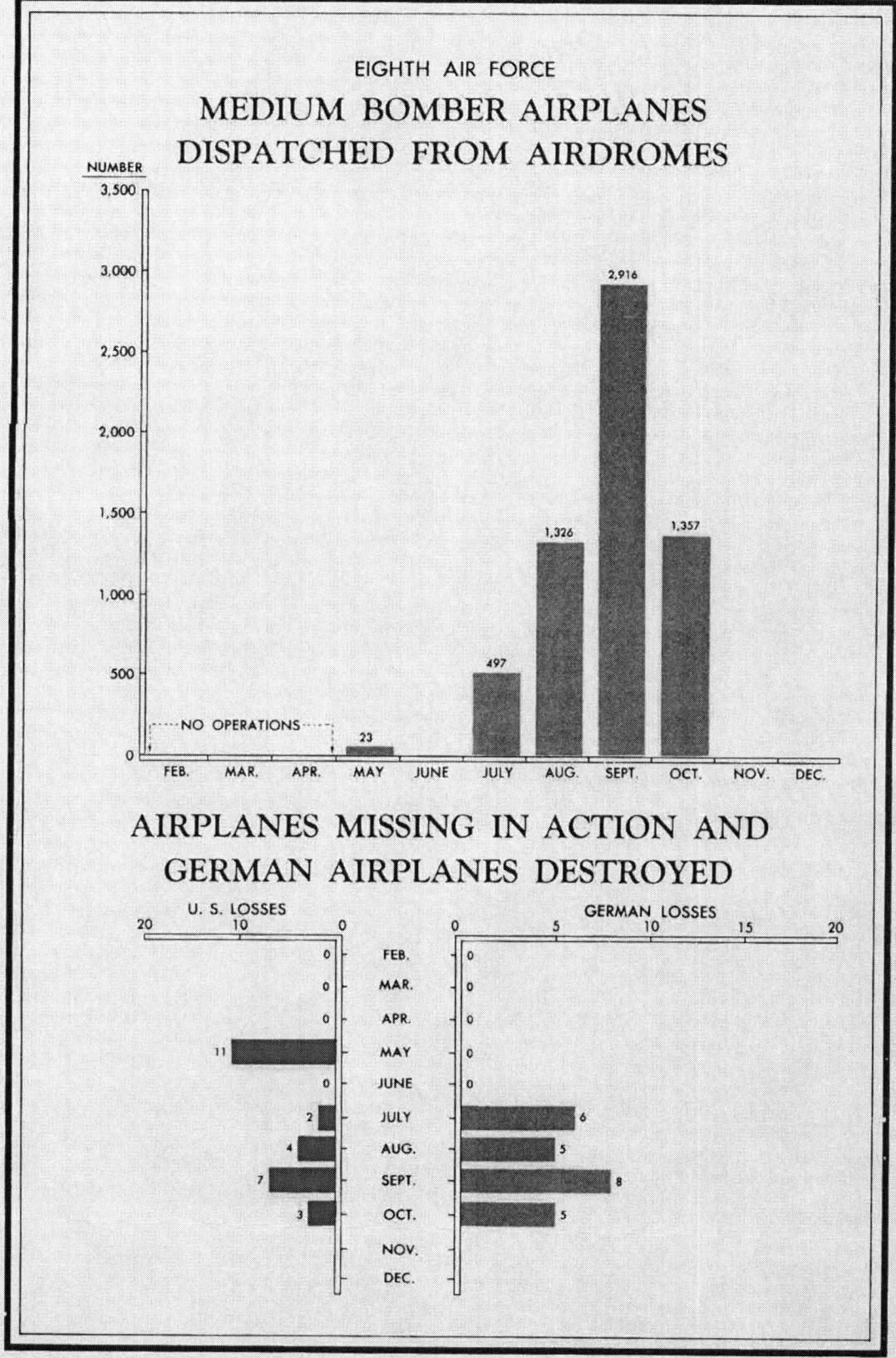

EIGHTH AIR FORCE

MEDIUM BOMBER AIRPLANES
DISPATCHED FROM AIRDROMES

AIRPLANES MISSING IN ACTION AND
GERMAN AIRPLANES DESTROYED

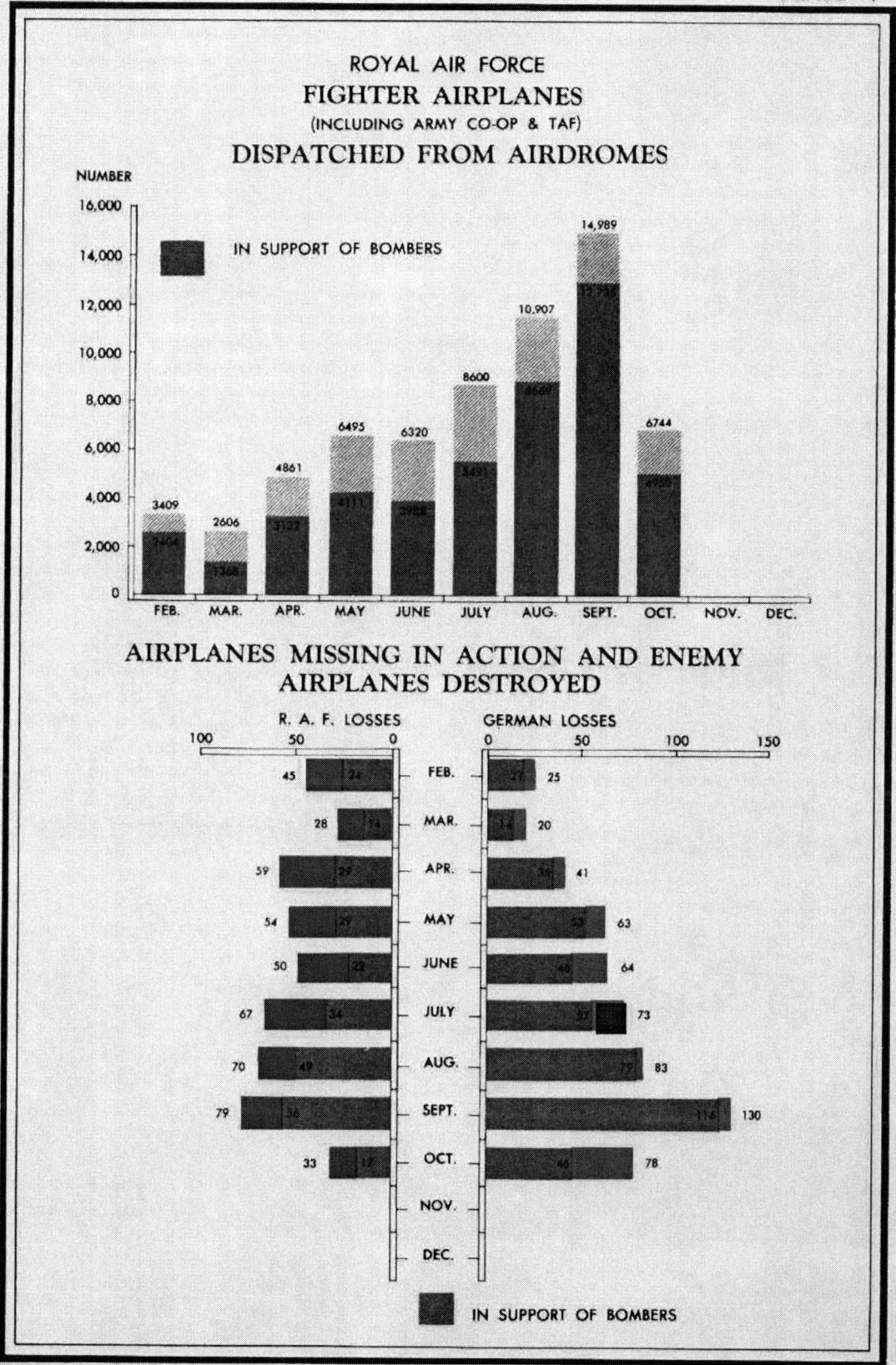

ROYAL AIR FORCE
FIGHTER AIRPLANES
(INCLUDING ARMY CO-OP & TAF)
DISPATCHED FROM AIRDROMES

AIRPLANES MISSING IN ACTION AND ENEMY
AIRPLANES DESTROYED

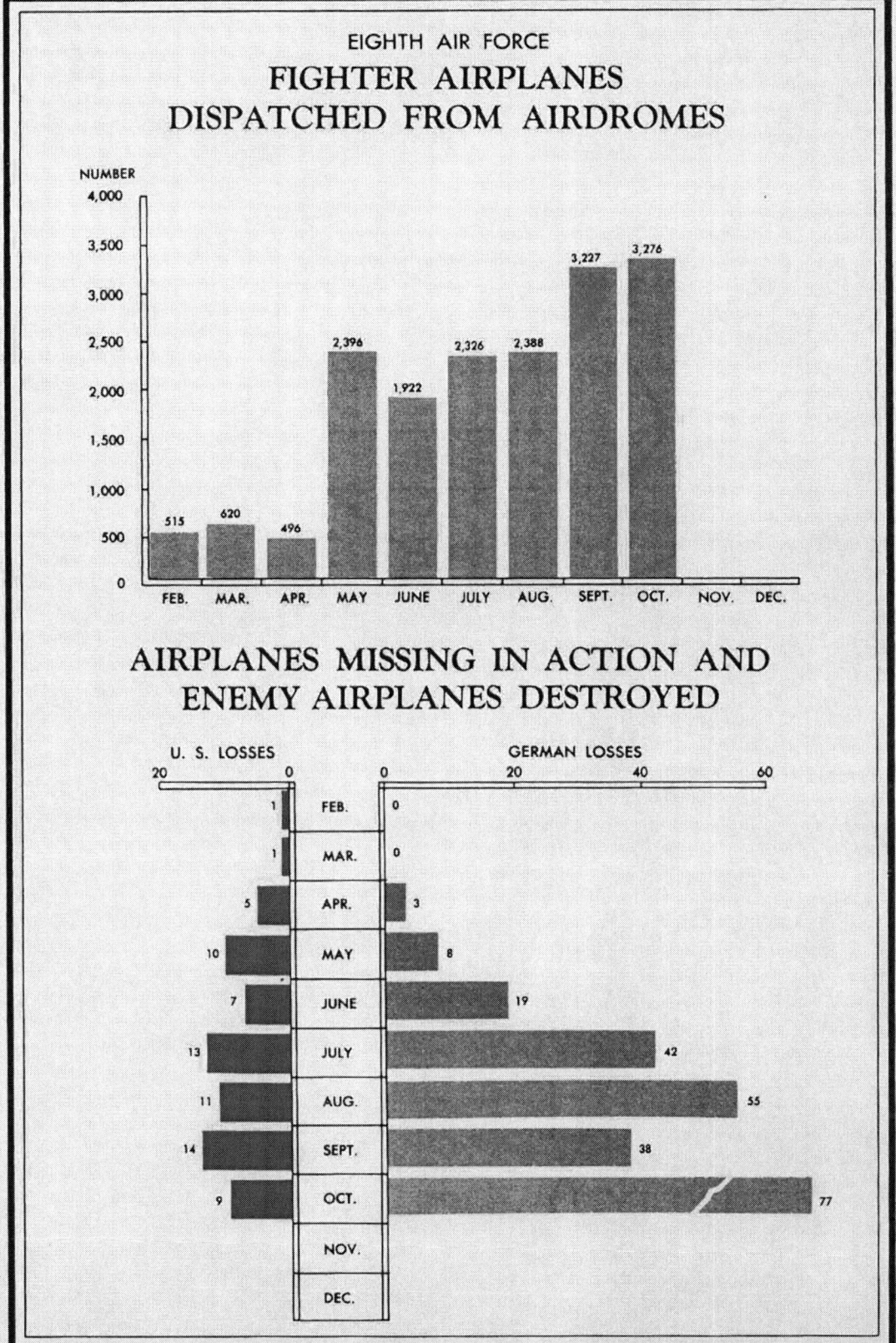

EIGHTH AIR FORCE
FIGHTER AIRPLANES
DISPATCHED FROM AIRDROMES

AIRPLANES MISSING IN ACTION AND
ENEMY AIRPLANES DESTROYED

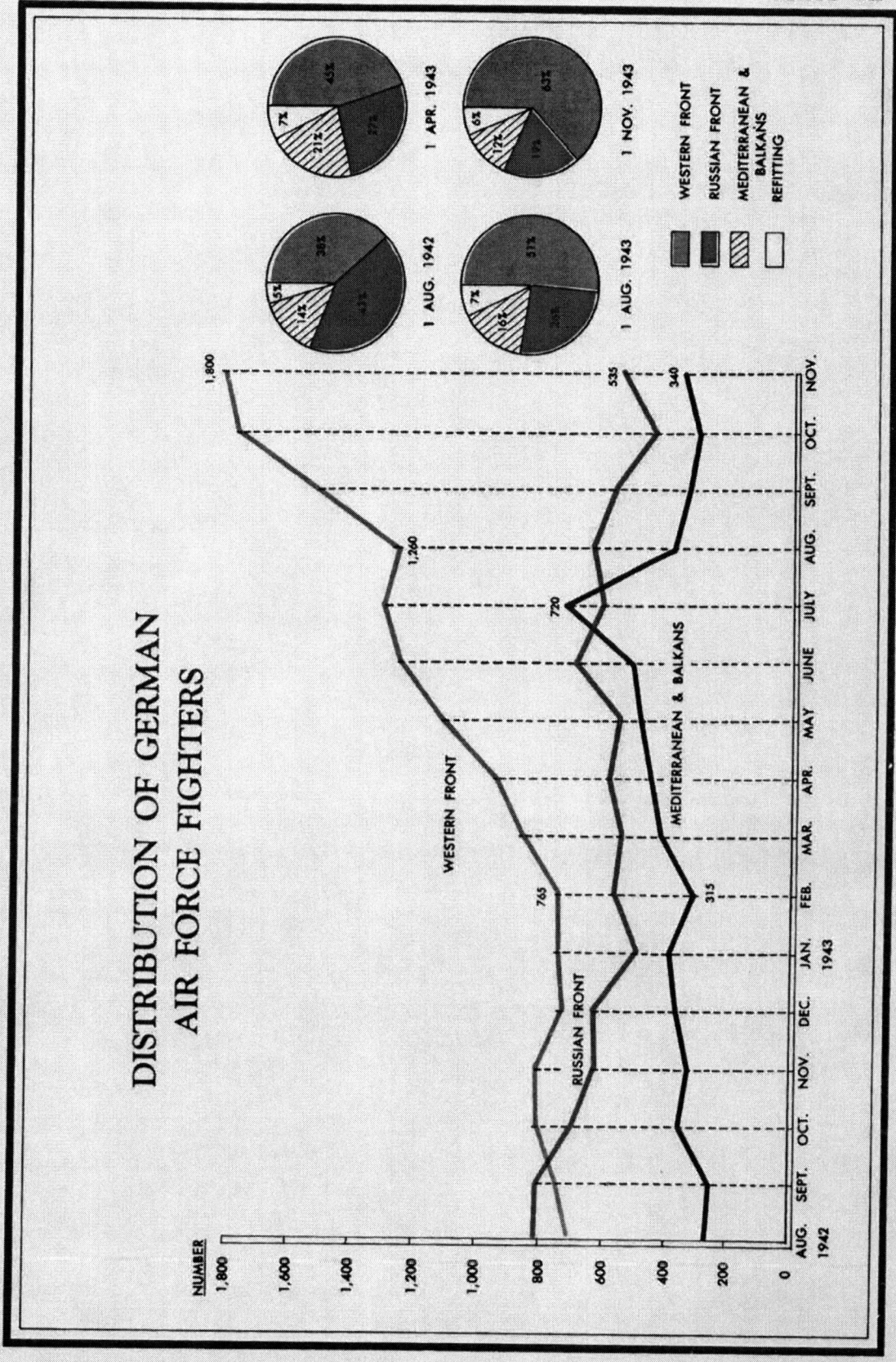

DISTRIBUTION OF GERMAN AIR FORCE FIGHTERS

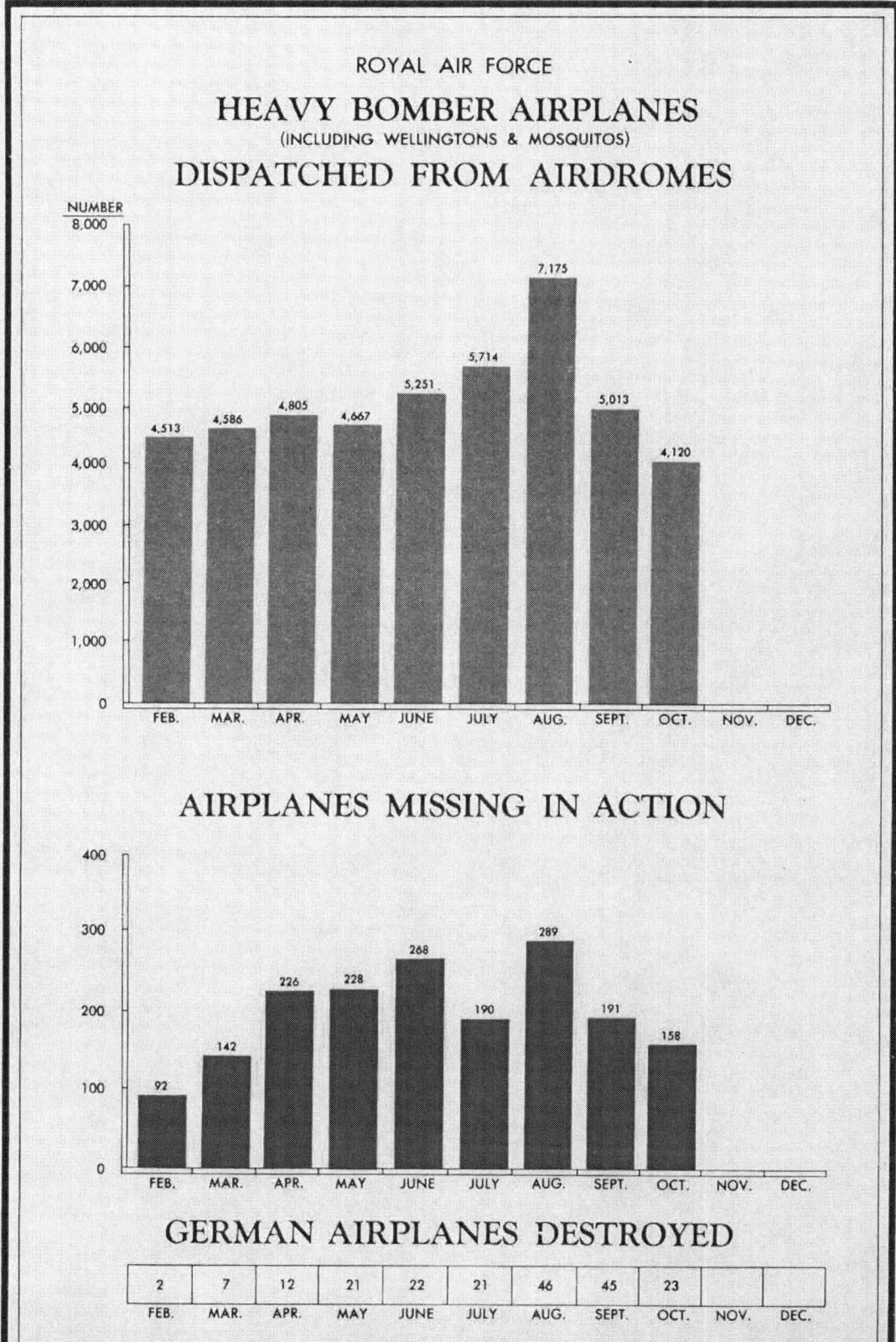

ROYAL AIR FORCE

HEAVY BOMBER AIRPLANES
(INCLUDING WELLINGTONS & MOSQUITOS)
DISPATCHED FROM AIRDROMES

AIRPLANES MISSING IN ACTION

GERMAN AIRPLANES DESTROYED

2	7	12	21	22	21	46	45	23		
FEB.	MAR.	APR.	MAY	JUNE	JULY	AUG.	SEPT.	OCT.	NOV.	DEC.

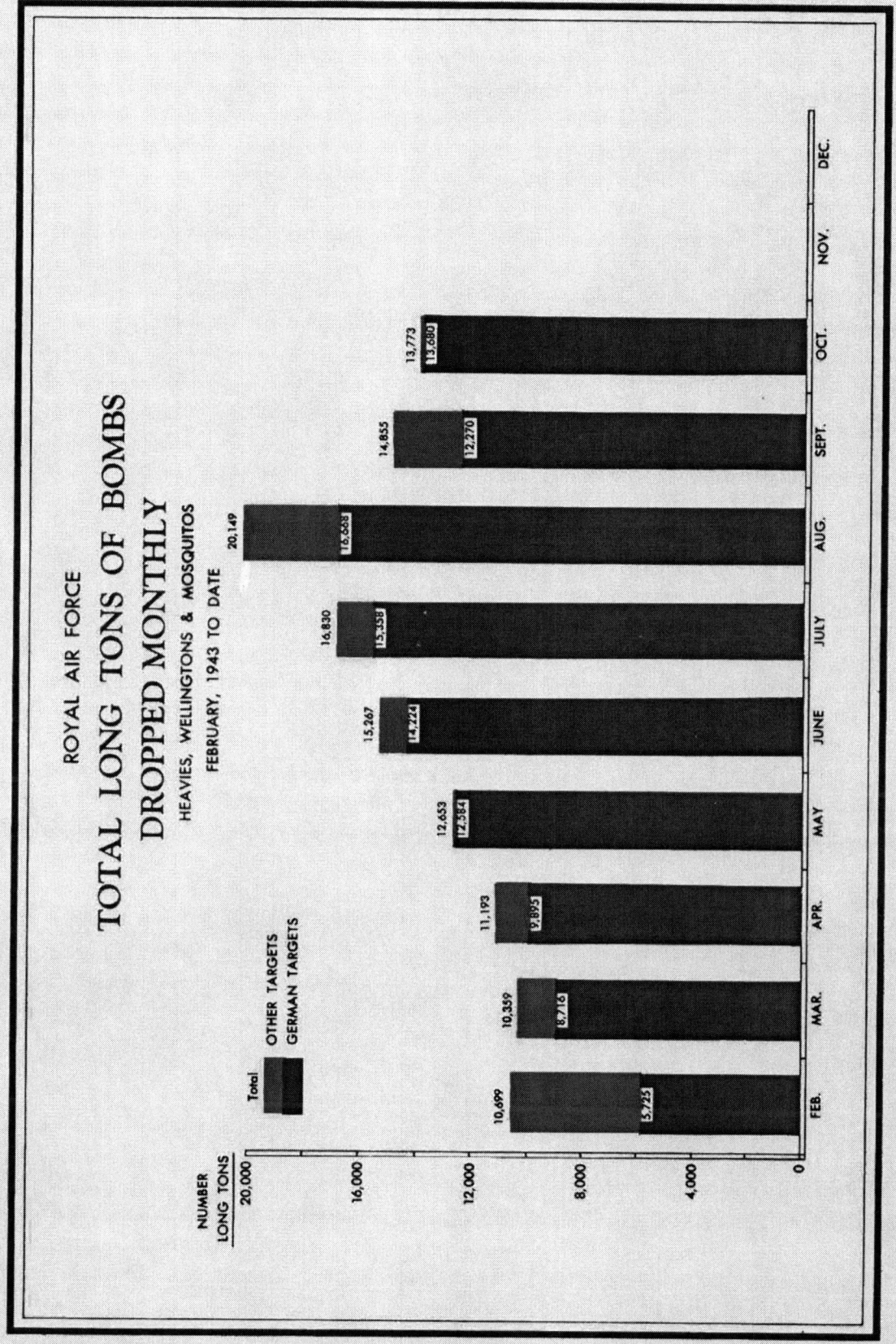

ROYAL AIR FORCE
TOTAL LONG TONS OF BOMBS
DROPPED MONTHLY
HEAVIES, WELLINGTONS & MOSQUITOS
FEBRUARY, 1943 TO DATE

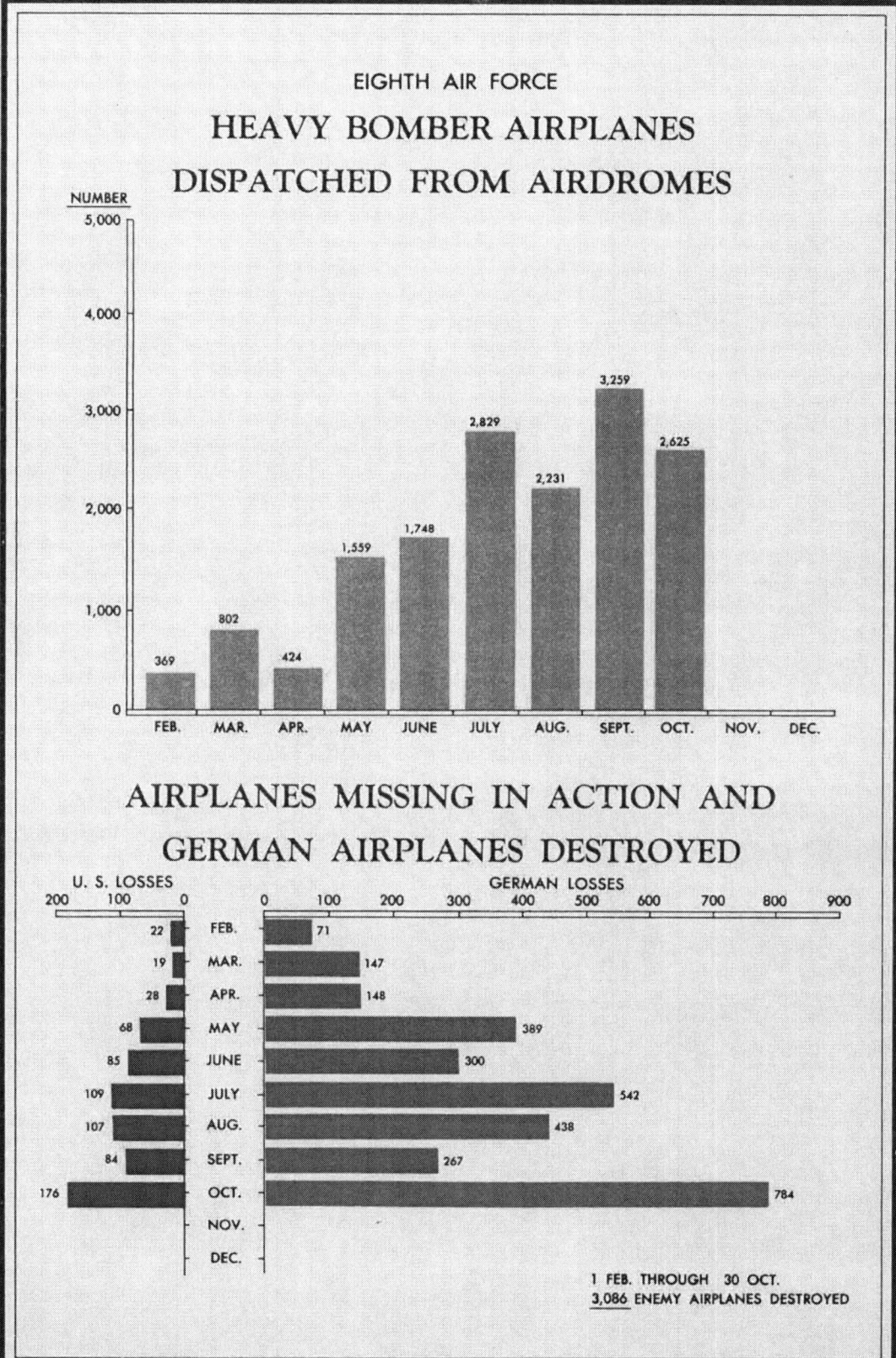

EIGHTH AIR FORCE

HEAVY BOMBER AIRPLANES
DISPATCHED FROM AIRDROMES

AIRPLANES MISSING IN ACTION AND
GERMAN AIRPLANES DESTROYED

1 FEB. THROUGH 30 OCT.
3,086 ENEMY AIRPLANES DESTROYED

145

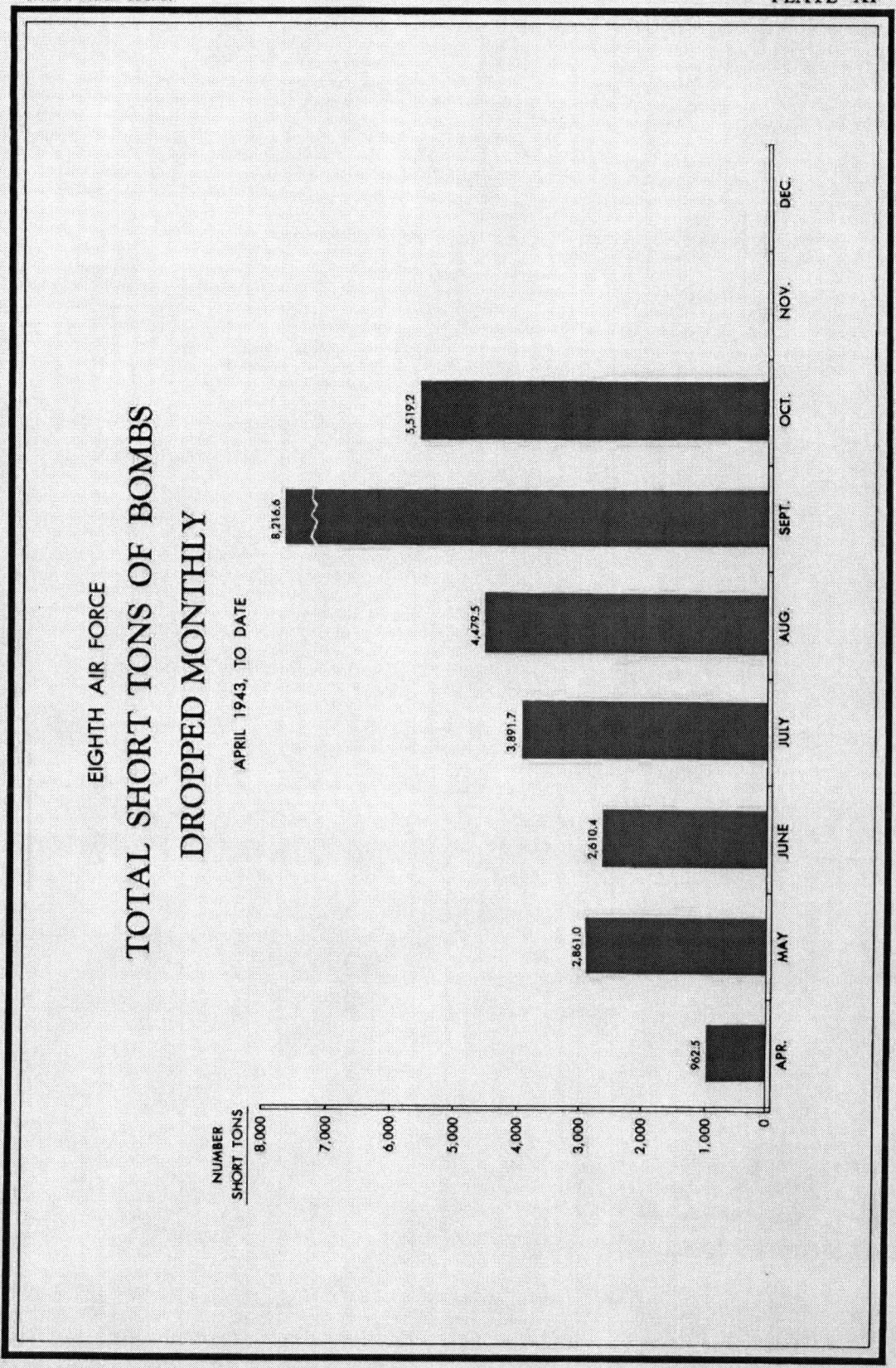

EIGHTH AIR FORCE

TOTAL SHORT TONS OF BOMBS
DROPPED MONTHLY

APRIL 1943, TO DATE

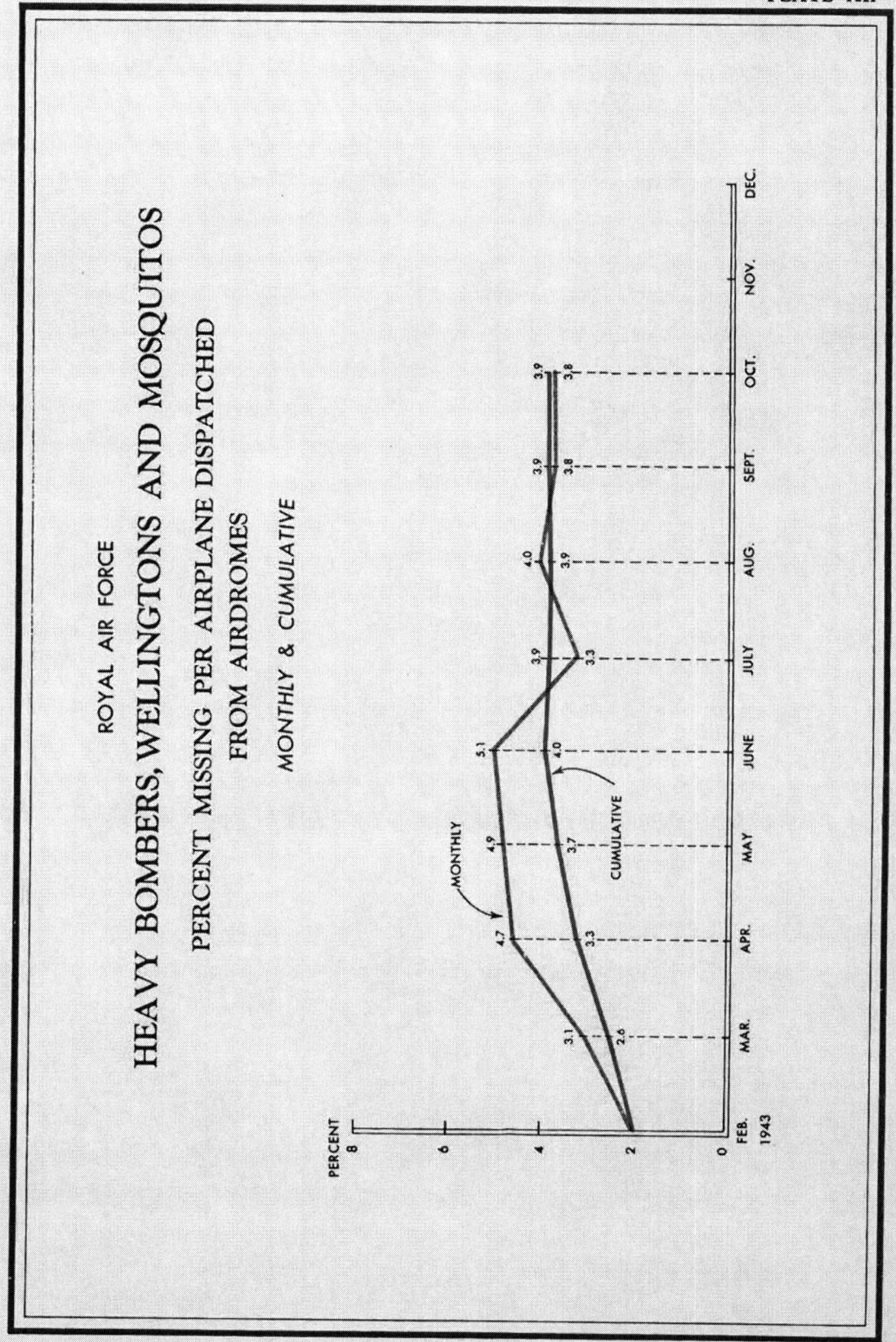

ROYAL AIR FORCE

HEAVY BOMBERS, WELLINGTONS AND MOSQUITOS

PERCENT MISSING PER AIRPLANE DISPATCHED
FROM AIRDROMES

MONTHLY & CUMULATIVE

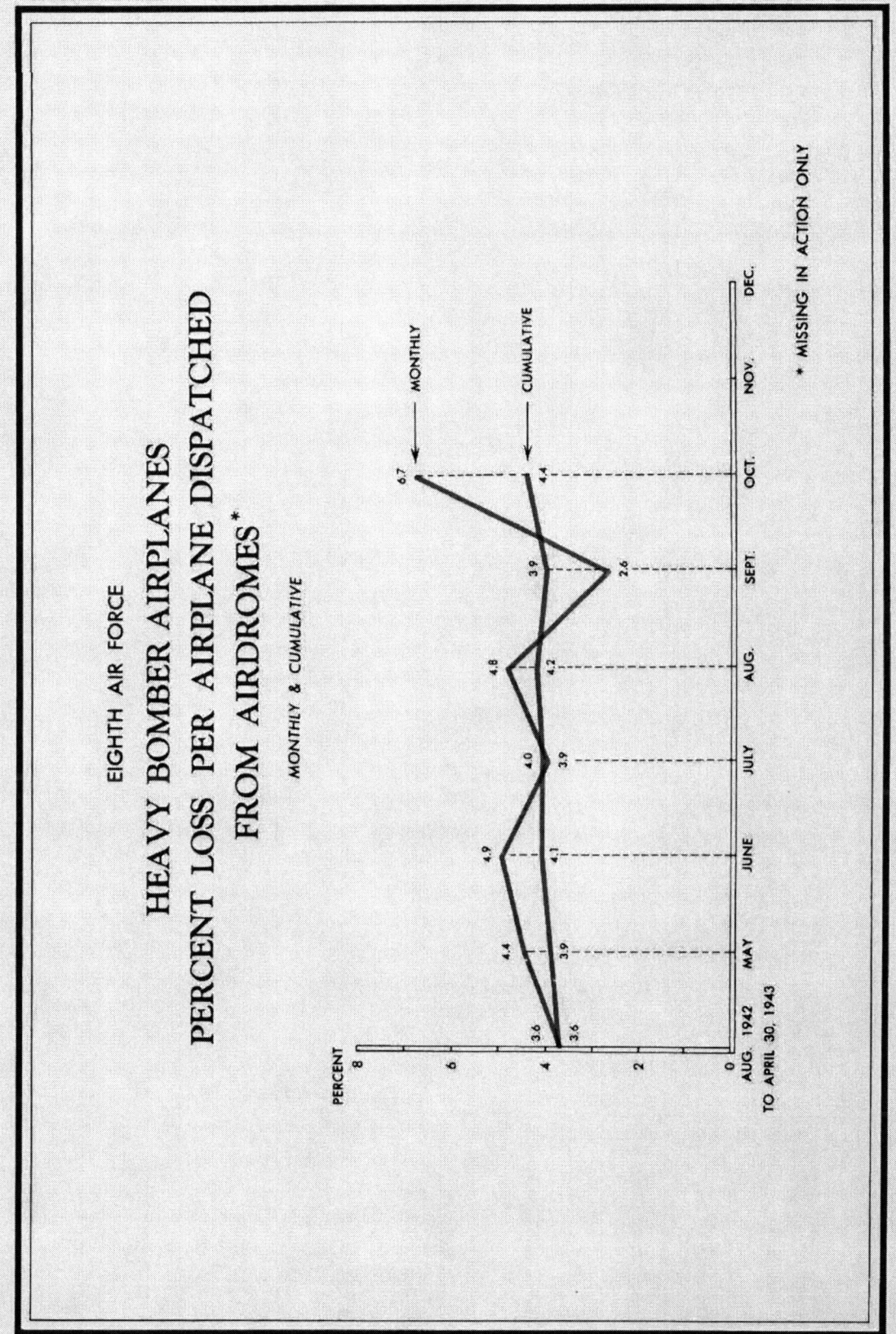

EIGHTH AIR FORCE

HEAVY BOMBER AIRPLANES
PERCENT LOSS PER AIRPLANE DISPATCHED
FROM AIRDROMES*

MONTHLY & CUMULATIVE

* MISSING IN ACTION ONLY

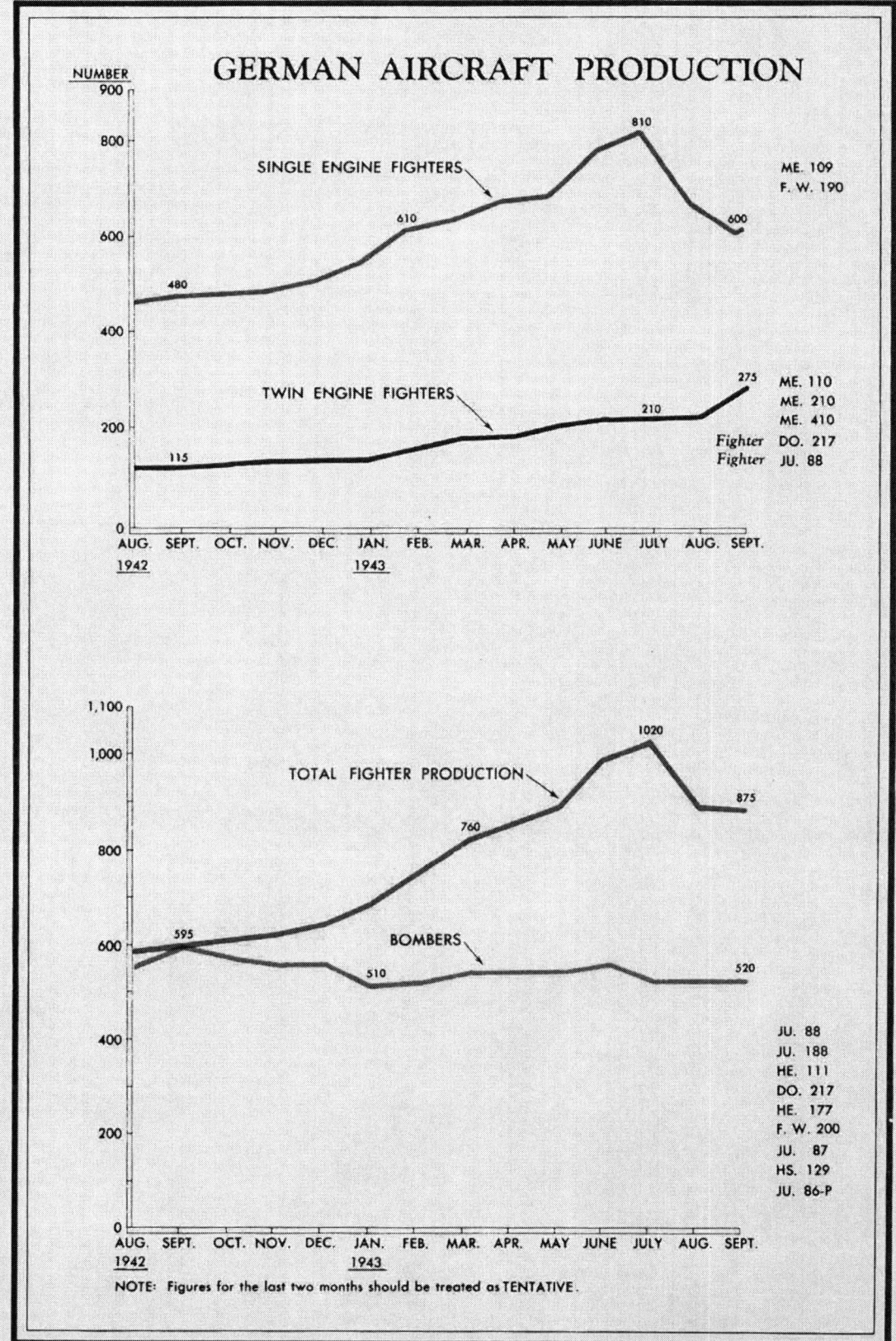

GERMAN AIRCRAFT PRODUCTION

NUMBER

SINGLE ENGINE FIGHTERS

ME. 109
F. W. 190

TWIN ENGINE FIGHTERS

ME. 110
ME. 210
ME. 410
Fighter DO. 217
Fighter JU. 88

TOTAL FIGHTER PRODUCTION

BOMBERS

JU. 88
JU. 188
HE. 111
DO. 217
HE. 177
F. W. 200
JU. 87
HS. 129
JU. 86-P

AUG. SEPT. OCT. NOV. DEC. JAN. FEB. MAR. APR. MAY JUNE JULY AUG. SEPT.
1942 · 1943

NOTE: Figures for the last two months should be treated as TENTATIVE.

153

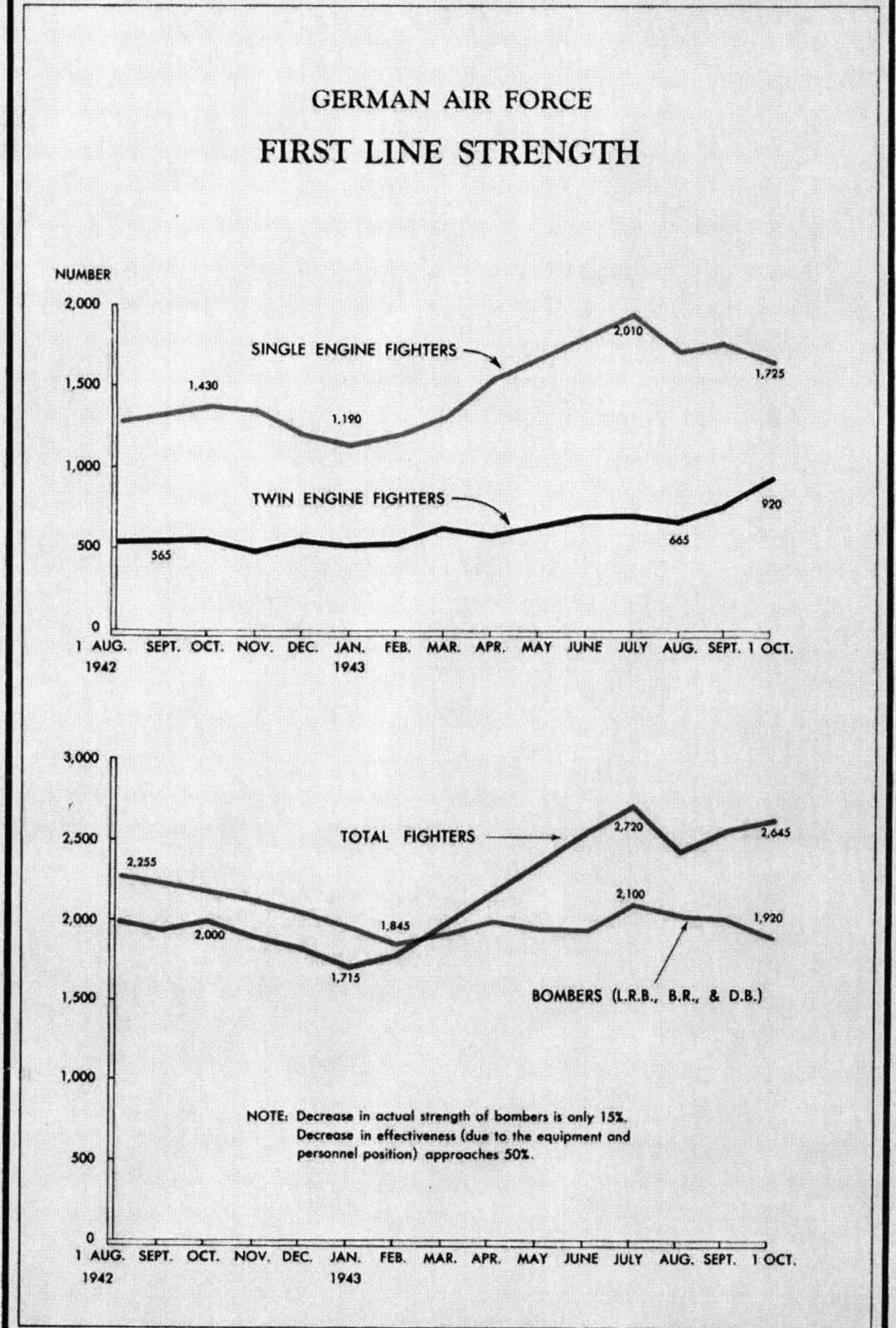

GERMAN AIR FORCE
FIRST LINE STRENGTH

NUMBER

SINGLE ENGINE FIGHTERS

1,430

1,190

2,010

1,725

TWIN ENGINE FIGHTERS

565

665

920

1 AUG. SEPT. OCT. NOV. DEC. JAN. FEB. MAR. APR. MAY JUNE JULY AUG. SEPT. 1 OCT.
1942   1943

TOTAL FIGHTERS

2,255

2,000

1,845

1,715

2,720

2,645

2,100

1,920

BOMBERS (L.R.B., B.R., & D.B.)

NOTE: Decrease in actual strength of bombers is only 15%.
Decrease in effectiveness (due to the equipment and
personnel position) approaches 50%.

1 AUG. SEPT. OCT. NOV. DEC. JAN. FEB. MAR. APR. MAY JUNE JULY AUG. SEPT. 1 OCT.
1942   1943

155

C.C.S. 403/1   3 December 1943

COMBINED CHIEFS OF STAFF

PROGRESS REPORT ON COMBINED BOMBER OFFENSIVE

Note by the Secretaries

The attached note on the Combined Bomber Offensive has been prepared by the British Chief of Air Staff and is circulated for information. On 3 December 1943, at their 133rd Meeting, the Combined Chiefs of Staff discussed Passages A, B and C. It was generally agreed that General Eaker should be ordered to proceed with the present plan up to the limit which can be achieved without seriously outrunning the supply of replacement aircraft and crews in prospect for the units which he has at any time.

H. REDMAN,

F. B. ROYAL,

Combined Secretariat.

ENCLOSURE

THE COMBINED BOMBER OFFENSIVE

Note by the British Chief of Air Staff

General Eaker and I have prepared in accordance with the request of the Combined Chiefs of Staff the report (C.C.S. 403) which is before you. It contains, largely in the form of diagrammatic charts, statistical information of many kinds. It also contains appreciations by the British Ministry of Economic Warfare, Air Intelligence and the Political Warfare Executive stating what they believe to be the effects of the bombing on Germany to date.

I do not of course intend to take you through the report in detail, but I will try to give you a brief summary of what has been achieved, and then I will deal shortly with certain features of the report which deserve particular attention.

This is a short summary of what has been done. First, mainly as a result of the successful attacks on 7 factories, German single-engined fighter production has been reduced by some 40 percent below what the Germans had planned that it should be at the present time. This is equivalent to a strength of about 750 less than the planned strength.

Secondly, attacks on other factories and industrial areas have seriously affected the German capacity for armament manufacture, chiefly in respect of ball-bearings, rubber, electrical equipment, vehicles, machine tools, steel, shipbuilding and heavy industry. It is not possible to assess the loss accurately, but Appendix "C" contains some approximate estimates. Of course damage to capacity is not immediately reflected in shortages with the fighting forces, especially with the heavy industries, but there is very good evidence that actual shortages exist in certain important finished products and the field of these shortages will doubtless steadily widen.

Thirdly, the effects of the Combined Bomber Offensive on German morale, though incidental, are nevertheless of tremendous importance, are summed up as follows in Appendix "F":

"We conclude that during the period under review:

(i) Fear of air attack has been the dominant pre-occupation of a large part of the German civilian population, and has contributed to produce a situation in which fear of the consequences of continuing the war is becoming greater than fear of the consequences of defeat.

(ii) Air attacks on Germany have resulted in social disruption on a scale which has greatly impaired the German ability to prosecute the war and threatens the structure of the entire home front.

(iii) Though the forces of repression, the hopes of a compromise with one or other of the belligerents, and the favorable climatic conditions of the past three months have so far prevented any general break in morale, it is not reasonable to infer that no such break in morale can occur, and we do not exclude the possibility that, in conjunction with further large-scale military reverses and with the advent of winter air operations may exercise a decisive influence on conditions inside Germany."

I will give you a few statistics not recorded in the report which form a solid basis for the above opinion. Some 38 German cities have now been more or less seriously attacked. They aggregate a population of 18 millions. These cities contain 84,000 acres or 133 square miles of built-up area. Of this total 20,700 acres or 32½ square miles have been devastated. This does not include the heavy damage in industrial areas or suburbs, which is additional.

Ninety percent of the above has been done in 1943.

It is approximately equivalent to the devastation of three-fourths of the total built-up area comprised in the 10 largest cities in England and Scotland, excluding only London. I have brought to this Conference two books containing photographs of these German cities and transparencies showing the devastation achieved at each of them and a comparison, on the same scale, of what the Germans did at Coventry. Perhaps 6,000,000 people or more have been made homeless and have spread alarm and despondency in the areas into which they have gone. They are crowding into areas as yet unbombed, and huts are being built for some of them, but the replacement of their clothing and moveable goods destroyed in these devastating attacks is either impossible or can only be done at the direct expense of the war effort. There is no shadow of doubt that morale is at an extremely low ebb.

159

I do not think it is optimistic to suggest that we are now at least half-way along the road of industrial devastation towards the point where Germany will become unable to continue the war. With the winter coming on we may be even further along the road towards morale breakdown, though measurement of the destruction of morale is impossible.

I now come to one or two points in the report to which I would like to direct your attention.

You will remember that the essence of the first stage of the *POINT-BLANK* Plan was the progressive destruction of the German fighter force. This was to be achieved in three ways:

(a) By destruction of assembly plants by day bombing;

(b) By general destruction of the industrial facilities on which aircraft production depends;

(c) By the attrition resulting from air fighting.

Now if the *POINTBLANK* operations had proceeded exactly in accordance with the plan and had achieved exactly the planned effect the strength of the German fighter force, as then estimated, would have been reduced at the 1st July 1943 from a possible 2,480 to 2,450 and at the 1st November from a possible 2,900 to 2,250. You will note that very little effect was expected by the 1st July.

In fact, the rate of increase of the German single-engined fighter strength had not been accurately appreciated at the time the plan was formulated. The actual strength SEF and TEF on the 1st July was 2,720 and on the 1st November 2,850. I should nevertheless point out that had it not been for the *POINTBLANK* Plan, and had the observed rate of production in April, May and June been maintained, the total strength might well have been 2,760 in July and would certainly by now have mounted off the graph altogether, probably to over 3,500. If you will look at Plate XIV, annexed to C.C.S. 403 (blue line), you will see very clearly how single-engined fighter production has declined as a result of *POINTBLANK*.

Of course there are several things to account for the incomplete fulfillment of our hopes.

One of the most important is shown in Plate II, annexed to C.C.S. 403, where the black line shows the U.S. heavy bombers required by the Plan and the broken line the aircraft assigned to the U.K. The red line in relation to the green reflects the serviceability rate and the availability of crews.

I must say that I regard the achievements of the Eighth Air Force in relation to the resources available to them as highly creditable. Moreover, there is a concealed achievement which is, of course, to a considerable extent shared by the R.A.F. in that an ever-increasing proportion of the German fighter strength has been drawn away from other fronts to the immense advantage of the fighting in Russia and the Mediterranean.

In emphasizing the extent to which the *POINTBLANK* Plan has fallen short in one direction of what was intended of it I am not in any way minimizing what has been done towards achieving the primary object of the Combined Bomber Offensive which is stated in paragraph 5 of Appendix "B."

You will see from Plates IX and XI, annexed to C.C.S. 403, the total of bombs dropped and from Appendix "C" some of the results.

The R.A.F. Bomber Command has of course had its own difficulties to contend with in supporting the *POINTBLANK* Plan. The short summer nights virtually limited its effort for two months to the Ruhr. The mounting scale of defence caused a sharp rise in the casualty rate as shown in Plate XII, annexed to C.C.S. 403. The towns where twin-engined fighters are mainly constructed are distant and hard to find at night, yet the scale of assault on Germany mounted steadily until autumn weather of an unusually unfavorable kind set in during Septeml

I would refer you for a moment to Plate I, annexed to C.C.S. 403, which shows how the provision of crews is related to the scale of effort to be expected.

The weather in April was actually better than that in August and the aircraft on strength were almost exactly the same in the two months. The increase in crews (blue) is reflected not only in the increase available (red) but much more strikingly in the sorties and bomb delivery, which rose from 4,805 to 7,175 (Plate VIII) and from 11,193 tons to 20,149 (Plate IX) respectively.

There are two factors which affect the effort which can be sustained:

(a) The availability of aircraft and crew replacements.

(b) The casualty rate.

British heavy bomber production is now about 400 a month with corresponding crew output and it can only increase very slowly. Our casualty rate as you see from Plate XII is at the moment stabilized at just under 4% of sorties. Whether we can keep it there or not will depend largely on the success of *POINTBLANK*.

The Eighth Bomber Command casualty rate, which was fluctuating between 3½% and 5% until August, dropped sharply in September to 2.6% and then rose sharply to 6.7% in October as a result of the deep penetration undertaken during that month against ever-increasing strength of the defence. (See Plate XIII).

The only other charts deserving mention are Plates V and VI, which illustrate how far we have employed the fighter forces in U.K. in support of the day bombers.

In August, September and October the R.A.F. flew over 26,000 and the U.S. fighters nearly 9,000 sorties on this work and destroyed 241 and 170 enemy aircraft respectively.

I now come to the point where I must ask for a decision on policy.

At the inception of the *POINTBLANK* Plan it was pointed out most clearly that the planned result could not be achieved unless the forces required were provided. This is how it was put:

> "The task requires the force called for. The provision of a lesser force will not accomplish a proportionate result. For example, if only 75% of the force called for is made available, 75% of the result cannot be expected. If only 75% of the force called for is made available, less than 50% of the result outlined can be accomplished."

A   According to my calculations about 89% of the planned strength was provided for the first phase, 76% for the second phase and 67% for the first half of the third phase, where we now are. With this force 90% of the sorties required by the Plan have been despatched, but it has not been possible for them all to be against targets in the Plan. Nevertheless, 58% of the planned successful sorties have been flown against targets in the Plan and 54% against the G.A.F. targets in the Plan. The hard fact is that we are almost exactly three months behind schedule and German fighter production and strength are both higher than the Plan contemplated. This is in spite of the most gallant and successful efforts on the part of the squadrons to use surprise instead of numbers for achieving penetrations which were only intended to be attempted in the later stages of the Plan and with far greater strength.

The question is what is to be done in view of the arrears and the dependence of *OVERLORD* on *POINTBLANK*.

B

I think it is necessary for the Combined Chiefs of Staff to take responsibility for laying down a policy for the use of the Eighth Bomber Command in the remainder of Phase III and during Phase IV of the *POINTBLANK* Plan.

Is the Commander to go out for the completion of the present phase regardless of the fact that, being 26% short of planned strength, he must expect to suffer disproportionate losses?

Or on the other hand is he to be given a modified objective which is believed to be within the compass of the force he will have?

Or is some middle course possible?

After discussing this question at some length with General Eaker, I would advise against the modification of the Plan and also against his being ordered to complete it regardless of loss.

I would advise the following:

(a) The greatest possible increase in the force at General Eaker's disposal in respect of both formed units and replacement aircraft and crews. I suggest it may be necessary to give the Eighth Air Force priority over the Fifteenth Air Force in new groups until the spring.

C

(b) Subject to (a) above, General Eaker should be ordered to proceed with the present Plan up to the limit which can be achieved without seriously out-running the supply of replacement aircraft and crews in prospect for the units which he has at any time.

A decision to the above effect would enable General Eaker to feel his way and perhaps to achieve more than we at present dare to expect. It will also serve to sustain morale and to prevent the undue dissipation of the forces now in action which by its accumulated experience must form the basis of future expansion.

APPENDIX "A"

C.C.S. 166/1/D
January 21, 1943

"CASABLANCA DIRECTIVE"

COMBINED CHIEFS OF STAFF

THE BOMBER OFFENSIVE FROM THE UNITED KINGDOM

Directive to the appropriate British and United States Air Force Commanders, to Govern the operation of the British and United States Bomber Commands in the United Kingdom.

(Approved by the Combined Chiefs of Staff at their 65th Meeting on January 21, 1943).

YOUR primary object will be the progressive destruction and dislocation of the German military, industrial and economic system, and the undermining of the morale of the German people to a point where their capacity for armed resistance is fatally weakened.

2.   Within that general concept, your primary objectives, subject to the exigencies of weather and of tactical feasibility, will for the present be in the following order of priority:-

(a) German submarine construction yards.

(b) The German aircraft industry.

(c) Transportation.

(d) Oil plants.

(e) Other targets in enemy war industry.

The above order of priority may be varied from time to time according to developments in the strategical situation. Moreover, other objectives of great importance either from the political or military point of view must be attacked. Examples of these are -

(i)   Submarine operating bases on the Biscay coast. If these can be put out of action, a great step forward will have been taken in the U-boat war which the C.C.S. have agreed to be a first charge on our resources. Day and night attacks on these bases have been inaugurated and should be continued so that an assessment of their effects can be made as soon as possible. If it is found that successful results can be achieved, these attacks should continue whenever conditions are favourable for as long and as often as is necessary. These objectives have not been included in the order of priority, which covers long-term operations, particularly as the bases are not situated in Germany.

(ii) Berlin, which should be attacked when conditions are suitable for the attainment of specially valuable results unfavourable to the morale of the enemy or favourable to that of Russia.

3.   You may also be required, at the appropriate time, to attack objectives in Northern Italy in connection with amphibious operations in the Mediterranean theatre.

4.   There may be certain other objectives of great but fleeting importance for the attack of which all necessary plans and preparations should be made. Of these, an example would be the important units of the German Fleet in harbour or at sea.

5.   You should take every opportunity to attack Germany by day, to destroy objectives that are unsuitable for night attack, to sustain continuous pressure on German morale, to impose heavy losses on the German day fighter force and to contain German fighter strength away from the Russian and Mediterranean theatres of war.

6.   When the Allied Armies re-enter the Continent, you will afford them all possible support in the manner most effective.

Appendix "A"

7.   In attacking objectives in occupied territories, you will conform to such instructions as may be issued from time to time for political reasons by His Majesty's Government through the British Chiefs of Staff.

Appendix "A"

APPENDIX "B"

AIR MINISTRY,

LONDON, S.W. 1.

MOST SECRET

S.46368/A.C.A.S. (Ops.)   10th June, 1943.

Sir,

       I am directed to refer to Directive C.C.S. 166/1/D dated 21st January, 1943, issued by the Combined Chiefs of Staff and forwarded to the Commanding General, Eighth Air Force and the Air Officer Commanding-in-Chief, Bomber Command under cover of Air Ministry letter S.46368/A.C.A.S. (Ops.) dated 4th February, 1943. This directive contained instructions for the conduct of the British and American bomber offensive from this country.

2.   In paragraph 2 of the directive, the primary objectives were set out in order of priority, subject to the exigencies of weather and tactical feasibility. Since the issue of this directive there have been rapid developments in the strategical situation which have demanded a revision of the priorities originally laid down.

3.   *The increasing scale of destruction which is being inflicted by our* night bomber forces and the development of the day bombing offensive by the Eighth Air Force have forced the enemy to deploy day and night fighters in increasing numbers on the Western Front. Unless this increase in fighter strength is checked we may find our bomber forces unable to fulfil the tasks allotted to them by the Combined Chiefs of Staff.

4.   *In these circumstances it has become essential to check the growth* and to reduce the strength of the day and night fighter forces which the enemy can concentrate against us in this theatre. To this end the Combined Chiefs of Staff have decided that first priority in the operation of British and American bombers based in the United Kingdom shall be accorded to the attack of German fighter forces and the industry upon which they depend.

Appendix "B"

5.   The primary object of the bomber forces remains as set out in the original directive issued by the Combined Chiefs of Staff (C.C.S. 166/1/D dated 21st January, 1943) i.e.:-

"the progressive destruction and dislocation of the German military, industrial and economic system, and the undermining of the morale of the German people to a point where their capacity for armed resistance is fatally weakened."

6.   In view however, of the factors referred to in para. 4 the following priority objectives have been assigned to the Eighth Air Force:-

Intermediate objective:

German Fighter strength

The Air Officer Commanding-in-Chief, Bomber Command
The Air Officer Commanding-in-Chief, Fighter Command
The Commanding General, Eighth Air Force.

Primary objectives:

German submarine yards and bases
The remainder of the German aircraft industry
Ball bearings
Oil (contingent upon attacks against Ploesti
    from the Mediterranean)

Secondary objectives:

Synthetic rubber and tyres
Military motor transport vehicles.

While the forces of the British Bomber Command will be employed in accordance with their main aim in the general disorganisation of German industry their action will be designed as far as practicable to be complementary to the operations of the Eighth Air Force.

7.   In pursuance of the particular requirements of para. 6 above, I am to request you to direct your forces to the following tasks:-

(i) the destruction of German air-frame, engine and component factories and the ball-bearing

Appendix "B"

industry on which the strength of the German fighter force depend

(ii) the general disorganisation of those industrial areas associated with the above industries

(iii) the destruction of those aircraft repair depots and storage parks within range, and on which the enemy fighter force is largely dependent.

(iv) the destruction of enemy fighters in the air and on the ground.

The list of targets appropriate to these special tasks is in Appendix 'A' forwarded under cover of Air Ministry letter S.46368/III/D.B. Ops. dated 4th June, 1943. Further copies of this list, which will be amended from time to time as necessary, will be forwarded in due course.

8.　　Consistent with the needs of the air defence of the United Kingdom the forces of the British Fighter Command will be employed to further this general offensive by:-

(i) the attack of enemy aircraft in the air and on the ground

(ii) the provision of support necessary to pass bomber forces through the enemy defensive system with with the minimum cost.

9.　　American fighter forces will be employed in accordance with the instructions of the Commanding General, Eighth Air Force in furtherance of the bomber offensive and in co-operation with the forces of Fighter Command.

10.　　The allocation of targets and the effective co-ordination of the forces involved is to be ensured by frequent consultation between the Commanders concerned. To assist this co-ordination a combined operational planning committee has been set up. The suggested terms of reference under which this Committee is to operate is outlined in Air Ministry letter CS.19364/A.C.A.S. (Ops.) dated 10th June, 1943.

11.　　It is emphasised that the reduction of the German fighter force is of primary importance; any delay in its prosecution will make the task progressively more difficult. At the same time it is necessary to direct the maximum

Appendix "B"

effort against the submarine construction yards and operating bases when tactical and weather conditions preclude attacks upon objectives associated with the German Fighter Force. The list of these targets is in Appendix 'B' forwarded with the Appendix 'A' referred to in paragraph 7 above.

I am, Sir,

Your obedient Servant,

(Sgd) N. H. BOTTOMLEY.

Air Vice Marshal,

Assistant Chief of the Air Staff (Operations)

Appendix "B"

APPENDIX "C"

JOINT REPORT BY MINISTRY OF ECONOMIC WARFARE
AND AIR INTELLIGENCE ON EFFECTS OF
BOMBER OFFENSIVE

The effects of bombing do not fall evenly on the various parts of the Enemy's war potential, and, to some extent, they are redistributed according to the immediate requirements of the consumers of material having the highest priority in Germany. There is a cushion represented by the margin over the bare minimum demands required by the workers and the armed forces, which is now being deeply depressed by aerial attack.

2. It is difficult to estimate the overall effect in quantitative terms but it is considered to be now in the region of 10% of the total war potential. A total decline of 20% in overall effort may well be fatal. Contributing to this average decline is a very much greater decline in some individual industries (e.g. Ball-bearings and rubber) which may be near the point where they could cause the collapse of the whole war machine. Moreover, the housing situation and the general morale are both so bad that either might cause a collapse before industry became unable to sustain the war effort.

Aircraft.

3. Direct attack on fighter-aircraft assembly and component plants did not begin until the end of July. Between that date and the end of October the eight attacks that were made by the U.S.A.A.F. on the Me. 109 works at Wiener Neustadt* and Regenburg and on the F.S. 190 works at Oschersleben, Warnemunde, Anklam, Marienburg and Kassel have been highly successful. They were aided by a night attack by Bomber Command on Kassel in October, which damaged the Bettenhausen components plant.

4. Single-engined fighter production in the months of September and October was on a lower level than for the month of July, notwithstanding the high degree of priority accorded to single-engined fighter production and the

---

* Two attacks by N.A.A.F.

Appendix "C"

considerable planned expansion in output. Damage to assembly factories alone in the above attacks has resulted in a production loss of 880 aircraft and production in October was between 600 and 700 against an estimated planned production of 1,000.

U-Boats.

5.   The regular attacks on U-Boat construction and components manufacture have caused a direct loss of at least 22 vessels in 1943 out of the total of about 200 that would have been launched by the end of October. The delayed action of attacks on areas producing materials and components for U-Boats appears now to be having an effect on the average rate of completion.

Industrial Damage.

6.   Up to the Spring of this year bombing appears to have had only a small effect on *Coal* output. Between April and July inclusive, however, Ruhr coal production probably declined by 10%. In spite of this, and presumably because consumers were harder hit than producers, supply still more than covers essential demand. *Coke* continues to be a limiting factor in steel production. There is increasing stringency in the supply of *liquid fuels* caused at least in part by the raid on Ploesti. At the peak of the Summer attack Ruhr *steel* output probably declined by 30-40%. This was partly offset by increased output in France, Belgium and Luxembourg, so that the maximum net drop was not less than 10% in German Europe. Bombing has also helped the shortage of ferro-alloys to reduce the quality and quantity of *special-steel* output. The decrease in the supplies of crude and special steels has made itself felt in *armaments* output, including aircraft, which has also been directly reduced by damage to the heavy-engineering industries of the Ruhr and other areas.

7.   Virtually no *rubber* has been received through the blockade during the past nine months and consequently the raw material for *tyres* has been reduced in quantity and wearing quality. The destruction of the Huls plant has deprived Germany of 15% of her total rubber requirements and pressure has been increased by heavy losses of stocks at tyre factories.

8.   Manufacturing centres for *textiles* have suffered heavily and the greater part of the remaining textile output is now reserved for essential military and industrial requirements. The civilian clothes ration has been

Appendix "C"

cancelled and parachute cloths, cords and harness have been affected. Losses of stocks have probably been an important factor in producing immediate effects.

9. *Electrical engineering* has suffered more heavily than any other branch of the engineering industry owing to the direct effects of factory damage and a high degree of concentration of the industry in a few concerns. There is evidence of continuing shortage of signals equipment in the Wehrmacht.

10. A few raids have resulted in damage to *ball-bearing* factories on a scale which may cause a 50% loss of production over the next six months, and in addition, by producing bottlenecks in an even shorter period, is likely severely to affect particular types of bearings required in the armaments and aircraft industry.

Housing.

11. Damage to housing, combined with evacuation, has resulted in the final saturation of all suitable accommodation in Germany. In the coming Winter the problem of housing evacuees, many of whom have hitherto been in temporary dwellings unsuitable to Winter conditions, will put upon the home administration a burden that it may not be able to support.

Land Transportation and Shipping.

12. Damage to the Western European communications system and its equipment, although heavy throughout the year, has declined of late; and this, coupled with the withdrawal on the Russian front and the reduction in traffic to Italy, has caused some easing in the general transport position. New construction of locomotive and wagons now probably more than offsets losses by bomb damage.

13. Damage to ports on Germany's Western seaboard has necessitated a most inconvenient reorientation of sea-borne and internal transport.

Mining.

14. In Northern waters the continued mining offensive has further decreased the enemy's shipping potential by sinking many of his ships and by causing him to divert tonnage from his now slender reserves to mine-sweeping. It has also contributed to the enforced reorientation of transport.

Appendix "C"

Immobilization of Enemy Resources, etc.

15.   The employment of a considerable and increasing number of full-time adult personnel in anti-aircraft and civil defence, factory repair and reconstruction, and first-aid to housing, represents a serious drain on Germany's industrial man-power that might otherwise have been employed on production.

Morale.

16.   The maintenance of morale is the gravest single problem confronting the home authorities. The full effects of air attack since the devastation of Hamburg have become known in all parts of the country. The increasing death roll is an important factor and coupled with military failures the general attitude is approaching one of "peace at any price" and the avoidance of the wholesale destruction of further cities in Germany.

4th November, 1943.

APPENDIX "D"

WAR CABINET

JOINT INTELLIGENCE SUB-COMMITTEE

EFFECTS OF BOMBING OFFENSIVE ON GERMAN WAR EFFORT

Report by the Joint Intelligence Sub-Committee

CONCLUSIONS

1. All the great industrial centres of the Ruhr and Rhineland have been so devastated by bombing that they are openly regarded as front line zones whose essential activities must somehow be kept going. The task of evacuating less essential personnel is being pressed forward on the highest priority, but is clearly meeting with very grave difficulties. A.R.P. services, even though reinforced, are increasingly inadequate to meet the strain of prolonged bombardment, and relief measures have lost much of their earlier efficiency. The willingness to hold out has been seriously lowered in the heavily bombed areas; in the less heavily bombed areas morale has most certainly been affected. The morale of the fighting forces has suffered in consequence of the plight of their relatives but there is as yet no evidence that their fighting spirit has been impaired.

2. The problem of housing workers in the heavily bombed industrial areas, and of housing refugees elsewhere is very acute. The effect of the offensive on transportation and administration and on the supply of consumer goods, though not calculable, is known to be severe and cumulative.

3. Though the physical destruction of productive capacity in Germany has been considerable, it comprises as yet only a small proportion of the total industrial capacity available to Germany. Indeed only about one-third of German industry has been under really heavy attack and that for only about three months.

4. No individual industry, with a few exceptions, has yet suffered the complete loss of a critical number of the factories on which it depends. There are also

Appendix "D"

still some small reserves of manufacturing capacity and some possible spheres of retrenchment with which to "cushion" munitions production from the effects of bomb damage. Such "cushioning", however, involves serious repercussions on capital construction, housing, repairs and consumer goods production. These in turn react on future production plans and on morale.

5.   The reduction in steel production must already be having its effect on armament output; some other industries producing finished materials for the armed forces have already suffered immediate consequences as a result of the offensive. The chief of these are industries producing submarines, W/T, and other signals equipment, motor transport and perhaps heavy guns and ammunition. In other departments, it has so far been possible to maintain the supply of finished armaments to the forces by the expedients mentioned, and by depleting stocks.

6.   The greater part of the damage has fallen on industries producing or processing for other industries. This means a time lag of weeks or even months before the impact is fully felt by industries producing finished equipment. Thus the final effect of the damage done to Krupps in March and April will not be seen until the Autumn or even the Winter of 1943.

7.   On the other hand our offensive must have taken immediate effect on German plans by making production prospects both more adverse and largely incalculable at the very time when an unexpectedly high rate of military wastage had to be made good, and thus increasingly limiting German strategy.

8.   Our bombing offensive has been a major factor in forcing Germany to adopt a defensive air strategy. It has forced the Germans to make a special effort to increase the production of fighter types and it has tied down fighter units on the Western Front in spite of a vital need for them elsewhere.

9.   Our bomber offensive has made very heavy demands on skilled manpower for Radar and fighter defences. Large A.R.P. and fire services have had to be maintained at a high level of efficiency. The effect on Germany's military manpower in causing men to be diverted from the armed forces or retained in civil life instead of being called up appears so far to have been very small. The Germans, however, appear to be now realising that their policy in this respect has been mistaken and members of the Todt organization have already been recalled from Norway and Russia to the Ruhr.

Appendix "D"

10.   Although the rate of "softening" does not admit of numerical calculation without far greater knowledge of German policy and of the indirect results of bombing than we possess at present, enough is known to show that considerable progress has already been made, the effect of which is still developing.

> (Signed)   E.G.N. RUSHBROOKE
> F.H.N. DAVIDSON
> A.F. INGLIS
> C.G. VICKERS
> A. NOBLE (for Mr. Cavendish-
> Bentinck).

Offices of the War Cabinet, S.W.1.

22ND JULY, 1943.

Appendix "D"

APPENDIX "E"

WAR CABINET

JOINT INTELLIGENCE SUB-COMMITTEE

EFFECTS OF BOMBING OFFENSIVE ON GERMAN WAR EFFORT

Report by the Joint Intelligence Sub-Committee
(November, 1943)

CONCLUSIONS

1.   The extreme gravity with which the German High Command view the extension of the air offensive during the past three months is evidenced by changes effected between 1st July and 1st October in the distribution of the German fighter force. Whereas at the beginning of this period approximately 50% of the total German fighter strength was employed on the Western front, today the fighter defenses of the Reich comprise not less than 70% of the total fighter resources of the G.A.F. This policy of concentrating fighter forces for home defence has been pursued at the direct expense of the Russian and Mediterranean fronts and has contributed to the severe military reverses which Germany has suffered on these fronts.

2.   The Allied air offensive has inflicted heavy casualties on the civilian population. In addition by compelling the German authorities to evacute not only raided areas but also major cities throughout Greater Germany, it has spred alarm throughout the Reich, and has dislocated the social and economic life of the country. It has also greatly reinforced the effect of military reverses in convincing an increasing majority of the German people that defeat is now probable. Despite the strength of the Gestapo control and the increasing use of and publicity about the death sentence, often for minor offences, the discipline of the German people now shows signs of considerable weakening; in particular their co-operation in civil defence, in helping with the difficulties of evacuation and in complying with the direction of labour has been found wanting. The masses are still carrying on owing to fear of the Gestapo and to fear of the consequences of defeat. The sense of hopelessness, however, and still more the voluntary and involuntary withdrawal of support for the war effort

Appendix "E"

already seriously impedes the German leaders in their conduct of the war. The extent to which this is attributable to Allied bombing has conspicuously increased in the last quarter.

3.   Probably five to six million people have by now been rendered temporarily or permanently homeless by bombing. This, coupled with evacuation of many large cities under the threat of further bombing has resulted in final saturation of all existing accommodation in Germany. The authorities are now being forced to divert labour and materials to the erection of large numbers of emergency hutments. Simultaneously, destruction of stocks of clothing in factory, shop and home have compelled the suspension of the clothing ration for adults. Lastly, the shortage of consumer goods has been so accentuated that even the needs of air-raid victims cannot be met. By the end of September, it is estimated that the number of workers displaced by bombing from their normal productive activities in industry, or engaged in rehabilitation work necessitated by bombing had reached the million mark (6½% of the industrial labour force). In addition a substantial carry-over of lost production and repair work has been created so that if the continuity of the attack can be maintained, there is every prospect that this figure will increase.

4.   Since June the offensive has been directed primarily against the single-engined fighter industry and by the middle of October had deprived the G.A.F. of over 900 S.E.F.

5.   Since the beginning of the year, five U-Boats have been destroyed by bombing of the yards. In addition damage to the yards and to the cities in which they are situated will result in the further loss of production of 17 U-Boats before September, 1944. Of the total of 22 U-Boats denied, 10 are attributable to attacks in the third quarter.

6.   Although the shortage of A.F.V's., and Signals equipment is primarily due to the high rate of wastage, the inadequacy of production has been aggravated by bombing, particularly in the case of signals equipment for the G.A.F. It is probable that as a result the arming and equipping of new divisions is now a greater problem than manning them.

7.   The attack on the Schweinfurt ball-bearing factories early in October is likely to produce a decline in Axis supplies by 15% - 20% over the next six months and may well begin to affect the production of aircraft, A.F.V's., and other military equipment after two months.

Appendix "E"

8.   Over the past twelve months, Axis steel production as a whole has shown a net decline of 5% - 7% and high-grade steel production for armament purposes an even larger decrease due to the concentration of damage in the Ruhr where the decline in steel output at the height of the offensive amounted to 30%-40%.

9.   The bombing of synthetic oil plants and the temporary dislocation in distribution of oil from Ploesti have contributed to maintaining the stringency of the German oil supply position.

10.   As a direct result of bombing during the third quarter, combined with the enemy's lack of success in blockade running operations since the beginning of the year, the rubber position has deteriorated severely and has produced an acute shortage of tyres, the effects of which have not yet been fully felt.

11.   In other industries damage has been distributed too widely to make a deep impression on any one of them. In its overall effort (i.e., allowing for bombing offensive resulted by the end of September, 1943, in a reduction of output of 10% - 15% as compared with the level of early 1943. Armament production as a whole has been reduced over this period perhaps to the same extent. In view of the wastage of equipment which the German armed forces, particularly the Army, have been and are incurring, and of the other factors operating after four years of blockade and intense military effort to impair Germany's economic potential, such a decline at this critical stage of the war is undoubtedly causing the greatest concern to the higher direction of the German war effort.

(Signed) V. CAVENDISH - BENTINCK
E. G. N. RUSHBROOKE
F. H. N. DAVIDSON
F. F. INGLIS
C. G. VICKERS

Offices of the War Cabinet,
S.W.1.

12th November, 1943.

Appendix "E"

APPENDIX "F"

REPORT BY AIR MINISTRY INTELLIGENCE

IN CONSULTATION WITH

POLITICAL WARFARE EXECUTIVE

ALLIED AIR ATTACKS AND GERMAN MORALE - IV

1.   This paper appreciates the effect of Allied air attacks on German morale during the period July 15th - October 15th.

2.   In these three months the Allied air offensive has increased in weight and has included night attacks on targets in Central, Southern and South-Western Germany and day attacks on targets in East Prussia, Austria and Bavaria. In North-Western Germany Hamburg was devastated between July 24th and August 3rd by four attacks of an unparalleled intensity; Hanover became the target of four successful attacks on September 22nd/23rd and 27th/28th, and October 8th/9th and 18th/19th; and notably effective single night attacks were made on Essen on July 25th/26th, Remscheid on July 30th/31st, Munchen-Gladbach on August 30th/31st, Bochum on September 29th/30th, Hagen on October 1st/2nd, and Kassel on October 3rd/4th. In South-Western Germany three very successful attacks were made on Mannheim on 9th/10th August and 5th/6th and 23rd/24th September, and Stuttgart and Frankfurt were raided on the nights of October 4th/5th and 7th/8th. In Southern Germany an ineffective attack on Munich on September 6th/7th was followed by a heavy and concentrated attack on October 2nd/3rd, and Nuremburg was raided on August 10th/11th and 27th/28th. In Central Germany two moderately effective attacks on Berlin at the end of August culminated in a very successful attack on September 3rd/4th; and on 20th/21st October a scattered attack was for the first time made on Leipzig. By day aircraft of the U.S.A.A.F. have attacked targets as widely dispersed as Hamburg (July 25th and 26th), Kiel (July 29th), Kassel (July 29th and 30th), Bonn (12th August), Regensburg (17th August), Wiener-Neustadt (13th August and 1st October), Schweinfurt (17th August and 14th October), Stuttgart (6th September), Emden (September 27th and October 2nd), Frankfurt

Appendix "F"

(October 4th), Bremen (October 8th), Gdynia, Anklam and Marienburg (October 9th), and Munster (October 10th).

3.   It was concluded in mid-July that attacks during the preceding two months had transformed what had previously been serious local difficulties into a threat affecting the entire structure of the German home front, and had caused a decline in morale which if it continued might prejudice the conduct of the war. It is appreciated that since that time the decline in morale as a direct and indirect result of air attack has been accelerated and that the tendencies noted in the earlier period are now present in a much exacerbated form. We single out for special notice the following reports:-

(i) A reliable and somewhat conservative Berlin source indicated in the third week of August that bombing was having a progressive and extremely detrimental effect on morale, and that among the whole population it had given rise to an increasing desire for peace.

(ii) It was learned in mid-September that in the view of a responsible official the moral effect of Allied air attacks on Germany had been greatly increased by their systematic nature, since the Germans now had the impression that the Allies could wipe out any town district by district as they chose.

(iii) A collated Swiss report prepared during the second half of September concluded that air attacks were having a more lowering effect on morale than the withdrawal in Russia. It was being said that even victory (which was generally regarded as unattainable) would not be worth achieving at the cost of the destruction of so many German towns.

(iv) It was reliably indicated on 14th October that Allied air attacks were the main topic of conversation in Berlin. It was said that if no means could be found of putting an end to these attacks, the deterioration of economic conditions and morale would render a general collapse inevitable. The feeling in the bombed areas was that the war must be terminated regardless of what the terms might be, since even were Germany able to hold out in the hope of attaining a compromise peace, destruction would be on a scale which would preclude a return to normal conditions for an indefinite period.

We consider that these reports accurately describe the evolution of opinion in Germany since the attacks on Hamburg at the end of July.

Appendix "F"

182

4.   Concurrently with the last of the Hamburg attacks the German authorities inaugurated a system of large-scale precautionary evacuation from Berlin and other threatened areas. Initiated at short notice and conducted in confusion, these evacuation measures gave rise to alarm verging on panic in the towns concerned. Described by *Das Reich* as "a movement of millions of individuals", they involved the wholesale removal of non-essential personnel *inter alia* from Berlin, Hamburg, Stettin, Nuremburg, Munich, Mannheim, Hannover, Kassel, Stuttgart, Augsburg, Leipzig, Vienna, Graz and Linz, and were accepted as a tacit admission on the part of the German Government that the security of centres of civilian population could no longer be ensured. An account of the evacuation of Berlin from an objective resident mentions the confusion resulting from the sudden recension of restrictions on individual movement, the appearance on the roads of large numbers of cars and lorries which had been laid up as a result of fuel rationing, the despatch of administrative departments to one point and of their archives to another, the unco-ordinated evacuation of industrial concerns without regard to technical considerations, and the temporary inability to trace evacuated offices.

5.   On the disastrous long-term effects of this precautionary evacuation all sources are agreed. Earlier reports of the results of the evacuation of raided areas in the Ruhr described the tension which had arisen between evacuees and the inhabitants of evacuation areas. This has now become apparent on a national scale. Thus a responsible source reporting in late August describes the difficulties that had arisen from the tendency of evacuees to regard themselves as state pensioners, and to drift back to evacuated districts as a result of the discomfort to which they were subjected in evacuation areas and the quarrels to which their presence there had given rise. Another source refers to the hostility with which evacuees were greeted in Eastern Germany, to the lack of preparation which had necessitated their sleeping in sheds, and to the dislocation of the supply system of the smaller towns as a result of the influx of the evacuated population. A third source refers to the fear of evacuees that they might be despatched to Poland, which was generally regarded as a danger zone. Statements made by a German business man towards the beginning of September also pay tribute to the influence on morale of the movement of large numbers of civilians from place to place, and to the effect upon them of a period of residence in strange surroundings when they are regarded as intruders. That demoralisation extends to the residents of evacuation areas as well as to evacuees is suggested in a report of early September, which describes the latter as "about as welcome as the plague" in the areas to which they are despatched. A detrimental effect has undoubtedly been

Appendix "F"

exercised on local morale by the contagious despondency of refugees from raided areas. In this connection there is good evidence that the advent of evacuees from North-Western Germany resulted in an epidemic of defeatism in the Sudetenland. It was in these circumstances that Himmler in August assumed control of the Ministry of the Interior.

6.   So far-reaching have been the consequences of evacuation and so complex the problem of housing, feeding and controlling the evacuated population, that a number of reports compare the low standard of living necessitated by evacuee conditions with Russian Communism. A responsible German business man, for example commented in the first week of September on the fact that evacuees who lost all their possessions constituted in effect a new proletariat, and on the inclination of residents in evacuation areas to regard the newcomers as Communists. The same theme recurs in a responsible report received in late October, which describes the automatic drift of this homeless, migratory population towards a Communist mentality. The danger that Europe might be "proletarianised by dispropriation through bombing" has also been mentioned in the German press. While it cannot be precluded that some of these references and reports are in the nature of propaganda addressed to Great Britain and the U.S.A. we believe that the tendency described has some basis in fact.

7.   While it is difficult to provide firm figures for the number of individuals in Germany affected by evacuation, some conception of the magnitude of the problem which confronts the German authorities can be gained from reports estimating the evacuated population at between four and six millions and eight millions respectively. An index to the scale of evacuation following specific attacks is provided by Hannover, from which 250,000 homeless were transferred after the attack of October 8th/9th.

8.   In conjunction with heavy residential damage, large-scale evacuation has contributed to the complete absorption of the housing resources of the Reich. The results of this are apparent both in raided districts and in evacuation areas. Thus during August evacuation from Hamburg caused a crisis in accommodation in Danzig, while by the third week of September (when evacuation to the Ostland was suspended) serious congestion had arisen in East Prussia, whither evacuees from the triangle Bremen - Hamburg - Berlin were moved, and where life was described as completely disorganised. From raided areas there is evidence that as late as 4th October essential personnel in Mannheim were living in air raid shelters for want of alternative accommodation, that in October further dwelling space was being requisitioned in

Appendix "F"

Bochum, and that in Bremen supplementary registration was in progress in anticipation of heavy air attacks. In late September the problem of housing the evacuated population during the winter months was reported to be causing the authorities the gravest concern, since in many areas *refugees were accommodated in temporary wooden barracks.* An official solution in the form of a German Housing Relief Scheme was announced by Ley on October 30th. This somewhat nebulous plan which provided for the large-scale construction of pre-fabricated emergency dwellings "in the form of summer houses" for evacuated families, had the merit of reassuring the evacuated population as to their chances of securing occupation of independent premises and even of returning to the vicinity of their native towns, and the disadvantage of an admission that since construction had only recently begun on an appreciable scale, it would be some time before the scheme was fully operative.

9.   The regionalism noted in the Ruhr in a previous report as one of the administrative consequences of a heavy series of attacks have assumed more significant proportions. Separatist tendencies are reliably reported to be attracting official attention in Bavaria,Wurtemberg and Baden where deep-rooted hostility towards the Prussians is becoming evident. In Southern Germany during the first week of October demoralisation was stated to have *expressed itself in growing anti-Prussian feeling.* While it would be a mistake to attach undue importance to this point, sources agree that this development is largely due to the effect of air attacks on Nuremberg and Munich and to the transfer to Bavaria of large numbers of evacuees *from raided areas in North-Western Germany.*

10.   Not unnaturally the authorised evacuation of non-essential civilian personnel led to the unauthorised evacuation of large numbers of civilians in essential occupations. In Vienna and other centres, which have not yet been attacked, a large section of the population is reported to sleep outside the town. In Berlin *non-evacuated workmen are described as crowded into camps within* a fifty mile radius of the city returning to the city daily for their work, while in Mannheim it proved necessary to institute a special check on motor-cars and trucks "loaded with goods as camouflage", *which were transporting the* inhabitants into the country at night. A serious view is taken by the German authorities of this practice on the ground that it places an unnecessary strain on local communications and results in a depletion of the A.R.P. services. Absconding A.R.P. workers have been threatened that their ration cards will be withdrawn if the practice does not stop.

Appendix "F"

11.   A by-product of the Hamburg raids was the diffusion of rumours on a scale and of a kind unparalleled in earlier periods. Lurid accounts of men and women with their clothes on fire running like living torches through the town seem to have gained immediate currency, and every effort has been made by the German authorities to dispel an illusion that liquid phosphorous was sprayed over the town by the attacking aircraft. An unprecedented number of injunctions against rumour mongering have been delivered, warnings have been issued against retailing sensational stories in shelters during air attacks, and heavy sentences have been imposed on individuals stabbing the home front in the back. There is no doubt that in the minds of the authorities the new credulity with which the German public discusses the effects of air attack is an important factor in undermining civilian resistance.

12.   There is good evidence that the number of fatal casualties incurred in raids has greatly increased during this period. In the case of four attacks on Cologne in June and July the German press admitted a total of over 4,000 deaths; and in the case of the Hamburg attacks of 28,000 dead. There is some reason to think that in the latter instance the admitted casualties were about 50% of the true figures, and many reports from Hamburg have mentioned totals of between 100,000 and 120,000. At Hannover 3,000 were killed in a single raid. While there is no means of forming an accurate estimate of aggregate casualties for any specific series of attacks, it is clear that in Germany casualties are believed greatly to exceed the totals admitted by the authorities. The fact that it is found necessary to deny the "gruesome figures" in current circulation indicates that in the eyes of the public the expectation of life of the average German civilian has sharply declined.

13.   This has no doubt contributed to reduce the effort of the A.R.P. and fire-fighting services. That impaired efficiency is not confined to any one locality is indicated by reports from Hamburg, Bremen and Berlin, by the threats of punishment meted out to defaulting A.R.P. personnel in Dusseldorf, Breslau, Chemnitz, Munich and Stettin, by press admissions of the failure of the fire-fighting services in Stuttgart during the attack of October 4th/5th and by a local announcement that the material losses incurred at Frankfurt on October 7th/8th could have been reduced by 25% had the fires been fought in a more energetic and determined way.

14.   The organisation of relief in raided areas varies greatly in efficiency from town to town. Whereas in Hannover the relief organisation evidently functioned reasonably well, in Mannheim and Ludwigshafen hitches seem to

Appendix "F"

have occurred. At Hamburg the distribution of food and commodities broke down after the first two attacks, while the non-availability of drinking water and the dislocation of the drainage system presented major medical problems, with which Conti, the Reich Health Leader, was called upon to deal. As late as the first week of October the Hamburg press contained references to the "open ditch latrines", which had had to be instituted, and to living conditions, which suggest that the rate of recovery, even in the quite exceptional circumstances obtaining, was very slow. Contributory evidence of a decline in the rate of repairs comes from Stuttgart, where the population were asked in mid-October to show understanding of the situation. The need to use the existing retail supply system after air attacks accounts for the cancellation during August of the order providing for the closure of surplus retail establishments.

15.   The shortage of consumer goods mentioned in earlier reports as a factor in intensifying and prolonging the effect of raids has become progressively more serious with the advent of evacuation and the extension of attacks. It was alleged, for example, in a collated Swiss intelligence report, that two-fifths of the entire July production of consumption goods were commandeered in factories for the bombed areas. Following the Hamburg attacks, the sale of textiles was suspended throughout the whole of Germany, but as late as the third week of September this does not seem greatly to have alleviated the textile supply position in Hamburg itself. Elsewhere at the end of September the impossibility of obtaining goods not sold on the card system was popularly attributed to the results of air attack.

16.   One outcome of the shortage of consumer goods has been an increase in the incidence of looting after raids. Cases have been reported *inter alia* from Berlin, Cologne, Hannover, Frankfurt, Mannheim, Karlsruhe, and Oldenburg. First-hand observers have alluded to the prevalence of looting in Hamburg, in which the police were alleged to have participated. Looting on the part of the police has also been reported on by Russian prisoners-of-war in Bremen.

17.   Of the effect of raids on industrial morale there is cumulative evidence. Reporting in early August, a Hamburg business man mentions a marked deterioration in the industrial situation as a result of the effect of air attacks upon the workers; in this lack of sleep, a sense of insecurity, and changes in living and factory conditions played their part. An authoritative report of mid-September also testifies to the decline in working capacity of raided or evacuated personnel, and in general it appears that nervousness and overstrain have served appreciably to reduce industrial effort. French workers

Appendix "F"

in Germany (whose statements must, however, be treated with reserve), have consistently reported on the low state of industrial morale. To this the presence of foreign workers has contributed. Thus a source who left Hamburg before the July attacks mentioned that at that time the foreign workers, many of whom were Communists, were already fomenting unrest amongst the German workmen, while a member of the staff of I. G. Farben indicated that an armed organisation had been formed from German staff to handle foreign workmen in the event of any crisis. That these apprehensions are not altogether unfounded is confirmed by the difficulty known to have been experienced in rounding up conscripted workmen and prisoners-of-war after attacks.

18. The anti-Party bias noted in the preceding period as an effect of air attack has assumed more formidable proportions. A Berlin source indicated in late September that Hitler was more or less openly criticised as a result of his responsibility for the deteriorating military position on the Eastern Front and for the continuance of air attacks. Another source reported in mid-August that Hitler's personal prestige had greatly declined. Accounts of anti-Nazi slogans chalked up after raids come from a number of sources. A Spaniard reported in mid-September that in the Berlin factory in which he was employed he observed a diminution in Hitler's influence with the workers and the growth of a new antipathy towards the regime. A similar report emanates from a French workman in a North-West German factory. According to some sources, resentment in Hamburg was also directed in the first instance against Hitler and the Party. In press and public statements the Fuehrer's personal interest in the home front has been increasingly insisted on, and a somewhat defensive tone has been adopted in respect of local Party leaders. Only in the post-war period, it is insisted, will the achievements of National Socialism receive the appreciation and esteem which is their due. Instances of a new effort to counter the prevailing impression that the Fuehrer is not interested in events in Germany are Ley's statement that Hitler was responsible for devising the Housing Relief Scheme and Hitler's own participation in the much publicised conference on the home front held at his headquarters in the third week of October.

19. Whereas during the preceding period there was little evidence as to disturbances after attacks, in the present period the number of first-hand reports of demonstrations after raids has tended to increase. A circumstantial report from Nuremburg describes an anti-Nazi demonstration after the attack of August 10th/11th, which resulted in a hundred or more arrests; this report is the more credible in view of a tendency to panic during the attack reported on by many sources notwithstanding the small scale of damage caused. Small-scale anti-Nazi demonstrations were also reported from Aachen. At Hamburg

Appendix "F"

incidents broke out in connection with the distribution of relief, and sources described the defacement of pictures of Hitler "to the accompaniment of extremely coarse language." Difficulties are reliably reported to have arisen at Cologne, where a body of workmen downed tools after a heavy attack, a number being shot and the remainder transported to other areas, and disturbances have also occurred at Mannheim (as the result of a delay in carrying out evacuation), Munich and Frankfurt. Tension in Munich is mentioned by several sources.

20. First-hand observers continue to express the view that the German security forces remain strong enough to deal with such disturbances as may occur. It was appreciated by an officer of the German Intelligence Service in early October that the repressive measures adopted would not lose their efficacy until the end of 1944, and by a German business man a month earlier that the sporadic disturbances which had occurred were relatively insignificant in face of the repressive measures which were used to check the growing desperation following attacks. In Mid-August (when panic was at its worst) reports were circulating in Berlin of the arrival in the capital of some 60,000 S.S. troops, and of an incident a month earlier at Essen in which a clash with the S.S. had led to many deaths. While it is a fact that repressive measures have so far lost little or nothing of their efficacy and that there is as yet no indication of organised revolt, it would none the less be a mistake to accept these indications in too literal a way. On the one hand, the slight weakening of control recorded earlier in the Ruhr has become apparent in other areas, notably in Hannover, and on the other it is credibly reported that S.S. units brought in to raided areas from Eastern Germany are relieved as rapidly as possible in order to minimise the danger of any form of disaffection. It is also stated that in early August a secret investigation was instituted into the reliability of S.S. officers. In addition, evacuation and the extension of attacks should have resulted in some thinning out of the forces of control.

21. The attempt to stimulate flagging morale by creating a demand for retaliation has continued, and references to coming reprisals have been a feature of Ley's speeches to factory workers and other quasi-official pronouncements. The consensus of evidence suggests that despite the hysterical vilification of the attacking air forces, which has been noticeable in the local press in Frankfurt and elsewhere, reprisals are viewed rather as a vague means of averting further attacks than in a strictly retaliatory spirit. It was indicated by a Swiss source in late July that the middle classes in particular were placing what hopes they had upon reprisal action. Elsewhere press threats seem to

Appendix "F"

meet with scepticism. A significant sentence in a Munich paper reads: "Remembering the binding statements of the Reich leaders, the German people awaits the hour of retaliation with set teeth lest this frantic terror should become an unassailable law against us."

22.   The general tendency of propaganda, however, has been to divert attention to Allied losses in aircraft and personnel as a limiting factor on the development of operations. Propaganda of this type reached its climax with the U.S.A.A.F. attack on Schweinfurt on October 15th, when the loss of 121 four-engined bombers was claimed in the official communique and the loss of 199 in unofficial statements put out on the German-controlled wireless. Concurrently with these announcements, a tone of cautious optimism became apparent in German press statements, which had for some time previously alluded to the strengthening of the German defensive system. At the same time no specific promise of immunity or even of an appreciable decline in the incidence of air attack within any specific period was made. Locally this line of propaganda has been followed out in public tributes to the leaders who had "built up new German air defences."

23.   The myth of the invulnerability of German industry, to which propaganda statements had adhered in the preceding period, has been abandoned, and a number of press articles have gone so far as to refer to the possibility that German industry will be unable to recover in the post-war period, and that the U.S.A.A.F. may "destroy all our factories in order to prevent German-European competition." This is one among a number of instances of the great moral effect exercised by day attacks.

24.   Mosquito attacks on Berlin and other towns have lost none of the effectiveness with which they were credited in the preceding two months, and we are satisfied that these are playing an important part in wearing down morale.

25.   Evidence as to the impact of air attacks on the morale of German troops on the war fronts or abroad is fragmentary. The most significant item is a categorical but uncorroborated statement in a Swiss intelligence report that an O.K.W. circular had been issued to troops in the East, assuring them that every possible measure was being taken to relieve the lot of the bomb victims, and exhorting them to stand firm in the belief in final victory. Unconfirmed reports refer to the deleterious influences exercised by air attacks on the morale of German troops in Oslo and on personnel of the Todt Organisation

Appendix "F"

190

at Bodo, while a report despatched in August from Crete stated that R.A.F. attacks had done more to lower the morale of the German occupying forces than military defeat. It may well be that this attitude is representative of that of garrison forces in other occupied areas.

26.   We conclude that during the period under review:—

  (i) Fear of air attack has been the dominant preoccupation of a large part of the German civilian population, and has contributed to produce a situation in which fear of the consequences of continuing the war is becoming greater than fear of the consequences of defeat.

 (ii) Air attacks on Germany have resulted in social disruption on a scale which has greatly impaired the German ability to prosecute the war and threatens the structure of the entire home front.

(iii) Though the forces of repression, the hopes of a compromise with one or the other of the belligerents, and the favourable climatic conditions of the past three months have so far prevented any general break in morale, it is not reasonable to infer that no such break in morale can occur, and we do not exclude the possibility that, in conjunction with further large-scale military reverses and with the advent of winter, air operations may exercise a decisive influence on conditions inside Germany.

7th November, 1943

Appendix "F"

APPENDIX "G"

MAJOR TARGETS ATTACKED BY R.A.F. BOMBER COMMAND

FEBRUARY 4 — OCTOBER 31, 1943

TARGETS IN THE RUHR AND RHINELAND

Target	Date	Sorties Desp'd	Bomb Tonnage	A/C Missing
Aachen	13/14 July	374	875	20
Barmen	29/30 May	719	1,895	33
Bochum	29/30 March	157	149	13
	13/14 May	442	1,056	24
	12/13 June	503	1,596	24
	29/30 Sept.	352	1,344	7
Cologne	14/15 Feb.	243	528	9
	26/27 Feb.	427	1,062	10
	16/17 June	212	718	14
	28/29 June	608	1,727	25
	3/4 July	653	1,878	30
	8/9 July	288	1,097	7
Dortmund	4/5 May	596	1,570	31
	23/24 May	826	2,248	38
Duisburg	26/27 March	455	944	6
	8/9 April	392	846	19
	9/10 April	109	321	8
	26/27 April	561	1,492	17
	12/13 May	572	1,554	34
Dusseldorf	25/26 May	759	2,038	27
	11/12 June	783	2,101	38
Elberfeld	24/25 June	630	1,746	34

(Table continued on following page)

Appendix "G"

Target	Date	Sorties Desp'd	Bomb Tonnage	A/C Missing
Essen	5/6 March	442	1,014	14
	12/13 March	457	1,027	23
	3/4 April	348	983	21
	30/1 May	305	839	12
	27/28 May	518	1,443	23
	25/26 July	705	2,032	26
Gelsenkirchen	25/26 June	470	1,391	30
	9/10 July	418	1,341	12
Hagen	1/2 Oct.	251	1,115	1
Krefeld	21/22 June	705	2,068	44
Leverkusen	22/23 Aug.	462	1,729	5
Mulheim	22/23 June	557	1,643	35
Munchen-Gladbach	30/31 Aug.	660	2,353	25
Oberhausen	14/15 June	203	645	17
Remscheid	30/31 July	273	778	15
Ruhr Dams (Moehne & Eder)	16/17 May	19	61	8

BERLIN

Date	Sorties Desp'd	Bomb Tonnage	A/C Missing
1/2 March	302	665	17
27/28 March	396	883	9
29/30 March	329	606	21
23/24 Aug.	719	1,772	57
31/1 Sept.	612	1,448	47
3/4 Sept.	316	999	22

(Table continued on following page)

Appendix "G"

THE CENTRAL COMPLEX, THE "BERLIN ROAD," THE NORTH SEA AND BALTIC PORTS

Target	Date	Sorties Desp'd	Bomb Tonnage	A/C Missing
Bremen	21/22 Feb.	143	424	—
	8/9 Oct.	119	252	3
Hamburg	3/4 Feb.	263	393	16
	3/4 March	417	922	10
	24/25 July	791	2,397	12
	27/28 July	787	2,417	17
	29/30 July	777	2,383	28
	2/3 Aug.	740	1,426	30
Hannover	22/23 Sept.	711*	2,503	26
	27/28 Sept.	678*	2,358	38
	8/9 Oct.	504	1,762	27
	18/19 Oct.	360	1,697	17
Kassel	3/4 Oct.	547	1,601	24
	22/23 Oct.	569	1,806	43
Kiel	4/5 April	577	1,381	13
Leipzig	20/21 Oct.	358	1,045	16
Stettin	20/21 April	339	847	22
Wilhelmshafen	11/12 Feb.	177	432	3
	18/19 Feb.	195	596	4
	19/20 Feb.	338	781	11
	24/25 Feb.	115	193	—

(* Including 5 U.S. Fortresses. 1 reported missing on night 27/28 Sept.)

(Table continued on following page)

Appendix "G"

THE UPPER RHINE AND THE SOUTHERN COMPLEX

Target	Date	Sorties Desp'd	Bomb Tonnage	A/C Missing
Frankfurt	10/11 April	502	1,060	20
	4/5 Oct.	409*	1,088	10

(* Including 3 U.S. Fortresses)

Target	Date	Sorties Desp'd	Bomb Tonnage	A/C Missing
Mannheim	16/17 April	271	362	18
	9/10 Aug.	457	1,723	9
	5/6 Sept.	605	1,586	34
	23/24 Sept.	630*	1,974	32

(* Including 5 U.S. Fortresses)

Target	Date	Sorties Desp'd	Bomb Tonnage	A/C Missing
Munich	9/10 March	264	579	8
	6/7 Sept.	404	1,045	17
	2/3 Oct.	298*	979	8

(* Including 4 U.S. Fortresses)

Target	Date	Sorties Desp'd	Bomb Tonnage	A/C Missing
Nuremburg	25/26 Feb.	337	758	9
	8/9 March	335	798	7
	10/11 Aug.	653	1,671	16
	27/28 Aug.	674	1,773	33
Stuttgart	11/12 March	314	821	11
	14/15 April	462	801	23
	7/8 Oct.	342	1,235	4

(Table continued on following page)

Appendix "G"

195

IMPORTANT WAR FACTORIES ATTACKED IN GERMANY
AND OCCUPIED TERRITORY

Target	Date	Sorties Desp'd	Bomb Tonnage	A/C Missing
Jena (Zeiss Works)	27 May	14	7	3
Peenemunde (Experimental Station)	17/18 Aug.	597	1,937	40
Pilsen (Skoda Works)	16/17 April	327	617	37
	13/14 May	168	527	9

FRANCE

Target	Date	Sorties Desp'd	Bomb Tonnage	A/C Missing
Arnage (Renault Works)	9 March	15	13	1
Le Creusot (Schneider Works)	19/20 June	287	751	2
Montbeliard (Peugeot Works)	15/16 July	165	391	5
Montlucon (Dunlop Works)	15/16 Sept.	376*	1,016	3

(* Including 5 U.S. Fortresses)

NORWAY

Target	Date	Sorties Desp'd	Bomb Tonnage	A/C Missing
Knaben (Molybdenum Mines)	3 March	10	9	1

SEA-MINING OPERATIONS

No. of Aircraft Despatched	Mines Laid	No. of Aircraft Missing
4,094	10,752	98

(Table continued on following page)

Appendix "G"

LEAFLET OPERATIONS

No. of Aircraft Despatched	*No. of Aircraft Missing*
1,056	13

Of the Total Effort, 89.8% was expended on Bomb Raids, 8.1% on Sea-Mining and 2.1% on Leaflets.

Appendix "G"

APPENDIX "H"

MAJOR TARGETS ATTACKED BY VIII BOMBER COMMAND

FEBRUARY 4 — NOVEMBER 1, 1943

Date of Attack	TARGET ATTACKED	A/C Attacking	Tonnage on Target
16 Feb.	ST. NAZAIRE—Submarine Base	65	160.0
26 Feb.	WILHELMSHAVEN—Submarine Building Yards	64	161.5
27 Feb.	BREST—Submarine Base	60	155.0
4 Mar.	HAMM—Railway Marshalling Yard	14	35.0
6 Mar.	LORIENT—Submarine Base	63	157.5
6 Mar.	BREST—Submarine Base	15	44.5
18 Mar.	VEGESACK—Submarine Building Yard of Bremer Vulkan Schiffbau u Maschinen-Fabrik A.G. (Subsidiary of Vereinigte Stahlwerke A.G.)	97	268.0
22 Mar.	WILHELMSHAVEN—Submarine Building Yard	84	224.0
4 April	PARIS (BILLANCOURT)—Motor Vehicle and Armament Works of Soc. des Usines Renault	85	251.0
5 April	ANTWERP (MORTSEL) — Aircraft and Aero Engine Works of Erla Maschinewerk G.m.b.H. (formerly Soc. Nouvelle des Automobiles Imperia) (formerly S.A. Minerva Motors)	82	245.5
16 April	LORIENT—Submarine Base	59	147.0
16 April	BREST—Submarine Base	18	49.0

(Table continued on following page)

Appendix "H"

Date of Attack	TARGET ATTACKED	A/C Attacking	Tonnage on Target
17 April	BREMEN (NEUENLAND)—Bomber Aircraft Assembly Factory of Focke Wulf Flugzeugbau A.G.	106	263.0
1 May	ST. NAZAIRE—Submarine Base	25	49.0
4 May	ANTWERP—Motor Assembly Plant of Ford Motor Co. Motor Assembly Plant of General Motors	65	161.5
13 May	MEAULTE Nr. ALBERT—Aircraft Factory of Soc. Nationale de Constructions Aeronautiques du Nord (S.N.C.A.N.) (formerly Avions et Hydravions Potez-C.A.M.S.)	88	218.0
14 May	KIEL—Submarine and Warship Building Yard of Fried Drupp Germania-Werft	126	293.6
14 May	ANTWERP—Motor Assembly Plant of Ford Motor Co. Motor Assembly Plant of General Motors	38	89.0
15 May	HELIGOLAND—Submarine Base	76	186.0
17 May	LORIENT—Submarine Installations	80	197.5
17 May	KEROMAN—Submarine Base	38	92.0
19 May	KIEL—Submarine and Warship Building Yard of Deutsche Werke Kiel A. G.	103	236.9
19 May	FLENSBURG—Submarine Building Yard of Flensburger Schiffsbaugesellschaft A. G.	55	134.0
21 May	WILHELMSHAVEN—Submarine Building Yards	77	190.5
21 May	EMDEN — Submarine Building Yard of Nordseewerke G. m. b. H. (Subsidiary of Vereinigte Stahlwerke A. G.)	45	111.0
29 May	ST. NAZAIRE—Submarine Base	147	277.0
29 May	LA PALLICE—Submarine Base	34	99.0

(Table continued on following page)

Appendix "H"

Date of Attack	TARGET ATTACKED	A/C Attacking	Tonnage on Target
29 May	RENNES—Submarine Installations	57	132.5
11 June	WILHELMSHAVEN — Submarine Building Yards	168	417.0
13 June	BREMEN—Submarine and Warship Building Yard of Deutsche Schiff u Maschinenbau A. G. (Deschimag)	102	253.7
13 June	KIEL—Submarine and Warship Building Yard of Deutsche Werke Kiel A. G.	44	99.7
22 June	HULS Nr. RECKLINGHAUSEN—Synthetic Rubber (Buna) Works of Chemische Werke Huls G.m.b.H.	181	422.0
22 June	ANTWERP—Motor Assembly Plant of General Motors	39	95.5
28 June	ST. NAZAIRE—Submarine Base	158	301.0
29 June	LE MANS—Aero Engine Factory of Societe des Moteurs Gnome et Rhone	74	181.5
4 July	LE MANS—Aero Engine Factory of Societe des Moteurs Gnome et Rhone	103	254.5
4 July	NANTES—Aircraft Assembly Plant of Societe Nationale de Constructions Aeronautiques du Sud-Ouest (S.N.C.A.S.O.) (formerly S.A. des Ateliers d'Aviation Louis Breguet	61	145.0
4 July	LA PALLICE—Submarine Base	69	137.5
14 July	VILLACOUBLAY — Aircraft Factories of Breguet	101	202.5
14 July	LE BOURGET Nr. PARIS—Aircraft Repair Installations	52	122.8
17 July	AMSTERDAM—Aircraft Factory of Fokker Aircraft Co.	21	51.5

(Table continued on following page)

Appendix "H"

Date of Attack	TARGET ATTACKED	A/C Attacking	Tonnage on Target
24 July	HEROYA (68 miles S.S.W. of Oslo) — Aluminum Works of Nordisk Lettmetal A/S	167	414.2
24 July	TRONDHEIM—Submarine Base	41	81.0
25 July	HAMBURG—Submarine Building Yard of Blohm & Voss K.G.	51	100.0
25 July	HAMBURG (MONFLETH)—Aero Engine Works of Klockner Flugmotorenbau A.G.	17	34.0
25 July	KIEL—Submarine and Warship Building Yard of Deutsche Werke Kiel A.G. and Submarine and Warship Building Yard of Howaldtswerke A.G.	67	155.3
26 July	HANNOVER—Tyre and Tube Factory of Continental Gummiwerke A.G.	42	98.3
26 July	HANNOVER—(NORDHAFEN)—Synthetic Rubber (Buna) Processing Works of Continental Gummiwerke A.G.	50	115.5
26 July	HAMBURG—Submarine Building Yard of Blohm & Voss A.G.	39	89.2
26 July	HAMBURG (MONFLETH)—Aero Engine Works of Klockner Flugmotorenbau A.G.	15	37.0
28 July	KASSEL (BETTENHAUSEN)—Fighter Aircraft Components Factory of Fieseler Flugzeugbau G.m.b.H.	49	137.0
28 July	OSCHERSLEBEN—Fighter Aircraft Assembly Factory of AGO Flugzeugwerke A.G.	37	90.4
29 July	KIEL—Submarine and Warship Building Yard of Deutsche Werke Kiel A.G.	42	94.9
29 July	KIEL—Submarine and Warship Building Yard of Howaldtswerke A.G.	50	115.5

(Table continued on following page)

Appendix "H"

201

Date of Attack	TARGET ATTACKED	A/C Attacking	Tonnage on Target
29 July	WARNEMUNDE—Fighter Aircraft Assembly Factory and Airfield of Ernst Heinkel Flugzeugwerke G.m.b.H. (formerly Arado Flugzeugwerke G.m.b.H.)	54	129.0
30 July	KASSEL (BETTENHAUSEN)—Fighter Aircraft Components Factory of Fieseler Flugzeugbau G.m.b.H.	95	222.0
30 July	KASSEL (WALDAU)—Fighter Aircraft Assembly Factories of Fieseler Flugzeubau G.m.b.H.	37	87.0
16 August	LE BOURGET (Nr. PARIS)—Aircraft Repair Installations	168	397.4
17 August	SCHWEINFURT — Ball-bearing Works of Kugelfischer Schweinfurt; Undercarriage, Clutch and Cycle Accessories Works of Fichtel & Sachs A.G.; Ball-bearing Works of Vereinigte Kugellagerfabriken A.G. (Werk I and II)	183	424.4
17 August	REGENSBURG — Fighter Aircraft Assembly Factory of Messerschmitt A.G.	127	299.3
24 August	VILLACOUBLAY (Nr. PARIS) — Aircraft Factories of Breguet	86	257.3
3 Sept.	ROMILLY-SUR-SEINE—Air Park and Airfield	100	294.0
3 Sept.	MEULAN-LES-MUREAUX — Aircraft Factory of Soc. Nationale de Constructions Aeronautiques du Nord (S.N.C.A.N.) (formerly Avions et Hydravions Potez C.A.M.S.)	38	114.0
3 Sept.	PARIS—Aircraft Components Factory of S.A. des Avions Caudron-Renault	20	60.0

(Table continued on following Page)

Appendix "H"

Date of Attack	TARGET ATTACKED	A/C Attacking	Tonnage on Target
7 Sept.	BRUSSELS (EVERE) — Aircraft Repair Works of Erla Maschinenwerk G.m.b.H. (formerly S.A.B.C.A.)	104	282.0
15 Sept.	ROMILLY-SUR-SEINE—Air Park and Airfield	76	246.0
15 Sept.	PARIS—Aircraft Components Factory of S.A. des Avions Caudron-Renault and Automobile Engine and Lorry Assembly Works of S.A. Andre Citroen	40	118.8
15 Sept.	PARIS (BILLANCOURT)—Motor Vehicle and Armament of Soc. Des Usines Renault	21	63.0
15 Sept.	PARIS—Aero Engine Factory of Societe Hispano-Zuiza and Ball Bearing Works of Compagnie d'applications Mecaniques (C.A.M.)	78	229.0
16 Sept.	NANTES—Naval Installations	79	233.0
16 Sept.	LA PALLICE—Submarine Base	53	131.8
23 Sept.	NANTES—Naval Installations	61	134.0
23 Sept.	NANTES—Naval Installations	46	130.0
26 Sept.	REIMS/CHAMPAGNE—Aircraft Assembly and Repair Plant of Junkers Flugzeug und Motorenwerke A.G.	40	118.0
2 Oct.	EMDEN — Submarine Building Yard of Nordseewerke Emden G.m.b.H.	341	953.0
4 Oct.	FRANKFURT (HEDDERNHEIM—Aircraft Components Works of Vereinigte Deutsche Metallwerke A. G. (V. D. M.) Heddernheim Kupferwerke	77	216.3
4 Oct.	FRANKFURT—Built up area of City	37	88.3

(Table continued on following Page)

Appendix "H"

Date of attack	TARGET ATTACKED	A/C Attacking	Tonnage on Target
8 Oct.	BREMEN—Submarine and Warship Building Yard of Deutsche Schiff u Maschinenbau A.G. (Deschimag)	44	130.0
8 Oct.	BREMEN (OSLEBHAUSEN)—Bomber Aircraft Assembly Factory of Weser Flugzeubau G.m.b.H.	33	81.0
8 Oct.	BREMEN—Center of City	197	471.9
8 Oct.	VEGESACK—Submarine Building Yard of Bremer Vulkan Schiffbau u Maschinenfrabrik A.G.	48	142.5
9 Oct.	ANKLAM—Trainer, Reconnaissance and Bomber Aircraft Components Factory of Arado Flugzeugwerke G.m.b.H.	102	185.5
9 Oct.	MARIENBURG—G.A.F. Station	96	218.0
9 Oct.	DANZIG—Naval Installations	23	50.0
9 Oct.	GDYNIA—Naval Installations	127	308.0
10 Oct.	MUNSTER—Railway Junctions	138	354.0
14 Oct.	SCHWEINFURT—Ball Bearing Works of Kugelfischer Undercarriage Clutch and Cycle Accessories. Works of Fichtel and Sachs A.G. Ball Bearing Works of Vereinigte Kugellagerfabriken A.G. (Werk I) Ball Bearing Works of Vereinigte Kugellagerfabriken A.G. (Werk II) Ball Bearing Cage Works of Deutsche Star		

Appendix "H"

C.C.S. 404 and 404/1

AGENDA FOR SEXTANT

References:

CCS 127th Meeting, Item 2

CCS 133d Meeting, Item 3

On 22 November 1943, the United States Chiefs of Staff proposed an agenda for *SEXTANT* (C.C.S. 404). The British Chiefs of Staff circulated C.C.S. 404/1. In their 127th Meeting, the Combined Chiefs of Staff accepted the proposals for the main subjects for discussion on the *SEXTANT* agenda as set out in paragraph 2 of C.C.S. 404/1.

On 2 December 1943, the Secretaries circulated a draft agenda for the remainder of the *SEXTANT* Conference. The Combined Chiefs of Staff in their 133d Meeting agreed that all but the most essential items should be excluded from the *SEXTANT* agenda and listed in their decision the priority in which the remaining conference items should be dealt with.

C.C.S. 404   22 November 1943

COMBINED CHIEFS OF STAFF

AGENDA FOR "SEXTANT"

Memorandum by the United States Chiefs of Staff

The attached proposed agenda is presented for the consideration of the Combined Chiefs of Staff.

ENCLOSURE

PROPOSED AGENDA FOR "SEXTANT"

1. Agreement as to conference procedure.

2. Over-All Objective; Over-All Strategic Concept for the Prosecution of the War; Basic Undertakings in Support of Over-All Strategic Concept.

3. *European-Mediterranean*

    a. Estimate of the enemy situation.

    b. Report on the Combined Bomber Offensive.

    c. Report on anti-U-boat operations.

    d. Report on status of development of facilities in the Azores, air and naval.

    e. Readiness report on *OVERLORD, RANKIN,* and *JUPITER.*

    f. Report on Mediterranean operations, including the Middle East.

    g. Plans for U.S.-British-U.S.S.R. military collaboration.

    h. Specific operations for the defeat of Germany and her Satellites, 1943-44.

i. Policies with respect to military considerations in dealing with neutral, liberated and occupied countries, including agreement as to division of responsibility between the United Nations.

4. *Japan*

a. Estimate of the enemy situation, 1944, Japan (giving consideration to Russian and Chinese intentions).

b. Short Term Plan for the defeat of Japan.

c. Report on the general situation in the Southeast Asia Command.

d. Report on operations in China.

e. Report on Pacific operations.

f. Transfer of United Nations efforts to the defeat of Japan upon the defeat of Germany.

g. Specific operations for the defeat of Japan, 1944, including amphibious operations in Southeast Asia.

5. Relation of resources to plans.

6. Final report to President and Prime Minister.

7. Preparation and approval of any directives arising from conference decisions and of any reports to other Allies.

8. Discussion as to the next conference.

C.C.S. 404/1   22 November 1943

COMBINED CHIEFS OF STAFF

SEXTANT AGENDA

Memorandum by the British Chiefs of Staff

1. We have considered the Agenda for *SEXTANT* proposed by the United States Chiefs of Staff (C.C.S. 404) and while we have no specific objections to the subjects set out in their memorandum, we suggest that a more simple agenda would meet the case.

2. We, therefore, propose that the main subjects for discussion should be as follows:

    I. REAFFIRM OVER-ALL OBJECTIVE, OVER-ALL STRATEGIC CONCEPT AND BASIC UNDERTAKINGS
(C.C.S. 319/5, paragraphs 2-5 and paragraphs 6, as subsequently amended by agreement between Combined Chiefs of Staff (see C.C.S. 380/2))

    II. SOUTHEAST ASIA OPERATIONS

    III. "OVERLORD" AND THE MEDITERRANEAN

    IV. THE WAR AGAINST JAPAN

    V. PROGRESS REPORTS

3. Discussion of the above main subjects would include the introduction of most, if not all, of the points put forward in the American agenda. The arrangements for dealing with the detailed subjects would, however, be made from day to day.

4. It will be noted that Southeast Asia operations have been placed second on the list, in view of the intention to bring the Generalissimo and Admiral Mountbatten into the discussions at the earliest stage.

5. It is thought that the Progress Reports should be left to the end of the Conference when the main items have been disposed of. This procedure will not, of course, preclude points being raised for discussion when the Progress Reports are taken.

(Signed)   A. F. BROOKE,

C. A. PORTAL,

A. B. CUNNINGHAM.

CAIRO.

22 November 1943

C.C.S. 405

ROLE OF CHINA IN DEFEAT OF JAPAN

Reference:

CCS 128th Meeting, Item 2

C.C.S. 405 circulated a memorandum from Lt. General Stilwell, 22 November 1943. The Combined Chiefs of Staff considered this memorandum in their 128th Meeting and agreed that operations proposed in paragraphs 2 *a* to *d* inclusive are in general, in consonance with the present concept of operations against Japan as expressed in C.C.S. 397, Specific Operations for the Defeat of Japan, 1944. They further agreed that operations proposed in paragraphs 2 *e* to *h* inclusive go beyond the present concept of operations in China and require detailed examination and study with particular reference to logistic difficulties. This study, when completed, to be incorporated in the over-all plan for the defeat of Japan.

C.C.S. 405   22 November 1943

COMBINED CHIEFS OF STAFF

ROLE OF CHINA IN DEFEAT OF JAPAN

Memorandum from Lt. General Stilwell, USA

1. At *QUADRANT* an outline plan for operations against Japan was presented in Annex "I" to C.C.S. 319/2. These operations culminated in an invasion of Japan some time after 1947.

2. The question at hand which concerns the China Theater is "what operations can be mounted from China which will have the greatest effect on the course of the war in the Pacific?" This question can be answered as follows:

   a. Assist S.E.A.C. in operations against North Burma—Current.

   b. Develop land route to China and improve internal communications—Current.

   c. Continue to train and improve combat effectiveness of Chinese Army—Current.

   d. Initiate intensive bombing of Japan by V.L.R. bombers — Early 1944.

   e. Recapture Canton and Hongkong — November 1944-May 1945.

   f. Carry out intensive bombing of Formosa and P.I., deny use of Straits of Formosa and South China Sea to Japan and furnish land-based air support to any U.S. Navy activities in these areas—October 1944-

   g. Attack Formosa if required — May 1945-November 1945.

   h. Offensive operations towards Shanghai—November 1945.

The above operations are tactically and logistically feasible. The cost is low. There is no competition with other theaters for specialized equipment and there is no conflict with operations projected by other theaters. These operations will:

   (1) *PROVIDE GREATEST AID POSSIBLE TO OTHER THEATERS,* and

212

(2) *CUT DOWN "QUADRANT" TIME TABLE FOR FINAL DEFEAT OF JAPAN BY ONE TO TWO YEARS.*

3. *REQUIREMENTS*

a. One U.S. Infantry Division in India by March 1944. Two additional divisions about a month apart thereafter. (These to be definitely earmarked for China Theater.)

b. Continuation of supply program from U.S. for equipping Chinese troops.

c. Setting up India as a base for both China and Southeast Asia Theaters. All U.S. Troops now in India except those necessary for operation of the Communication Zone to be moved to China after recapture of North Burma.

C.C.S. 406 and 406/1

COMBINED CHIEFS OF STAFF — UNITED CHIEFS OF STAFF

References:

CCS 127th Meeting, Item 4

CCS 128th Meeting, Item 5

CCS 129th Meeting, Item 3

C.C.S. 406 circulated a memorandum from the United States Chiefs of Staff 23 November. The British Chiefs of Staff circulated their reply 24 November. The Combined Chiefs of Staff in their 129th Meeting took note of C.C.S. 406 and 406/1 and agreed to a reply to the Chinese and/or U.S.S.R. if the question of machinery for closer military cooperation should be raised.

C.C.S. 406   23 November 1943

COMBINED CHIEFS OF STAFF

COMBINED CHIEFS OF STAFF — UNITED CHIEFS OF STAFF

Reference: CCS 127th Meeting, Item 4

Memorandum by the United States Chiefs of Staff

1. The discussion in the C.C.S. 127th Meeting concerning the Chinese military representatives meeting with the Combined Chiefs of Staff was the first of a series of such problems which will arise, particularly as our cooperation with the Soviets and Chinese develops. It would seem highly desirable to find a solution which will permanently (a) *maintain the exclusive American-British character of the Combined Chiefs of Staff* while avoiding these embarrassing complications and (b) furnish adequate and satisfactory machinery for discussions by the principal Allies at the Chiefs of Staff level, as military problems arise or political considerations make such meetings desirable.

2. As a solution it is suggested:

   a. That the Combined Chiefs of Staff be recognized as an exclusive American and British Body, and

   b. That a "United Chiefs of Staff" be set up at the Chiefs of Staff level to include the principal Allies — that is, for the present, the four "Moscow" powers.

3. The United Chiefs of Staff would function only when necessity arose, and would provide for attendance either by all members or by only those concerned in the problems to be discussed. This arrangement would give an "out" to China or Russia as the case might be. The proposed United Chiefs of Staff should consist of a single representative of the Chiefs of Staff of each nation. This representative would not necessarily have to be the same official at all meetings. Our Allies could not complain of being left out of Combined Chiefs of Staff discussion, since in theory, at least, the Combined Chiefs of Staff would be the lesser of the two bodies.

4. Such a "United Chiefs of Staff" should be considered as a flexible organization designed to meet situations as they develop, including possible inclusion of other Allies at a later date, on the same basis of participation when concerned.

C.C.S 406/1   24 November 1943

COMBINED CHIEFS OF STAFF

COMBINED CHIEFS OF STAFF — UNITED CHIEFS OF STAFF

Memorandum by the British Chiefs of Staff

We have studied the question of the possible formation of a United Chiefs of Staff organization and, alternatively, of the possible representation on the Combined Chiefs of Staff of powers other than the U.S. and the British. We appreciate, moreover, the need for us all to have our minds made up on this subject, in view of the increasing pressure that is likely in the future. Our views are as follows:

a. The chief need is that the best possible coordination of our military effort with that of the Russians and of the Chinese should be ensured. We feel strongly that, whereas the integration of U.S. and British forces is complete and worldwide, this is in no way the case with regard to the Russians or the Chinese, whose outlook, indeed, is largely confined to their own particular main front. We feel, therefore, that no change whatever should be made in the present Combined Chiefs of Staff standing organization, and that it should remain essentially U.S.-British.

b. We have considered whether there should be any other organization, such as a United Chiefs of Staff, and have come to the conclusion that it would not be desirable to establish any form of *standing* machinery. Relations of such a body to the Combined Chiefs of Staff would be very difficult. It might even claim to be the more representative body, and therefore to exercise jurisdiction over the Combined Chiefs of Staff. The representatives of such a body would not have the authority to make big decisions, and in consequence, such an organization could serve no useful purpose, excepting as a means of improving liaison. This could be done better by improving the arrangements already existing in Washington, London, Moscow and Chungking.

c. Our final conclusion, therefore, is that the best way of ensuring inter-Allied coordination and at the same time meeting the Russian and Chinese susceptibilities, is to ensure that whenever the Combined Chiefs of Staff meet for a big conference such as *SEXTANT*, they should be invited to attend to discuss the military problems with which they are concerned, as has been done on the present occasion.

C.C.S. 407 (Revised) and 407/1

COLLABORATION WITH THE U.S.S.R.

References:

CCS 127th Meeting, Item 4

CCS 129th Meeting, Item 4

CCS 131st Meeting, Item 5

The Combined Chiefs of Staff in their 131st Meeting amended and accepted C.C.S. 407. The amended paper, in which are incorporated the conclusions on this subject reached at the C.C.S. 129th Meeting, was circulated as C.C.S. 407 (Revised).

C.C.S. 407/1 circulated an agenda of items which are currently under discussion as a result of the Moscow Conference and which should be discussed between the United States and British Military Missions in Moscow and the Soviet authorities concerned.

C.C.S. 407 (Revised)   26 November 1943

COMBINED CHIEFS OF STAFF

COLLABORATION WITH THE U.S.S.R.

Memorandum by the Combined Chiefs of Staff

1. During the forthcoming conference with the Soviets it is recommended that the following broad lines of action be adopted:

a. That the Combined Chiefs of Staff agree upon the U.S.-British strategy in Europe and seek the approval of the President and Prime Minister before meeting the Soviets.

b. That the Soviets be urged to enhance the effectiveness of the United Nations offensive by effective coordination with *OVERLORD*.

c. That the Combined Chiefs of Staff should agree to consult together before making reply to proposals upon which there has been no previous agreement.

d. That, specifically, an agreed answer be obtained to any Soviet proposals which involve the undertaking of major operations through the Balkans or the Aegean.

e. That a common policy be adopted concerning Turkey, to include briefly the support of the Soviet proposal to force Turkey into the war but to stand firm on the principle that no diversion of forces or supplies for Turkey can be accepted to the prejudice of approved operations elsewhere.

2. Throughout the deliberation with the Soviets it should be made clear that the United States and Great Britain are involved in military operations not only in the European Theater but also in the Pacific-Asiatic Theater, and that their heavy commitments of resources throughout the world compel them to decide on operations only after careful analysis of the over-all situation.

3. At the Moscow Conference, the United States and British representatives were primarily engaged in explaining and defending their own position. In the future, the United States and Great Britain should make specific requests on the Soviets.

4. A proposed agenda is attached as an enclosure.

ENCLOSURE

PROPOSED AGENDA FOR U.S.-BRITISH-U.S.S.R. CONFERENCE

1. *COORDINATION OF MILITARY EFFORT*

The coordination of Soviet operations with Anglo-American operations in Europe.

2. *ITALY*

Discuss current and planned military operations in and from Italy.

3. *TURKEY*

Turkish action on entry into the war.

4. *SUPPLIES TO RUSSIA*

5. *STRATEGIC BOMBING*

Discussion of Soviet capabilities to initiate strategic bombing of targets in Germany or her satellites in extension of *POINTBLANK*. (Current intelligence indicates German fighter strength is extremely weak on the Russian front — 130 serviceable fighters.)

6. *JAPAN*

On the assumption that the U.S.S.R. will bring up for discussion its entry into the war against Japan after the defeat of Germany, the following should be considered:

a. Request Soviets to furnish combat intelligence information concerning Japan; if agreed to we will present specific questions through the military mission at Moscow.

b. Request Soviets to indicate whether they consider it desirable at this time to set in hand arrangements to base Soviet submarine force in U.S. territory.

c. Request Soviets to indicate what direct or indirect assistance they will be able to give, if it is found possible to launch an attack on the Northern Kuriles.

d. Soviets to indicate what ports, if any, they could allow the Allies to use. Request Soviets to furnish data on ports through Military Mission in order that we may determine the size and type of Naval Task Forces we can employ.

e. Soviets to indicate what air bases, if any, they could allow our air forces to use for operations against Japan, and what facilities, including gasoline and bombs, could be supplied. What air routes to these bases could be provided?

U. S. SECRET
BRITISH MOST SECRET

C.C.S. 407/1   26 November 1943

COMBINED CHIEFS OF STAFF

COLLABORATION WITH THE U.S.S.R.

Note by the Secretaries

1. The Combined Chiefs of Staff at their 131st Meeting, Item 5, agreed that the following items, which are currently under discussion as a result of the Moscow Conference, should be discussed between the United States and British Military Missions in Moscow and the Soviet authorities concerned:

A. *SHUTTLE BOMBER BASES*

(1) When will the U.S.S.R. be prepared to designate air bases for our use? What are presently available locations, facilities, and capabilities? The United States tentatively desires 10 bases so distributed as to permit shuttle bombing from Italy and United Kingdom.

(2) When may we begin sending the required service personnel into the U.S.S.R. to the designated bases?

(3) What is Soviet proposal for handling the close operational liaison required?

(4) What signal communications with the United Kingdom and Italy can be provided?

B. *AIR TRANSPORT ROUTES*

Request establishment of U.S. Air Transport Service on a minimum frequency basis of one round trip weekly on three routes in the following order of priority:

(1) *ALSIB*
In order that the U.S. may have a direct and independent air line of communications with the U.S.S.R.

In order that the basic machinery may be set up and be in operation to provide a direct U.S.-U.S.S.R. aerial route of supply to support any future U.S.S.R. military air operations.

(2) *U.S.-U.K.-MOSCOW*

Primarily to support shuttle bombing operations.

(3) *TEHRAN-MOSCOW*

In order to transport munitions and spare parts required in connection with shuttle bombing operations and to connect Moscow with our Mediterranean and S.E. Asia fronts. This will provide an alternative during the winter months when the nothern route (U.S.-U.K.) is not operating regularly.

C. *WEATHER INFORMATION*

(1) Request Soviet basic weather ciphers in order to interpret weather broadcasts. The U.S. will furnish weather ciphers desired by the U.S.S.R.

(2) Alternatively if foregoing is not acceptable to the Soviets, U.S. desires weather data on specific areas, using special ciphers as follows:

(a) Shuttle bombing areas.

(b) Tehran transport route; data west of Long. 75° E.

(c) From 60° E. to 160° E., (for operations in China).

(d) From 90° E. to 180°, (for the Alsib route).

(3) Request U.S.S.R. to indicate the procedure they suggest in the mutual exchange of weather information. We propose exchange of meteorological liaison officers for coordination of technical details and arrangements for distribution of weather codes and ciphers.

2. The Combined Chiefs of Staff desire their respective missions to make periodic reports to the Combined Chiefs of Staff regarding progress made in the negotiations on the above subjects.

H. REDMAN,

F. B. ROYAL,

Combined Secretariat.

C.C.S. 408 and 408/1

COMMAND OF BRITISH AND U.S. FORCES
OPERATING AGAINST GERMANY

C.C.S. 408 circulated a proposal by the United States Chiefs of Staff, 25 November 1943. The reply from the British Chiefs of Staff was circulated 26 November as C.C.S. 408/1.

C.C.S. 408   25 November 1943

COMBINED CHIEFS OF STAFF

COMMAND OF BRITISH AND U.S. FORCES
OPERATING AGAINST GERMANY

Memorandum by the United States Chiefs of Staff

1. Current operations in the war against Germany and those approved for the immediate future are grouped geographically and functionally into three categories:

    a. Operations in the Mediterranean area involving combined forces with land, sea, and air components.

    b. Operations in the northwestern part of Europe, also involving combined forces with land, sea, and air components.

    c. Operations against interior Germany involving combined strategic air forces based both in the Mediterranean area and in northwestern Europe.

2. Each of these operations is an entity requiring unity of command over the forces which are engaged.

3. These operations are all intimately related to each other, with a common, over-all objective — DEFEAT OF GERMANY. Events in the Mediterranean area attract enemy forces and affect enemy capabilities, which in turn have an important bearing upon our capabilities in northwestern Europe, and vice versa. Strategic air operations against interior Germany strongly affect our capabilities in both areas. Furthermore, the flexibility of the strategic air forces permits their employment in varying degree to assist the Allied forces in either area.

4. The United States Chiefs of Staff now consider that the war in Europe has reached a stage where the necessity for command direction over all these forces, in conformity with general directives of the Combined Chiefs of Staff, is clearly indicated. This command should be vested in a single commander, and he should exercise command over the Allied force commanders in the Mediterranean, in northwest Europe, and of the strategic air forces. The

immediate appointment of this commander is, in our opinion, most urgently necessary. Even if he is appointed now, it is improbable that he will be able to organize his staff and begin to function before the end of January 1944. The situation which may develop in Europe by that time requires a more positive over-all command arrangement than that now functioning under the Combined Chiefs of Staff. Any delay in setting up such a command may lead to confusion and indecision at a critical time, thus delaying the attainment of early victory in Europe.

5. In matters pertaining to strategic bombing, it is imperative that unified Allied command be established. The rapidity with which decisions regarding air operations must be made demands command control, as opposed to general directives or occasional direct action by the Combined Chiefs of Staff. We cannot escape the responsibility for adopting every means known to us to save the lives of our men and the planes they fly. The one effective method is to insure the rapid coordinated employment, on a day-to-day operational basis, of the United States Air Forces in both the U.K. and Mediterranean by day and R.A.F. bomber units by night in order to obtain the maximum dispersion of enemy air and anti-aircraft defense, and to take the greatest possible advantage of weather conditions in both theaters. This unified command must, therefore, be established without delay and must embrace all the strategic air forces engaged against Germany, including the United States Eighth and Fifteenth Air Forces and the British Bomber Command.

6. The British Chiefs of Staff have proposed the establishment of unified command in the Mediterranean area. We are in accord with this proposal, with the proviso that the U.S. Fifteenth Air Force should be specifically excepted and commanded as in paragraph 5 above.

7. The United States Chiefs of Staff propose to the British Chiefs of Staff:

a. That a Supreme Commander be designated at once to command all United Nations operations against Germany from the Mediterranean and the Atlantic under direction from the Combined Chiefs of Staff.

b. That an over-all commander for northwestern European operations be appointed, under the Supreme Commander.

c. That a strategic air force commander be appointed, under the Supreme Commander, to exercise command over the U.S. Eighth and Fifteenth Air Forces and the British Bomber Command.

d. That the Commander of the Allied Forces in the Mediterranean shall come under the Supreme Commander.

8. The United States Chiefs of Staff further propose that the Supreme Commander be directed to carry out the agreed European strategy, and

a. Be charged with the location and timing of operations;

b. Be charged with the allocation of the forces and materiel made available to him by the Combined Chiefs of Staff; and

c. That his decisions on the above questions be subject to reversal by the Combined Chiefs of Staff.

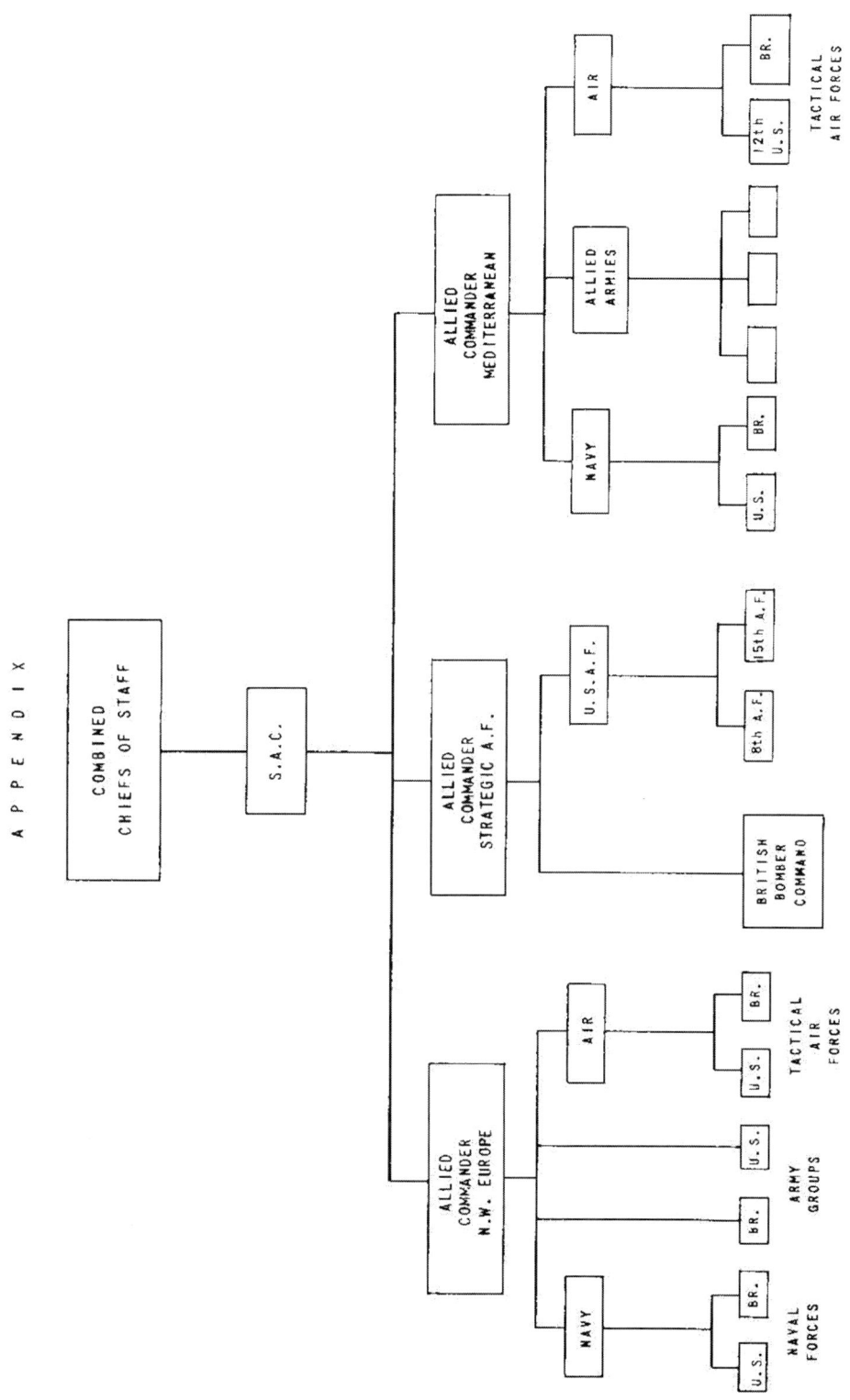

229

C.C.S. 408/1   26 November 1943

COMBINED CHIEFS OF STAFF

COMMAND OF BRITISH AND U.S. FORCES
OPERATING AGAINST GERMANY

Memorandum by the British Chiefs of Staff

1. The British Chiefs of Staff have given careful consideration to the proposal put forward by the United States Chiefs of Staff in C.C.S. 408 that "a Supreme Commander be designated at once to command all United Nations operations against Germany from the Mediterranean and the Atlantic." This proposal has immense political implications and is clearly a matter for the most earnest consideration of the U.S. and British Governments. Nevertheless, the British Chiefs of Staff must say at once that, from the military point of view, they profoundly disagree with the proposal. Their reasons are set out in the paragraphs that follow.

2. Total war is not an affair of military forces alone, using the word "military" in the widest sense of the term. There are political, economic, industrial, and domestic implications in almost every big war problem. Thus it seems clear that the Supreme Commander for the war against Germany will have to consult both the U.S. and the British Governments on almost every important question. In fact, it boils down to this, that he will only be able to make a decision without reference to high authority on comparatively minor and strictly military questions, such as the transfer of one or two divisions, or a few squadrons of aircraft, or a few scores of landing craft, from one of his many fronts to another. He will thus be an extra and unnecessary link in the chain of command.

3. There is no real analogy between the position of Marshal Foch in the last war and the position now contemplated for the Supreme Commander against Germany. Marshal Foch was responsible only for the Western Front and the Italian Front. His authority did not extend to the Salonika Front, the Palestine Front, or the Mesopotamian Front. Under the arrangements now contemplated, the Supreme Commander will have not only *OVERLORD* and the Italian Front under his authority, but also the Balkan Front and the Turkish Front (if this is opened). There must be some limit to the responsibili-

ties which Allied Governments can delegate to a single soldier and the sphere now proposed seems to exceed these limits considerably.

4. The United States Chiefs of Staff propose (see paragraph 8 c) that the decisions of the Supreme Commander should "be subject to reversal by the Combined Chiefs of Staff." If the main object of this new arrangement is to insure rapid decisions, it looks as though the above proviso will lead to deplorable consequences. Instances will occur in which the Supreme Commander has issued orders and the troops have marched in accordance with these orders, only to be followed by a reversal of the order by the Combined Chiefs of Staff and consequent confusion. Again it may happen that the British Chiefs of Staff agree with a decision taken by the Supreme Commander, while the United States Chiefs of Staff totally disagree with it. What happens then? Or again, the Combined Chiefs of Staff may wholeheartedly support on military grounds a decision taken by the Supreme Commander, only to find that one or other of the Governments concerned is not prepared to ratify it. Then what happens?

5. If the Supreme Commander is going to exercise real control, he will need to assemble the whole paraphernalia of Intelligence, Planning and Administration on an unprecedented scale. This staff will merely be a great pad between the theater commanders and the Combined Chiefs of Staff.

6. Finally, it is not admitted either that the existing machinery for the higher direction of the war has failed, or that the situation which now confronts us is so inherently different as to demand a revolutionary change.

7. The conclusion to be drawn from the above arguments is that the Supreme Commander of the war against Germany will never have, under the system of government which now obtains in the U.S.A. and U.K., authority to deal with anything but strictly military, and comparatively minor, problems. He will be boosted by the Press and public opinion as a superman who is going to lead the two nations to victory. This is a mere delusion. His position will be a sham. In important matters, he will not be able to do anything more than is now done by the theater commanders.

8. If the well tried machinery that has led us safely through the last two years has failed in the smaller problems, it would be better to examine that machinery and see how it could be speeded up and adjusted, rather than to embark upon an entirely novel experiment, which merely makes a cumbrous and unnecessary link in the chain of command, and which will surely lead to disillusionment and disappointment.

C.C.S. 409

"OVERLORD" AND THE MEDITERRANEAN

References:

CCS 130th Meeting, Item 4

CCS 131st Meeting, Item 4B

CCS 132d Meeting

C.C.S. 409 circulated a memorandum by the British Chiefs of Staff 25 November 1943. The Combined Chiefs of Staff resolved this subject in their 132d Meeting at *EUREKA*.

C.C.S. 409   25 November 1943

COMBINED CHIEFS OF STAFF

"OVERLORD" AND THE MEDITERRANEAN

Note by the British Chiefs of Staff

1. For some time past it has been clear to us, and doubtless also to the United States Chiefs of Staff, that disagreement exists between us as to what we should do now in the Mediterranean, with particular reference to the effect of future action on *OVERLORD*. The point at issue is how far what might be termed the "sanctity of *OVERLORD*" is to be preserved in its entirety, irrespective of developments in the Mediterranean Theater. This issue is clouding the whole of our future strategic outlook, and must be resolved at *SEXTANT*.

2. At the outset we must point out that, since the decisions taken at *QUADRANT*, there have been major developments in the situation. The Russian campaign has succeeded beyond all hope or expectations and their victorious advance continues. Italy has been knocked out of the war; and it is certainly not beyond the bounds of possibility that Turkey will come in on our side before the New Year. In these changed conditions, we feel that consideration of adjustments of, if not actual departures from, the decisions taken at *TRIDENT* and *QUADRANT* are not only fully justified but positively essential.

3. Nevertheless, we emphasize that we do not in any way recoil from, or wish to sidetrack, our agreed intention to attack the Germans across the Channel in the late spring or early summer of 1944, or even earlier if *RANKIN* conditions were to obtain. We must not, however, regard *OVERLORD* on a fixed date as the pivot of our whole strategy on which all else turns. In actual fact, the German strength in France next spring may, at one end of the scale, be something which makes *OVERLORD* completely impossible and, at the other end, something which makes *RANKIN* not only practicable, but essential. Consequently, to assume that the achievement of a certain strength by a certain date will remove all our difficulties and result in shortening the duration of the war is entirely illusory. This policy, if literally interpreted, will inevitably paralyze action in other theaters without any guarantee of action across the Channel.

4. With the Germans in their present plight, the surest way to win the war in the shortest time is to attack them remorselessly and continuously in

234

any and every area where we can do so with superiority. The number of places at which we can thus attack them depends mainly on the extent to which they are stretched. Our policy is therefore clear; we should stretch the German forces to the utmost by threatening as many of their vital interests and areas as possible and, holding them thus, we should attack wherever we can do so in superior force.

5. If we pursue the above policy we firmly believe that *OVERLORD* (perhaps in the form of *RANKIN*) will take place next summer. We do not, however, attach vital importance to any particular date or to any particular number of divisions in the assault and follow-up, though naturally the latter should be made as large as possible consistent with the policy stated above. It is, of course, valuable to have a target date to which all may work, but we are firmly opposed to allowing this date to become our master, and to prevent us from taking full advantage of all opportunities that occur to us to follow what we believe to be the correct strategy.

6. In the light of the above argument, we submit the following proposals for action in the Mediterranean:

a. Unification of Command

Unification of Command in the Mediterranean, as outlined in C.O.S. (W) 919 is an essential and urgent measure which should be put into effect irrespective of any other decisions taken about this theater.

b. The Italian Campaign

The Offensive in Italy should be nourished and maintained until we have secured the Pisa-Rimini line.

c. Yugoslavia, Greece, and Albania

Our policy should be to place on a regular military basis and to intensify our measures to nourish the Partisan and irregular forces in these countries.

d. Turkey

We should bring Turkey into the war this year.

e. The Dardanelles

We should aim to open the Dardanelles as soon as possible.

f. *The Balkans*

We should undermine resistance in the Balkan States and do everything possible to promote a state of chaos and disruption in the satellite Balkan countries.

7. If the above measures necessitate putting back the date upon which the forces agreed to be necessary for *OVERLORD* will be available in the United Kingdom, this should be accepted since it does not by any means follow that the date of the invasion of France will be put back to the same extent.

8. To sum up, our policy is to fight and bomb the Germans as hard as possible all through the winter and spring; to build up our forces in the United Kingdom as rapidly as possible consistent with this; and finally to invade the Continent as soon as the German strength in France and the general war situation gives us a good prospect of success.

C.C.S. 410

THE EFFECT OF WEATHER ON OPERATION "OVERLORD"

Reference:

CCS 131st Meeting, Item 4B

C.C.S. 410 circulated a memorandum by the British Chiefs of Staff 25 November 1943. The Combined Chiefs of Staff took note of this subject in their 131st Meeting.

C.C.S. 410   25 November 1943

COMBINED CHIEFS OF STAFF

THE EFFECT OF WEATHER ON OPERATION "OVERLORD"

Memorandum by the British Chiefs of Staff

1. The following examination has been made regarding the limitations imposed by weather conditions on the postponement of Operation *OVERLORD*.

2. Suitable weather conditions are required for two phases of the operation, firstly, the assault for which a four-day fine weather period is required; secondly, the maintenance and build-up period for which suitable weather for a decreasing degree of beach maintenance is required for about three months.

THE ASSAULT

3. In order to launch the assault a quiet spell of four days with winds of force 3 or less is desirable. Over ten consecutive years there were quiet spells for four or more consecutive days on the following number of occasions:

April	18 times
May	21 times
June	19 times
July	16 times
August	23 times
September	17 times
October	14 times

It will be seen that there is no serious deterioration in the chances of launching the assault between the months of May and September with the exception of July, where the incidence of a fine spell is only slightly less than in the month of June. It is therefore considered that, purely from the assault aspect, the operation could be postponed up to the month of September.

4. For tidal reasons the assault is limited in each lunar month to two periods of five or six days, which occur at times of full and new moon. The air lift can only be carried out in the full moon period. It therefore follows that if the full moon period is missed on account of the weather conditions being unsuitable, the assault must be postponed for 24 days. By sacrificing the air lift this postponement could be reduced to 10 days.

AIR FACTORS AFFECTING THE ASSAULT

5. *a.* For fully effective operation of air forces the following conditions must be satisfied:

	Night	*Day*
Minimum horizontal visibility	5 miles	5 miles
Minimum cloud base above ground level	3,000 feet	11,500 feet
Maximum cloud	6/10	10/10
Maximum wind at ground level	20 m.p.h.	20 m.p.h. (if airborne forces are used by day)
Minimum moon		5 days each side of full. Moon 20° above horizon.

b. If high level bombing is abandoned, the cloud conditions by day are then limited by the requirements of the fighter cover over shipping and beaches. These are 10/10 at not less than 5,000 feet.

c. The chances of obtaining these conditions are not yet available, but it is evident that they will lengthen the odds against launching the assault to some extent, although settled summer weather suitable for the landing will most probably be suitable for the air operations.

MAINTENANCE AND BUILD-UP PERIOD

6. *COSSAC* has stated that, making full use of every captured port, large and small, 18 divisions must be maintained over the beaches during the first month of the operations, 12 divisions during the second month, and a number rapidly diminishing to nil during the third month. It is believed that the use of *MULBERRIES* will approximately halve this commitment for beach maintenance. Therefore, during this period there will be at first a considerable, and later a gradually dwindling dependence on fine weather conditions. In assessing suitable weather for carrying out beach maintenance any day with wind of not more than Force 3 on shore and not more than Force 4 off shore has been accepted. In the *OVERLORD* area the average number of suitable days per month is as follows:

April	21
May	23
June	25
July	25
August	24½

September	23½
October	18½
November	20
December	20

It is apparent from the above figures that a marked deterioration does not occur until October. Although *the months of October, November, and December* appear to provide a reasonable number of quiet days, it is considered that this proportion cannot be fully relied on owing to the severe weather which may occur during unsuitable days, thereby producing conditions of sea or swell which will render beach maintenance impracticable on the subsequent quiet day or days.

7. It is impossible to calculate what loss in expectation of suitable maintenance days can be accepted by *COSSAC* during the second and third months of the beach maintenance period without a very intimate knowledge of his maintenance and build-up plan; but it would appear that weather should be suitable for sufficient beach maintenance at least up to the end of September and possibly, in view of the dwindling commitment in this respect, up to the middle or end of October.

CONCLUSION

8. It is not possible to submit a firm recommendation on this subject, but *from the limited facts* available for this brief examination, there does not appear to be any overriding reason why the assault could not be carried out up to about the middle of July.

9. This means that the target date should be in the middle of June to *allow for a postponement of 24 days in case weather conditions are unsuitable.*

10. Thus if the target date is mid-June and the air lift is not sacrificed, only two periods of four or five days when Moon and Tide conditions are suitable will occur in 1944; and these must coincide with a four day spell of fine weather.

C.C.S. 411/2 and 411/5

OPERATIONS IN THE SOUTHEAST ASIA COMMAND

References:

CCS 128th Meeting, Item 6
CCS 129th Meeting, Items 5 and 7
CCS 130th Meeting, Item 1
CCS 131st Meeting, Item 1
CCS 132d Meeting
CCS 138th Meeting, Item 8
1st Plenary Meeting

At their 130th Meeting the Combined Chiefs of Staff invited Admiral Mountbatten to prepare a list of the points with regard to operations in the Southeast Asia Command on which Generalissimo Chiang Kai-shek's concurrence should be obtained before his departure from *SEXTANT*. C.C.S. 411 circulated the draft prepared by Admiral Mountbatten 25 November 1943. Amendments proposed by the Combined Chiefs of Staff were circulated as C.C.S. 411/1. The Combined Chiefs of Staff, in their 131st Meeting approved the memorandum as amended (subsequently circulated as C.C.S. 411/2).

C.C.S. 411/3 and 411/4 circulated memoranda by the Deputy Chief of Staff, Southeast Asia Command proposing an amendment to paragraph 4, C.C.S. 411/2, also stating that it is understood that C.C.S. 411/2 was explained to the Generalissimo but not handed to him.

C.C.S. 411/5, 7 December, circulated a memorandum by the United States Chiefs of Staff suggesting a solution to the proposal contained in C.C.S. 411/3 and 411/4. The Combined Chiefs of Staff, in their 138th Meeting, accepted C.C.S. 411/5.

C.C.S. 411/2   2 December 1943

COMBINED CHIEFS OF STAFF

OPERATIONS IN THE SOUTHEAST ASIA COMMAND

Note by the Secretaries

The enclosure, a list of points with regard to operations in the Southeast Asia Command on which Generalissimo Chiang Kai-shek's concurrence is to be sought, was approved by the Combined Chiefs of Staff in their 131st Meeting and is circulated herewith for information.

H. REDMAN,

F. B. ROYAL,

Combined Secretariat.

ENCLOSURE

POINTS ON WHICH GENERALISSIMO'S AGREEMENT
SHOULD BE OBTAINED

1. Since the Combined Chiefs of Staff are unable to find the 535 additional transport aircraft which are required for the Mandalay plan, it is agreed that the plan presented by Admiral Mountbatten at the First Plenary Session shall be accepted.

2. The stipulation which the Generalissimo has made that an amphibious operation is to be carried out in March is noted, and will be taken into consideration by the Combined Chiefs of Staff when amphibious operations in all parts of the world are reviewed in about a week's time. Meanwhile preparations are being pushed forward in the Southeast Asia Theater for an amphibious operation to meet this date, should approval be subsequently given.

3. A fleet of adequate strength to cover such an operation and to obtain command of the Bay of Bengal will be assembled by the beginning of March.

4. The Supreme Commander, Southeast Asia Command, will be authorized to divert not more than an average of 1,100 tons per month from tonnage over the "hump" to the requirements of the Burma campaign. Diversions in excess of this figure may be made by him only to meet sudden and critical emergencies of the battle or by permission of the highest authority. The Air Transport Command will use its utmost energy to raise the efficiency of its operation and increase the "hump" tonnage to a full 10,000 tons per month into China by the late winter and a further increase in the spring.

5. The Supreme Allied Commander is delegating his command over the Chinese-American Task Force starting from Ledo to Lieutenant General Slim, commanding the 14th British Army, until the main body reaches Kamaing, when he will place the force under the command of Lieutenant General Stilwell.

6. It is the intention to resume the offensive in October 1944, when the monsoon stops; it is, however, too far ahead to decide the precise resources which will be available.

CCS 411/5   7 December 1943

COMBINED CHIEFS OF STAFF

OPERATIONS IN THE SOUTHEAST ASIA COMMAND

Memorandum by the United States Chiefs of Staff

1. In order to settle the question of tonnage lift to China versus availability of aircraft from A.T.C. India-China Wing, it is recommended that the Combined Chiefs of Staff accept the following in lieu of the solution recommended in C.C.S. 411/4, *SEXTANT*, 5 December 1943:

   a. The Combined Chiefs of Staff recognize the principle that the Supreme Allied Commander, Southeast Asia Command must have control over resources allocated to him for the accomplishment of the assigned objectives.

   b. The Combined Chiefs of Staff also recognize the necessity of firm commitments of tonnage over the "hump" into China during the next six months. The Combined Chiefs of Staff direct:

   (1) That the tonnage over the "hump" be maintained on the following basis of transport plane allotments:

	C-87's	C-46's	Tons Delivered
December	40	97	8,858
January	40	107	9,535
February	48	120	11,066
March	55	25	5,614
April	52	46	6,716
May	50	96	9,686

   (2) They further direct that transport plane allotments to the Supreme Allied Commander, Southeast Asia Command, for *TARZAN*, be on the following basis:

15 Dec to 31 Jan—	18 C-47's or 12 C-46's
1 Feb to 28 Feb—	11 C-47's or 8 C-46's
1 Mar to 31 Mar—	188 C-47's or 126 C-46's
1 Apr to 15 Apr—	183 C-47's or 122 C-46's
16 Apr to 15 May—	114 C-47's or 76 C-46's
16 May to 30 Jun—	43 C-47's or 29 C-46's

Note: The above subparagraph is based on the assumption that 35 additional C-47's will be available in the theater by 1 February. (Now allotted to the 10th Air Force)

c. The Combined Chiefs of Staff direct that any shortages in delivery of transport aircraft into the theater on present allottment bases be pro-rated in proportion to the allotments outlined in *b* (1) and (2) above. Excess in numbers of A. T. C. aircraft over the expectations outlined in (1) and (2) above will be allocated by direction of the Commanding General, U.S.A.A.F., India, during the above period.

C.C.S. 413 and 413/2

FRENCH PARTICIPATION IN CAIRO CONFERENCE

C.C.S. 413 circulated a memorandum from the Commander in Chief, Allied Force Headquarters 26 November. The Secretaries' proposed reply was circulated as C.C.S. 413/1. The Combined Chiefs of Staff amended and approved, informally, the proposed reply which was subsequently circulated for information, as C.C.S. 413/2.

C.C.S.   26 November 1943

COMBINED CHIEFS OF STAFF

FRENCH PARTICIPATION IN CAIRO CONFERENCE

Memorandum from Commander in Chief, Allied Force Headquarters

An extract of a letter received today by the Commander in Chief Allied Forces, from General Giraud, is quoted for the information of the Allied Chiefs of Staff and such action as they desire to take:

"The conversation which I had with you this morning has confirmed my conviction that the point of view of the French High Command should be explained at the Cairo Conference, before any decision determines definitely the conduct of operations in Western Europe.

"Indeed, if France is to be the theater of new operations, you will understand, I am sure, how anxious I am to contribute to the studying of these operations with all the competence which a thorough knowledge of our territory has given me, and also to take my share of responsibility in the operation where the use of underground forces and resistance groups share the preponderant role.

"If it is not considered necessary that I go personally to this Conference, though I do hold myself at the disposal of President Roosevelt and of the British Prime Minister, I would consider it most useful to have one officer of my staff present to explain my views before the Allied Chiefs of Staff.

"In the event where such a solution would not be possible, I do rely upon you to defend the interests of France and the French Army with the friendship and understanding which you have always shown us."

C.C.S. 413/2   22 December 1943

COMBINED CHIEFS OF STAFF

FRENCH PARTICIPATION IN CAIRO CONFERENCE

Note by the Secretaries

The attached message (FAN 282), as sent to General Eisenhower from the Combined Chiefs of Staff on 4 December 1943, is circulated for information.

> H. REDMAN,
>
> F. B. ROYAL,
>
> Combined Secretariat.

ENCLOSURE

SECURITY CONTROL

PRIORITY

From: SEXTANT
To: AGWAR   10116
          Algiers   FP30
          USFOR   MP 60
4 December 1943   FAN 282.

With reference to letter from Giraud suggesting he attend *SEXTANT*, you should reply on following lines:

General Giraud's offer to come to Cairo very much appreciated by Combined Chiefs of Staff, who feel, however, that it is unnecessary to ask the General to undertake the journey, since discussions on global strategy are of the broadest possible nature and the details of operations in France are not under consideration. Please inform him that the Combined Chiefs of Staff believe that your presentation here included an accurate and sympathetic explanation of his views.

The Combined Chiefs of Staff have the interest of France and of the French Armed Forces much at heart.

C.C.S. 415/3

THE PROVISION OF MERCHANT SHIPPING FOR THE BRITISH FLEET FOR THE WAR AGAINST JAPAN

Reference:

CCS 138th Meeting, Item 4

C.C.S. 415, 26 November 1943, circulated a memorandum by the British Chiefs of Staff who recommended that the Combined Staff Planners formulate and coordinate the service demands for merchant ship types required for the war against Japan. Reply from the United States Chiefs of Staff was circulated as C.C.S. 415/1, 4 December. Further memorandum from the British Chiefs of Staff (C.C.S. 415/2) was circulated 5 December.

The Commander in Chief, United States Fleet and the First Sea Lord presented a suggested formula for this problem (C.C.S. 415/3) which was approved by the Combined Chiefs of Staff in their 138th Meeting.

C.C.S. 415/3 6 December 1943

COMBINED CHIEFS OF STAFF

THE PROVISION OF MERCHANT SHIPPING FOR THE
BRITISH FLEET FOR THE WAR AGAINST JAPAN

Memorandum by the Commander in Chief,
United States Fleet and First Sea Lord

The Combined Chiefs of Staff are requested to approve that the Ministry of War Transport and the War Shipping Administration should take into consideration the need for Fleet Auxiliaries for the British Fleet for operations in the war against Japan, and that they should take steps to provide the requisite ships after agreement in detail between the Commander in Chief, United States Fleet and the First Sea Lord.

C.C.S. 417

OVER-ALL PLAN FOR THE DEFEAT OF JAPAN

References:

CCS 130th Meeting, Item 3
CCS 134th Meeting, Item 4
CCS 137th Meeting, Item 4
1st Plenary Meeting
2d Plenary Meeting

C.C.S. 417 circulated the report by the Combined Staff Planners 2 December 1943. The Combined Chiefs of Staff in their 134th Meeting amended C.C.S. 417. In their 137th Meeting the Combined Chiefs of Staff approved C.C.S. 417 in principle as amended by C.C.S. 417/1 less paragraph 4 (certain changes submitted by the Combined Staff Planners). They directed that the Combined Staff Planners prepare a plan of campaign for the Chinese theater proper together with an estimate of the forces involved.

C.C.S. 417 as published herein is corrected as amended.

C.C.S. 417   2 December 1943

COMBINED CHIEFS OF STAFF
OVER-ALL PLAN FOR THE DEFEAT OF JAPAN

References:

     a. CCS 319/5, paras. 43, 44

     b. CCS 130th Meeting, Item 3

Report by the Combined Staff Planners

Pursuant to reference *b*, the report of the Combined Staff Planners is forwarded for the consideration of the Combined Chiefs of Staff.

E N C L O S U R E

DEFEAT OF JAPAN

Report by the Combined Staff Planners

PROBLEM

1. To prepare an over-all plan for the defeat of Japan.

ASSUMPTIONS

2. Our studies of this subject have taken account of:

a. The possibility that invasion of the principal Japanese islands may not be necessary and the *defeat of Japan may be accomplished by sea and air blockade and intensive air bombardment from progressively advanced bases.* The plan must, however, be capable of expansion to meet the contingency of invasion.

b. The possibility that Germany may be defeated as early as the spring of 1944.

c. The possibility that the U.S.S.R. may enter the war against Japan early after the defeat of Germany, and our plan proposes that all possible preparations should be made to take advantage of such a development. Further progress is dependent upon staff conversations with the Soviets.

d. The possibility that a full campaign in Burma may have to be carried out following on the *TARZAN* operation.

OVER-ALL OBJECTIVE

3. To obtain objectives from which we can conduct intensive air bombardment and establish a sea and air blockade against Japan, and from which to invade Japan proper if this should prove to be necessary.

GENERAL CONCEPT

4. The main effort against Japan should be made in the Pacific.

CONCEPT WITHIN THE PACIFIC

5. The advance along the New Guinea-N.E.I.-Philippine axis will proceed concurrently with operations for the capture of the Mandated Islands. These two series of operations will be mutually supporting. United Nations naval forces can be deployed to support successive operations along each axis, and to prevent interference by hostile surface units with simultaneous operations in the two areas. Transfer of forces and resources from one area to the other is contemplated. When conflicts in timing and allocation of means exist, due weight should be accorded to the fact that operations in the Central Pacific promise at this time a more rapid advance toward Japan and her vital lines of communication; the earlier acquisition of strategic air bases closer to the Japanese homeland; and, of greatest importance, are more likely to precipitate a decisive engagement with the Japanese Fleet.

The aim should be to advance along the New Guinea-N.E.I.-Philippine axis and to complete the capture of the Mandated Islands in time to launch a major assault in the Formosa-Luzon-China area in the spring of 1945 (i.e., before the onset of the typhoon season), from a distant base.

CONCEPT WITHIN OTHER AREAS

6. Operations in the North Pacific, the South Pacific, China and the Southeast Asia Theater should be conducted in support of the main operations in the

Central and Southwest Pacific. In the event of the U.S.S.R. entering the war, operations in the North Pacific may assume far greater importance and may involve a major redeployment of forces.

GENERAL CONDUCT OF OPERATIONS

7. The conduct of operations should be designed to:

   a. Destroy the Japanese Fleet at an early date.

   b. Secure the maximum attrition of enemy air forces.

   c. Intensify air, submarine and mining operations against enemy shipping and lines of communication.

   d. Enable us to launch shore-based and carrier-borne air attack on Japan.

   e. Keep China in the war.

   f. Insure that the sequence of operations remains flexible and that preparations are made to take all manner of short cuts made possible by developments in the situation.

   g. Take advantage of the earliest practicable reorientation of forces from the European Theater.

SPECIFIC OPERATIONS IN 1944

8. For operations planned for 1944, see schedule in C.C.S. 397, Specific Operations for the Defeat of Japan, 1944 (To be revised). These operations are in accordance with the over-all concept. In brief they contemplate:

Central Pacific

   a. Capture of the Mandated Islands and conduct of V.L.R. strategic bombing of Japan proper from the Marianas (Guam, Tinian and Saipan).

Southwest Pacific

   b. Continuing the advance along the New Guinea-N.E.I.-Philippine axis. Intensification of air bombardment of targets in the N.E.I.-Philippine area.

North Pacific

c. Preparations to conduct very long range strategic bombing against the Kuriles and Northern Japan. (Preparations for the possible entry of the U.S.S.R. into the war are discussed in Annex I, page 261).

Southeast Asia Theater

d. Operations for the capture of Upper Burma in the spring of 1944 in order to improve the air route and establish overland communications with China, and an amphibious operation at approximately the same time. Continuance of operations during the autumn of 1944 within the limits of the forces available (see paragraph 14) to extend the position held in Upper Burma.

e. Should the means be available, additional ground, sea and air offensive operations, including carrier-borne raids, with the object of maintaining pressure on the enemy, forcing dispersion of his forces, and attaining the maximum attrition practicable on his air and naval forces and shipping.

CHINA AREA

f. Conducting V.L.R. air operations from the Chengtu area in China against vital targets in the Japanese inner zone.

g. Building up the U.S. Air Forces in China and the Chinese Army and air force with the object of intensifying land and air operations in and from China.

DISPOSITION OF FORCES

Naval Forces

9. Considering the British Naval forces shown below, we believe the combined naval forces will be adequate to conduct the operations envisaged for the defeat of Japan. We show in Annex II, page 262, the estimated dispositions of British Naval forces in the Indian Ocean and the Pacific after the completion of operation *BUCCANEER*, and the subsequent build-up of British Naval forces in the Pacific during 1944 and early 1945.

10. This allocation provides for sufficient forces in the Indian Ocean to maintain our communications with the Andamans, to act as a deterrent

against any attempt to recapture them by the Japanese and to carry out operations, raids and threats against Japanese possessions in S.E. Asia. All other available units, to the extent that they can be supported and profitably employed, will be concentrated for the main effort in the Pacific.

11. Though full details have not yet been worked out, we consider that the British naval forces shown can be supported logistically and should in general operate from advanced bases in the Bismarck and Solomons area so that they may either cover the operations along the New Guinea-N.E.I.-Philippines axis, or cooperate with the U.S. Fleet in the Central Pacific.

12. Logistic preparations should be made by the British for the increased British naval forces expected to become available for the long distance assault contemplated in the spring of 1945. Manpower limitations will probably prevent any new bases being manned by the British until after the defeat of Germany.

13. Our studies have reemphasized the importance of the provision of aircraft carriers of all sorts for our future operations against Japan.

Land Forces

14. Present plans contemplate the timely deployment in the Pacific of about 40 U.S. divisions and supporting troops. British/Indian land forces, which can be made available to Southeast Asia command up to the end of 1944 are likely to be fully committed in carrying out the operations recommended for the season 1943/44, and subsequently extending the area of occupation in Burma and in carrying out additional operations against the enemy. This concept is subject to alteration in the light of the progress of the 1943/44 operations and of detailed examination of the forces which will be required for 1944/45, but included in the forces retained in the theater there should be at least one amphibious division.

15. After the defeat of Germany the number of additional British divisions from the European Theater and the dates by which they can be made available for the war against Japan cannot yet be assessed, but it is estimated that some nine months will be required for the necessary reorganization, passage and training. Additional British forces may prove essential for Burma. In the Pacific, the target should be to provide four British divisions based on Australia for service in that theater as early as possible after the defeat of Germany. At least two of these divisions should be amphibiously trained.

16. After providing for paragraph 15 above, additional British forces becoming available will probably be best placed in reserve at the disposal of Southeast Asia, ready for additional offensive operations in that area.

17. Australian and New Zealand forces should continue to be employed in Pacific operations. The employment of Canadian forces should be discussed with the Canadian Government.

18. We believe that the combined land forces to be made available as outlined in paragraphs 14, 15, 16 and 17 above will be adequate to conduct the operations envisaged for the defeat of Japan.

Assault Shipping and Landing Craft

19. Present plans contemplate an eventual U.S. assault lift of 12 divisions in the Pacific. The British should maintain in the Southeast Asia Theater an assault lift for at least one division. As soon as the war with Germany is over the British should aim to provide in the Southwest Pacific as large an assault lift as possible (probably between two and three divisions simultaneously).

Air Forces

20. British and U.S. air forces are sufficient for plans at present contemplated although if the U.S.S.R. enters the war the demand on our resources for the establishment of a bomber force in the Maritime Provinces may conflict with the development of our air effort against Japan through China.

The large air forces which will be available when Germany is defeated must be redeployed against Japan as quickly as possible. The general principles which we consider should govern this redeployment are in Annex III, page 263. Immediate examinations of the problems involved in this redeployment of British and U.S. air forces should be made. Studies are now under way to determine the best employment of the B-29 aircraft against Japan.

Appendix "A" to Annex III shows the U.S. and British air forces which may be available for deployment against Japan after the defeat of Germany.

PREPARATION OF BASES IN INDIA

21. The preparation of the bases in India required for approved operations in the Southeast Asia and China Theater should continue in consonance with provisions of paragraphs 4, 5 and 6.

RECOMMENDATIONS

22. It is recommended that the Combined Chiefs of Staff:

   a. Approve the over-all plan for the defeat of Japan and direct that the necessary preparations be initiated.

   b. Approve the specific operations set out in C.C.S. 397, Specific Operations for the Defeat of Japan, 1944. (To be revised).

ANNEX I

NOTE ON PREPARATIONS THAT SHOULD BE MADE FOR POSSIBLE RUSSIAN ENTRY INTO THE WAR

1. We should urge the U.S.S.R. to come in as early as possible; ask them to tell us when they propose to come in; what they propose to do when they come in; and what they want us to do to help.

2. Meanwhile, in so far as they do not conflict with the operations in the Central and Southwest Pacific, preparations should be made by the spring or early summer of 1944 so that we can assist her:-

   a. By building up supplies by trans-Pacific shipment, sea and air.

   b. By insuring that her defenses and means in Kamchatka are adequate. If she wants our forces there we should be prepared to move them in, especially air.

   c. By furnishing aircraft and air units released from the European front, both from the East and the West.

3. If and when conversations with the Soviets can be arranged, plans should also be made for operations:-

   a. To enter and develop bases in Kamchatka and the Maritime Provinces.

   b. To seize and hold the Northern Kuriles and to open a sea route to the Maritime Provinces.

   c. To supply and operate air forces from Siberian bases.

4. We must constantly review the situation so as to be ready to adjust our operations elsewhere when the U.S.S.R. come into the war.

Annex I

PROVISIONAL ANNEX II

(Subject to further Confirmation)

BRITISH FORCES IN THE INDIAN OCEAN AND PACIFIC AFTER COMPLETION OF *"BUCCANEER"*

1944	Indian Ocean	Pacific	
June	2 OBB (Queen Elizabeth & Valiant)	June	1 OBB (Renown)	WOOLWICH (DD Depot)
	1 AA Ship (Dutch Doubtful)		2 CV	RESOURCE (Fleet Repair Ship)
	1 CV		6 CL	UNICORN (Aircraft Repair)
	3 CVE (Assault)		4 CVE (Assault)	7 Armament Supply Ships
	1 CVE (A/S)		1 CVE (A/S)	3 Armament Carriers
	3 CA		2 or 3 VCE (Ferries)	3 Victualling Supply Ships
	4 CL (1 Dutch)			8 to 10 Fleet Tankers
	12 Fleet DD		16 Fleet DD	1 Naval Store Issuing Ship
	6 Frigates		12 Frigates	2 Naval Store Carriers
	14 SS (to be based Australia when possible)			1 Air Store Issuing Ship.
	9 SS (Based I.O.)			

Notes and additions (reading down each column):

Indian Ocean:

Add July

August Last Quarter — Except for CVE's, no ships below this line can be manned for certain until after the defeat of Germany nor can the needs of the Atlantic (if Germany is still fighting) be estimated at this time.

1945 First Quarter

Second Quarter

Pacific:

Add July 2 CV

? Fleet DD
1 Air Store Issuing Ship
1 Hospital Ship

August Last Quarter
1 BB (Howe)
1 BB (KGV)
2 CVL
3 CVE (Assault)
6 CVE (A/S)

? CL
? Frigates
1 Naval Store Issuing Ship.
1 Victualling Supply Ship.
3 Armament Supply Ships.
? 1 Hospital Ship

1945 First Quarter
1 BB (Anson fully modn.)
1 CVL

Second Quarter
1 BB (Duke of York fully modernized)
2 CVL

Appropriate CVE's, CL's, DD's, DE's.

(Revised 2 December 1943)

Provisional Annex II

262

ANNEX III

AIR FORCES

AVAILABILITY OF AIR FORCES

1. Appendix "A" shows the British and U.S. air forces that may become available for the war against Japan on the alternative assumptions that Germany is defeated in March or October 1944.

These large air forces must be deployed against Japan as quickly as possible.

REDEPLOYMENT OF AIR FORCES

Pacific

2. We should speedily increase our air forces in the Central, Southwest and North Pacific. The air forces in the Central Pacific will be U.S.; those in the Southwest and possibly in the North Pacific will be both British and U.S.

Southeast Asia

3. In Southeast Asia we must deploy sufficient air forces to insure the security of the area, protect our sea communications and to meet the requirements of operations. These will be predominantly British.

U.S.S.R. and China

4. A study is now being made to determine the best employment of B-29 aircraft in the war against Japan.

In so far as operations from China are concerned, we have under consideration the *DRAKE* Plan for V.L.R. bombing from the Kweilin area and a plan for V.L.R. bombing from the Chengtu area (plan *MATTERHORN*). We recommend approval of the *MATTERHORN* plan on the understanding that it is not permitted to interfere materially with other approved operations.

The preparations now underway for the Chengtu operations are also preliminary for the *DRAKE* plan.

Annex III

Further study of the *DRAKE* plan is required, especially with regard to the logistic features.

5. With respect to whether we carry out *DRAKE* operation from China or V.L.R. bombing from the U.S.S.R., we consider that:

a. If the U.S.S.R. enters the war, grants us facilities and we are able to establish and maintain a bomber force in the Maritime Provinces, the establishment and operation of such force should have priority over the *DRAKE* plan.

b. If the U.S.S.R. enters the war but it does not prove feasible to establish and maintain a bomber force in the Maritime Provinces, we should proceed with the *DRAKE* plan. In this case the requirement in Chinese divisions for the defense of the forward area should be considerably reduced below the figure of 50 stipulated by General Stilwell. If 20 divisions only were required we might start bombing Japan by autumn 1945.

c. If the U.S.S.R. does not enter the war, we should proceed with the *DRAKE* plan. If the full figure of 50 divisions is necessary, bombing could not start before the end of 1946.

EXAMINATIONS REQUIRED

6. We do not consider that at this stage we can go further than the above. We recommend, however, that the following examinations should be carried out as a matter of urgency:

a. A proposed redeployment of the British and U.S. air forces in the light of the above principles, after the defeat of Germany, setting out the types and strengths required in the various areas.

b. *DRAKE Plan*

(1) To be examined by S.A.C.S.E.A. and Commander in Chief, India.

(2) A study as to the extent to which Lancaster/Halifax aircraft could take the place of the B-24 aircraft on which our staff study has been based.

c. It is most desirable to examine as early as practicable with the Soviets the problems involved in establishing and maintaining a U.S.-British air force in the Maritime Provinces of the U.S.S.R., leading to conclusions as to the size of force that may be achieved and the effort required to maintain it by sea, land and air routes. This will depend upon staff conversations with the Soviets.

Annex III

APPENDIX A TO ANNEX III

AMERICAN AND BRITISH AIR FORCES AVAILABLE FOR DEPLOYMENT AGAINST JAPAN AFTER THE DEFEAT OF GERMANY

U.S.A.A.F.

	Air Forces outside the Pacific and South East Asia which will be available for deployment against Japan providing Germany defeated by March 1944.		Air Forces outside the Pacific and South East Asia which will be available for deployment against Japan providing Germany defeated by October 1944.		Air Forces which will already be deployed against Japan in the Pacific and South East Asia under present plans, in October 1944.		Ultimate total of U.S. and British Air Forces that will be available for deployment against Japan in October 1944.	
	GROUPS	AIRCRAFT U.E.	GROUPS	AIRCRAFT U.E.	GROUPS	AIRCRAFT U.E.	GROUPS	AIRCRAFT U.E.
VERY HEAVY BOMBERS					8	224	8	224
HEAVY BOMBERS	57½	2012	63½	3048	10½	492	73 3/4	3540
MEDIUM & LIGHT BOMBERS	10	570	10	640	9¼	592	19 1/4	1232
FIGHTER & FIGHTER BOMBERS	38	2850	38½	3825	18½	1825	56 1/2	5650
NIGHT FIGHTERS	2	96	2½	108	1½	60	3 1/2	168
RECONNAISSANCE & LIAISON	6	342	6	384	5½	352	11 1/2	736
TROOP CARRIERS	14½	754	13½	702	7	364	20 1/2	1066
TOTALS	128	6624	133½	8707	59½	3909	193	12616

R.A.F.

	SQUADRONS	AIRCRAFT	SQUADRONS	AIRCRAFT	SQUADRONS	AIRCRAFT	SQUADRONS	AIRCRAFT
HEAVY BOMBERS (DAY)	3	48	5	80	5	80	10	160
HEAVY BOMBERS (NIGHT)	30	600	34 (a)	680	—	—	50	1000
MEDIUM & LIGHT BOMBERS	6	96	6	96	8	128	14	224
S.E. FIGHTERS	54	864	54	864	31	496	85	1360
T.E. DAY & NIGHT FIGHTERS	8	128	8	128	5	80	13	208
PHOTOGRAPHIC RECONNAISSANCE	4	80	4	80	2	40	6	120
COASTAL FIGHTERS	4	64	4	64	3	48	7	112
G.R. LAND PLANES	15	240	15	240	6	88	21	528
FLYING BOATS	3	27	3	27	12	108	15	135
TORPEDO AIRCRAFT	6	96	6	96	3	48	9	144
TRANSPORT & TROOP CARRIERS	9	180	9	180	10	250	19	430
TOTALS	142	2423	148	2535	85	1366	249	4221

(a) An additional 16 squadrons will be available by December, 1944. A proportion may be converted to freighters.

Appendix "A" to Annex III

265

APPENDIX "B" TO ANNEX III

"DRAKE" PLAN

1. The plan is to bomb Japan with B-29 aircraft supplied through India and operating through forward airfields in the Kweilin area of China. This forward area would be protected by U.S. equipped Chinese divisions and the augmented 14th Air Force.

2. Twenty-seven airfields would be constructed (or converted) in Bengal. These would be supplied with gasoline by pipelines direct from the port. This would necessitate considerable expansion of the port facilities of Calcutta (both for dry stores and for gasoline) and communications in India, including the Bengal/Assam L. of C. In addition, the plan would require the construction of the Ledo-Paoshan-Kunming road and the projected pipelines from India to China.

3. Simultaneously with the above, fifteen airfields would be constructed in the Kunming area, using Chinese labor and local resources.

4. On the completion of these projects supplies would be moved from India into China by approximately 2,000 transport aircraft (our plan is based on B-24's), the Ledo-Kunming road and the oil pipelines. These supplies would equip and maintain Chinese forces and the augmented 14th Air Force. As soon as sufficient forces have been built up to protect the Kweilin area, airfields would be constructed there for use by the B-29 aircraft.

5. General Stilwell has stipulated that he would require 50 U.S. equipped and trained Chinese divisions before he could secure the Kweilin area sufficiently to allow airfield construction to be started. On this basis bombing could not start before the autumn of 1946. If a lesser force were acceptable, bombing could start correspondingly earlier (e.g., if 20 divisions would suffice, bombing might start in autumn 1945). The above dates assume the defeat of Germany by 1 October 1944.

6. The maximum B-29 force which we could operate would be eight groups (224 aircraft).

7. The plan allows for the Chengtu project, preparations for which have already been ordered.

Appendix "B" to Annex III

8. The plan would be dependent upon the following assumptions:

a. That operations in North Burma in 1943/44 enable construction of the Ledo-Paoshan-Kunming Road and pipelines to be completed by 1 January 1945.

b. That sufficient airfield sites (27) in Bengal and port and communication facilities can be made available.

c. That the Bengal/Assam L. of C. is expanded as directed at *QUAD-RANT*.

d. That we can construct suitable airfields (15) in China with local labor and materials.

e. That during 1944, 7,000 tons a month (including 5,000 already allotted to the 14th Air Force) are made available from the capacity of the existing A.T.C. route to China.

f. That the necessary U.S. personnel and equipment are made available by the dates required.

C.C.S. 418/1

ENTRY OF TURKEY INTO THE WAR

References:

CCS 133d Meeting, Item 2 (2)
CCS 133d Meeting, Item 4
1st EUREKA Plenary Meeting
2d EUREKA Plenary Meeting

C.C.S. 418 circulated a memorandum by the British Chiefs of Staff 2 December 1943. The Combined Chiefs of Staff in their 133d Meeting, amended and approved C.C.S. 418 (subsequently circulated as C.C.S. 418/1).

U. S. SECRET
BRITISH MOST SECRET

C.C.S. 418/1   3 December 1943

COMBINED CHIEFS OF STAFF

ENTRY OF TURKEY INTO THE WAR

Memorandum by the British Chiefs of Staff

1. The object of this paper is to discuss the role that Turkey might be called upon to adopt if she agrees to come into the war, and the extent of our commitments likely to be involved.

TURKEY'S ROLE IN THE WAR

2. We consider that our object in the Balkans should be to bring about the surrender of Bulgaria and open a short sea route to Russia.

3. The surrender of Bulgaria is most likely to be achieved by:

   a. Air action.

   b. Russian diplomatic and subversive action.

   c. The psychological effect of Turkey becoming an active ally of the United Nations.

4. We do not propose that Allied forces should be concentrated in Thrace to cooperate with the Turks. In Thrace, therefore, the Turks must be persuaded to stand on the defensive and to concentrate their forces for the protection of the Straits. To assist them we would continue to bomb the Bulgarians.

5. The opening of a short supply route to Russia through the Dardanelles would achieve a considerable economy in shipping, but might also enable us to take the strain off the Persian supply route. The Turks should be called upon to provide us with the bases from which to protect the convoys.

COMMITMENTS INVOLVED

6. The commitments which would be involved in the above policy can be considered under two headings:

a. Minimum air and anti-air assistance to the Turks, who make a great point of the necessity for protecting their main cities, communications and industries from German air attack.

b. Action, within the capacity of the forces that can be made available, for opening the Aegean Sea, the capture of Rhodes and the other Dodecanese Islands.

Assistance to the Turks

7. We can provide a reasonable scale of air defense for Turkish key points.

Opening the Aegean

8. In addition to 6 *a* above, we can find the necessary air forces to provide air cover for convoys in the Aegean and the Marmora, without any serious effect on operations elsewhere.

9. The naval forces required for escorting and minesweeping for a fortnightly convoy cycle would have to be provided from outside the Mediterranean.

10. With the above naval and air forces it should be possible to pass occasional convoys through the Aegean without first capturing Rhodes. In these circumstances, however, the losses in ships might be considerable, and for the passage of regular convoys it would be necessary to capture Rhodes and highly desirable to clean up Kos, Leros, Samos, Khios, Mytilene and Lemnos. From the military point of view it would be an immense advantage if the Turks could cooperate in the assaults on the islands other than Rhodes.

11. The forces required for the capture of Rhodes over and above those *now* in M.E. Command would be:

a. Naval forces for the assault.

b. One British division.

c. The assault shipping and craft for one division, two brigades assaulting.

d. Two parachute battalions and the necessary air lift for them amounting to 90 transport aircraft.

12. As far as can be foreseen at present the land and air forces for this operation could be found from resources in the Mediterranean Theater.

13. There are two possible sources for the necessary assault shipping and craft: the Mediterranean Theater, and the Southeast Asia Theater.

14. The two parachute battalions and the 90 transport aircraft could only come from the Central Mediterranean and their release would depend on the requirements of the situation in Italy, and the preparations for operations against Southern France.

15. From the point of view of the weather it might be possible to stage an assault on Rhodes towards the end of February, but other factors are likely to affect this date.

C.C.S. 420

GENERAL PROGRESS REPORT ON RECENT OPERATIONS

AND FUTURE PLANS IN THE PACIFIC

Reference:

CCS 133d Meeting, Item 5

C.C.S. 420, 4 December 1943, circulated a report by the United States Chiefs of Staff for the information of the Combined Chiefs of Staff.

C.C.S. 420   4 December 1943

COMBINED CHIEFS OF STAFF

GENERAL PROGRESS REPORT ON RECENT OPERATIONS
AND FUTURE PLANS IN THE PACIFIC

Memorandum by the United States Chiefs of Staff

The enclosure, compiled from reports of the area commanders in the Pacific, is presented to the Combined Chiefs of Staff for their information.

E N C L O S U R E

GENERAL PROGRESS REPORT ON RECENT OPERATIONS
AND FUTURE PLANS IN THE PACIFIC

PROGRESS OF PACIFIC AND SOUTHWEST PACIFIC OPERATIONS
15 AUGUST—15 NOVEMBER 1943

North Pacific

1. The Kiska operation was begun on 15 August. A combined United States-Canadian Task Force, involving naval, ground, and air units, effected an unopposed occupation as the Japanese had previously evacuated without the knowledge of our forces. This evacuation eliminated the Japanese from the Aleutians where they had begun seizure of bases in June 1942.

2. Subsequently an aircraft strike was made against Paramushiru in August and another in September. These strikes inflicted some damage on Japanese shore installations, aircraft, and ships, and provided some information on the extensive development and fortification underway in this area. The aircraft losses in these strikes were disproportionate to results obtained. Accordingly the small air forces now allotted to this area have assumed a generally defensive

role for the time being. The North Pacific Force, in addition to carrying out the usual patrols, is proceeding with the development of bases and plans for the capture of Paramushiru and for follow-up in the Kuriles or, in case of Soviet participation, in Kamchatka or Sakhalin, or both.

Central Pacific

3. Activities in this area have mainly been limited, generally to support of the submarine campaign and the operations in the North and South Pacific Areas, and to preparation of forces for island operations.

4. A carrier task force raided Marcus Island on 31 August effecting complete surprise and meeting opposition only from anti-aircraft fire. Enemy installations were heavily damaged and some enemy aircraft, which were caught grounded, were destroyed.

5. Similarly, on 18 September, Tarawa, Makin, and Apamama in the Gilberts were attacked by a carrier task force. This attack was coordinated with one by U.S. Army planes from Canton and Guadalcanal on Tarawa and Nauru, respectively. Enemy shore facilities and considerable aircraft were destroyed in these raids.

6. On 5 and 6 October, Wake Atoll was attacked by aircraft and bombarded by ships of a task force of six carriers, seven cruisers, and supporting destroyers. U.S. Navy planes temporarily based at Midway also attacked Wake during these two days. Damage was estimated as 55 percent of enemy shore installations and 67 enemy planes destroyed.

7. In preparation for operations against the Gilberts and the Marshalls, Baker, Nukufetau, and Nanomea were occupied between 1 and 15 September. Airfields for heavy bombers on Baker and Nukufetau, and for fighters on Nanomea have been prepared.

South and Southwest Pacific

8. On 15 August the forces of the South and Southwest Pacific, under the strategic direction of the CinC, SWPA, were engaged in the *CARTWHEEL* Operations. (Map, facing page 280). In these operations the Eastern Axis (Phases A, B and C) was assigned to the South Pacific Forces, while the Western Axis (Phases 1, 2 and 3) was assigned to the Southwest Pacific Forces.

9. By 5 August, Munda airfield on New Georgia had been captured, but mopping up of scattered enemy resistance continued for several weeks. Continuing with Phase A, Vella Lavella was occupied on 12 August, thus by-passing the enemy strength on Kolombangara. Initial landings on Vella Lavella on 12 August met little resistance and our ground strength was quickly built up. This outflanking move, involving air attacks against enemy airfields, personnel, and landing barges, and numerous naval engagements, prevented reinforcements and supplies reaching Japanese garrisons, and forced enemy evacuation of Kolombangara and nearby islands. The battle of New Georgia was officially terminated on 16 October, completing Phase A of *CARTWHEEL*. In the course of these operations, 5 airfields were captured or constructed in this area, thus permitting more effective employment of aircraft in support of further operations.

10. On 26 October, Phase B was begun by enveloping operations against the strong enemy position in the south Bougainville area. Allied forces from the South Pacific, including New Zealand troops, occupied two islands in the Treasury Group. One day later U.S. troops landed in northwest Choiseul as a diversion. On 1 November a large-scale landing was made on the northern shores of Empress Augusta Bay. Coincident with this landing, carrier and shore-based aircraft struck Buka and Bonis airfields and surface craft bombarded in the Buka and Shortland areas. Air forces from the Southwest Pacific gave support by operations against the airfields in New Britain. Early on the morning of 2 November a United States force of cruisers and destroyers made contact with several groups of Japanese cruisers and destroyers west of Empress Augusta Bay. Preliminary reports on this engagement indicate possibly five Japanese ships, including a cruiser of the SENDAI class, were sunk and four damaged. We lost no ships although some damage was received. On 5 November a carrier task force conducted an air strike against shipping in Rabaul harbor, inflicting damage on six Japanese heavy cruisers, two light cruisers, and two destroyers with only minor U.S. plane losses. One of the Japanese heavy cruisers is reported to have blown up. These strikes were coordinated with the operations of the air forces from the Southwest Pacific which hit Rabaul immediately after the carriers. Subsequently air groups from two carrier task forces again struck at naval vessels and shipping in and near Rabaul inflicting damage on the enemy while receiving little themselves. Despite Japanese surface ship, aircraft, and ground reaction, the Bougainville operations are progressing satisfactorily and approximately 27,000 troops have been landed.

11. On the Western Axis, Phase 1 was initiated on 30 June, by simultaneous unopposed landings on Kiriwina and Woodlark Islands by forces from the Southwest and South Pacific respectively. An airfield on Woodlark was completed for fighter operation by 5 July. Two large airdromes were ready for full operational use on Kiriwina by 11 October. On 12 October the first full-scale fighter-escorted daylight raid on Rabaul was launched, using Kiriwina to stage the fighters and medium bombers. This attack was initiated by escorted low-level bombing and strafing of the airdromes by the medium bombardment and followed up with a high level bombardment of shipping by 84 heavy bombers. The attack was eminently successful and similar attacks are being continued as weather permits and in conjunction with the operations on the Eastern Axis.

12. On 30 June one U.S. regiment was landed at Nassau Bay to assist the Australians in the capture of Salamaua which was finally occupied on 11 September.

13. Phase 2 of the Western Axis was initiated on 4 September by shore to shore assault of the 9th Australian Division 14 miles east of Lae. This assault was closely followed by seizure of the Nadzab airdrome on 5 September by a U.S. Parachute Regiment. Seizure of Nadzab permitted the airborne movement of the 7th Australian Division into the Markham Valley, completing the double envelopment of Lae. Heavy bombardment of Lae and its perimeter defenses with 1,000-lb. bombs so softened these defenses and demoralized the Japanese that Lae fell to the advancing 7th Australian on 16 September.

14. As Lae was occupied, the 9th Australian changed direction and effected a landing 6 miles north of Finschhafen on 22 September and, by a pincer movement, cleared the coastal area to include the tip of the Huon Peninsula. Construction was begun on a fighter strip on the south shore of Langemak Bay about 20 October. Remnants of scattered Jap forces, reassembled and reinforced at Satelberg, are still being cleaned out by the Australians.

15. The 7th Australian by a combination of airborne and overland operations moved rapidly up the Ramu Valley seizing Kaipit by 19 September and advancing their outpost line west to Kasawai and north to the Finisterres. Construction of airfields at Kaipit and Dumpu are now in progress.

16. During all of Phase 2 extensive air operations were maintained against Japanese supply lines, particularly barges and all airfields within striking

distance of the operation. These air operations were effective in pushing back the Jap air concentrations and destroying Jap air forces, as indicated by the fact that during the month of October an estimated 660 Japanese aircraft were destroyed and 245 probably destroyed and damaged, against a loss of 34 Allied planes destroyed and 6 damaged. In addition, these air attacks sank 4 destroyers, 1 subchaser, 1 gunboat, 44 miscellaneous merchant vessels, 86 small craft and luggers and 50 barges; probably sank 2 destroyers, 1 gunboat, 4 merchant vessels and 12 barges; damaged 1 cruiser, 1 destroyer, 1 submarine, 1 destroyer tender, 1 submarine tender, 12 merchant cargo vessels and 14 schooners and barges.

17. In the Northwestern Sector of the Southwest Pacific, continual harassing bombardment and fighter sweeps were conducted by the Allied air units stationed around Darwin. These attacks were concentrated on Jap installations, shipping and aircraft on Timor and the islands of the Arafura Sea. Several long range attacks on targets such as Balikapapan, Soerabaya, Ambon, and Ceram were carried out. One heavy bombardment group at approximately two-thirds strength is now maintained in this area in addition to R.A.A.F. fighter squadrons and Dutch and R.A.A.F. medium bombardment squadrons.

18. Naval forces in the Southwest Pacific area escorted supply and troop ships from Australia to New Guinea and along the northeast New Guinea coast. They also participated in amphibious operations at Kiriwina, Woodlark, Salamaua, Lae and Finschhafen. No opposition was met at any beaches but several assaults withstood air attacks. One destroyer was lost by torpedoing. There was small loss in landing craft.

19. All preparations have been completed and units are in position for initiation of Phase 3, which will consist of ship-to-shore and shore-to-shore assaults on the Cape Gloucester and Gasmata areas. Present target date is 4 December. At Gloucester, assaults will be made by the 1st U.S. Marine Division and at Gasmata by the 32d U.S. Infantry Division. At Gloucester the assault will receive its close fighter cover from the strip now being completed at Langemak Bay near Finschhafen and the Gasmata assault from Kiriwina. The 503rd Parachute Regiment will again be used if necessary in the Cape Gloucester operation. The initial assaults of Phase 3 will be followed by successive infiltration movements to secure the line Talasea-Gasmata.

Submarine Operations

20. During the period 15 August-1 November, U.S. submarines have continued to operate against Japanese shipping in the Pacific from bases in Hawaii and Australia. These offensive patrols extended to Japanese Empire waters, to Japanese Mandates, the South China Sea-Philippine waters, and the New Guinea-Bismarck Archipelago waters. All reports for October have not been received but results continue to be satisfactory. Indications are that September, with approximately 262,000 tons of shipping sunk and 203,000 tons damaged, was the outstanding month of those for which complete reports have been received. Japanese anti-submarine measures and tactics have been intensified, but escort vessels are still limited and our losses have not increased. New submarines are reporting at the rate of about six per month, and proportionate future effectiveness in patrol areas is expected.

PROGRESS OF FUTURE PLANS IN THE PACIFIC

21. In general future planning for the over-all Pacific campaign has been directed towards the exploration of ways and means to accelerate the defeat of Japan after the collapse of Germany. Studies to date have indicated the necessity for immediate action to provide a large increase in assault shipping to insure the success of that campaign beyond 1944. This will tax the shipbuilding facilities of the United States. Future planning for 1944 has covered the development of Staff studies for operations which had been approved at the *QUADRANT* Conference. The actual operational planning is being done by the area commanders.

North Pacific Area

22. The Joint Chiefs of Staff have decided that the target date for planning purposes for the capture of the Paramushiru area should be the spring of 1945, as studies have shown that the advance into the Northern Kuriles is an operation of such magnitude that it cannot be integrated with other approved operations for the Pacific during 1944. Plans for such an advance are actively continuing in order that it may be possible to take advantage of unforeseen events. Plans for 1944 contemplate the continuance of bombing and photographic

missions in the Paramushiru area, and the development of base facilities in the Aleutians to provide B-29 airfields and staging areas, to facilitate any operations that may be projected against the Kuriles in 1945.

Central Pacific Area

23. The Area Commander's plans for seizure of the Gilbert Islands have reached the final phase. These plans include preliminary air strikes by carrier and shore-based aircraft on objectives in the Marshalls and Gilberts, followed by the simultaneous seizure on 20 November of Makin, Tarawa, and Apamama after sustained air and gunfire bombardment. While complete reports are not yet available, these operations are proceeding satisfactorily.

24. His plans for seizing control of the Marshall Islands are nearing completion. At present, these plans envisage the simultaneous capture of Wotje, Maloelap, and Kwajalein and control of Mille and Jaluit, followed shortly by the seizure of Eniwetok and the control of Kusaie. Wake will be by-passed initially. The target date for the initial Marshall assault has been deferred from 1 January to 17 January, mainly in order to allow more time for the movement of material to mounting areas, essential training, and rehabilitation of ships involved in the Gilbert Islands operation. Both the Gilbert and the Marshall Islands operations will require the full employment of all available assault shipping in the Pacific over and above that assigned to the South and Southwest Pacific, plus the support of the Fifth Fleet.

25. Plans for operations in the Mandates west of the Marshalls are now in the exploratory and preliminary phases. At the present time no change in the objectives as outlined at *QUADRANT* for 1944 is foreseen. However, it is expected that the *QUADRANT* target dates may be anticipated.

South and Southwest Pacific Area

26. The schedule of 1944 post-*CARTWHEEL* operations as approved in *QUADRANT* Conferences include the seizure of Kavieng, the Admiralty Islands, the neutralization of Rabaul and an advance along the north New Guinea coast to the Vogelkop area. Detailed plans and requirements for these operations have been submitted to the Joint Chiefs of Staff by the Commander in Chief, Southwest Pacific Area, entitled Reno III.

PROGRESS OF CARTWHEEL OPERATIONS

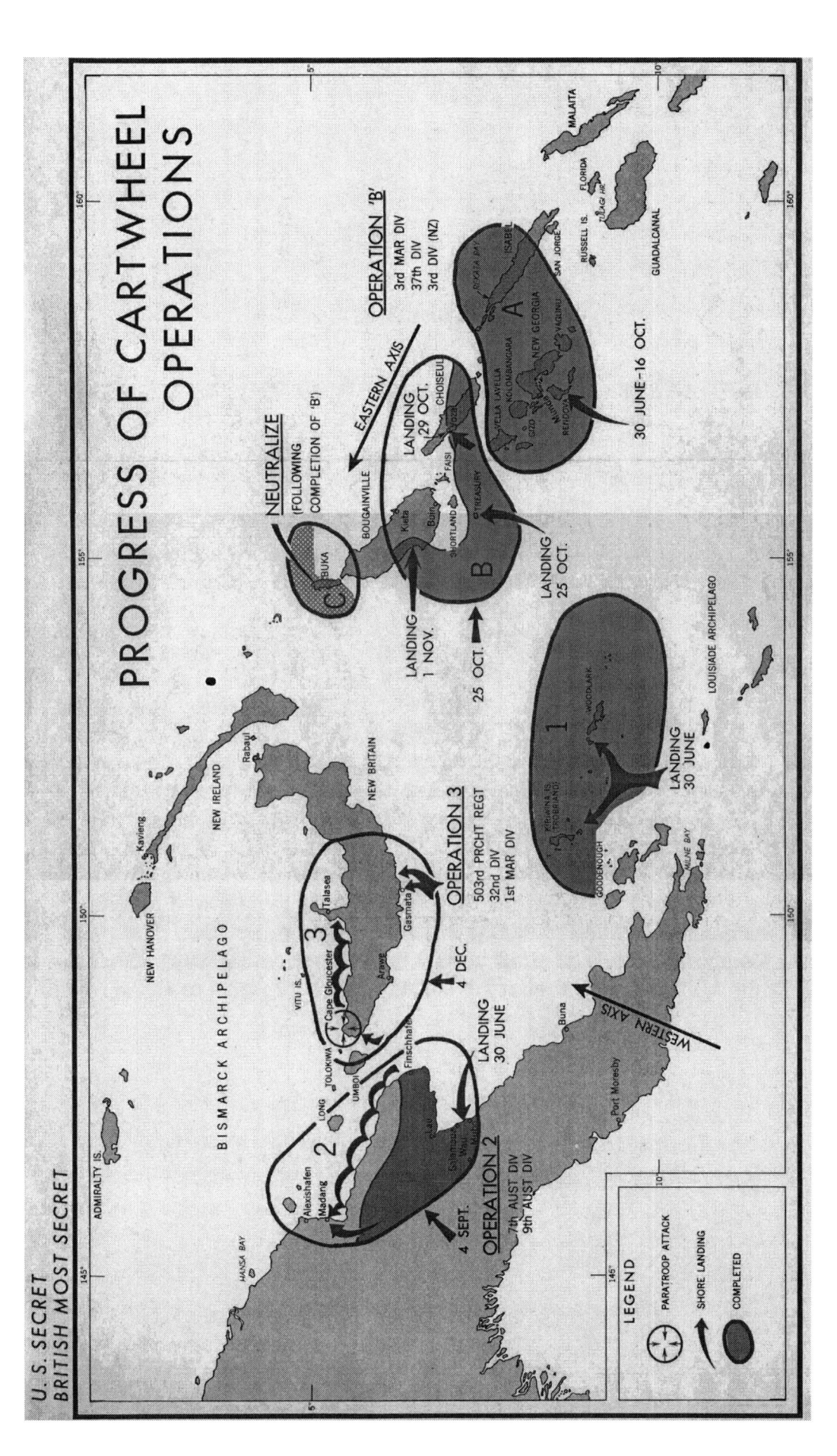

C.C.S. 423/2

DRAFT AGREEMENT BY THE COMBINED CHIEFS OF STAFF

References:

CCS 134th Meeting, Item 8
CCS 135th Meeting, Item 2
4th Plenary Meeting
CCS 426/1
CCS 427

The Combined Chiefs of Staff, in their 134th Meeting agreed that the U.S. and British Chiefs of Staff, respectively, should draw up a paper setting out a draft of matters of high policy regarding the European Theater and the Southeast Asia Command. Subsequently, the memorandum submitted by the British Chiefs of Staff, C.C.S. 423 and the memorandum submitted by the United States Chiefs of Staff, C.C.S. 423/1 were considered by the Combined Chiefs of Staff in their 135th Meeting. An agreed memorandum for the President and Prime Minister, setting out the various points of agreement and disagreement was circulated as C.C.S. 423/2, 5 December 1943. The resolutions of the Combined Chiefs of Staff following their meeting with the President and Prime Minister (4th Plenary Meeting) are contained in C.C.S. 426/1.

C.C.S. 423/2   5 December 1943

COMBINED CHIEFS OF STAFF

Report by the Combined Chiefs of Staff

OPERATIONS IN THE EUROPEAN THEATER

1. *OVERLORD* and *ANVIL* are the supreme operations for 1944. They must be carried out during May 1944. Nothing must be undertaken in any other part of the world which hazards the success of these two operations.

2. *OVERLORD* as at present planned is on a narrow margin. Everything practicable should be done to increase its strength.

3. The examination of *ANVIL* on the basis of not less than a two-division assault should be pressed forward as fast as possible. If the examination reveals that it requires strengthening, consideration will have to be given to the provision of additional resources.

4. Operations in the Aegean, including in particular the capture of Rhodes, are desirable, provided that they can be fitted in without detriment to *OVERLORD* and *ANVIL*.

5. Every effort must be made by accelerated building and conversion, to provide the essential additional landing craft for the European Theater.

6. The decisions made by the Combined Chiefs of Staff at the *QUADRANT* Conference covering the bombing of German industrial targets and the destruction of the German air force, as set forth in paragraph 10 of C.C.S. 319/5, are reaffirmed.

OPERATIONS IN SOUTHEAST ASIA THEATER

Views of U.S. Chiefs of Staff

7. Political and military considerations and commitments make it essential that Operation *TARZAN* and an amphibious operation in conjunction therewith should take place. Apart from political considerations, there will be serious military repercussions if this is not done, not only in Burma and China, but also in the Southwest Pacific.

8. The Supreme Commander, Southeast Asia Command, should be told that he must do the best that he can with the resources already allocated to him.

Views of British Chiefs of Staff

7. We fully realize that there are political and military implications in the postponement of *BUCCANEER*. As regards the political implications, we must leave these to be taken into consideration by the President and Prime Minister. As regards the military disadvantages, these are overridden by the far greater advantages to be derived from a successful invasion of the Continent, and the collapse of Germany.

C.C.S. 424

AMPHIBIOUS OPERATION AGAINST THE SOUTH OF FRANCE

References:

CCS 132d Meeting
CCS 133d Meeting, Item 2 (4)
CCS 135th Meeting, Item 5
CCS 136th Meeting, Item 2
3d Plenary Meeting
4th Plenary Meeting
1st *EUREKA* Plenary Meeting
1st *EUREKA* Military Meeting
2nd *EUREKA* Plenary Meeting

C.C.S. 424 circulated the report of the Combined Staff Planners prepared with the collaboration of the Combined Administrative Committee. The Combined Chiefs of Staff, in their 136th Meeting, amended and approved C.C.S. 424 and directed that the draft directive contained in Appendix "B" be forwarded to General Eisenhower.

C.C.S. 424 5 December 1943

COMBINED CHIEFS OF STAFF

AMPHIBIOUS OPERATION AGAINST THE SOUTH OF FRANCE

Note by the Secretaries

The enclosure is a report by the Combined Staff Planners prepared with the collaboration of the Combined Administrative Committee.

H. REDMAN,

F. B. ROYAL,

Combined Secretariat.

ENCLOSURE

AMPHIBIOUS OPERATION AGAINST THE SOUTH OF FRANCE

Reference: CCS Memo Directive
1 December 1943

1. In accordance with the instructions of the Combined Chiefs of Staff, we have examined the agreed operations against the South of France on the following premises:

a. That this operation should be carried out with a minimum of two assault divisions.

b. That the necessary resources shall not be found at the expense of *OVERLORD*.

2. We have in addition assumed:

a. That operation *ANVIL* will approximately coincide with *OVERLORD*.

b. In Italy we have reached the Pisa-Rimini line and thereafter as strong pressure as possible is maintained consistent with the provision of forces for *ANVIL*.

c. The Mediterranean forces will not be engaged in offensive operations elsewhere.

3. We have made tentative estimates, in the absence of any detailed operational plan, of the resources which will be required for the operation under two hypotheses where these apply:

a. That the assault is carried out within range of shore-based fighter aircraft.

b. That the assault is carried out beyond the range of shore-based fighter aircraft.

4. It appears that the following cannot be found from the resources which under present agreements will be available to General Eisenhower in the Mediterranean at the time of the operation:

A. *Naval Forces*

On the assumption that adequate shore-based, short-range fighter cover is provided:

(1) Additional escorts, probably 10 to 20.

(2) 2 AA fighter direction ships.

(3) In the event that the build-up exceeds one division before D plus 8, nine A/S A/A escorts will be required for each extra division.

This indicates that if a rapid build-up is necessary, more escorts will be required.

In the event that adequate shore-based short-range air cover can not be provided the following will be needed in addition to those above.

(1) 9 to 12 escort carriers with fighters.

(2) 6 AA cruisers.

(3) 18 screening vessels.

To meet these deficiencies, we must draw on other theaters, most probably from the Atlantic. *It might prove possible for four CVE and six escorts which are taking part in BUCCANEER to return to the Mediterranean in time.* This, however, will be conditioned by the availability of fighters for reequipping these escort carriers. We have assumed that port parties will be provided from within the Mediterranean.

B. *Land Forces*

Certain service forces, the number and type of which cannot be determined without careful study by AFHQ.

On the assumption that French divisions will participate, the requirement will be lessened if, as recommended by General Eisenhower, some of the French divisions scheduled for activation are not formed but are converted to service forces.

C. *Air Forces*

The troop carrier resources in the Mediterranean will only be sufficient to lift one brigade and if the detailed plan requires a second brigade lift, this will have to be provided.

D. *Shipping*

(1) Personnel Shipping.

The *QUADRANT* allotment of personnel shipping for 80,000 troop lift in the Mediterranean expires on 31 March. Initially, personnel shipping for 32,000 will be required until after the assault, and during the period of build-up, a total personnel lift for 15,000 will be necessary. It is proposed to use cargo ships for personnel lift to the maximum extent possible.

(2) MT/Stores Shipping.

The following sailings within the Mediterranean will be required in addition to those required for the maintenance of the remainder of the theater:

First month	—	128
Second month	—	90
Third month	—	75
Fourth and subsequent months	—	40

This can obviously be provided but until the present shipping examination is completed, we cannot assess the cost.

E. *Assault Shipping and Craft*

Assault lift for two divisions can be provided. Methods of providing this are shown in Appendix "A."

5. We consider that General Eisenhower should be directed to prepare an outline plan for the agreed operation against the South of France as a matter of urgency. We have accordingly prepared a directive to General Eisenhower, and this is attached at Appendix "B."

RECOMMENDATION

6. That the directive in Appendix "B" be sent to General Eisenhower.

APPENDIX "A"

1. We have examined the resources available for the agreed operation against the South of France on the following premises:

a. That this operation should be carried out with a minimum of two assault divisions, and;

b. That the necessary resources shall not be found at the expense of *OVERLORD*.

2. The assault shipping and craft which we estimate will be available and serviceable in the Mediterranean for an assault on Southern France at about the time of *OVERLORD* is as follows:

	Assault Shipping Craft			*Lift*	
	British	*U.S.*	*Total*	*Personnel*	*Vehicles*
L.S.I.(L)	3	—	3	3,600	—
L.S.T.	10	22	32	10,000	1,920
L.C.T.	30	30	60	1,800	600
L.C.I.(L)	45	55	100	20,000	—
L.S.I.(M)	1	—	1	400	—
L.S.I.(H)	1 (a)	—	1		2,000 (by using the
M.T. Ships	16	—	16)		LCT for unloading
L.S.C.	1	—	1)	3,200	other ships after the
L.S.G.	1	—	1)		LCT have discharged
					their original lift as
L.C.M.	85*	—	85)		shown above.)
* U.S. and British				39,000	4,520

(a) Fitted as a brigade headquarters ship. The British state that its allocation is not firm.

3. The above lift in terms of divisions is estimated to be as follows:

a. U.S. - A task force to include one division in the assault and 2/3 of a division embarked as a follow-up or the equivalent thereof;

OR

b. British - 3 assault and 2 follow-up Brigades.

4. It is estimated that, to meet the full requirements of a minimum of two assault divisions, a total force of 45,500 personnel and 7,740 vehicles should be provided. The lift available is short by 6,500 personnel and 3,220 vehicles.

5. The above deficit can be overcome by the provision of 3 combat loaders, 12 MT ships, 26 LST and 31 LCT so that all required vehicles are available on D-day. If required, these 26 LST's can bring with them 12 to 15 sets of pontoon strips.

6. We find that from U.S. resources 26 LST and 26 LCT can be supplied from early spring production previously allocated Pacific and arrive in the Mediterranean by 15 April. The remaining 5 LCT can be supplied from U.S. LCT's now in the Mediterranean and scheduled for *OVERLORD*. The United States is sending 24 additional LCT's to *OVERLORD* beyond the *QUADRANT* commitment, hence these 5 LCT's are not materially at the expense of that operation. The United States can supply 3 XAP's. We consider that the additional MT ships can be supplied from the shipping of that category now pooled in the Mediterranean under AFHQ.

7. The above LST's and LCT's sent from the United States represent a one month's allocation to the Pacific the majority of which were due to be available for the *TRUK* operation in July. It may be possible by withdrawing some of these craft from the South Pacific to make up the *TRUK* deficiency thus created, otherwise the operation may be delayed.

8. The requirement for LSH (AGC) are 2 ; *OVERLORD* requires 3. There are 2 British* and 3 U.S.** available which can be allocated to meet these requirements.

* H.M.S. LARGS

   H.M.S. HILARY

** U.S.S. ANCON

   U.S.S. BISCAYNE

   U.S.S. COTOCTIN

9. Special landing craft types for the assault support must come from those now available in the Mediterranean. Since these are few, the naval forces must be arranged to properly provide close support for the assault.

Appendix "A"

APPENDIX "B"

DRAFT DIRECTIVE TO GENERAL EISENHOWER

1. The Combined Chiefs of Staff have agreed that an operation is to take place in conjunction with *OVERLORD*, with the object of establishing a bridgehead on the South Coast of France and subsequently to exploit in support of *OVERLORD*.

2. You will prepare in consultation with *COSSAC* and submit to the Combined Chiefs of Staff, as a matter of urgency, an outline plan for the operation.

3. The exact date for *OVERLORD* has not yet been decided upon, but it is to take place at the most suitable date during May 1944. You will be informed of the date once this has been decided, and operation *ANVIL* will be timed approximately to coincide with operation *OVERLORD* — the exact date to be determined in consultation with *COSSAC*.

4. You will be given the assault shipping and craft for a lift for at least two divisions (each with two brigades in the assault).

5. You will inform the Combined Chiefs of Staff of your requirements which cannot be met from the resources which will be at your disposal in the Mediterranean on that date. In assessing your resources you should assume that your forces have reached the Pisa-Rimini line and that as strong pressure as possible is maintained, consistent with the forces required for *ANVIL;* also that Mediterranean forces will not be engaged in offensive operations elsewhere.

C.C.S. 425

DIRECTIVE FOR INTENSIFICATION OF SUPPORT OF PARTISAN FORCES IN YUGOSLAVIA

References:

CCS 133d Meeting, Item 2 (1)

CCS 135th Meeting, Item 6

2d *EUREKA* Plenary Meeting

C.C.S. 425 circulated the report by the Combined Staff Planners 4 December 1943. The Combined Chiefs of Staff, in their 135th Meeting approved the draft directive, enclosure to C.C.S. 425, and directed that it be included in the directive to the Supreme Commander, Mediterranean (subsequently circulated as C.C.S. 387/3).

C.C.S. 425   4 December 1943

COMBINED CHIEFS OF STAFF

DIRECTIVE FOR INTENSIFICATION OF SUPPORT
OF PARTISAN FORCES IN YUGOSLAVIA

References: a. CCS 387/1

b. CCS Memo Inf. No. 165,
2 December 1943.

c. CCS 133d Mtg., Item 2.

Report by the Combined Staff Planners

1. As directed by reference c and after consideration of reference a, Unification of Command in the Mediterranean, the Combined Staff Planners have prepared a proposed directive to the Commander in Chief, Allied Forces in North Africa, with regard to the support of the Partisans in Yugoslavia.

2. It is submitted herewith to the Combined Chiefs of Staff with the recommendation that it be approved and forwarded to the Commander in Chief, Allied Forces in North Africa.

E N C L O S U R E

DRAFT DIRECTIVE TO COMMANDER IN CHIEF, ALLIED FORCES

IN NORTH AFRICA

It was agreed at the *EUREKA* Conference that our support of the Partisans in Yugoslavia, which now falls within the area in which you are responsible for Allied operations, should be intensified in order to increase their effectiveness.

You will be responsible for supporting them to the greatest practicable extent by increasing the supply of arms and equipment, clothing, medical stores, food and such other supplies as they may require. You should also support them by commando operations and by furnishing such air support as you may consider advisable in the light of the general situation.

You should examine the possibility of continuing to supply the Partisans with Italian equipment, in the use of which they are already experienced, making good deficiencies in Italian formations to such extent as may be necessary with available British or American equipment.

We consider that this mission is of such importance that it would best be controlled on a regular basis by a special commander and joint staff.

C.C.S. 426/1

REPORT TO THE PRESIDENT AND PRIME MINISTER

Reference:

CCS 136th Meeting, Item 4

CCS 137th Meeting, Item 7

5th Plenary Meeting

The Combined Chiefs of Staff considered a draft report to the President and Prime Minister (C.C.S. 426) in their 137th Meeting. The report as amended and approved by them was subsequently circulated as C.C.S. 426/1.

The President and Prime Minister approved C.C.S. 426/1 in their 5th Plenary Meeting.

C.C.S. 426/1   6 December 1943

COMBINED CHIEFS OF STAFF

REPORT TO THE PRESIDENT AND PRIME MINISTER

Note by the Combined Chiefs of Staff

The enclosure is the report of the Combined Chiefs of Staff on the *SEXTANT* Conference.

ENCLOSURE

REPORT TO THE PRESIDENT AND PRIME MINISTER OF THE AGREED SUMMARY OF CONCLUSIONS REACHED BY THE COMBINED CHIEFS OF STAFF AT THE "SEXTANT" CONFERENCE

1. The agreed summary of the conclusions reached at *SEXTANT* Conference is submitted herewith:—

I. *OVER-ALL OBJECTIVE*

2. In conjunction with Russia and other Allies to bring about at the earliest possible date the unconditional surrender of the Axis Powers.

II. *OVER-ALL STRATEGIC CONCEPT FOR THE PROSECUTION OF THE WAR*

3. In cooperation with Russia and other Allies to bring about at the earliest possible date the unconditional surrender of the Axis in Europe.

4. Simultaneously, in cooperation with other Pacific Powers concerned to maintain and extend unremitting pressure against Japan with the purpose of continually reducing her military power and attaining positions from which her ultimate surrender can be forced. The effect of any such extension on the over-all objective to be given consideration by the Combined Chiefs of Staff before action is taken.

5. Upon the defeat of the Axis in Europe, in cooperation with other Pacific Powers and, if possible, with Russia, to direct the full resources of the United States and Great Britain to bring about at the earliest possible date the unconditional surrender of Japan.

III. *BASIC UNDERTAKINGS IN SUPPORT OF OVER-ALL STRATEGIC CONCEPT*

6. Whatever operations are decided on in support of the over-all strategic concept, the following established undertakings will be a first charge against our resources, subject to review by the Combined Chiefs of Staff in keeping with the changing situation.

a. Maintain the security and war-making capacity of the Western Hemisphere and the British Isles.

b. Support the war-making capacity of our forces in all areas.

c. Maintain vital overseas lines of communication, with particular emphasis on the defeat of the U-boat menace.

d. Continue the disruption of Axis sea communications.

e. Intensify the air offensive against the Axis Powers in Europe.

f. Concentrate maximum resources in a selected area as early as practicable for the purpose of conducting a decisive invasion of the Axis citadel.

g. Undertake such measures as may be necessary and practicable to aid the war effort of Russia, including the coordinated action of our forces.

h. Undertake such measures as may be necessary and practicable in order to aid the war effort of China as an effective Ally and as a base for operations against Japan.

i. Undertake such action to exploit the entry of Turkey into the war as is considered most likely to facilitate or accelerate the attainment of the over-all objectives.

j. Continue assistance to the French and Italian forces to enable them to fulfill an active role in the war against the Axis Powers.

k. Prepare to reorient forces from the European Theater to the Pacific and Far East as soon as the German situation allows.

IV. *EXECUTION OF THE OVER-ALL STRATEGIC CONCEPT*

THE U-BOAT WAR

7. We have received from the Chiefs of the two Naval Staffs encouraging reports regarding the U-boat war. (C.C.S. 399 and 399/1)

THE DEFEAT OF THE AXIS IN EUROPE

THE COMBINED BOMBER OFFENSIVE

8. *a.* We have received a most encouraging report covering the combined bombing operations against Germany. (C.C.S. 403)

b. The progressive destruction and dislocation of the German military, industrial and economic system, the disruption of vital elements of lines of communication, and the material reduction of German air combat strength by the successful prosecution of the Combined Bomber Offensive from all convenient bases is a prerequisite to *OVERLORD* (barring an independent and complete Russian victory before *OVERLORD* can be mounted). This operation must therefore continue to have highest strategic priority.

c. We are agreed that the present plan for the Combined Bomber Offensive should remain unchanged except for revision of the bombing objectives which should be made periodically. The intensity of the operations of the 8th Air Force should be limited only by the aircraft and crews available.

"EUREKA" DECISIONS

9. At the *EUREKA* Conference, the following military conclusions were approved by the President, the Prime Minister and Marshal Stalin. The Conference:

a. Agreed that the Partisans in Yugoslavia should be supported by supplies and equipment to the greatest possible extent, and also by commando operations.

b. Agreed that, from the military point of view, it was most desirable that Turkey should come into the war on the side of the Allies before the end of the year.

c. Took note of Marshal Stalin's statement that if Turkey found herself at war with Germany, and as a result Bulgaria declared war on Turkey or attacked her, the Soviet would immediately be at war with Bulgaria. The Conference further took note that this fact could be explicitly stated in the forthcoming negotiations to bring Turkey into the war.

d. Took note that Operation *OVERLORD* would be launched during May 1944, in conjunction with an operation against Southern France. The latter operation would be undertaken in as great a strength as availability of landing craft permitted. The Conference further took note of Marshal Stalin's statement that the Soviet forces would launch an offensive at about the same time with the object of preventing the German forces from transferring from the Eastern to the Western Front.

e. Agreed that the military staffs of the three Powers should henceforward keep in close touch with each other in regard to the impending operations in Europe. In particular, it was agreed that a cover plan to mystify and mislead the enemy as regards these operations should be concerted between the staffs concerned.

10. In the light of the above *EUREKA* decisions, we have reached agreement as follows regarding operations in the European Theater:

a. OVERLORD and *ANVIL* are the supreme operations for 1944. They must be carried out during May, 1944. Nothing must be undertaken in any other part of the world which hazards the success of these two operations.

b. OVERLORD as at present planned is on a narrow margin. Everything practicable should be done to increase its strength.

c. The examination of *ANVIL* on the basis of not less than a two-division assault should be pressed forward as fast as possible. If the examination reveals that it requires strengthening, consideration will have to be given to the provision of additional resources.

d. Operations in the Aegean, including in particular the capture of Rhodes, are desirable, provided that they can be fitted in without detriment to *OVERLORD* and *ANVIL*.

e. Every effort must be made, by accelerated building and conversion, to provide the essential additional landing craft for the European Theater.

OPERATIONS AGAINST SOUTHERN FRANCE

11. We have examined the operations to be undertaken against Southern France. We have instructed the Supreme Allied Commander, Mediterranean Theater, in consultation with *COSSAC*, to submit, as a matter of urgency, an outline plan for the operation. He has been informed that it will take place at about the same time as Operation OVERLORD and that he will be given the assault shipping and craft for a lift of at least two divisions. He has been instructed to inform us of his requirements which cannot be met from the resources he will have at his disposal in the Mediterranean on that date.

OPERATIONS IN ITALY

12. We have agreed that in Italy the advance should be continued to the Pisa-Rimini line. We have informed the Supreme Allied Commander, Mediterranean Theater, that he may retain in the Mediterranean until the 15th January 1944 the 68 LST's due for return to the United Kingdom. This will still allow these landing craft to reach the United Kingdom in time for *OVERLORD*.

COMMAND IN THE MEDITERRANEAN

13. We have agreed to the unification of command in the Mediterranean Theater and have issued the necessary directive to General Eisenhower (C.C.S. 387/3).

SUPPORT TO THE BALKANS

14. We have issued special instructions to the Supreme Allied Commander, Mediterranean Theater, with regard to the assistance he should render to the Partisans (C.C.S. 387/3, Appendix "B").

TURKEY

15. We have examined the role that Turkey might be called upon to adopt if she agrees to come into the war* and the extent of our commitments that is likely to be involved. (C.C.S. 418/1).

* See paragraph 9 *b* above.

COORDINATION WITH THE U.S.S.R.

16. We have agreed that the necessary coordination of effort with the U.S.S.R. should be arranged through the United States and British Military Missions in Moscow. We have agreed that deception experts should proceed to Moscow to coordinate plans with the Soviet Staff.

EMERGENCY RETURN TO THE CONTINENT

17. In developing his plans for *RANKIN*, *COSSAC* has submitted a recommendation that under the general direction of the Supreme Allied Commander the territories to be occupied should be divided into two spheres, the British sphere, including Northwest Germany, Belgium, Luxembourg, Holland and Denmark; and the U.S. sphere, generally Southern Germany and France, with Austria a U.S. sphere, initially under the Mediterranean command. Planning by *COSSAC* is now proceeding on this basis.

18. The United States Chiefs of Staff now propose that these spheres be changed as follows:

a. U.S. sphere. The general area Netherlands, Northern Germany as far east as the line Berlin-Stettin, Denmark, Norway and Sweden. The boundary of this area is to be as follows: southern boundary of the Netherlands; thence to Dusseldorf on the Rhine; down the east bank of the Rhine to Mains; thence due east to Beyreuth; thence north to Leipzig; thence northeast to Cottbus; thence north to Berlin (exclusive); thence to Stettin (inclusive).

b. British sphere. Generally the territory to the west and south of the American western boundary.

19. We have agreed that *COSSAC* be directed to examine and report on the implications of revising his planning on the basis of the new allocation of spheres of occupation.

20. We have further agreed that the Combined Intelligence Committee be instructed to keep the situation in Europe under constant review in relation to *RANKIN* and to report on the first of each month regarding this to the Combined Chiefs of Staff.

THE WAR AGAINST JAPAN

LONG TERM STRATEGY

21. Active study continues regarding the Over-all Plan for the Defeat of Japan, and we have approved in principle C.C.S. 417 and 417/1 (less paragraph 4 of the enclosure to C.C.S. 417/1) as a basis for further investigation and preparation, subject to final approval by the Combined Chiefs of Staff.

We have directed the Combined Staff Planners to plan a campaign for the Chinese Theater proper, together with an estimate of the forces involved.

SPECIFIC OPERATIONS IN 1943-1944

22. We have approved the Specific Operations for the Defeat of Japan in 1944 (C.C.S. 397 Revised) with the exception of the references contained therein to *BUCCANEER*.

HIGHER DIRECTION OF OPERATIONS IN SOUTHEAST ASIA COMMAND

23. We agree that it is undesirable for the Combined Chiefs of Staff to enter into details of various operations in this theater, but consider that the Combined Chiefs of Staff in the exercise of their general jurisdiction over strategy in this theater must reach decisions as to which of several courses of action are to be undertaken and their sequence and timing.

OPERATIONS IN THE S.E. ASIA COMMAND

24. We have agreed to delay major amphibious operations in the Bay of Bengal until after the next monsoon and divert the landing craft now assigned to *BUCCANEER* to Operations *ANVIL* and *OVERLORD*.

25. We have decided:—

  a. To make all preparations to conduct *TARZAN* as planned less *BUCCANEER*, for which will be substituted naval carrier and amphibious raiding operations simultaneous with the launching of *TARZAN*; and to carry out air bombardment of the Bangkok-Burma railroad and the harbor of Bangkok, in the meantime maintaining naval control of the Bay of Bengal—

OR ALTERNATIVELY

b. To postpone *TARZAN*, increase to a maximum with planes available the air lift to China across the "hump," and intensify the measures that will enable the B-29's to be brought to bear on the enemy.

26. The choice between alternatives *a* and *b* above will be made at a later date by the Combined Chiefs of Staff after obtaining an expression of opinion by the Generalissimo and the Supreme Allied Commander, Southeast Asia Command.

RELATION OF AVAILABLE RESOURCES TO THE OPERATIONS DECIDED UPON

27. We have now in process of examination a study of the available resources of the United Nations with a view to assessing our ability to carry out the operations decided upon.

V. CONCLUSIONS ON MISCELLANEOUS SUBJECTS

UNITED CHIEFS OF STAFF

28. We have studied proposals for the possible formation of a United Chiefs of Staff organization and, alternatively, the possible representation on the Combined Chiefs of Staff of powers other than the U.S. and the British. We have agreed that the Combined Chiefs of Staff should not take the initiative in putting forward either of the above proposals. We feel that if the U.S.S.R. or China should raise the question, the difficulties of and objections to any form of standing United Chiefs of Staff Committee should be frankly explained to them. It should then be pointed out that the Combined Chiefs of Staff in Washington are responsible for the day-to-day conduct of the Anglo-American forces which are closely integrated in accordance with the broad policy laid down at the formal conferences such as *CASABLANCA, TRIDENT, QUADRANT*

and *SEXTANT*, which are convened from time to time; and that the U.S.S.R. and/or the Chinese Governments will be invited to join in any formal conferences which may be convened in the future, to take part in the discussion of any military problems with which they are specifically concerned.

NOTE

The matters still under study and decisions which have yet to be taken, notably in paragraphs 11, 15, 19, 21, 25, and 27, will be duly brought to your attention for approval.

C.C.S. 427 and 427/1

AMPHIBIOUS OPERATIONS IN SOUTHEAST ASIA
ALTERNATIVE TO "BUCCANEER"

References:

CCS 129th Meeting, Items 5 and 7
CCS 130th Meeting, Item 1
CCS 136th Meeting, Item 1
CCS 137th Meeting, Items 2 and 6
CCS 138th Meeting, Item 3
1st Plenary Meeting
3d Plenary Meeting
4th Plenary Meeting
5th Plenary Meeting

C.C.S. 427 circulated a report by the Combined Staff Planners, 5 December 1943. The Combined Chiefs of Staff took note of C.C.S. 427 in their 137th Meeting.

C.C.S. 427/1 circulated a message received from the Supreme Allied Commander, Southeast Asia Command. The Combined Chiefs of Staff, in their 138th Meeting, resolved this subject and their conclusions are contained in C.C.S. 426/1.

C.C.S. 427   5 December 1943

COMBINED CHIEFS OF STAFF

AMPHIBIOUS OPERATIONS IN SOUTHEAST ASIA

ALTERNATIVE TO "BUCCANEER"

Report by the Combined Staff Planners

Pursuant to C.C.S. 136th Meeting, Item 1, the Combined Staff Planners enclose their report on the subject for the consideration of the Combined Chiefs of Staff.

E N C L O S U R E

AMPHIBIOUS OPERATIONS IN SOUTHEAST ASIA

ALTERNATIVE TO "BUCCANEER"

Draft Report by Combined Staff Planners

PROBLEM

1. On the assumption that the amphibious lift available for *BUCCANEER* is reduced in certain respects, to consider what minor amphibious operations or raids might be carried out in the Southeast Asia Theater, in order to harass Japanese communication, destroy Japanese installations and equipment, or alternatively to support the land advance on the Arakan coast and obtain airfields with which to support further operations in Burma.

RESOURCES AVAILABLE

2. An appendix is attached showing a list of the resources which we assume will be left in Southeast Asia. This list is based on the assumption that the bulk

of LST and LSI (L) will be withdrawn together with a proportion of the naval forces and escort carriers now allotted to *BUCCANNER*, as these are the resources which are chiefly required in the European Theater.

3. With resources remaining in the Southeast Asia Theater it would be possible to land a force of one infantry battalion group up to one brigade group, depending on the scale of transport to be landed.

POSSIBLE OPERATIONS

4. Detailed study by the Force Commanders of intelligence maps and photographs is necessary before any definite opinion can be formed as to the practicability of any operations.

5. From a general survey of the possibilities however we consider that the following merit examination and might assist Operation *TARZAN:*

a. Amphibious operations along the Arakan coast in conjunction with the land advance of the 15th Army Group on Indin-Rathedaung-Kyauktau, which is timed to start in mid-January and be completed in February.

b. An amphibious operation to capture and secure the northern tip of Ramree Island, prior to the beginning of the 1944 monsoon. This operation might be covered by shore-based aircraft at Maungdaw. Maintenance of a garrison in this area by sea might prove costly as convoys will be subject to air attack. It might be possible to extend air operations against Japanese communications in Burma, and to infiltrate on the Taungup-Sandaway coast. The provision of fighter support to any such operations would have to be carefully balanced against the requirements of *TARZAN*.

6. Unless a target can be found to justify the landing of a raiding force, we do not believe that any raids should be attempted other than carrier-borne air raids.

APPENDIX

AMPHIBIOUS OPERATIONS IN SOUTHEAST ASIA
ON A REDUCED SCALE

Forces to remain in *Southeast Asia*	*Forces released for* *European Theater*
a. *Land and Shore Based Air Forces*	
As available for *BUCCANEER*	Nil
b. *Naval Forces*	
2 Old Battleships	4 CVE
1 Battle Cruiser	
2 CV	
5 CVE (3 assault)	
Destroyers)	A number of Destroyers
Cruisers) As required	Cruisers
Escorts)	Escorts
c. *Assault Shipping and Landing Craft*	
3 to 6 LSI (L) with Landing Craft	3 to 6 LSI (L) with Landing
1 Brigade HQ Ship or HQ Ship	Craft
3 LST (1)	15 LST (2)
2 LSD	1 HQ Ship or Brigade HQ Ship
1 LSC	
15 LCT (5)	
12 LCI (L)	
3 LSP if required	
120 LCM	
101 LCP	

Appendix

C.C.S. 427/1   6 December 1943

COMBINED CHIEFS OF STAFF

AMPHIBIOUS OPERATIONS IN SOUTHEAST ASIA
ALTERNATIVE TO "BUCCANEER"

Reference:

CCS 136th Meeting, Item 1

Note by the Secretaries

The attached message has been received from the Supreme Allied Commander, Southeast Asia Command in reply to the message sent to him on 5 December 1943 (Annex to C.C.S. 136th Meeting Minutes) .

H. REDMAN,

F. B. ROYAL,

Combined Secretariat.

ENCLOSURE

SEACOS 38   90211 SEACOS.   6th December, 1943

Following for COS from Mountbatten

1. Your 051430 Dec. para 2 we have examined proposal very carefully and consider that no small amphibious operation can be carried out for the following reasons:

    a. In view of enemy's powers of concentration our seaborne air requirements will be the same whether the operation is large or small.

    b. BUCCANEER was selected as objective for amphibious operation because it was the only worth while operation which could be carried out with the forces allotted.

    c. There is no other objective which could be seized and held with the landing craft and assault shipping likely to be available under your para 1.

2. I am totally opposed to landing troops and withdrawing them since the psychological effect of such withdrawal is considerable and in this theater I regard this aspect as of the greatest importance.

3. Possibility remains of hit and run operations by carriers with a view to containing enemy air and possibly surface forces. This may reduce pressure on the SW Pacific and is being examined. Least force which would be necessary for operation of this type is Fleet carriers 2, Unicorn 1, Escorts 3.

4. The utility of extending inshore operations on the Arakan coast is being examined but they cannot be represented as amphibious operations or be considered to be of great significance. Such operations in order to be in any degree effective would require 12 LCI(L), 15 LCT(5), 6 LCS(M), 3 LCA Flotillas, 2 LCM Flotillas, 1 LCP Flotilla. Some of these forces might however be more profitably employed in some other theater other than SEAC.

5. Cancellation of *BUCCANEER* must inevitably lead to collapse of *TARZAN* since Generalissimo has only agreed to reduction in "hump" tonnage and cooperation on Yunnan force if amphibious operation is staged at the same time. I have carried out a rapid examination of what could be done in the light of these circumstances and assuming that we could get the additional 25 first line transport aircraft promised by General Arnold in China a rough forecast is as follows:

a. That *TARZAN* in its original form will not be possible. In particular there will not be enough transport aircraft to fly in the 60th Parachute Brigade and the 26th Infantry Division to Indaw or to maintain them by air.

b. It will still be possible to employ all the LRPG's but in conjunction with

c. An advance by 4th Corps down the Kabaw Valley and through the Chin Hills on to the Kalemyo Kalawa area.

d. The Arakan operations would remain as in *TARZAN*.

e. The Ledo force would still be available to advance if the Generalissimo gave permission and they prove capable of doing so.

7. It is realized that this new operation the code word for which is given in my immediately following telegram will not enable me to achieve the *QUADRANT* Directive of opening up the land route to China but it has certain merits.

a. It enables the LRPG's to operate thus confusing the Japanese and helping to inflict casualties.

b. It will still produce a considerable amount of air fighting.

c. The capture of the Kalemyo Kalewa area will give us a starting point from which to begin land operations against Mandalay.

d. It does not repeat not necessarily commit us to further operations in the center of Burma.

8. The original plan was based on the high fighting qualities believed to be possessed by the Ledo Force. If, however, they fail to advance in accordance with the general program the fly in to Indaw would have to be cancelled even after the starting of *TARZAN* so as to avoid leaving the 26th Division entirely isolated in Central Burma.

C.C.S. 428 (Revised)

RELATION OF AVAILABLE RESOURCES TO AGREED OPERATIONS

References:

CCS 136th Meeting, Item 3

CCS 137th Meeting, Item 8

CCS 138th Meeting, Item 5

C.C.S. 428 circulated an interim report prepared by the Combined Administrative Committee and shipping and logistics experts 7 December 1943. The Combined Chiefs of Staff, in their 138th Meeting amended and accepted C.C.S. 428 in principle (amended report subsequently circulated as C.C.S. 428 (Revised)).

C.C.S. 428 (Revised)   15 December 1943

COMBINED CHIEFS OF STAFF

RELATION OF AVAILABLE RESOURCES TO AGREED OPERATIONS

Note by the Secretaries

The enclosed report relating available resources to agreed operations has been prepared by the Combined Administrative Committee and shipping and logistics experts, and is circulated for consideration by the Combined Chiefs of Staff.

H. REDMAN,

F. B. ROYAL,

Combined Secretariat.

ENCLOSURE

IMPLEMENTATIONS OF ASSUMED BASIC UNDERTAKINGS AND SPECIFIC OPERATIONS FOR THE CONDUCT OF THE WAR 1943-1944

AVAILABILITY OF RESOURCES TO MEET THE REQUIREMENTS OF CRITICAL STRATEGY

Report by the Combined Administrative Committee

THE PROBLEM

1. To examine the available means of the United Nations with the object of assessing our ability to carry out the operations and undertakings indicated in C.C.S. 426/1.

FACTS BEARING ON THE PROBLEM

2. The basis of investigation is given in Annex I.

3. We would emphasize that the purpose of this investigation is to examine whether the operations decided on at *SEXTANT* are within our resources, and not to imply binding commitments or decisions on the part of the Combined Chiefs of Staff.

4. Military operations shall take precedence over civil relief and rehabilitation of occupied territories.

5. The employment of Dominion forces will be a matter of discussion between governments concerned.

CONCLUSIONS

6. *GROUND FORCES* (Annex II)

The necessary ground forces for approved operations can be made available. Certain types of service units may be a critical factor but in no case should preclude the operations.

7. *NAVAL FORCES* (Annex III)

So far as can be foreseen, British and United States naval forces adequate to accomplish all approved operations for 1944 will be available. The situation will be tight particularly as to destroyers, escorts and escort carriers in the early part of the year but should be considerably eased by new construction as the year progresses. The defeat of Germany will make available an increase in naval forces for the prosecution of the war in the Pacific.

8. *AIR FORCES* (Annex IV)

The air resources to meet the operations specified in Annex I will be available with the following exceptions:

a. A deficiency in troop carrier squadrons in the Mediterranean if the detailed plan to be made for *ANVIL* requires more than a one brigade lift.

b. A possible deficiency of land-based aircraft for certain operations in the Pacific if the war with Germany is not concluded in time to release the additional resources required.

c. A possible deficiency of aircraft for the approved lift into China if diversions are made to supply forces operating in North Burma.

Such support can be given to the resistance groups in Europe as will not interfere with the intensification of the bomber offensive.

9. *ASSAULT SHIPPING AND LANDING CRAFT* (Annex V)

Production of combat loaders, LST's and LCT's still continues to be the bottleneck limiting the scope of operations against the enemy and our ability to carry out operations will continue to be limited by this fact. In 1944 there should be sufficient landing craft available to carry out approved operations.

The shortage of landing craft impels the earliest practicable release of assault shipping and craft after assaults to permit proper maintenance of material, rest for personnel and reorientation to other assignments.

10. *SUPPLY OF CRITICAL ITEMS* (Annex VI)

In the absence of detailed plans for certain of the approved operations it is impossible to determine exact requirements for supplies and equipment. Certain shortages will exist as indicated in Annex VI. In no case, however, is it considered that shortages will be so serious as to preclude the mounting of approved operations.

11. *SHIPPING* (Annex VII)

Examination of personnel and cargo shipping position indicates our ability to support approved naval and military operations. In addition it will be noted that provision has been made to execute Operation *HERCULES* in spring 1944. In the event that this operation is not undertaken, this shipping can be made available for approved operations. While the statement of the shipping position covering the first nine months of 1944 does not include presently indefinable demands or relief requirements except for Italy, there is now no reason to expect any interference with approved military and naval operations. This applies both to personnel shipping as well as to dry cargo resources.

12. *OIL* (Annex VIII)

An examination of the oil position has revealed that the most critical petroleum products are 100 octane aviation gasoline and 80 octane motor gasoline. The situation with respect to 100 octane gasoline continues to improve and the gap between production and consumption will be closed during February 1944. It is believed that the indicated shortage of 80 octane motor gasoline will be avoided by using gasolines with lower octane numbers and will be further reduced by continued acceleration of the aviation gasoline plant building program.

In all theaters there continues to exist a shortage of small tankers or small ships suitable for use as such. There appear to be sufficient large ocean-going tankers in existence and coming from new construction to meet requirements for bulk movements of petroleum products.

ANNEX I

BASIS OF INVESTIGATION

Reference: CCS 426.

The following operations and undertakings have been used as a basis for this investigation. They are not arranged in order of priority.

I—BASIC UNDERTAKINGS

1. The following list of our basic undertakings, selected from Section III of the Final Report to the President and Prime Minister (C.C.S. 426/1) in-volves *continuing commitments which must be regarded as a first charge upon our resources:*—

a. Maintain the security and war-making capacity of the Western Hemisphere and the British Isles.

b. Support the war-making capacity of our forces in all areas.

c. Maintain vital overseas lines of communication with particular emphasis on the defeat of the U-boat menace.

d. Continue the disruption of Axis sea communications.

e. Intensify the air offensive against the Axis Powers in Europe.

f. Concentrate maximum resources in a selected area as early as practicable for the purpose of conducting a decisive invasion of the Axis citadel.

g. Undertake such measures as may be necessary and practicable to aid the war effort of Russia.

h. Undertake such measures as may be necessary and practicable in order to aid the war effort of China as an effective Ally and as a base for operations against Japan.

i. Undertake such action to exploit the entry of Turkey into the war as is considered most likely to facilitate or accelerate the attainment of the over-all objectives.

j. Continue assistance to the French and Italian forces to enable them to fulfill an active role in the war against the Axis Powers.

Annex I

k. Prepare to reorient forces from the European Theater to the Pacific and Far East as soon as the German situation allows.

II—OTHER UNDERTAKINGS

l. Provide for the maintenance of prisoners of war.

m. Provide for the economic support of countries occupied by the United Nations.

III—THE DEFEAT OF THE AXIS IN EUROPE

2. *The Combined Bomber Offensive* from all convenient bases. This operation continues to have the highest strategic priority.

3. *OVERLORD and ANVIL. OVERLORD* and *ANVIL* are the supreme operations for 1944. They must be carried out during May, 1944 and for planning purposes D-day will be assumed to be the same for both operations. Nothing must be undertaken in any other part of the world which hazards the success of these two operations.

a. OVERLORD as at present planned is on a narrow margin. Everything practicable should be done to increase its strength. The approved plan allows for the employment of the following:—

Assault   5 divisions (simultaneously loaded in landing craft)
       2 divisions—follow-up
       2 airborne divisions

Subsequent Build-up — At least 20 divisions.

Total   — At least 29 divisions.

Thereafter, an additional build-up of 4 divisions a month.

b. ANVIL. The object of this operation is to establish a bridgehead on the south coast of France and to exploit in support of *OVERLORD.* There is no approved plan, but resources should allow for an assault of at least two divisions plus such additional lift as can be released from resources now allotted to Southeast Asia, building up to ten divisions.

Annex I

4. *Operations in Italy.* In Italy the advance will be continued to the Pisa-Rimini line. Thereafter such pressure as is consistent with the provision of the necessary resources for *ANVIL.* 68 LST's due by *QUADRANT* agreement for return to the U.K. may be retained in the Mediterranean until 15 January 1944.

5. *Use of the Azores Islands.* Facilities in the Azores available to the British are extended to the United States.

6. *Resistance Groups in Europe.* Continue the support of resistance groups in Europe, in particular the Partisans in Yugoslavia who will be supported by supplies and equipment to the greatest practicable extent and also by commando and air operations.

7. *Turkey and the Aegean.* Efforts will continue to bring Turkey into the war with a view to bringing about the collapse of Bulgaria and opening a short sea route to Russia. Commitments will be limited.

   a. The minimum air and anti-air assistance for protection of Turkish main cities, communications and industries (paragraph 6, C.C.S. 418/1).

   b. Operations in the Aegean, including in particular the capture of Rhodes, are desirable, provided that they can be fitted in without detriment to *OVERLORD* and *ANVIL.*

IV — THE WAR AGAINST JAPAN

8. *Operations in the Pacific*

   a. Northern Pacific. Plans for the North Pacific involve the augmentation of base facilities and defensive installations in the Aleutians in preparation for entry into the Kuriles and Soviet territory in the event of Russian collaboration. Naval surface and submarine action, including raids on the Japanese fishing fleet will be carried out. Preparations will be made for executing very long range strategic bombing against the Kuriles and Northern Japan.

   b. Central, South and Southwest Pacific. Operations will be conducted as follows:

Annex I

Target Dates	Central Pacific	Southwest Pacific
1-31 January 1944	Seizure of the Marshalls, including Eniwetok and Kusaie	Complete the seizure of Western New Britain; continue neutralization of Rabaul
1 February 1944		Seizure of Hansa Bay area.
20 March 1944		Capture of Kavieng
20 April 1944		Seizure of Manus
1 May 1944	Seizure of Ponape	
1 June 1944		Seizure of Hollandia (Humboldt Bay)
20 July 1944	Seizure of Eastern Carolines (Truk area)	Initiate V.L.R. bombing of vital targets in the Netherlands East Indies
15 August 1944		Advance to westward along north coast of New Guinea to include Vogelkop
1 October 1944	Seizure of Guam and Japanese Marianas	
31 December 1944	Initiate V.L.R. bombing of vital targets in Japanese "Inner Zone" from bases in the Marianas	

c. *British Naval Forces.* Such preparations as are necessary at this time will be made for British Naval Forces to move to the Southwest Pacific as envisaged in C.C.S. 417.

9. *Operations in China.* Efforts in the China area should have as their objective the intensification of land and air operations in and from China and the build-up of the U.S.A.A.F. and the Chinese Army and Air Forces in accordance with the approved program. Operation *MATTERHORN* has been approved (C.C.S. 397, Appendix, and C.C.S. 401/2). Target date 15 May 1944.

10. *Operations in Southeast Asia.* Preparations for Operation *TARZAN* should be continued until a decision on this operation has been reached by the

Annex I

Combined Chiefs of Staff. Target date, March 1944. Similarly, preparations should continue for minor amphibious operations or raids to harass Japanese communications, destroy Japanese installations and equipment, or alternatively to support the land advance on the Arakan coast.

11. *Preparation of India as a base.* Preparation of the bases in India required for approved operations in the Southeast Asia and China Theaters should continue in consonance with the provisions of paragraphs 4, 5 and 6 of C.C.S. 417.

Annex I

ANNEX II

LAND FORCES

SECTION I — UNITED KINGDOM

FORCES AVAILABLE

1. The forces available in the United Kingdom on 1 May 1944, will be as follows:

British	U.S.	Total
15-2/3 divisions	14 ex U.S.	36-2/3 divisions
2 airborne divisions	3 divisions ex Mediterranean	
	2 airborne divisions (one from U.S. and one from Mediterranean)	

2. Of the above, five American divisions which will be in the U.K. or en route will not be operationally available on 1 May 1944. These five American divisions will, however, be operationally available two months from their date of arrival and can, therefore, be used in the build-up subsequent to the initial assault. During May, June and July, 1944, reception and dispatch of facilities in the United Kingdom will limit the build-up to two, one and one divisions respectively making a total number of American divisions in the United Kingdom and on the Continent approximately 23 by August 1944. Thereafter, it is assumed that direct dispatch from the United States to the lodgment area may be begun at the rate of four divisions per month.

FORCES OPERATIONALLY AVAILABLE ON 1 MAY 1944

3. The total forces which will therefore be operationally available on 1 May 1944, are as follows:

British (incl. Canadians)	American	Airborne	Total
15-2/3 divisions	12 divisions	4 divisions (2 British and 2 American)	31-2/3 divisions

In addition to the above, 28 American divisions will be available for the subsequent build-up which should continue at the rate, if practicable, of four divisions per month starting about August 1944, through ports made available on the Continent.

SECTION II — MEDITERRANEAN

FORCES AVAILABLE

4. There will be the following forces available in the Mediterranean on 1 January 1944:

British	U.S.	French (native)	Total
19 divisions (including 2 Polish)	7 divisions	7 divisions	33 divisions

Of the above, three British divisions will be required for internal security commitments in Cyrenaica, Palestine, Syria and Cyprus. The garrison commitments in North Africa can be filled until May by U.S. and French divisions in training for *ANVIL*.

5. The balance on 1 January 1944, will be as follows:

British	U.S.	French (native)	Total
16 divisions (including 2 Polish)	7 divisions	7* divisions	30 divisions

6. After 1 January 1944, 4 further French (native) divisions may become available making a total of 11 divisions by June 1944. Of this total of 11 divisions, 3 may be broken up to find service troops for the French (native) forces in which event the total divisions in the Mediterranean available for operations would amount to 31.

7. The British divisions shown as available in paragraph 4 above, are exclusive of some 12 independent brigades** which are the equivalent of 4 divisions but have no supporting troops. These brigades will be available to assist both in the internal security commitments shown in paragraph 4 above and, to a limited extent, in operations.

---

* 3 of these are not yet adequately trained for offensive operations but should be ready for *ANVIL*.

** Includes one airborne brigade.

Annex II

OPERATIONS AGAINST THE SOUTH OF FRANCE

8. In the absence of a plan for *ANVIL* we have assumed that 10 divisions will be required for this operation. Of the total of 31 divisions (which includes 8 French) in the Mediterranean we estimate that 15 may be required to hold the Pisa-Rimini line. Providing that this line is reached in time to allow the necessary regrouping and reorganization of forces for *ANVIL,* we consider that sufficient divisions should be available within the Mediterranean. It appears, however, that adequate service troops are not now available in the theater. No British service troops will be available from outside the Mediterranean. The full requirements in service troops will therefore have to be found from within the resources now at the disposal of the Allied Commander in Chief, supplemented in so far as possible by service units from the United States.

TURKEY AND THE AEGEAN

9. If Turkey enters the war on the side of the Allies and our commitments are limited to:

a. The minimum air and anti-air assistance for protection of Turkish main cities, communications and industries; and

b. Operations in the Aegean including in particular the capture of Rhodes;

then the forces required can be found from the total resources in the Mediterranean Theater. The requirement in service troops is numerically small but would inevitably have to be furnished at the expense of other Mediterranean operations.

SECTION III — THE AZORES

10. No significant land forces are required.

SECTION IV

THE WAR AGAINST JAPAN

11. *OPERATIONS IN THE PACIFIC*

a. NORTHERN PACIFIC

American Forces now present in Alaska are adequate to effect the augmentation of base facilities and defensive installations.

Annex II

b. CENTRAL, SOUTH AND SOUTHWEST PACIFIC

(1) Resources Available

The following major Allied ground forces are present in, or projected for, the area as of 1 January 1944:

Central Pacific	1 Marine Infantry Division
	5 Infantry Divisions
South Pacific	2 Marine Infantry Divisions
	4 Infantry Divisions
	1 New Zealand Division
Southwest Pacific	1 Marine Infantry Division
	3 Infantry Divisions
	1 Cavalry Division (dismounted)
	11 Australian Divisions.

NOTE: Three Australian Infantry Divisions (6th, 7th and 9th) are available for offensive operations. There are also six Australian Infantry Divisions and two Australian Armored Divisions (militia) presently assigned for defense.

(2) Requirements for Contemplated Operations and Available From U.S. Resources*

	Required in addition to allocations above
Central Pacific	3 Infantry Divisions
Southwest Pacific	1 Infantry Division
South Pacific	4 Infantry Divisions
	1 Airborne Division

12. OPERATIONS IN CHINA

American Forces now present in and projected for the China area are adequate to implement the approved operations.

---

* Operation in contiguous areas, and movements through the Central Pacific as a staging area, may alter the subtotals but will not change the over-all requirements and availability indicated.

Annex II

13. *OPERATIONS IN S.E. ASIA*

    a. REQUIRED FOR OPERATION "TARZAN"

British	Chinese
6-2/3 British/Indian divisions	13 divisions
7 Long range penetration brigades (of which one is American)	
1 Parachute brigade	

The forces required can be made available from British resources now in India. The Chinese forces available amount to 22 divisions (assuming 10,000 to a division) which will allow of a reserve of nine divisions.

    b. MINOR AMPHIBIOUS OPERATIONS OR RAIDS

(1) The necessary forces can be found from those available in India.

(2) At present the forces which India will receive in addition to those at present available in India, are 82nd West African Division and two East African Brigades, total 1-2/3 equivalent divisions. These additional resources will be inadequate for post-monsoon operations in Northern Burma when assessed against the Supreme Allied Commander's additional requirements.

14. *PREPARATION OF INDIA AS A BASE*

Forces present in and projected for India are adequate to prepare those bases required for approved operations in Southeast Asia and China.

ANNEX III

NAVAL FORCES

1. The British intend to provide the forces for *OVERLORD* by:

a. Using Fleet destroyers from the Home Fleet not required for the Atlantic covering force, as escorts.

b. Using eight Fleet destroyers at present allocated to the Eastern Fleet as escorts.

c. Withdrawing one Monitor and two Fighter Direction ships from the Eastern Fleet.

d. Withdrawing nearly all escorts from the Atlantic and Home Commands. The U-boat threat is steadily diminishing but a possible increase in shipping losses may have to be accepted.

e. Possibly requesting some assistance from U.S. forces.

2. The British can provide the forces estimated as required for *ANVIL* at the expense of the Eastern Fleet to the scale of:

> 1 — 6" cruiser
> 3 — 5.25" cruisers
> 37 — escorts
> 2 — A/A ships
> 3 — CVE Assault
> 1 — CVE spare hull without aircraft.

NOTE: If carrier-borne fighter support is required on the scale estimated, about seven British escort carriers will have to be withdrawn from the Atlantic and equipped with R.A.F. fighters from the *OVERLORD* Tactical Air Force reserve.

3. Present and prospective availability of combatant U.S. Naval Forces, including Naval Air, will meet the requirements of scheduled operations in the Pacific. The tempo of these operations can be stepped up by the addition of British Forces, shown below, to those U.S. Forces available in the South and Southwest Pacific. The situation concerning destroyer and carrier types will

Annex III

be close, however, and forces less than those stated as required by area commanders must be accepted for certain operations in early 1944. Any diversion of these types for operations in other areas will further aggravate a situation where stated requirements are not now being met.

4. After meeting the commitments for *OVERLORD* and *ANVIL* the Eastern Fleet will be reduced to about:

> 3 — OBB
> 2 — CV
> 3 — 8" cruisers
> 2 — 6" cruisers
> 20 — Fleet destroyers
> 70 — Escorts
> 3 — CVE Assault
> 2 — CVE A/S
> 8 — old cruisers for station duties until paid off.

5. After operations in the Indian Ocean area in 1943-44, the Eastern Fleet will probably be divided as follows:

Indian Ocean	*Pacific*
2 — OBB	1 — OBB (RENOWN)
3 — 8" cruisers	2 — CV
8 — Fleet destroyers	2 — 6" cruisers
60 — escorts	12 — Fleet destroyers
(Reinforced very shortly by 1 CV	10 — escorts (frigates)
and 3 CVE (see paragraph 6 below))	3 — CVE (assault)
	2 — CVE A/S

6. The Eastern Fleet will be further reinforced during the second half of 1944 as follows:

> 2 — BB
> 3 — CV   )
> 5 — CVE) It will probably be impossible to man a
> 2 — CVL) number of these until Germany is defeated.

Annex III

As soon as the *OVERLORD* and *ANVIL* assaults are completed the following ships will also reinforce the Eastern Fleet:

> 3 — 6" cruisers
> 3 — 5.25" cruisers
> 12 — Fleet destroyers
> At least 40 to 50 — Escorts
> 2 — A/A ships
> 2 — FD ships
> 8 — CVE

7. Thus by the end of 1944 the Eastern Fleet might be divided between the Indian Ocean and the Pacific as follows:

Indian Ocean	*Pacific*
2 — OBB	2 — BB (RENOWN in U.K. for
1 — CV	modernization)
4 — CVE	4 — CV
3 — 8" cruisers	2 — CVL
8 — Fleet destroyers	14 — CVE
60 — escorts	5 — 6" cruisers
2 — A/A ships	3 — 5.25" cruisers
	24 — Fleet destroyers
	At least 50 to 60 — Escorts
	2 — FD ships

8. All the build-up of the Eastern Fleet referred to in paragraphs 5-7 above is dependent on the provision of the necessary fleet auxiliaries and base facilities.

ANNEX IV

AIR FORCES

1. The following appendices show the resources available for the various operations:

Appendix "A" — Combined Bomber Offensive from United Kingdom and cross-Channel Operation *OVERLORD*.

Appendix "B" — Operations from the Mediterranean.

Appendix "C" — Operations in the Pacific.

Appendix "D" — Air operations in and from China.

Appendix "E" — Operations in Southeast Asia.

Appendix "F" — Support of Resistance Groups in Europe and the Balkans.

2. Aircraft strength in this Annex is stated in terms of unit equipment (U.E.). Reserve aircraft are not included in the strength data.

APPENDIX "A"

COMBINED BOMBER OFFENSIVE FROM UNITED KINGDOM

AND CROSS-CHANNEL OPERATION "OVERLORD"

1. It is estimated that the following aircraft will be available in the United Kingdom by 1 May 1944.

	U.S.A.A.F.		*R.A.F.*	
	Groups	*Aircraft U.E.*	*Squadrons*	*Aircraft U.E.*
Heavy Bombers	40	1400-1920*	80	1600
Medium and Light Bombers	11	627	17	306
S.E./T.E. Fighters	35	2625	90	1630
Night Fighters	3/4	36	22	396
Torpedo Fighters	—	—	5	100
Reconnaissance	3	168	15	264
G.R. (Patrol Bomber)	—	—	29	415
Transport and Troop Carrier	13½	702	15	330
Air/Sea Rescue	—	—	8	210
TOTAL	103¼	5558	281	5251

NOTE: U.S.A.A.F. fighter groups include 3 fighter groups transferred from North Africa.

* These groups will be increased from a U.E. of 35 aircraft to a U.E. of 48 aircraft per group as rapidly as the present policy of providing two crews per aircraft will permit.

2. *Combined Bomber Offensive*

   a. Of the above U.S. forces, 40 heavy bomber groups and 15 fighter groups, one reconnaissance group and half a transport group are provided for the combined bomber offensive.

Appendix "A" to Annex IV

b. Of the above R.A.F. forces 80 heavy bomber squadrons and such fighter squadrons as can be spared from the tactical air forces and the defense of the U.K. and Northern Ireland will be available for the support of the combined bomber offensive.

c. The 15th U.S. Strategic Air Force and R.A.F. heavy bomber squadrons in the Mediterranean will be employed primarily on the combined bomber offensive. These forces will also be available for the support of land operations on the mainland of Italy and for *ANVIL*.

3. *Build-up for the Combined Bomber Offensive—Estimated Heavy Bomber Strength in Aircraft U.E.*

United Kingdom Bases	December	February	April
United States	980	1120	1400
British	1240	1420	1600
Mediterranean Bases			
United States	446	656	735
British	32	32	48
TOTAL	2698	3228	3783

NOTE: The above totals exclude medium and fighter bombers since these are not employed in the bomber offensive deep into Germany.

4. *Conclusion on Availability of Air Forces*

There will be sufficient forces available for *OVERLORD* and the intensification of the Combined Bomber Offensive as planned.

The deficiencies of transport aircraft for *OVERLORD* previously estimated at *QUADRANT* have been overcome and the requirement for 1,004 transport aircraft for this operation will be met.

Appendix "A" to Annex IV

APPENDIX "B"

OPERATIONS FROM THE MEDITERRANEAN

1. It is estimated the following air forces will be available in the Mediterranean area by 1 May 1944:

	U.S.A.A.F.		R.A.F.	
	Groups	Aircraft U.E.	Squadrons	Aircraft U.E.
Heavy Bombers	21	735	3	48
Medium and Light Bombers	7	399	14	248
S.E. and T.E. Fighters	10	750	51	816
Night Fighters	1	48	7	112
Torpedo Fighters	—	—	2	32
Reconnaissance	3	171	8	104
G.R. (Patrol Bomber)	—	—	16	256
Transport and Troop Carrier	3	156	4	100
Air/Sea Rescue	—	—	4	52
TOTAL	45	2259	109	1768

NOTE: The above figures make allowance for the transfer from the Mediterranean of three fighter groups to the U.K., two fighter groups to China, and one medium bomber group to Southeast Asia.

CONCLUSION ON AVAILABILITY OF AIR FORCES

2. The forces in the Mediterranean will be sufficient:

a. To support the Combined Bomber Offensive.

b. To support the land advance to the Pisa-Rimini line.

c. To provide the minimum defenses for Turkey if necessary and if so decided to support an amphibious operation for the capture of Rhodes except for the diversion of heavy bombers which this would demand.

Appendix "B" to Annex IV

3. When the Pisa-Rimini line has been secured, air forces in the Mediterranean will be sufficient for Operation *ANVIL* subject to the following qualifications:

    a. The troop carrier resources in the Mediterranean will only be sufficient to lift one brigade, and if the detailed plan for the assault on Southern France requires a second brigade lift, this will have to be provided from the United States. Sufficient individual aircraft and crews can be provided from this source but they would have to be superimposed on existing units and could not arrive in time to be fully trained.

    b. That if the assault for *ANVIL* takes place beyond the range of land-based, short range fighters, escort carriers with fighters will have to be provided.

APPENDIX "C"

AIR OPERATIONS IN THE PACIFIC

1. *South and Southwest Pacific*

   a. Operations:

   (1) Complete the seizure of Western New Britain; continue neutralization of Rabaul 1-31 January 1944.

   (2) Seizure of Hansa Bay area, capture of Kavieng and seizure of Manus 1 February 1944 to 20 April 1944.

   (3) Seizure of Hollandia (Humboldt Bay) 1 June 1944.

   (4) Advance to westward along north coast of New Guinea to include Vogelkop starting 15 August 1944.

   b. There is no approved plan for these operations stating aircraft requirements .The theater commander has submitted a plan entitled *RENO III* which has not yet been approved. Aircraft requirements stated in *RENO III* are:

H/B	M/B	L/D/B	F	F(N)	T/C	Photo Recon	TOTAL
240	640	736	1650	60	272	256	3854
384	576	564	1850	72	396	352	4194
480	800	800	1850	72	492	352	4846

   c. It is estimated that aircraft will be available in the theater as follows:

1 January 1944 & 1 February 1944	H/B	M & L/B	F & F/B	F(N)	Recon	T/C	TOTAL
AAF	248	342	675	36	171	273	1745
NAVY		288	216	12	306	48	870
RAAF	0	159	361	0	215	57	792
*NZAF							
TOTAL	248	789	1252	48	692	378	3407

   *Note: Some of these aircraft are obsolescent types. Figures shown are those as of 31 December 1943. Build-up during 1944 not known at this time.

Appendix "C" to Annex IV

1 June 1944	H/B	M & L/B	F & F/B	F(N)	Recon	T/C	TOTAL
AAF	248	342	675	36	171	273	1745
NAVY		288	216	12	306	36	858
RAAF							
*NZAF	0	159	361	0	215	57	792
TOTAL	248	789	1252	48	692	366	3395

15 August 1944							
AAF	248	384	900	36	192	273	2033
NAVY		288	216	12	306	30	852
RAAF							
*NZAF	0	159	361	0	215	57	792
TOTAL	248	831	1477	48	713	360	3677

*NOTE: Some of these aircraft are obsolescent types. Figures shown are those as of 31 December 1943. Build-up during 1944 not known at this time.

   d. Air resources available for these operations exceed the requirements estimated at *QUADRANT* (C.C.S. 329/2) except for a shortage in heavy bombardment and a slight shortage in night fighters for operation 1 *a* (4) unless the war in Europe is over in sufficient time to permit redeployment of European forces. Air resources available will be less than requested by the theater commander in *RENO III*.

2. *Central Pacific*

   a. *Operations:*

   (1) Seizure of the Marshalls, including Eniwetok and Kusaie 1-31 January 1944.

   (2) Seizure of Ponape 1 May 1944.

   (3) Seizure of Eastern Carolines (Truk area) 20 July 1944.

   (4) Seizure of Guam and Japanese Marianas 1 October 1944.

Appendix "C" to Annex IV

b. There is no approved plan for these operations stating aircraft requirements. The Joint War Plans Committee has prepared a tentative plan which indicates the following requirements:

	H/B	M/B	L/D/B	F	T/C	Photo Recon	TOTAL
2 *a* (1)	118	93	198	444	49	34	931
2 *a* (2)	142	177	252	570	74	52	1267
2 *a* (3)	252	232	404	896	74	100	1958
2 *a* (4)	276	268	666	1268	86	118	2682

c. With present allocations it is estimated that aircraft will be available in the theater as follows:

1 January 1944	H/B	M & L/B	F & F/B	F(N)	Recon	T/C	TOTAL
AAF	70	57	175	12	28	28	370
*NAVY		234	270	12	192	36	744
TOTAL	70	291	445	24	220	64	1114

1 May 1944							
AAF	70	57	175	12	28	28	370
*NAVY		372	360	48	312	48	1140
TOTAL	70	429	535	60	340	76	1510

1 July 1944							
AAF	105	64	200	12	28	28	437
*NAVY		582	612	72	396	48	1710
TOTAL	105	646	812	84	424	76	2147

1 October 1944							
AAF	105	64	200	12	28	28	437
*NAVY		870	936	120	438	60	2424
TOTAL	105	934	1136	132	466	88	2861

*NOTE: These figures include garrison forces of islands in the Central and South Pacific areas.

Appendix "C" to Annex IV

d. Land based aircraft will be available for these operations assuming that excess patrol bombers make up the deficiency in heavy bombers. (See naval Annex for carrier borne aircraft.)

3. *V.L.R. Bombing*

a. B-29 groups in addition to those provided for *MATTERHORN* will become available for movement to theaters as follows:

October 1944	3 Groups
November 1944	2 Groups
December 1944	3 Groups.

b. Therefore, three groups in November and two groups in December can be deployed and ready to commence bombing in either the Southwest or Central Pacific areas, depending upon availability of suitable facilities.

c. To provide the necessary troops for V.L.R. bombing an increase is required in the troop allotment to the A.A.F. for the supporting service units, including construction troops, for the first four groups and for all personnel for subsequent groups.

APPENDIX "D"

AIR OPERATIONS IN AND FROM CHINA

1. It is estimated that the strength of the 14th U.S.A.A.F. in China as of February 1944 will be as follows:

Heavy Bombers	1 Group	(35)
Medium Bombers	1 Group	(57)
Fighter and Fighter Bombers	4 Groups	(300)
Reconnaissance	1/2 Group	(28)

Included in the above table are two high altitude fighter groups to be transferred from North Africa.

2. It will be possible to initiate V.L.R. bombing from China in accordance with the time schedule, provided the required shipping is made available and assuming that the necessary air bases and facilities are provided in accordance with existing directives, C.C.S. 401 and 401/1. For this purpose B-29 groups will become available as follows:

April 1944	4 Groups	(112)
August 1944	2 Groups	(56)
September 1944	2 Groups	(56)

3. In addition to the above American Forces, it is expected that Chinese Air Forces will attain during the first quarter of 1944 the following strength:

Chinese Air Forces		*Composite Wing*	
1 H.B. Group	(30)	8 Fighter Squadrons	(96)
1 M.B. Group	(48)	4 M.B. Squadrons	(48)
2 Fighter Groups	(96)		
1 Recon Squadron	(15)		
1 Transport "	(9)		

4. On the assumption:

   a. That *TARZAN* takes place;

Appendix "D" to Annex IV

 b. That an additional 35 C-47's are available in the theater by 1 February 1944;

sufficient aircraft will be available to deliver the following tonnage over the "hump":

December 1943	8,858 tons
January 1944	9,535 tons
February 1944	11,066 tons
March 1944	5,614 tons
April 1944	6,716 tons
May 1944	9,686 tons

and in addition to provide the Supreme Allied Commander, Southeast Asia, with the following U.S. transport aircraft:

15 Dec. to 31 Jan.	18 C-47's or	12 C-46's
1 Feb. to 28 Feb.	11 C-47's or	8 C-46's
1 Mar. to 31 Mar.	188 C-47's or	126 C-46's
1 Apr. to 15 Apr.	183 C-47's or	122 C-46's
16 Apr. to 15 May	114 C-47's or	76 C-46's
16 May to 30 June	43 C-47's or	29 C-46's

APPENDIX "E"

OPERATIONS IN SOUTHEAST ASIA

1. The following air forces will be available in S.E. Asia in February 1944:

	U.S.A.A.F.		R.A.F.	
	Groups	Aircraft U.E.	Squadrons	Aircraft U.E.
Heavy Bombers	1	35	3	48
Medium and Light Bombers*	1	57	8	128
S.E. & T.E. Fighters**	2	150	35	560
Night Fighters	—	—	2	32
Torpedo Aircraft	—	—	2	32
Reconnaissance Photo	½	28	2	40
G.R. (Patrol Bomber)	—	—	18	156
Troop Carriers	1	52	5	125
Air/Sea Rescue	—	—	1	25
	5½	322	76	1146

NOTES: * One U.S.A.A.F. medium group will be transferred from North Africa in February and is included in above table.

** Assumes one R.A.F. T.E. fighter squadron is transferred from North Africa by February.

CONCLUSION ON AVAILABILITY OF AIR FORCES

2. Aircraft requirements for operations in the Southeast Asia Command should be sufficient for *TARZAN* and approved operations. Action has already been taken to provide two additional troop carrier squadrons to meet the requirements of *TARZAN*. These squadrons are included in the above table.

Appendix "E" to Annex **IV**

APPENDIX "F"

SUPPORT OF RESISTANCE GROUPS IN EUROPE AND BALKANS

1. The following aircraft are allocated to the support of resistance groups in Europe and the Balkans and at present are based as follows:

	Heavy Bombers
United Kingdom Bases	16
Mediterranean Bases	42
	—
	58

2. In addition it has been agreed to form within the 8th Air Force in the U.K., two squadrons of Liberators not suitable for combat duties by day.

3. Only such support can be given to the resistance groups in Europe as will not interfere with the intensification of the bomber offensive.

ANNEX V

ASSAULT SHIPPING AND CRAFT

GENERAL SITUATION

1. Appendices "A" and "B" contain tables showing production and estimated availability of U.S. and British landing ships and craft, respectively.

2. The planned allocations shown in the tables are not commitments and may be varied at any time to meet strategic requirements.

3. There is still a general shortage of assault shipping and craft, particularly in combat loaders and LST's.

4. There will be need for a general reassessment and reallocation of landing ships and craft remaining in the European-Mediterranean Theaters after the defeat of Germany in the light of the numbers and types available for reorientation to the Pacific and the situation in Europe at the time.

"OVERLORD" AND "ANVIL"

5. Planned allocations for these operations at *QUADRANT* are being augmented as follows:

Type	OVERLORD U.S.	OVERLORD British	ANVIL U.S.	ANVIL British
LST	23	3 extra from Med.	36 (a)	5 (From SE Asia)
LCI(L)	24	—	—	—
LCT	19 (c)	45 (d)	31 (b)	—
XAP	—	—	3	—
LSI(L)	—	—	—	6 (From SE Asia)

NOTES: (a) 26 LST from the U.S., 10 from S.E. Asia. Some of those coming from the U.S. are from spring production previously planned

Annex V

for the Pacific for use in the *TRUK* operation in July. It is believed that by pooling within Pacific areas, the *TRUK* deficiency can be offset and that the operation need not be delayed.

(b) Five of these LCT are from those previously scheduled to be sent from Mediterranean to *OVERLORD*, the remaining are to come from U.S.

(c) 24 LCT as now directed will be sent from U.S. The 5 LCT previously scheduled from the Mediterranean will not be sent; increase to *OVERLORD*—19.

(d) British production of LCT 3 and 4 in April, May and June amounts to 139. Although this will not all be available for the assault in May, it will all come into service progressively during the build-up period in June, July and August.

6. The above increases should provide a satisfactory lift both for *OVERLORD* and *ANVIL*. The 68 LST now in the Mediterranean will be released to *OVERLORD*, 15 January.

OTHER OPERATIONS IN THE MEDITERRANEAN

7. Specific allocation of landing ships and craft will not be made for operations in the Aegean. Resources if necessary must be provided without detriment to *OVERLORD* and *ANVIL* from those available in the Mediterranean at the time of the operation.

PACIFIC (CENTRAL, NORTH AND SOUTH PACIFIC AREAS)

8. Approved U.S. programs should provide minimum requirements of assault shipping and craft to carry out approved operations in the war against Japan from the Pacific in 1944. Any augmentation from survivors of European operations will improve the situation. It will be necessary to pool the combat loaders in all the Pacific Theaters and to pool the LST in the South and Southwest Pacific. It is considered that the timing of the operations will permit the shift of combat loaders from one operation to another and, to a certain extent, the LST and other special types such as LSD. Because of the close timing of some of the operations, assault shipping and craft must be released promptly after assaults to permit time for proper maintenance of material, and rest for personnel, and reorientation.

Annex V

SOUTHEAST ASIA

9. Assault shipping and craft originally made available for *BUCCANEER* are now available for *ANVIL* and *OVERLORD*. It is planned to divert to *ANVIL* at least 15 LST, 3 Pontoon Causeways, 1 ARL and 6 LSI(L)s. The U.S. LSD previously assigned *BUCCANEER* is planned for retention in Central Pacific.

10. No additional commitments for this theater as tentatively allocated at *QUADRANT* and as shown in Table III in Appendix "A" herein, are necessary for approved operations. The 68 additional LST's tentatively allocated to this theater can be made available to the Central Pacific.

11. It appears likely that the assault lift necessary to maintain one division for amphibious operations in S.E. Asia can be supplied from British resources after Germany is defeated. The remaining portion of the British assets will be available for deployment in S.W. Pacific. British estimates in this respect are:

Ship to shore assault — no balanced lift.
Shore to shore assault — 1 Brigade in the assault.
No follow-up.

SOUTHWEST PACIFIC

12. By pooling South and Southwest Pacific assault ships and craft, together with augmentation by combat loaders from the Pacific pool for specific operations, it is considered that there will be sufficient resources to carry out 1944 operations mounted from this area.

13. It is considered that U.S. assault ships and craft presently planned for operations, augmented by U.S. and British resources remaining available after the defeat of Germany, will be available and are adequate to provide the necessary assault lift for the amphibious divisions which it is expected will be employed in this area.

FUTURE PRODUCTION

14. Production programs in the U.S. and U. K. are proceeding to their maximum extent without unacceptable interference to other programs to

Annex V

overcome limitations in landing ships and craft for approved operations. The British plan to build LST's to come into service in 1945.

CONCLUSIONS

15. Production of combat loaders, LST's and LCT's still continues to be the bottleneck limiting the extent and scope of operations against the enemy and our ability to carry out operations will continue to be limited by this fact. In 1944, there should be sufficient landing craft available to carry the approved operations.

APPENDIX "A"

This Appendix contains 5 tables showing tentative allocations and availability of U.S. Assault ships and craft as follows:

Tables I and II   —   APA and AKA

        III — LST

        IV — LCI(L)

        V   — LCT(5) & (6)

ESTIMATED PRODUCTION, ALLOCATION AND AVAILABILITY OF A.P.A.'s AND A.K.A.'s
(REVISED 19 NOVEMBER, 1943)

TABLE I

This table is based on present approved conversion and building programs. See notes.

A.K.A.'s — AS OF THE LAST OF THE MONTH

DATE OF THIS STUDY 5 NOV., 1943 (CORRECTED AS OF 19 NOV., 1943)	1943 OCT.	NOV.	DEC.	1944 JAN.	FEB.	MAR.	APR.	MAY	JUNE	JULY	AUG.	SEPT.	OCT.	NOV.	DEC.
COMPLETED DURING MONTH	1	0	1	0	1	4	1	0	1	1/2	0/4	2/4	1/4	0/4	0/4
TOTALS COMPLETED (CUMULATIVE)	19	19	20	20	21	25	26	26	27	28/2	28/6	30/10	30/14	31/18	31/22
PRESENT AND PROSPECTIVE ASSIGNMENTS															
PACIFIC AREA	13	13	13	13	15	19	20	20	21	22/2	22/6	24/10	25/14	25/18	25/22
ATLANTIC AREA	6	6	7	6	6	6	6	6	6	6	6	6	6	6	6
ESTIMATED AVAILABILITY IN AREA (SEE NOTES)															
PACIFIC AREA	11	12	13	14	15	14	14	15	19	20	21	22/2	22/6	22/6	24/10
ATLANTIC AREA	6	6	6	6	6	6	6	6	6	6	6	6	6	6	6
FITTING-OUT, IN SHAKEDOWN, IN TRANSIT, OR TRAINING IN AREA (SEE NOTES)	2	1	1	1	2	5	6	5	2	2/2	2/6	3/10	3/12	3/17	1/12

A.P.A.'s — AS OF THE LAST OF THE MONTH

	1943 OCT.	NOV.	DEC.	1944 JAN.	FEB.	MAR.	APR.	MAY	JUNE	JULY	AUG.	SEPT.	OCT.	NOV.	DEC.
	1	4	2	1	2	0	2	1	2	2	2/2	2/3	2/3	0/2	1/3
	41/2	45/7	47/2	48/2	50/2	50/2	52/2	53/2	55/2	57/2	59/4	61/7	63/10	63/12	64/15
PRESENT AND PROSPECTIVE ASSIGNMENTS															
	31/2	35/2	36/2	37/2	43/2	43/2	45/2	45/2	46/2	48/2	50/2	52/4	54/7	56/10	57/15
	10	10	11	11	7	7	7	7	7	7	7	7	7	7	7
ESTIMATED AVAILABILITY IN AREA (SEE NOTES)															
	29/2	30/2	30/2	30/2	34/2	40/2	41/2	43/2	43/2	45/2	46/2	48/2	50/2	52/4	54/7
	10	10	11	11	7	7	7	7	7	7	7	7	7	7	7
	2	5	6	7	9	3	4	3	5	5	6/2	6/5	6/8	4/8	3/6

TABLE II

This table is based on present approved conversion and building programs plus new proposed Maritime Commission additional building program (See notes)

A.K.A.'s

	1943 OCT.	NOV.	DEC.	1944 JAN.	FEB.	MAR.	APR.	MAY	JUNE	JULY	AUG.	SEPT.	OCT.	NOV.	DEC.
COMPLETED DURING MONTH	1	0	1	0	1	4	1	0	1	1/2	5/4	6/4	8/4	7/4	7/4
TOTALS COMPLETED (CUMULATIVE)	19	19	20	20	21	25	26	26	27	28/2	33/6	39/10	47/14	54/18	61/22
PRESENT AND PROSPECTIVE ASSIGNMENTS															
PACIFIC AREA	13	13	13	14	15	19	20	20	21	22/2	27/6	33/10	41/14	48/18	55/22
ATLANTIC AREA	6	6	7	6	6	6	6	6	6	6	6	6	6	6	6
ESTIMATED AVAILABILITY IN AREA—NO ATTRITION (SEE NOTES)															
PACIFIC AREA	11	12	13	14	15	14	14	15	19	20	21	22/2	27/6	33/10	
ATLANTIC AREA	6	6	6	6	6	6	6	6	6	6	6	6	6	6	6
FITTING-OUT, IN SHAKEDOWN, IN TRANSIT, OR TRAINING IN AREA (SEE NOTES)	2	1	1	1	2	5	6	5	2	2/2	7/6	12/10	19/12	21/12	22/12

A.P.A.'s

	1943 OCT.	NOV.	DEC.	1944 JAN.	FEB.	MAR.	APR.	MAY	JUNE	JULY	AUG.	SEPT.	OCT.	NOV.	DEC.
	1	4	2	1	2	0	2	1	3	11	15/2	23/3	21/3	50/2	37/3
	41/2	45/7	47/2	48/2	50/2	50/2	52/2	55/2	57/2	82/4	105/7	128/10	156/14	193/15	
PRESENT AND PROSPECTIVE ASSIGNMENTS															
	31/2	35/2	36/2	37/2	43/2	43/2	45/2	46/2	49/2	60/2	75/4	98/7	119/10	149/12	186/15
	10	10	11	11	7	7	7	7	7	7	7	7	7	7	7
ESTIMATED AVAILABILITY IN AREA—NO ATTRITION (SEE NOTES)															
	29/2	30/2	30/2	30/2	34/2	40/2	41/2	43/2	43/2	45/2	46/2	49/2	60/2	75/4	98/7
	10	10	11	11	7	7	7	7	7	7	7	7	7	7	7
	2	5	6	7	9	3	4	3	6	15	29/2	49/5	59/8	74/8	88/8

NOTES

(1) All ships are pooled in the Atlantic and Pacific areas assuming they will be moved to areas as required for Operation. Initial distribution assignment in Pacific is 1 in SWPAC, 8 in SOPAC and 20/2 in CENTRAL PACIFIC. SWPAC has 3 old slow Australian ships converted to APA's for training purposes, not shown in this table.

(2) Where two figures are shown in a block, the left hand figure, represents large APA's and A.K.A.'s, while the right hand figure represents the small types, as DOYEN and FELAND and the Maritime Commission program of 32/32.

(3) All estimates are based on present estimates of deliveries which are subject to change monthly. 6xAP's available in the Atlantic for emergency use as APA's are not included in the tables.

(4) No attrition has been applied.

(5) In estimating availability in the area, 3 months has been allowed for fitting-out, shakedown, transit to area, additional training in the area, and unforseen contingencies. In many cases this 3 month allowance may be excessive and the probabilities are that more ships will be available in any one month for full employment in operations. The availability figures are therefore conservative provided the estimated completion dates are met.

(6) 7 APA's and 6xAKA's assigned to Atlantic may become available for transfer to the Pacific during the summer or fall of 1944 upon completion of the operations for which they are scheduled.

(7) 4 APA's and 1AKA in Atlantic are scheduled to be assigned to the Pacific in January or February 1944 after completion of Army training on the East Coast.

C. Maritime Commission's approved building program of 32 small APA's and 32 small AKA's. Present estimated dates of completion are as follows for 1944 and 1945.

1944	AKA	APA
July	2	0
Aug.	4	3
Sept.	4	3
Oct.	4	3
Nov.	4	3
Dec.	4	3
Sub-Totals	22	13
1945	AKA	APA
Jan.	4	5
Feb.	4	5
Mar.	2	4
Apr.	0	4
May	0	1
Sub-Totals	10	19

D. Proposed new Maritime Commission's building program to meet as nearly as possible the estimated deficits given in a Joint Staff Planners study. This program has not yet been approved. The estimated dates of completion given below are approximate only and should be used only for long-ranged planning studies.

1944	APA	AKA
June	1	0
July	9	0
Aug.	13	5
Sept.	21	7
Oct.	19	7
Nov.	36	7
Dec.	30	7
Sub-Totals	129	30

And with capacity to continue at a rate of about 48 ships per month thereafter.

NOTE: Programs A,B & C were used in making TABLE I of the tabulation. Programs A,B,C & D were used in making TABLE II.

DATA ON PRESENT APPROVED CONVERSION AND BUILDING PROGRAM AND ON PROPOSED NEW MARITIME COMMISSIONS ADDITIONAL BUILDING PROGRAM FOR 1944-1945

A. The so-called 24-6 conversion program (24A.P.A.'s and 6 A.K.A.'s,) is nearly finished-the last vessel completing in May, 1944. Therefore detailed data is not given here.

B. The approved conversion program for 8APA's and 6AKA's, to be completed as soon as possible in 1944 and a continuing program of 1 APA per month and 1 AKA every two months thereafter. Present estimates of completion dates for this program through 1944 are as follows:

1944	APA	AKA
Jan.	0	1
Feb.	0	0
Mar.	0	4
Apr.	1	1
May	2	0
June	1	1
July	2	1
Aug.	2	2
Sept.	2	1
Oct.	2	0
Nov.	0	0
Dec.	1	0
Totals	13	11

TABLE III

L S T

DATE OF TABLE 6 NOV. 1943	1943			1944												1945			TOTAL
	31 OCT	30 NOV	31 DEC	31 JAN	29 FEB	31 MAR	30 APR	31 MAY	30 JUNE	31 JULY	31 AUG	30 SEPT	31 OCT	30 NOV	31 DEC	31 JAN	28 FEB	31 MAR	
ESTIMATED TOTAL BUILT AS OF DATES INDICATED (a)	354	374	398	422	445	470	495	520	545	570	595	620	645	670	695				695
PLANNED ALLOCATIONS (b) *[FIGURES IN PARENTHESIS SHOW ALLOCATION OF THE MONTH'S ESTIMATED PRODUCTION]*																			
CENTRAL & NORTH PACIFIC	66	66	66	66	72	80	86	93	100	106	113	122	130	139	148				148
SOUTH PACIFIC	42	42	42	42	48	65	65	71	71	71	71	71	71	71	71				71
SOUTHWEST PACIFIC	36	36	36	36	42	48	54	60	66	72	79	88	96	105	114				114
SOUTHEAST ASIA (x)	10	10	10	10	10	10	10	10	10	16	22	28	37	50	57				78
MEDITERRANEAN	76	64	28	28	28	28	28	28	28	28	28	28	28	28	28				28
OVERLORD		12	28	122	128	135	135	135	135	135	135	135	135	135	135				135
AMPHIBIOUS TRAINING U.S.	19	19	19	19	19	18	18	18	18	18	18	18	18	18	18				18
ALLOCATED TO BRITISH	84	84	84	84	84	84	84	84	84	84	84	84	84	84	84				84
CONVERSIONS TO ARB, ARL, AGP.	9	7	11	12	14	16	17	17	17	17	19	19	21	21	21				21
ESTIMATED ON STATION (g) *[AND LOSSES CONSIDERED]*																			
CENTRAL & NORTH PACIFIC	32	41	59	66	66	65	66	72	80	86	93	100	106	113	122	130	139	148	148
SOUTH PACIFIC	24	29	30	42	42	42	42	48	54	59	65	71	71	71	71	71	71	71	71
SOUTHWEST PACIFIC	33	34	35	36	36	36	36	42	48	54	60	66	72	79	88	96	105	114	114
SOUTHEAST ASIA	10	10	10	10	10	10	10	10	10	16	22	28	37	50	57	64	71	78	78
MEDITERRANEAN	76	64	28	28	28	28	28	28	28	28	28	28	28	28	28	28	28	28	28
OVERLORD	2	14	60	78	90	128	135	133	135	133	135	133	135	135	135	133	133	135	135
AMPHIBIOUS TRAINING U.S.	19	19	19	19	19	18	18	18	18	18	18	18	18	18	18	18	18	18	18
BRITISH ALLOCATIONS	84	84	84	84	84	84	84	84	84	84	84	84	84	84	84	84	84	84	84
CONVERSIONS TO ARB, ARL, AGP.	9	9	11	13	15	15	15	17	17	17	19	19	19	19	19	21	21	21	21
																			TOTAL 695
ESTIMATED AVAILABILITY IN THEATERS (KNOWN LOSSES AND EST. ATTRITION CONSIDERED)																			
CENTRAL & NORTH PACIFIC	30	39	56	60	57	54	52	66	72	68	64	72	74	77	82	86	91	95	
SOUTH PACIFIC	23	28	28	39	30	35	33	48	42	49	45	52	52	52	52	52	52	52	
SOUTHWEST PACIFIC	33	33	32	31	30	28	27	32	36	40	44	48	52	56	62	67	73	79	
SOUTHEAST ASIA	10	10	10	10	5	9	8	8	8	14	20	26	37	48	57	50	53	55	
MEDITERRANEAN	72	60	24	23	22	21	20	17	17	17	17	17	17	17	17	17	17	17	
OVERLORD	2	14	60	78	100	128	133	73	73	73	73	73	73	73	73	73	73	73	
AMPHIBIOUS TRAINING U.S.	19	19	19	19	18	18	18	18	16	18	16	18	18	18	18	18	18	18	

NOTES:

(a) Based upon Bureau of Ships predicted deliveries at the building yards under latest accelerated program as directed by Cominch serial 03770 of 1 Nov. 1943.

(b) Allocations tentative. They may be altered to meet the requirements of changes in the strategic situation.

(c) Losses not considered. 12 U.S. LST sent to *OVERLORD* from Med. in November (NAF 461).

(d) 36 U.S. LST scheduled to sail from Med. to *OVERLORD* in Dec. There is a possibility that 12 of these may sail in Jan.

(e) As per *QUADRANT* allocations. At *SEXTANT* 26 LST were planned to be sent from U.S. to *ANVIL*. Some of the 26 will come from Feb. & March production, some may come from training.

(f) 1 LST from Amphibious Training to *OVERLORD*.

(g) Time from building yard to station estimated as 3 mos. for Pacific Areas, 6 weeks to 2 mos. for *OVERLORD*.

(h) 14 previously arrived, 36 from Med. 10 for U.S.

(i) Plan to sail 10 from U.S. to *OVERLORD* in Dec., 18 in Jan., 22 in Jan., 22 in Feb., 28 in Mar., and 5 in April.

NOTE (x)

The 10 U.S. LST in Southeast Asia are to return to the Mediterranean for *ANVIL*. It is planned to shift the allocations shown from April on to Central Pacific.

Attrition estimated at rate of 5% per month for Pacific Areas.

Attrition 53 out of 148, 28%

Attrition 18 out of 71, 25%: not carried beyond Sept.

Attrition 35 out of 114, 30%

Attrition 23 out of 78, 30%

(j) Attrition winter and spring @ 15%

(k) Attrition in So. France @ 15%

OVERLORD attrition 6C, 45% (*OVERLORD* combined est.)

(l) Considered available for Pacific at this time

LCI (L)

TABLE IV

DATE OF TABLE 6 NOV. 1943	1943			1944												1945		
	31 OCT.	30 NOV.	31 DEC.	31 JAN.	29 FEB.	31 MAR.	30 APR.	31 MAY	30 JUNE	31 JULY	31 AUG.	30 SEPT.	31 OCT.	30 NOV.	31 DEC.	31 JAN.	28 FEB.	31 MAR.
ESTIMATED TOTAL BUILT AS OF DATES INDICATED (a)	398	422	448	475	504	534	564	594	624	654	684	714	744	774	804			
PLANNED ALLOCATIONS (b) (FIGURES IN PARENTHESIS SHOW ALLOCATION OF THE MONTH'S ESTIMATED PRODUCTION)																		
CENTRAL & NORTH PACIFIC	50	55	62	68	72	87	97	107	117	137	157	177	197	217	237			
SOUTH PACIFIC	40	40	40	40	40	40	46	56	66	76	86	86	86	86	86			
SOUTHWEST PACIFIC	36	36	36	36	36	41	51	61	71	81	91	101	111	121	131			
MEDITERRANEAN	66 (c)	66	66	66	66	66	66	66	66	66	66	66	66	66	66			
OVERLORD	24 (c)	24	24	64	64	64	64	64	64	64	64	64	64	64	64			
AMPHIBIOUS TRAINING U.S.	21	21	21	21	33	42	42	42	42	42	42	42	42	42	42			
ALLOCATED TO BRITISH	152	157	161	168	168	168	168	168	168	168	168	168	168	168	168			
ESTIMATED ON STATION (d) (NO LOSSES CONSIDERED)																		
CENTRAL & NORTH PACIFIC	17	35	38	60	56	52	68	77	87	97	107	117	137	157	177	197	217	237
SOUTH PACIFIC	50	54	38	40	40	40	40	45	56	66	76	86	86	86	86	86	86	86
SOUTHWEST PACIFIC	25	33	35	36	36	36	36	42	51	61	71	81	91	101	111	121	131	141
MEDITERRANEAN	66 (c)	66	66	66	66	66	66	66	66	66	66	66	66	66	66	66	66	66
OVERLORD	24 (c)	24	24	36 (e)	55 (e)	64 (e)	64	64	64	64	64	64	64	64	64	64	64	64
AMPHIBIOUS TRAINING U.S.	16	21	21	21	33	41	42	42	42	42	42	42	42	42	42	42	42	42
ALLOCATED TO BRITISH	152	157	161	167	168	168	168	168	168	168	168	168	168	168	168	168	168	168
																TOTAL		804
ESTIMATED AVAILIBILITY IN THEATERS (KNOWN LOSSES AND EST. ATTRITION CONSIDERED)																		
CENTRAL & NORTH PACIFIC	17	35	37	47	51	55	59	65	72	79	85	91	107	122	136	150	163	175
SOUTH PACIFIC	50	33	35	37	36	34	33	38	45	54	62	69	66	63	60	60	60	60
SOUTHWEST PACIFIC	25	32	33	33	32	31	30	34	41	49	57	64	71	78	84	90	96	101
MEDITERRANEAN	65 (c)	65	63	61	59	57	55 (f)	47 (g)	47	47	47	47 (i)	47	47	47	47	47	47
OVERLORD	24 (c)	74	24	36 (c)	55 (e)	64 (e)	64 (e)	35 (h)	35	35	35	35 (i)	35	35	35	35	35	35
AMPHIBIOUS TRAINING U.S.	16	21	21	21	33	41	42	42	42	42	42	42	42	42	42	42	42	42

NOTES:

(a) Based upon Bureau of Ships predicted deliveries at the building yards under latest accelerated program as directed by Cominch serial 03770 of 1 Nov. 1943.

(b) Allocations tentative. They may be altered to meet the requirements of changes in the strategic situation.

(c) 24 sailed from Med. to OVERLORD in Oct. No losses considered

(d) Time from building yard to station estimated as 3 mos. for Pacific Areas, 2 mos. for OVERLORD.

(e) Plan to sail 12 from U.S. to OVERLORD in Jan., 10 in Feb., and 9 in March.

Attrition estimated at rate of 5% per month for Pacific Areas.
Attrition 62 out of 237, 27%
Attrition 26 out of 86, 30%
Attrition 40 out of 141, 28%

(f) Attrition in Med. estimated at 15% until May.
(g) Attrition in So. France 15%.
(h) OVERLORD attrition 29, 45% (OVERLORD combined est.)
(i) Considered available for Pacific at this time.

TABLE V

L C T (5 & 6)

DATE OF TABLE 6 NOV. 1943

	1943			1944												1945		
	31 OCT.	30 NOV.	31 DEC.	31 JAN.	29 FEB.	31 MAR.	30 APR.	31 MAY	30 JUN.	31 JULY	31 AUG.	30 SEPT.	31 OCT.	30 NOV.	31 DEC.	31 JAN.	28 FEB.	31 MAR.
ESTIMATED TOTAL BUILT AS OF DATES INDICATED (a)	541	587	621	657	693	729	765	691	837	873	909	945	981	1017	1053			
PLANNED ALLOCATIONS (b) [FIGURES IN PARENTHESIS SHOW ALLOCATION OF THE MONTH'S ESTIMATED PRODUCTION]																		

Note (x)

ESTIMATED ON STATION (NO LOSSES CONSIDERED):

	31 OCT.	30 NOV.	31 DEC.	31 JAN.	29 FEB.	31 MAR.	30 APR.	31 MAY	30 JUN.	31 JULY	31 AUG.	30 SEPT.	31 OCT.	30 NOV.	31 DEC.	31 JAN.	28 FEB.	31 MAR.
CENTRAL & NORTH PACIFIC	25	44	44	56	56	56	57	58	70	82	94	106	130	154	178	202	225	250
SOUTH PACIFIC	49	54	55	62	67	76	85	93	105	117	129	141	141	141	141	141	141	141
SOUTHWEST PACIFIC	52	53	64	55	60	72	82	90	102	114	126	138	150	162	174	186	198	210
SOUTHEAST ASIA	10	10	10	10	10	10	10	10	10	10	10	10	10	10	10	10	10	10
MEDITERRANEAN	20	70	50	50	50	50	50	50	50	50	50	50	50	50	50	50	50	50
OVERLORD	20	44	50	115	137	165	175	170	170	170	170	170	170	170	170	170	170	170
AMPHIBIOUS TRAINING U.S.	60	60	60	60	60	60	60	60	60	60	60	60	60	60	60	60	60	60
ALLOCATED TO BRITISH	162	162	162	162	162	162	162	162	162	162	162	162	162	162	162	162	162	TOTAL 1053

ESTIMATED AVAILABILITY IN THEATERS (KNOWN LOSSES AND EST. ATTRITION CONSIDERED):

	31 OCT.	30 NOV.	31 DEC.	31 JAN.	29 FEB.	31 MAR.	30 APR.	31 MAY	30 JUN.	31 JULY	31 AUG.	30 SEPT.	31 OCT.	30 NOV.	31 DEC.	31 JAN.	28 FEB.	31 MAR.
CENTRAL & NORTH PACIFIC	24	43	54	51	48	45	42	41	50	58	66	74	93	111	129	145	161	177
SOUTH PACIFIC	49	52	51	61	58	64	72	78	88	97	106	114	110	106	102	99	95	94
SOUTHWEST PACIFIC	52	51	50	49	52	62	69	74	83	91	99	106	113	129	126	132	138	144
SOUTHEAST ASIA	10	10	10	10	7	7	7	7	7	7	7	7	7	7	7	7	7	7
MEDITERRANEAN	84	72(e)	43(f)	41	39	37	35(n)	28(o)	26	28	28	28(q)	28	28	28	28	28	28
OVERLORD	20	44(k)	93(l)	115(m)	137(m)	165(m)	170(m)	94(p)	94	94	94	94(c)	94	94	94	94	94	94
AMPHIBIOUS TRAINING U.S.	60	60	60	60	60	60	60	60	60	60	60	60	60	60	60	60	60	60

NOTES:

(a) Based upon Bureau of Ships predicted deliveries at the building yards under latest accelerated program as directed by Cominch serial 03770 of 1 Nov. 1943.

(b) Allocations tentative. They may be altered to meet the requirements of changes in the strategic situation.

(c) Pacific allocations, Oct. through Jan. are entirely from expected West Coast production.

(d) 10 sent from Med. to Southeast Asia.

(e) Losses not considered, 12 going to OVERLORD from Med. in Nov.

(f) 29 scheduled to be sent from Med. to OVERLORD in Dec.

(g) Entire allocation may not be realized due to ice bound conditions in river and Lake region production.

(h) 7 from West Coast expected production, 11 from Midwest which, due to freezing of rivers, are not considered available for OVERLORD.

(i) Allocated Pacific because any March production would have to be sent to OVERLORD sectionalized late March or early April which makes arrival sectionalized too late.

(j) Time from bldg. yard to Pacific stations 3 mos.

(k) 12 from Med., 12 from U.S.

(l) 29 from Med., 20 from U.S.

(m) In addition to those scheduled above for OVERLORD, plan to send 22 in Jan., 22 in Feb., 28 in March, 5 in Apr.

Note (x)

It is planned to send 26 LCT's from early spring production and from amphibious training to Anvil, Med. column affected accordingly. Also Med. and OVERLORD columns affected as per notes (b)&(c) Para 5 Annex V.

Attrition estimated at rate of 5% per month for Pacific Areas.

(k) Attrition 73 out of 250, 31%.

(k) Attrition 47 out of 141, 33%.

(l) Attrition 66 out of 210, 31%.

Attrition 3, 30% Feb. operations.

(n) Attrition in Med. estimated at 20% until May.

(o) Attrition in So. France 20%.

(p) OVERLORD attrition 76, 45% (OVERLORD combined est.)

(q) Considered available for Pacific at this time.

APPENDIX B

ALLOCATIONS AND AVAILABILITY OF BRITISH ASSAULT SHIPS AND LANDING CRAFT FROM
1 DECEMBER 1943 TO 1 JANUARY 1945
(SUBJECT TO ALTERATION TO MEET THE NEEDS OF SPECIFIC OPERATIONS.)

		LANDING SHIPS								MAJOR LANDING CRAFT								
	2	3	4	5	6	7	8	9	10	11	12	13	14	15	16	17	18.	19
UNITED KINGDOM	(S)(L) Wh. Rd. En. En.	LSI (M)	LSI (S)	LSI (H)	LSH wh. En.	LST I	LST 2	LSD	LCT 3,4 & 8 6	LCT 5&	LCI (L)	LCH	LCI (S)	LCG (L)	LCG (M)	LCT (R)	LCF (L)	LCS (L)
1. Training and X.D.) on	–	–	–	1	–	–	1	–	53	21	–	–	3	–	–	1	–	–
2. Non-operational)1.12.	1	–	1	3	2	2	1	1	–	157	71	59	–	5	12	–	4	13	2
3. Operational) 43.	1	–	–	3	2	–	2	5	–	159	48	–	4	26	–	–	2	15	12
4. Moved to theatre by 1.4.44.	–	–	–	–	–	–	–	56	–	–	–	–	–	–	–	–	–	–
5. Production 1.12.43. to 1.4.44.	–	15	2	–	–	–	–	–	–	167	2	18	4	6	13	6	30	1	–
6. Losses and moved from Theatre 1.12.43. to 1.4.44.	1	2	–	–	–	–	–	4	–	–	–	4	–	–	–	–	–	–
7. Total 1,2,3,4,5 less 6	1	13	3	6	5	2	3	59	–	536	142	73	8	40	25	6	37	29	14
8. Training & X.D.) on	–	–	–	–	–	–	–	–	–	8	18	2	–	2	–	–	1	–	–
9. Non-operational)1.5.44.	–	–	–	–	–	–	–	–	–	92	–	25d	–	0	–	–	–	–	–
10. Allocated to) OVERLORD)	1	13	3	6	5	2	3	59	–	436	124	46	8	38	25	6	36	29	14
11. Casualties estimated in OVERLORD	–	3	1	2	1	1	1	25	–	187	57	21	2	9	6	1	9	7	3
12. Losses 1.4.44. to1.9.44.	–	–	–	–	–	–	–	2	–	108	6	16	–	4	5	2	1	2	7
13. Production(g)1.4.44.to 1.9.44 for craft and to 1.11.44 for ships	–	–	6	–	–	2	–	–	5	191	–	–	–	–	–	44	–	–	–
14. Total 7, 15 less 11 and 12	1	10	8	4	4	3	2	34	–	432	79	36	6	27	16	47	27	20	4
15. Training (1 Brigade Gp. & Basic R.N.) & experimental	–	–	–	4	–	–	–	2	–	53	14	4	2	2	2	2	1	2	2
16. Available for S.E. Asia or Pacific 1.9.44. for craft 1.11.44. for ships Line 14 less 15.	1	10	8	–	4	3	2	32	5	379 (h)	65	32	4	25	14	45	26	18	2
MEDITERRANEAN																		
17. Training) on	–	–	–	–	–	–	–	–	–	–	–	–	–	–	–	–	–	–
18. Non-operational)1.12.43	–	–	–	–	–	–	–	22	–	17	–	19	1	–	2	–	3	2	–
19. Operational)	–	–	1	–	1	–	–	45	–	30	–	50	2	–	4	–	3	4	–
20. Moved to theatre by 1.4.44.	2	7	–	–	–	1	–	9	–	–	–	–	–	–	–	–	–	–	–
21. Moved from theatre by 1.4.44. and losses 1.12.43. to 1.3.44.	–	–	–	–	–	–	–	59	–	7	–	2	–	–	–	–	–	–	–
22. Total 17,18,19,20 less 21 on 1.4.44.	2	7	1	–	1	1	–	17	–	40	–	67	3	–	6	–	6	6	–
23. Training (1 Brig.Gp.) or non-operational.	–	–	–	–	–	–	–	–	–	–	–	–	–	–	–	–	–	–	–
24. Allocated to ANVIL on 1.5.44.	2	7	1	–	1	1	–	17	–	40	–	67	3	–	6	–	6	6	–
25. Casualties estimated in ANVIL	–	2	–	–	–	–	–	3	–	14	–	20	1	–	2	–	2	2	–
26. Losses 1.3.44 to 1.9.44	–	4(b)	–	–	–	–	–	1	–	7	–	5	2	–	4	–	4	4	–
27. Total 22 less 25,26.	2	1	1	–	1	1	–	13	–	19	–	42	–	–	–	–	–	–	–
28. Training	–	–	–	–	–	–	–	2	–	19	–	4	–	–	–	–	–	–	–
29. Available for S.E. Asia or Pacific 1.9.44. Line 27 less 28.	2	1	1	–	1	1	–	11	–	–	–	38	–	–	–	–	–	–	–
S.E. ASIA.																		
30. TOTAL in India on 1.12.43.	2	8	–	–	1	1	3	5	–	–	5	12	–	–	–	–	–	–	–
31. Indian Production 1.12.43. or moved to theatre) to	–	–	–	–	–	–	–	2	3	–	–	–	–	–	–	–	–	–	–
32. Moved from theatre)1.2.44.	1	5	–	–	1	1	–	5	–	–	–	–	–	–	–	–	–	–	–
33. Total 30, 31 less 32	1	3	–	–	1	–	3	–	2	3	5	12	–	–	–	–	–	–	–
34. Training or non-) operational)1.3.44.	–	1	–	–	–	–	–	–	–	3	–	–	–	–	–	–	–	–	–
35. Available for) operations)	1	2	–	–	1	–	3	–	2	–	5	12	–	–	–	–	–	–	–
36. Estimated casualties in operations	–	1	–	–	–	–	–	–	–	–	2	2	–	–	–	–	–	–	–
37. Losses 1.2.44 to 1.1.45.	–	2(b)	–	–	–	–	–	–	–	3	1	2	–	–	–	–	–	–	–
38. Indian Production 1.2.44. to 1.1.45.	–	–	–	–	–	–	–	–	–	–	–	–	–	–	–	–	–	–	–
39. Total 33 less 36, 37 plus 38	1	–	–	–	1	–	3	–	2	–	2	8	–	–	–	–	–	–	–
40.)REQUIRED (From)by 1.1.45(British) (Sources	2	3	–	–	2	1	2	43	1	88	–	46	4	–	14	45	26	–	–
41. Total 39,40	3	4	–	–	3	1	5	43	3	88	2	38	4	–	14	45	–	–	–
42. Training (1Bde Gp. & Basic R.I.N.)	–	1	–	–	–	–	2	2	–	18	2	4	1	–	–	3	–	–	–
43. Non-operational	–	–	–	–	–	–	–1	–	1–	21	–	10	–	–	4	12	–	–	–
44. Operational (1Amph. Division)	3	3	–	–	3	1	3)	41(f)((3	3	49	–	24	3	–	10	30	–	–	–
PACIFIC																		
45. Available from British sources by 1.1.45.(g) Line 16,29 less line 40.	1	8	9	–	3	3	–	–	4	–	65	24	–	–	–	–	–	18	2

NOTES:
(a) Awaiting spares from U.S.A.
(b) Revert to Trooping.
(c) Available for Pacific
(d) 50 available for Pacific
(e) Will NOT be available by given date.
(f) The FULL Requirement is 53, i.e. there is a shortage of 12.
(g) Production in U.K. after 1.4.44 will be adjusted to meet active requirements in Pacific Theatre (C.P.S. 86/8).
(h) L.C.T. 3 & 4 may be able to get to S.E. Asia but NOT the Pacific.

APPENDIX "B"

This Appendix shows the allocations and availability of British assault ships and landing craft from 1 December 1943 to 1 January 1945 (subject to alterations to meet the needs of specific operations).

Appendix "B"
Annex V

ANNEX VI

SUPPLY OF CRITICAL ITEMS

1. Shortages of certain organizational (Class II) and project (Class IV) items of equipment may hamper directed operations throughout 1944. Generally speaking, adequate substitutes can be provided until standard items become available from production. It is considered that with the possible exception of provision of parachutes for *TARZAN*, shortages will in no case be so serious as to preclude the mounting of operations scheduled in C.C.S. 426/1.

2. *Organizational (Class II) Equipment*

The acceleration of Pacific operations, new requirements for V.L.R. bombing operations in the Southeast Asia Command and Pacific Areas, together with the increased scale of operations against Southern France will aggravate current shortages of organizational equipment. Increased demands for service troop units are expected, particularly port, depot, and certain construction units. Shortages are heaviest in the equipment for these types of units and in portable radar equipment. Generally speaking, except for certain signal items, production will meet requirements by mid-1944. It will be necessary to move some units with combat-serviceable (as opposed to new) cargo vehicles.

3. *Project (Class IV) Equipment*

Shortages of Class IV equipment are expected in the following categories:

> Heavy trucks, tipping lorries, and tires
> Cargo handling equipment
> Small tankers, fire-boats, tugs and other floating equipment
> Air compressors
> Gasoline driven generators
> Heavy engineer shop equipment
> Construction equipment
> > Heavy crawler cranes
> > Earth moving equipment
> > Pumps
> > Tractors
> > Pierced plank landing mat

Signal Equipment
Plant items
Long line equipment
Submarine cable
Water distillation units

Production of N.L. pontoon equipment has started in U.K. and India though the latter's production will be negligible for some time to come.

4. Pacific operations will require considerably increased numbers of landing vehicles tracked, (LVT) both armored and unarmored. Production of these vehicles is being accelerated in order to meet the demands; however, no increases can be realized until the latter half of 1944.

5. Operations in the Southeast Asia Command will require tugs, lighters, mobile cranes, railway flat cars, and N.L. pontoon equipment. Local production of these and similar items should be emphasized to reduce shipping requirements. Shortages of some of these items, as indicated in paragraph 3, above, will hamper L of C operations in this area. Due to the necessity for export of 300,000 tons of coal per month through the port of Calcutta, port construction supplies and equipment may be required for L of C operations in India. Since requirements are not yet firm, the exact degree of shortages cannot be assessed, but no insuperable difficulties are anticipated.

6. Requirements for operations in Europe are being met. The high priority of operations *OVERLORD* and *ANVIL* insure the provision of essential supplies and equipment. There is a possible requirement for small refrigerated ships for *OVERLORD*. Availability of such vessels is under investigation.

7. Requirements for support of resistance groups in Europe including a stockpile of light weapons for 150,000 personnel can probably be met. However, production should not be increased to meet these requirements except in specific instances approved by the Combined Chiefs of Staff.

AIR FORCE TECHNICAL SUPPLIES AND EQUIPMENT
OTHER THAN AIRCRAFT

8. Shortages of certain critical items of Air Force Technical Supplies and Equipment will continue to exist for some time. These shortages will in some

cases hamper operations but in no case will they be serious enough to preclude the mounting of operations in C.C.S. 426/1.

9. There will probably be a shortage of parachutes. Production of parachutes is being stepped up in the U.K. and in India. British requirements for *TARZAN* and other S.E.A.C. operations cannot be met without the help of U.S. production until the end of July 1944. A statement as to whether U.S. production will be able to meet the deficit cannot be made at this time.

10. Floating Air Depots (Aircraft repair ships) will be needed to support A.A.F. units in Pacific operations for which no provision has been made. Provision has been made to meet R.A.F. requirements.

ANNEX VII

SHIPPING

PART I — BRITISH DRY CARGO SHIPPING REQUIREMENTS

British Military Cargo Shipping requirements for the first three-quarters of 1944 have been reexamined in the light of the *SEXTANT* decisions and are now as follows:-

A. FOR MAINTENANCE AND BUILD-UP OF BRITISH FORCES OVERSEAS:-

THEATER	JAN. UK	JAN. US	FEB. UK	FEB. US	MAR. UK	MAR. US	APR. UK	APR. US	MAY UK	MAY US	JUNE UK	JUNE US	JULY UK	JULY US	AUG. UK	AUG. US	SEPT. UK	SEPT. US	REMARKS
							SAILINGS FROM (BRITISH SHIPS)												
MEDITER-RANEAN	60	40	60	40	60	40	50	45	50	45	45	45	45	40	45	40	45	40	Including Coal to North Africa
INDIA	13	22	13	22	13	22	14	24	14	24	14	24	15	25	15	25	15	25	
PERSIAN GULF	2	3	2	3	2	3	2	3	2	3	2	3	2	3	2	3	2	3	
AID TO TURKEY	1	4	1	4	1	4	1	4	1	4	1	4	1	4	1	4	1	4	
AID TO RUSSIA	10	–	10	–	–	–	–	–	–	–	–	–	10	–	10	–	10	–	Northern Route

B. REQUIREMENTS IN RESPECT OF ALLIED OPERATIONS:

(1) Requirements within the Mediterranean for the maintenance of the Forces now within the Theater and for Operations *HERCULES* and *ANVIL* will involve the following monthly sailings:-

JAN.	FEB.	MAR.	APR.	MAY	JUNE	JULY	AUG.	SEPT.
140	140	140	60	175	130	105	75	75

It has been agreed that the number of vessels to be provided as a British commitment will be as follows:

Jan. — 70
Feb. — 70
Mar. — 70
Apr. — 30
May — 49
Jun. — 38
Jul. — 31
Aug. — 38
Sept. — 38

The U.S. contribution is stated in Part III of this Annex—U. S. Cargo Shipping Position.

(ii) For Operation *OVERLORD* 625,000 tons of Coastal Shipping will be required over a period of three months and at least 100,000 tons thereafter.

M.T. ships will be required for the carriage of M/T for both British and U.S. Forces as follows: As at *QUADRANT* it is agreed that M.W.T. and W.S.A. will each provide half of the total tonnage including coasters.

First month — 160
Second month — 100
Third month — 70

The U. S. controlled ships detained for this purpose are shown in Part III of this Annex—U.S. Cargo Shipping Position.

At the end of the third month these ships will be released relying on vehicle ferry in craft sufficient for the agreed "build-up."

Ocean-going vessels for the carriage of Stores with a D.W. of about 9,000 tons will require to be taken up about the middle of the second month to a total of 90 vessels on British account only, and these will be retained until the completion of the operation.

(iii) The build-up of the Pacific task force will call for large shipments of naval aircraft and landing craft to the Pacific in the second half of 1944. The transference of LST's from home waters will provide considerable assistance, but even so it is likely to be in excess of the lift possible in programmed sailings to Australia. The full extent of the commitment is, however, so uncertain that no useful program can be made at this stage.

6 December 1943.   Annex VII

PART II—AVAILABILITY OF BRITISH CONTROLLED DRY-CARGO
TONNAGE: (OF 1600 G.R.T. AND OVER)

1. Total shipping available is estimated to be as shown below:-

(Million deadweight tons)

Date	Estimated losses (at rates approved by C.C.S.) during preceding quarter year	Estimated new construction and transfers to British flag during preceding quarter year	Estimated tonnage at date
31 December 1943			20.30
31 March 1944	0.55	1.10	20.85
30 June 1944	0.55	1.00	21.30
30 September 1944	0.55	0.55	21.30
	Average for first half of 1944		20.85
	Average for third quarter of 1944		21.30

2. The estimated employment of this shipping is as follows:

(Million deadweight tons)

	First half of 1944	Third quarter of 1944
Estimated tonnage available:	20.85	21.30
Deduct average allowance for tonnage awaiting or undergoing repair:	2.60	2.65
	18.25	18.65

Deduct:

(1)   United Kingdom coastal tonnage: 0.45

(2)   Tonnage permanently abroad engaged in maintenance of war-making capacity of areas of British responsibility: 2.20

(Table continued on following page)

			First half of 1944	Third quarter of 1944
(Continued)				
(3)	Non-importing Naval and Military tonnage (including troopships)			
	Naval Commissioned vessels:	0.60		
	Naval, Military and R.A.F. auxiliaries:	0.60		
	Vessels carrying military cargoes and permanently in Mediterranean and Indian Ocean and vessels detained in N. Russia	0.50		
	Troopships and LSI(L)'s	1.35	3.05 5.70	5.70
			12.55	12.95

(Million deadweight tons)

	First half of 1944		Tihrd Quarter of 1944	
Tonnage required (expressed as an average over the period)				
(1) for the maintenance of the war-making capacity:				
(a) of the United Kingdom after allowing for imports for British a/c at the average rate of 1,500 tons per ship in scheduled *BOLERO* sailings:	7.40		7.60	
(b) of areas (other than U.K.) of British responsibility, additional to item (2) above:	0.90		0.90	
(2) for Military commitments:				
(a) build-up and maintenance as in (A) of Part I	5.90		5.90	
(b) in respect of Allied operations, as in (B) of Part I	1.05	15.25	1.40	15.80
NET DEFICIT		2.70		2.85

Annex VII

3. After allowing for (1) imports for British account in scheduled *BOLERO* sailings;

(2) the effect of the W.S.A./M.W.T. bareboat chartering scheme and

(3) for 10 customary sailings of W.S.A. ships monthly from North America to South and East Africa and Anzac area,

it is estimated that the following W.S.A. sailings will be required to meet the tonnage deficiency in the first half of 1944 shown above:-

(a) 10 Eastern customary sailings monthly from N. America to India and the Red Sea.

(b) 60 sailings monthly from N. America (including some from the Gulf) to the U.K.

(c) 16 flexible customary sailings monthly (the equivalent of 22 sailings monthly from N. America to the U.K.) from N. America, probably to Italy and N. Africa.

4. Of the sailings mentioned in paragraph 3 above, (a) and (b) are fully provided for in the United States statement of Part III. The sailings provided towards item (c) leave a small tonnage deficit which, after discussion with W.S.A., it is agreed should prove manageable.

5. In the above estimates no provision has been made for auxiliaries of the merchant ship type in connection with the deployment of the Royal Navy for the war against Japan beyond the immediate needs of the Eastern Fleet in the Indian Ocean and of the British Task Force in the Pacific.

6. The movement of coal to Italy will be met by arrangements effected through the M.W.T. and W.S.A. Subject to further review it is expected to be covered at the current level by allocations of W.S.A. ballasters during the 1st quarter of 1944 to lift available coal from the Indian Ocean principally from India.

7. The estimated deficiency in the 3rd quarter of 1944, which is given with considerable reserve, could be met by the same number of monthly sailings as mentioned in paragraph 3 with the exception of item (c), which becomes:-

19 flexible customary sailings monthly (the equivalent of 26 sailings monthly from North Africa to the U.K.)

8. This apparent deficiency will be discussed between the U.K. and U.S. and should not be difficult to resolve.

Annex VII

PART III

U.S. CARGO SHIPPING POSITION

1. The U.S. Military dry cargo requirements are based on known Army and Navy deployment programs within troop ship capabilities for the first half of 1944 and on the estimated deployment of U.S. Forces for the third quarter. Other requirements listed in the following summary include British dry cargo shipping requirements met by U.S. shipping and in addition incorporate retentions in overseas areas for operational use to the extent required after allowing for those provided from British controlled tonnage.

SUMMARY OF REQUIREMENTS FOR U. S. CARGO SHIPPING IN TERMS OF SAILINGS

(As determined at *SEXTANT* Conference)

Requirement	1st Qtr.	2d Qtr.	3d Qtr.
		1944	
1. To maintain the war making capacity of WESTERN HEMISPHERE	137	137	137
2. To maintain the war making capacity of BRITISH EMPIRE			
a. U.K. Import Program	261	223	222
b. Regular Lend Lease allocations	30	30	30
c. Ships bareboat chartered	58	35	
3. Lend Lease Allocations other than British			
a. Russian	120	75	75
b. French	12	12	12
c. China Defense	3	3	3
4. Rearm and re-equip FRENCH Forces	Included in Mediterranean requirements.		
5. Economic support of occupied countries (Italy)	64	110	110
6. Supply of equipment to TURKEY	Carried in British shipping.		
7. Maintenance of prisoners of war	Included in theater requirements on basis of requisitions from theater.		

Annex VII

	1st Qtr.	2d Qtr.	3d Qtr.
MILITARY OPERATIONS			

Support and maintenance of the war making capacity of U.S. Forces in all areas.

	1st Qtr.	2d Qtr.	3d Qtr.
8. Army and Navy requirements for minor areas.	57	54	54
9. U.K.-EUROPEAN (Army & Navy)	323	354	536
10. *MEDITERRANEAN (Army and Navy)*	174	155	154
11. *CENTRAL PACIFIC* Including Marshalls, Ponape, Carolines, and Guam-Marianas.			
Army	60	71	67
Navy	90	95	125
12. *SOUTH and S.W. PACIFIC* Including New Guinea, Bismarck, Manus.			
Army	165	181	194
Navy	126	117	109
13. *CHINA-BURMA-INDIA*	56	77	100
14. *ALASKA*			
Army	59	46	43
Navy	10	6	6
15. *OPERATIONAL USE* Average No. of Ships retained			
a. Mediterranean	(73)	(120)	(50)
b. U.K.	(33)	(100)	(16)
c. Pacific	(96)	(121)	(121)

Retentions not included in totals.

Available sailings have been adjusted.

	1st Qtr.	2d Qtr.	3d Qtr.
16. *TOTAL REQUIREMENT*	1805	1781	1977
17. *TOTAL AVAILABLE*	1811	1806	2035
18. *BALANCE*	+6	+25	+58

Annex VII

7 December 1943

COMMENTS BY LORD LEATHERS AND MR. L. W. DOUGLAS

ON THE DRY CARGO SHIPPING POSITION

The combined cargo shipping position for the first three quarters of 1944, while reflecting a necessarily heavy increase in the demand for ships on military account, including a very large tonnage indeed retained for operations in the active theaters, does not include a claim for shipping to provide relief for occupied and liberated areas other than for Italy. For this reason, the essential requirements for shipping may not be adequately stated. Particularly may this be the case for the last quarter of the period in question. But the situation after the first half of 1944 is susceptible of such wide and unpredictable changes that only by frequent review can any variations that promise materially to affect the position be satisfactorily disposed of. At the moment it seems reasonable, however, to anticipate no interference on shipping grounds with the approved military and naval operations.

/s/ LEATHERS   /s/ L. W. DOUGLAS

PART IV

PERSONNEL SHIPPING POSITION

BRITISH

1. In our consideration of the British personnel shipping position the following assumptions have been made:-

   a. That the British contribution to operational requirements will be as shown in the attached Table I: Operations *HERCULES* in March and *OVERLORD* and *ANVIL* in May, 1944, are covered; the allowance made for assault shipping remaining in Southeast Asia Command is adequate.

   b. That British personnel shipping will be required to carry out troop movements other than operational as detailed in Table II.

   c. That the available British personnel shipping in the Indian Ocean is capable of meeting local trooping requirements in that area except for the movement of East African troops to India for which special provision has been made.

   d. That the projected improved convoy cycle permitting troopships to proceed from the U.K. direct to Naples will become effective as from 1 January 1944, and will be maintained throughout the period; that all other convoy cycles remain as at present, and the numbers of ships permitted in these convoys remain unchanged.

   e. That the movement of personnel from North Africa and the Middle East to Italy can be covered by means of two groups of fast troopships making three round voyages each per 35-day period.

   f. That additions to the escorted class of troopship during the period under review will offset losses. Losses of unescorted troopships cannot be made good by new construction and no allowance has been made for losses in this class. Any retardation of completion dates of ships under conversion to troopships will affect the estimates.

2. It must again be stated that the *BOLERO* program is to a large extent dependent upon the intensive running of the large liner class of ship; there is no margin in that program for damage or unexpected delays of any sort and the whole program must be regarded as subject to this overriding contingency.

Annex VII

3. During the period since *QUADRANT* all British trooping movements have been subordinated to the achievement of the maximum possible *BOLERO/SICKLE* flow. This has necessitated the postponement of certain British troop movements for some of which allowance has now to be made in the period under review.

4. Table III details present estimates of British assistance to U.S. troop movements (i.e., over and above that rendered in the Mediterranean for the movement of U.S. and French personnel to Italy from North Africa).

The *BOLERO/SICKLE* figure is based upon a new target of a total of 1,366,100 U.S. personnel in the U.K. and en route by 1 May 1944.

Diversion of 16,000 capacity in U.S. ships for use in *ANVIL* to immediate follow-up and build-up may result in a reduction in United States contribution to the *BOLERO* program in April 1944. This reduction has, however, been covered by the British contribution of 386,000 during the period January to April 1944.

Accordingly, to any extent that this diversion is not necessary the British contribution to *BOLERO* may be reduced.

United States

5. The deployment of U.S. personnel shipping, and of British personnel shipping which is estimated to be available for the movement of U.S. troops, is shown in Table III. A comparison of capabilities with forecast requirements shows the following general position:

a. *Joint Army and Navy Requirements in the Pacific*

(1) Available trooplift will overcome present deficits during the 2d quarter of 1944. Trooplift capability in the 3d quarter will meet all estimated requirements. Troop units essential to planned operations can be moved into Pacific areas in time to be ready for scheduled target dates.

b. *Build-up of U.S. Forces in U.K.*

(1) The requirement for a balanced force of approximately 1,366,000 U.S. troops, including 19 divisions, in the U.K. by May 1944 can be met.

Annex VII

(2) The build-up of divisions in the U.K. during May, June and July 1944 is scheduled at two, one, and one in the respective months. Thereafter it is estimated that U.S. Forces will be moved into the European Theater at a rate of four divisions per month.

c. *Mediterranean Requirements*

(1) Requirements to this area can be met.

(2) Preliminary estimates indicate a requirement for 16,000 U.S. troop ship lift in the Mediterranean for *ANVIL* immediate follow-up and build-up. This requirement will be met by the use of the troop capacity in cargo ships to the maximum extent consistent with operational plans.

d. *China-Burma-India*

Troop capacity is available for the movement of units essential to operations and projects planned for this area.

e. *Alaska and Northwest Service Command*

The requirements for this area can be met.

f. *Other Areas* - Including Newfoundland, Greenland, Bermuda, Iceland, West and Central Africa, Caribbean and South Atlantic, Middle East and Persian Gulf.

Troop movements to these areas represent a very small proportion of the total and consist almost wholly of replacements. Total strengths show a gradual reduction.

TABLE I

OPERATIONAL REQUIREMENTS COUNTING AGAINST BRITISH CONTROLLED SHIPPING (INCLUDING L.S.I. (L)) FOR PLANNING PURPOSES

OPERATION	PERIOD REQUIRED	CAPACITY REQUIRED
1. In Indian Ocean Area.	January-September	6,000*
2. OVERLORD.	(a) Up to July 1944.	(a) 16,000 in 13 L.S.I. (L) (C.I.B's)
	(b) May/June 1944.	(b) 10,000. To be used in immediate follow-up, probably for one voyage only.
3. ANVIL.	(a) April/May 1944.	(a) 14,000 in 7 L.S.I. (L) including 5 reallocated from BUCCANEER. The other two are specially converted cargo ships.
	(b) April/May 1944.	(b) 16,000 - for use in immediate follow-up.
4. HERCULES.	March/April 1944.	24,000

*Includes L.S.I. (L) allocated for training only.

TABLE II

BRITISH TROOPING COMMITMENTS other than:

(1) Operational.

(2) In Indian Ocean, shipping.

(3) *BOLERO* and other direct U.S. assistance.

AREA	NUMBER	REMARKS
1. Canada & North America to U.K.	10,800 per month	Covers R.A.F., Canadian and miscellaneous requirements.
2. U.K. to Gibraltar,) West Africa, North) Africa, Italy,) Middle East, P.A.) I.C., India, East) and South Africa)	38,000 per month	
3. Internal Mediterranean movement-North Africa and Middle East to Italy	75,000 per month up to end of March, 1944. Reducing thereafter by May to 30,000 per month by end of May.	
4. Miscellaneous Movements:		
(a) W. Africa to India	1,700 per month to end of August, 1944: 3,400 per month thereafter. 36,000 to arrive in India in June, July and August, 1944.	Reinforcements for 81st W.A. Division and subsequently for 82nd W.A. Division. 82nd W. A. Division.
W. Africa to M.E.	2,000	Pioneer Corps Personnel
(b) Return of Falkland Islands garrison to U.K.	2,000	

(Table continued on following page)

Annex VII

AREA	*NUMBER*	*REMARKS*
(c) New Zealand to Middle East	4,300 to arrive by February 1944. 4,000 to arrive by July 1944.	Reinforcements for New Zealand Division.
(d) East Africa to India	9,000 in January/February, 1944 and 5,000 in June 1944.	East African troops

TABLE III

ESTIMATE OF AVAILABILITY OF BRITISH PERSONNEL SHIPPING

FOR THE MOVEMENT OF U.S. TROOPS JANUARY 1944

TO SEPTEMBER 1944

(CAPACITY IN THOUSANDS)

	Jan.	Feb.	March	April	May	June	July	August	Sept.
1. *BOLERO/SICKLE*									
U.S.A./U.K.	76.7	103.2	110.6	95.5	70.0	70.0	70.0	70.0	70.0
2. *MEDITERRANEAN*									
North Africa/India (ex USA)	6.0	6.0	6.0	6.0	6.0	6.0	6.0	6.0	6.0
U.S.A./North Africa	12.7	—	—	—	—	—	—	—	—

6.12.43.

Annex VII

369

TABLE IV

ESTIMATED U.S. TROOP MOVEMENT CAPABILITY

	Strength 1 Jan. 44	Jan.	Feb.	Mar.	Apr.	May	June	July	Aug.	Sept.
						1 9 4 4					
1. Troop movement of Naval Forces provided for in Pacific including Alaska	—	40,475	29,875	44,975	79,375	61,975	37,175	32,800	32,800	32,800
2. Troop movements to minor Areas (Army and Navy)		1,650	1,550	1,650	1,550	1,450	1,550	1,450	1,470	1,550
Cumulative Strength (Army Only)	(212,000)	209,100	206,100	203,100	200,100	197,900	195,700	193,500	190,200	186,900
3. U.K.-European Build-up (Army)										
Replacements—Attrition Pool		10,100	10,400	13,200	14,200	12,400	25,000	30,000	30,000	30,000
		8,100	19,100	5,800	5,800	47,600	35,000			
Troop Units		77,800	147,900	127,300	157,100	62,600	61,100	112,800	173,700	113,400
Cumulative Strength—End Month	(817,200)	903,100	1,070,100	1,203,200	1,366,100	1,476,300	1,572,400	1,685,200	1,858,900	1,972,300
Divisions		12	13	17	19	21	22	23	27	31
Navy movements in addition to above figures		7,600	7,600	7,600	1,400	1,400	1,400	1,400	1,400	1,400
4. Mediterranean (Army & Navy)	(590,500)	34,600	34,700	31,200	18,600	14,600	14,600	14,500	14,500	14,500
Army Cumulative—End Month		613,000	633,100	649,700	653,700	653,700	653,700	653,700	653,700	653,700
5. Central Pacific (Army Only)	(185,700)	30,500	26,700	19,100	41,200	35,200	29,700	17,800	17,800	17,800
Cumulative Strength—End Month		193,700	197,900	215,500	249,200	261,900	294,100	304,400	314,700	325,000
6. South and S.W. Pacific (Army Only)	(523,300)	57,400	69,000	69,400	59,300	40,900	19,000	50,400	50,400	45,400
Cumulative Strength—End Month		582,700	653,700	710,100	761,400	809,300	820,900	853,300	885,700	918,100
7. China-Burma-India (Army & Navy)	(108,600)	8,800	11,900	13,800	30,800	11,900	12,900	38,900	18,900	19,000
Army Cumulative—End Month		116,000	124,900	137,300	161,900	168,500	176,200	209,900	223,600	237,300
8. Alaska & N.W. Ser. Comd. (Army Only)	(139,000)	500	500	500	500	500	500	500	500	500
Cumulative Strength—End Month		132,400	123,500	115,500	107,500	100,600	97,500	97,500	97,500	97,500

NOTES: This table includes movement provided in British troopships.
Movements include replacements. Cumulative strength reflects net build-up present or en route.

ANNEX VIII

PETROLEUM

REQUIREMENTS

1. Studies of crude oil availability and refinery capacity recently made by a combined committee indicate that adequate facilities exist or can be made available by the use of idle refinery capacity and by absorbing the surplus from Persian Gulf Refineries, together with facilities now in process of construction or which can be made available in the course of the next eighteen months. This statement does not apply to high grade aviation gasoline (100 octane) and to a limited degree it does not apply to 80 octane motor gasoline.

HIGH GRADE AVIATION GASOLINE

2. The most critical petroleum product continues to be high grade (100 octane) aviation gasoline. The present total production of this grade of fuel is still inadequate to meet current requirements. Consequently, training planes and many others carrying heavy freight loads are required to operate on inferior grades of gasoline from 87 octane to 91 octane. Obviously, this deficit seriously curtails training programs and other associated activities. Steps have been taken by both the U.S. Army and Navy to assist Petroleum Administration for War in its aviation gasoline plant building program, but even so the schedule continues to lag critically. U.S. War and Navy Departments jointly have supported the uprating to AA-1 by W.P.B. of all materials required in the aviation gasoline plant building program for plants scheduled for completion by 31 December 1944.

3. The degree to which the present deficits in production for current requirements may be reduced will depend entirely upon the success which may be attained in accelerating the plant building program. The report of new worldwide estimates together with scheduled increases in production, indicates a shortage in production of 86,000 barrels per day during December 1943. The gap between requirements and production will be gradually closed during January and February 1944, until in March the study shows an excess of production over requirements of 30,000 barrels per day worldwide. The sur-

Annex VIII

plus increases gradually until July 1944 when it reaches 52,000 barrels per day and in December 1944, 93,000 barrels per day, based upon projected plant expansions being completed on schedule.

4. The *requirement* figures take into account the scheduled delivery of all Allied aircraft planned for operations during the period covered.

5. As additional quantities of high grade aviation gasoline become available the lower grades now used for certain phases of training and in transport planes will be replaced by the better gasoline. The upgrading of motor base stock to 87 octane gasoline will then be discontinued thus easing to some extent the indicated shortage of 80 octane motor gasoline. (See below)

6. It should be noted that stocks are inadequate in all theaters and that as surpluses materialize they should be allocated for stock building in keeping with C.C.S. approved priority of operations.

7. When stock building requirements are taken into consideration and the proper amount of high grade aviation gasoline is allocated for transport and training planes, no excess will exist, even after plant building program has been completed.

80 OCTANE MOTOR GASOLINE

8. A preliminary report just completed by the Army-Navy Petroleum Board Committee considering this subject indicates a possible shortage of 112,000 barrels per day by the end of 1944. However, from a practical point of view, it is believed that this shortage can be avoided by using gasolines with octane numbers as low as 72 where this is practicable, and by so accelerating the aviation gasoline plant building program as to make it unnecessary to use any of the higher components going into 80 octane gasoline for aviation gasoline purposes. Further, it is anticipated that with the higher percentages of lead and by the use of other additives, combined with the measures above mentioned, this situation will be satisfactorily met.

9. It is believed that by the measures outlined above sufficient 80 octane gasoline may be conserved for combatant areas.

Annex VIII

SEAGOING TANKERS

10. It is believed that seagoing tankers as necessary for agreed operations will be available provided they are judiciously employed. It is certain, however, that based upon agreed *SEXTANT* operations, the working surplus will be practically non-existent.

SMALL TANKERS

11. The need in all theaters for small tankers is more acute at this time than ever before. A preliminary report based upon the findings of a committee, representative of U.S. Army and Navy, W.S.A., and British interests, shows the deficit in vessels under 5,000 D.W.T. to be about 90,000 tons. The matter of prompt clearance for the providing of these additional units is important in connection with presently planned offensive operations.

Annex VIII

2 December 1943

COMBINED CHIEFS OF STAFF

MEMORANDUM FOR INFORMATION NO. 165

MILITARY CONCLUSIONS OF THE "EUREKA" CONFERENCE

Reference: CCS 133d Mtg., Item 2

Note by the Secretaries

The enclosure sets out the military conclusions of the *EUREKA* Conference, as signed by the President, the Prime Minister and Marshal Stalin on 1 December 1943.

H. REDMAN,

F. B. ROYAL,

Combined Secretariat.

ENCLOSURE

MILITARY CONCLUSIONS OF THE "EUREKA" CONFERENCE

THE CONFERENCE:

(1) Agreed that the Partisans in Yugoslavia should be supported by supplies and equipment to the greatest possible extent, and also by commando operations.

(2) Agreed that, from the military point of view, it was most desirable that Turkey should come into the war on the side of the Allies before the end of the year.

(3) Took note of Marshal Stalin's statement that if Turkey found herself at war with Germany, and as a result Bulgaria declared war on Turkey or attacked her, the Soviet would immediately be at war with Bulgaria. The Conference further took note that this fact could be explicitly stated in the forthcoming negotiations to bring Turkey into the war.

(4) Took note that Operation *OVERLORD* would be launched during May 1944, in conjunction with an operation against Southern France. The latter operation would be undertaken in as great a strength as availability of landing craft permitted. The Conference further took note of Marshal Stalin's statement that the Soviet forces would launch an offensive at about the same time with the object of preventing the German forces from transferring from the Eastern to the Western Front.

(5) Agreed that the military staffs of the three Powers should henceforward keep in close touch with each other in regard to the impending operations in Europe. In particular, it was agreed that a cover plan to mystify and mislead the enemy as regards these operations should be concerted between the staffs concerned.

MINUTES

OF

MEETINGS

SEXTANT CONFERENCE

MINUTES OF FIRST PLENARY MEETING, HELD AT THE VILLA KIRK,

ON TUESDAY, 23 NOVEMBER 1943 AT 1100

PRESENT

United States	*British*
The President (In the Chair)	The Prime Minister
Mr. Harry L. Hopkins	General Sir Alan Brooke
Admiral W. D. Leahy, USN	Air Chief Marshal
General G. C. Marshall, USA	Sir Charles F. A. Portal
Admiral E. J. King, USN	Admiral of the Fleet
General H. H. Arnold, USA	Sir Andrew B. Cunningham
Lt. General J. W. Stilwell, USA	Field Marshal Sir John Dill
Lt. General B. B. Somervell, USA	Admiral Lord Louis Mountbatten
Maj. General R. A. Wheeler, USA	Lt. General Sir Hastings L. Ismay
Maj. General G. E. Stratemeyer, USA	Lt. General A. Carton de Wiart
Maj. General C. L. Chennault, USA	
Maj. General A. C. Wedemeyer, USA	

China

Generalissimo Chiang Kai-shek

Madame Chiang Kai-shek
General Shang Chen
Lt. General Lin Wei
Lt. General Chu Shih Ming

SECRETARIAT

Brigadier L. C. Hollis
Captain F. B. Royal, USN

377

SOUTHEAST ASIA OPERATIONS

THE PRESIDENT, extending a warm welcome to the Generalissimo and Madame Chiang Kai-shek, and to the Chinese Delegation, said that this was an historic meeting and a logical consequence to the Four Power Conference recently concluded in Moscow. The effect of this meeting would, he hoped, not only bear fruit today and in the immediate future, but for decades to come. He suggested that Admiral Mountbatten might be asked to give a general survey of intended operations in Southeast Asia. The ground to be covered mainly concerned the land, since seagoing operations were in progress all the time. There was, he felt sure, unanimous agreement that every effort should be made to send more equipment to China, with a view to accelerating the process by which we could launch an air offensive against the heart of Japan itself.

ADMIRAL MOUNTBATTEN then outlined the operations he proposed for the coming campaign in Burma. Apart from current air operations by British-U.S. air forces and two Chinese divisions operating from Ledo, the first land movement would take place in mid-January. The 15th British Indian Corps would advance on the Arakan front with a view to taking up an improved line. This Corps would not, however, be restricted to a defensive role, but would exploit success wherever possible. For this purpose a West African brigade would be deployed on an outflanking movement. At the same time the 4th British Indian Corps (Imphal Force) would start operations with the object of capturing Minthami, Mawlaik, and Sittaung and advancing as far as possible to the southeast.

ADMIRAL MOUNTBATTEN then explained the natural difficulties with which the Allied Forces had to contend. Our lines of communication ran through one of the most difficult countries in the world, served by a one meter gauge railway which, nevertheless, had been worked up to carry 3,100 tons a day, with the hope that this might be increased by a further 500 tons a day. After leaving the railway and the Brahmaputra River, the communication was by roads now being built. All this was being done in thick jungle and across mountains running north and south across the line of communications. The Japanese in Burma were at the end of an excellent line of communication up the Irrawaddy from Rangoon, with a railway running through Indaw to Myitkyina. They had vast resources and adequate equipment and a force of some five divisions, which was likely to be augmented by a sixth division. In order to make good the disparity between our extremely difficult and the Japanese relatively good communications, we had adopted the expedient of air supply on a large scale.

In February General Wingate intended to make three thrusts with his Long Range Penetration Groups. One would be from Chittagong; the second would support the 4th Group in the Tamu area; and the third would help the Chinese forces operating from Ledo. It was hoped that the 3rd Group would, by the use of gliders operating ahead of the Yunnan forces, disrupt and muddle the Japanese. Meanwhile, the Ledo forces would move down in the Myitkyina direction to link up at Bhamo with the main operations of the Yunnan forces advancing on Lashio. In mid-March the 5th Indian Parachute Brigade would seize the airfield at Indaw, after which the 26th Indian Division would be flown in to Indaw by transport aircraft and thereafter be maintained by air.

It was hoped in these operations to surprise the Japanese by using novel methods of supply and by the boldness of our advance through what they might consider to be impassable country. Subject to the Generalissimo's permission, General Stilwell had agreed that the Ledo force should come under the 14th Army Commander until it reached Kamaing, after which it would revert to the command of General Stilwell. Admiral Mountbatten enquired whether this arrangement was agreeable to the Generalissimo.

THE GENERALISSIMO said that he would like to see the proposals illustrated on a map before giving his decision.

ADMIRAL MOUNTBATTEN then gave certain logistic information for the air route over the "hump." He had promised the Generalissimo to work the supply over this route up to 10,000 tons a month. For November and December the figure would be 9,700 tons. For January and February, however, it would drop to 7,900 tons. In March the figure should rise again to 9,200 tons. Twenty-five additional first-line transport aircraft were required and this demand had been put to the Combined Chiefs of Staff with, he understood, every prospect of the demand being met.

THE PRIME MINISTER said that these were important military operations of a much greater magnitude than ever previously contemplated for this theater. The plans had not yet been examined by the Chiefs of Staff, but this would be done at the earliest opportunity, possibly the same day. In all there was an Allied force of approximately 320,000 men who would apply pressure on the enemy in this theater. They would have a qualitative as well as a quantitative supremacy over the enemy. He had high hopes of these operations, the success of which largely depended on surprise and secrecy and ignorance on the part of the enemy as to the lines of approach and the points of attack.

Owing to the surrender of the Italian Fleet and other naval events of a favorable character, a formidable British Fleet would be established in due course in the Indian Ocean. This would ultimately consist of no less than 5 modernized capital ships, 4 heavy armored carriers, and up to 12 auxiliary carriers, together with cruisers and flotillas. This force would be more powerful than any detachment which it was thought that the Japanese could afford to make from their main fleet in the Pacific, having regard to the U.S. naval strength in the Pacific theater. In addition to all this, Admiral Mountbatten would have formed by the spring an amphibious "circus" for use in such amphibious operations as might ultimately be decided upon, but for which preparations were now going ahead with all speed.

THE GENERALISSIMO said that in accordance with the view he had expressed at Chungking, the success of the operations in Burma depended, in his opinion, not only on the strength of the naval forces established in the Indian Ocean, but on the simultaneous coordination of naval action with the land operations.

THE PRIME MINISTER said that naval operations in the Bay of Bengal would not necessarily be coordinated with and linked to the land campaign. Our naval superiority in this area should ensure the security of our communications and a threat to those of the enemy. It should be remembered that the main fleet base would be anywhere from 2,000 to 3,000 miles away from the area in which the armies were operating. Thus, no comparison could be made with these operations and with those carried out in Sicily, where it had been possible for the fleet to work in close support of the Army.

THE GENERALISSIMO considered that the enemy would reinforce Burma and that this could only be stopped by vigorous naval operations.

THE PRIME MINISTER said it would be disastrous if we could do nothing to prevent the Japanese bringing large reinforcements by sea through the Malacca and Sunda Straits. We could not guarantee to cut off reinforcements by sea entirely, but we should do everything to prevent their arrival.

THE GENERALISSIMO said he was not clear as to the timing of the concentration of the naval forces in the Indian Ocean. He was convinced that simultaneous naval and land operations gave the best chance of success for the operations. Burma was the key to the whole campaign in Asia. After he had been cleared out of Burma, the enemy's next stand would be in North China and, finally, in Manchuria. The loss of Burma would be a very serious matter to the Japanese and they would fight stubbornly and tenaciously to retain their hold on the country.

THE PRIME MINISTER said he was unable to agree that the success of the land operations entirely hinged on a simultaneous naval concentration. The fleet could not, in any event, be assembled by January, nor, indeed, until some time later. The ships had to be tropicalized and fitted with special equipment. Some would be starting soon, but the build-up to full strength would not be achieved until the late spring or early summer of 1944. It seemed, however, on the whole improbable that in the meanwhile the enemy would send naval forces in any strength to the Bay of Bengal.

THE PRESIDENT enquired about the railway communications between Siam and Burma.

ADMIRAL MOUNTBATTEN said that the Japanese had recently completed the railway from Bangkok to Thanbyuzayat, 15 degrees 55 minutes N., 97 degrees 40 minutes E. and this would improve their facilities for maintaining forces in Burma to an appreciable degree.

THE PRIME MINISTER thought that the Japanese were mainly relying upon road and rail communications from the Malay Peninsula to maintain their forces in Burma. As we did not possess shore air bases, it was not possible for us to threaten the Japanese communications in the Gulf of Siam. He wished to emphasize the great importance he attached to the operations in Southeast Asia, which would be driven forward with all vigor and dispatch. He hoped to have a further talk with the Generalissimo when some other details of the British naval situation would be communicated.

In conclusion, *THE PRESIDENT* said that the matter could not be carried any further that morning. He hoped that the Generalissimo would take this opportunity of meeting the Chiefs of the American and British Staffs and to discuss these important problems frankly with them.

SEXTANT CONFERENCE

Minutes of Second Plenary Meeting, Held at the Villa Kirk,
on Wednesday, 24 November 1943 at 1100

PRESENT

United States	*British*
The President (In the Chair)	The Prime Minister
Mr. Harry L. Hopkins	General Sir Alan Brooke
Admiral W. D. Leahy, USN	Air Chief Marshal
General G. C. Marshall, USA	Sir Charles F. A. Portal
Admiral E. J. King, USN	Admiral of the Fleet
General H. H. Arnold, USA	Sir Andrew B. Cunningham
Lt. General B. B. Somervell, USA	Field Marshal Sir John Dill
	Lt. General Sir Hastings L. Ismay
	Maj. General R. E. Laycock

SECRETARIAT

Brigadier L. C. Hollis
Captain F. B. Royal, USN

1. *OPERATIONS IN EUROPE AND THE MEDITERRANEAN*

THE PRESIDENT said that at this meeting he hoped there would be a preliminary survey of operations in the European Theater, including the Mediterranean. Final decisions would depend on the way things went at the conference shortly to be held with Premier Stalin. There were some reports that Premier Stalin had no thoughts beyond *OVERLORD*, to which he attached the highest importance as being the only operation worth considering. In other quarters it was held that Premier Stalin was anxious that in addition to *OVERLORD* in 1944, the Germans should be given no respite throughout the winter, and that there should be no idle hands between now and *OVERLORD*. The logistic problem was whether we could retain *OVERLORD* in all its integrity and, at the same time, keep the Mediterranean ablaze. In his view, Premier Stalin would be almost certain to demand both the continuation of action in the Mediterranean, and *OVERLORD*. As regards the Eastern Mediterranean, the question arose "where will the Germans go from the Dodecanese." The answer seemed to be "nowhere." If the same question was applied to ourselves, the answer seemed to depend on the action of Turkey. The entry of Turkey into the war would put quite a different complexion on the matter. This would be another question for discussion at the meeting with Premier Stalin.

THE PRIME MINISTER said he was in accord with the President's views. We had had a year of unbroken success in North Africa and the Mediterranean, in Russia, and in the Pacific. Alamein and *TORCH* had paved the way for the extermination of large German forces in Tunisia. This was followed by the highly successful Sicily operation, and subsequently by the daring amphibious landing at Salerno and the capture of Naples. Then came Mussolini's fall, the collapse of Italy and the capitulation of the Italian Fleet. In the whole history of warfare there had never been such a long period of joint Allied success, nor such a high degree of cooperation and comradeship extending from the High Command down to the troops in the field between two Allies. We should, however, be unworthy of these accomplishments and of the tasks lying ahead if we did not test our organization to see whether improvements could be made. That was the purpose of these periodical meetings.

As a contrast to the almost unbroken successes of the past year, the last two months had produced a series of disappointments. In Italy the campaign had flagged. We did not have a sufficient margin of superiority to give us the power to force the enemy back. The weather had been bad. The departure from the Mediterranean of certain units and landing craft had had, it seemed, a rather depressing effect on the soldiers remaining to fight the battle. The build-up of strategic air forces may also have contributed to the slow progress. The main objective was Rome, for "whoever holds Rome holds the title deeds of Italy." With Rome in our possession, the Italian Government would hold up its head. Moreover, we should then be in a position to seize the landing grounds to the northward.

He, *THE PRIME MINISTER*, had agreed, but with a heavy heart, to the return of seven divisions from the Mediterranean Theater. The 50th and 51st British Divisions, which were first-class troops, had had their equipment removed in preparation for embarkation. In the meanwhile, the 3rd U.S. Division had been no less than 49 days in constant contact with the enemy, and other U.S. and British units had been fighting without rest for long periods.

Passing across the Adriatic to Yugoslavia, more trouble had brewed up. It was a lamentable fact that virtually no supplies had been conveyed by sea to the 222,000 followers of Tito. These stalwarts were holding as many Germans in Yugoslavia as the combined Anglo-American forces were holding in Italy south of Rome. The Germans had been thrown into some confusion after the collapse of Italy and the Patriots had gained control of large stretches of the coast. We had not, however, seized our opportunity. The Germans had recovered and were driving the Partisans out bit by bit. The main reason for this was the artificial line of responsibility which ran through the Balkans. On the one hand, the responsibility for operations here lay with the Middle East Command but they had not the forces. On the other hand, General Eisenhower had the forces but not the responsibility. Considering that the Partisans and Patriots had given us such a generous measure of assistance at almost no cost to ourselves, it was of high importance to insure that *their resistance was maintained and not allowed to flag.*

Moving further east to the Aegean, the picture was equally black. When Italy fell, cheap prizes were open to us, and General Wilson had been ordered to "improvise and dare." Although we had not been able to seize Rhodes we had occupied Kos, Leros, Samos and others of the smaller islands. It had been *hoped to capture Rhodes in October, but when the time came only one Indian* division was available for the task, and this was considered an insufficient force to eject the 8,000 Germans in the island. The enemy had reacted strongly to our initial moves. He had ejected us one by one from the islands, ending up with the recapture of Leros where we had lost 5,000 first-class troops, with four cruisers and seven destroyers either sunk or damaged. Nevertheless, taking into account the German soldiers drowned and those killed by air attack and in the battle, neither side could claim any large superiority in battle casualties. The Germans, however, were now re-established in the Aegean.

As stated by the President, the attitude of Turkey would have a profound effect on future events in this area. With Rhodes once more in our possession and the Turkish airfields at our disposal, the other islands would become untenable for the enemy.

It was to be hoped that the Russians would share our view of the importance of bringing Turkey into the war. They should see that great possibilities would accrue and a chance to join hands with them by means of sending supplies through the Dardanelles. The effect on Hungary, Rumania and Bulgaria would be profound. All this might be done at quite a small cost, say, two divisions and a few landing craft. It might well be that a meeting with the Turkish Prime Minister could be arranged on the way back from meeting Premier Stalin.

Passing now to the Southeast Asia Theater, it was now clear that *FIRST CULVERIN* would require many more ships and craft than the British alone could supply. If it was thought by the United States Chiefs of Staff that *CULVERIN* was the best contribution to the Pacific war, then our resources would *have to be made up by help from America. If, on the other hand, CULVERIN was* thought to be too costly, it might be better to bring back from the Southeast Asia Theater to the Mediterranean sufficient landing craft for an attack on Rhodes. Thus the sequence would be, first Rome then Rhodes. He, the Prime Minister, wished to make it clear that the British had no idea of advancing into the Valley of the Po. Their idea was that the campaign in Italy should have the strictly limited objective of the Pisa-Rimini line. No regular formations were to be sent to Yugoslavia. All that was needed there was a generous packet of supplies, air support and, possibly, a few Commandos. This stepping-up of our help to the Patriots would not involve us in a large additional commitment. Finally, when we had reached our objectives in Italy, the time would come to take the decision whether we should move to the left or to the right.

Turning now to the knock-out blow, *OVERLORD, THE PRIME MINISTER* emphasized that he had in no way relaxed his zeal for this operation. We had profited very considerably in our experiences of amphibious operations and our landing appliances had improved out of all knowledge. There would be an anxious period during the build-up, when the Germans might be able to concentrate more quickly than we could. Nevertheless, the 16 British divisions would be ready when called upon. It seemed to him that the timing of the operation depended more on the state of the enemy than on the set perfection of our preparations. He agreed with the view that if the Germans did not throw in the sponge by February we should have to expect heavy fighting throughout the summer. In this event, it would have to be realized that the 16 British divisions were the limit of our contribution. The British could not meet any further calls on our manpower, which was now fully deployed on war service.

After reviewing all the various theaters of operations the relationships seemed to work out as follows.

OVERLORD remained top of the bill, but this operation should not be such a tyrant as to rule out every other activity in the Mediterranean; for example, a little flexibility in the employment of landing craft ought to be conceded. Seventy additional LCT's had been ordered to be built in British shipyards. We must see if we can do even better than this.

General Alexander had asked that the date of the return of the landing craft for *OVERLORD* should be deferred from mid-December to mid-January. The resources which were at issue between the American and British Staffs would probably be found to amount to no more than 10 percent of the whole, excluding those in the Pacific. Surely some degree of elasticity could be arranged. Nevertheless, he wished to remove any idea that we had weakened, cooled, or were trying to get out of *OVERLORD*. We were in it up to the hilt.

To sum up, the program he advocated was Rome in January, Rhodes in February, supplies to the Yugoslavs, a settlement of the Command arrangements and the opening of the Aegean, subject to the outcome of an approach to Turkey; all preparations for *OVERLORD* to go ahead full steam within the framework of the foregoing policy for the Mediterranean.

THE PRESIDENT said that we could not tell what the state of German military capabilities would be from month to month. The Russian advance, if it continued at its present rate, would bring our ally in a few weeks to the boundaries of Rumania. At the forthcoming conference, the Russians might ask what we intended to do in this event. They might suggest a junction of our right with their left. We should be ready to answer this question.

The Russians might suggest that we stage an operation at the top of the Adriatic with a view to assisting Tito.

Turning to manpower, *THE PRESIDENT* read out the figures for the U.S. and British air and land forces at present disposed overseas and in the respective home countries.

THE PRIME MINISTER said that the staffs had been giving much thought to how we should beat Japan when Hitler was finished. He was determined to solve this problem and the British Fleet would be disposed wherever it could make the best contribution towards this end. The air force build-up would also be studied.

THE PRESIDENT said that he shared the views expressed by Mr. Molotov that the defeat of Japan would follow that of Germany and more rapidly than at present was generally thought possible. It seemed that the Generalissimo had been well satisfied with the discussion held the previous day. There was no doubt that China had wide aspirations which included the re-occupation of Manchuria and Korea.

THE PRESIDENT then referred to the question of Command, remarking that he still received requests for the transfer of shipping and of air forces from one theater to another for a limited period of operations. In his view our strategic air forces from London to Ankara should be under one command. He cited the example of the command which Marshal Foch exercised in 1918.

THE PRIME MINISTER said that once we were across the Channel a united command would be established in the area of operations. He considered that the Combined Chiefs of Staff system had worked reasonably satisfactorily in taking the decision referred to by the President.

THE PRIME MINISTER paid a tribute to the accuracy and effectiveness of the U.S. daylight bombers operating from the United Kingdom.

THE PRESIDENT and *PRIME MINISTER* invited the staffs to study the problems as to the scope and dates of the operations to be carried out in the European and Mediterranean Theaters in 1944, with a view to arriving at an agreed view, if possible, before the coming meeting with the Russians.

SEXTANT CONFERENCE

MINUTES OF THIRD PLENARY MEETING, HELD AT THE VILLA KIRK,
ON SATURDAY, 4 DECEMBER 1943 AT 1100

PRESENT

United States	*British*
The President (In the Chair)	The Prime Minister
Mr. Harry L. Hopkins	The Rt. Hon. Anthony Eden
Admiral W. D. Leahy, USN	General Sir Alan Brooke
General G. C. Marshall, USA	Air Chief Marshal
Admiral E. J. King, USN	Sir Charles F. A. Portal
General H. H. Arnold, USA	Admiral of the Fleet
	Sir Andrew B. Cunningham
	Field Marshal Sir John Dill
	Lt. General Sir Hastings L. Ismay

SECRETARIAT

Captain Forrest B. Royal, USN

389

THE PRESIDENT said that he must leave Cairo on Monday morning. It was therefore necessary that all reports of the Conference should be signed by Sunday night. Apart from the question of Turkish participation in the war, which he felt should be brought about at some date between 15 February and 1 April, the only outstanding problem seemed to be the comparatively small one of the provision of about 20 landing craft or their equipment. It was unthinkable to be beaten by a small item like that, and he felt bound to say that it *must* be done.

THE PRIME MINISTER said that he did not wish to leave the Conference in any doubt that the British Delegation viewed the early separation of the *SEXTANT* Conference with great apprehension. There were still many questions of first-class importance to be settled. Two decisive events had taken place in the last few days. In the first place, Marshal Stalin had voluntarily proclaimed that the Soviet would make war on Japan the moment Germany was defeated. This would give us better bases than we could ever find in China, and made it all the more important that we should concentrate on making *OVERLORD* a success. It would be necessary for the Staffs to examine how this new fact would affect operations in the Pacific and Southeast Asia. The second event of first-class importance was the decision to do *OVERLORD* during May. He himself would have preferred the July date, but he was determined nevertheless to do all in his power to make the May date a complete success. *OVERLORD* was a task transcending all others. A million Americans were to be thrown in, and 500,000-600,000 British. Terrific battles were to be expected on a scale far greater than anything that we had experienced before. In order to give *OVERLORD* the greatest chance of success, it was necessary that Operation *ANVIL* should be as strong as possible. The critical time would come at about the thirtieth day, and it was essential that every possible step should be taken by action elsewhere to prevent the Germans from concentrating a superior force against our bridgeheads. As soon as the *OVERLORD* and *ANVIL* forces got into the same zone, they would come under the same Commander.

Reverting to *ANVIL*, *THE PRIME MINISTER* expressed the view that it should be planned on the basis of an assault force of at least two divisions. This would provide enough landing craft to do the outflanking operations in Italy and also, if Turkey came into the war soon, to capture Rhodes. But he wished to say at once that, in the face of the new situation, Rhodes had no longer the great importance which he had previously attached to it.

ADMIRAL KING intervened to remark that a two-division lift for *ANVIL* was in sight.

THE PRIME MINISTER, continuing, said that operations in Southeast Asia must be judged in their relation to the predominating importance of *OVERLORD.* He was astounded at the demands for *BUCCANEER* which had reached him from the Supreme Commander. Although there were only 5,000 Japanese in the island, 58,000 men were apparently required to capture it. As he understood it, the Americans had been fighting the Japanese successfully at odds of two and a half to one. In the face of Marshal Stalin's promise that Russia would come into the war, operations in the Southeast Asia Command had lost a good deal of their value; while on the other hand their cost had been put up to a prohibitive extent.

THE PRIME MINISTER concluded by observing that there were still very large differences of opinion between the British and American Delegations, and that it was of the first importance that these differences should be cleared away.

SIR ALAN BROOKE said that at all the previous Conferences there had been a number of military meetings, as a result of which reports had been submitted from time to time to the President and Prime Minister. The last stage of the Conference had always been the submission of a final report, followed by an examination of ways and means. *SEXTANT* had been a very different affair. In the first place there had been meetings with the Generalissimo. Then after a short interval, the principal members of both delegations had gone to Tehran where there had been a number of Plenary Conferences on political as well as military matters. Thus the Combined Chiefs of Staff had so far had very few opportunities of discussion at *SEXTANT.* The following matters were still outstanding: First, an examination of the landing craft position, without which it was impossible to say what operations could or could not be undertaken; second, the long term plan for the defeat of Japan, which in its turn was affected by the decisions to undertake operations in Upper Burma next March. The plan was also seriously affected by Marshal Stalin's promise to make war on Japan as soon as Germany was finished. It seemed essential that these problems should be resolved before the Combined Chiefs of Staff separated. The Mediterranean was of the greatest importance. It would be fatal to let up in that area. We should go on hitting the Germans as hard as we possibly could, and in every place that we could. Finally, the question of *ANVIL* was still under examination and it was essential to decide how the necessary resources could be provided.

SIR ANDREW CUNNINGHAM observed that, on a preliminary examination, our naval resources in cruisers, escort carriers, destroyers, and escorts were not adequate to undertake more than two amphibious operations at the same time, namely *OVERLORD* and *ANVIL*. It might be possible to arrange for some of the naval forces employed in *BUCCANEER* to get back in time for *ANVIL*, but a large proportion of them would have to remain in the Indian Ocean.

SIR CHARLES PORTAL said that, according to his information, there was only one good airfield in the Andamans. This was capable of operating squadrons of heavy bombers. There was another site which had been cleared by blasting the top off a hill, and a few strips might be made on the beach. Thus the value of the Andamans as a base for long distance bombing was strictly limited.

GENERAL MARSHALL expressed agreement with General Brooke's observations. There was no question that there were a number of important points to be settled. It was impossible to say how long this settlement would take; and thereafter there would be the business of surveying ways and means.

THE PRIME MINISTER said that he himself would at any rate be leaving on Tuesday. Would it not be possible for the Staffs to stay for two or three days and work out their problems together?

ADMIRAL LEAHY said that two or three days would not suffice for what they had to do, since the detailed problems to be worked out would take at least one or two weeks.

ADMIRAL KING remarked that the staffs were unlikely to reach agreement on certain problems which could only be resolved by the President-Prime Minister level.

THE PRIME MINISTER said that the Generalissimo had left Cairo under the impression that we were going to do *BUCCANEER*. The new facts were, firstly, that the Soviet had declared themselves ready to go to war with Japan immediately Germany collapsed; secondly, that it had been decided to do *OVERLORD* in May; and, thirdly, that *ANVIL* was also to be undertaken. He added that he was very anxious lest the Russian promise should leak out.

THE PRESIDENT agreed, and added that it was impossible to tell the Chinese. Continuing, he said that 18-20 additional landing craft must be provided by hook or by crook. As for the *BUCCANEER* assault, he thought that 14,000 instead of 58,000 men would be ample. The Supreme Commander in the

392

Far East should be told that he must do his best with the resources which had already been allocated to him. It should be possible for the staffs to settle their problems in principle, leaving the details to be worked out afterwards. They appeared already to have reached agreement on the objectives.

SIR ALAN BROOKE demurred. Many questions, such as shipping, landing craft, and naval resources would have to be examined in detail, as would the relation between *ANVIL* and *BUCCANEER*. The former was being examined on the basis of a two-division assault, whereas it might be found that the proper strategy was to divert landing craft from *BUCCANEER* to the Mediterranean and to increase this to say a three-division assault.

ADMIRAL KING said that landing craft and assault shipping for a two-division assault was already in sight, subject to certain complications. He added that, so long as the target date for *OVERLORD* was 1 May, it had been necessary to arrange for landing craft to be in the U.K. by 1 March. Consequently, the intention had been to send all new construction of landing craft after that date to the Pacific. Now that it had been decided to postpone *OVER-LORD* by 2-4 weeks, this new construction would come to the U.K. Nothing would be sent to the Pacific.

THE PRIME MINISTER observed that this was a fruitful contribution.

Some discussion followed on the subject of LSI(L)'s. Would it not be possible, asked *THE PRIME MINISTER*, to adapt merchant ships for this purpose instead of building special vessels?

ADMIRAL KING said that conversions of this character were in progress. The U.S. Navy used ships of 6,000-10,000 tons for this purpose, the monster liners being reserved for transportation of large bodies of troops across the Atlantic.

Some discussion followed about the increase of Japanese fighter strength in Southeast Asia, and, in connection with this matter, *ADMIRAL KING* pointed to the interrelation between the attack on Rabaul and *BUCCANEER*. The Japanese air force was going to be in difficulties at two widely separated points.

ADMIRAL LEAHY suggested that if it could be decided:

a. that *ANVIL* should go ahead on the basis of a two-division assault; and, *b.* that Admiral Mountbatten should be instructed to do the best he could with the resources already allocated to him;

the picture would begin to be filled in. Of course, if Admiral Mountbatten said that he could do nothing, some of his resources could be taken away from him for other purposes.

THE PRIME MINISTER suggested that *BUCCANEER* might be left until after the monsoon; in fact this solution of the problem might be forced upon us by facts and figures.

ADMIRAL KING said that there was a definite commitment to the Generalissimo that there should be an amphibious operation in the spring.

THE PRIME MINISTER recalled that at the Plenary Meeting with the Generalissimo, the latter had said that it was essential that an amphibious operation should be undertaken simultaneously with *TARZAN*. He *(THE PRIME MINISTER)* had said quite firmly that he could not agree. The Generalissimo could be under no illusion about this.

THE PRESIDENT suggested the following plan of action:

a. Accept *OVERLORD* and *ANVIL* as the paramount operations of 1944.

b. Make every effort to get the additional 18-20 landing craft for operations in the Eastern Mediterranean.

c. Let Admiral Mountbatten be told that he could keep what he has got, but is going to get nothing else; and that he must do the best that he can.

SIR CHARLES PORTAL remarked that *ANVIL* had only come seriously into the picture last week. At the present, nobody knew whether a two-division assault would, or would not, be enough. It was merely a yardstick for the planning staffs to work on. It might well be that the proper strategy would be to get a lift for at least another division out of the Southeast Asia Command.

SIR ALAN BROOKE said that for *OVERLORD* the assault was only 3½ divisions; and for *ANVIL* only a two-division assault was at present contemplated. Surely it would be better to employ all the *BUCCANEER* resources to strengthen up the European front.

ADMIRAL LEAHY entirely agreed with the idea of strengthening up the European front, but observed that *BUCCANEER* had been decided on a higher level than the Chiefs of Staff.

THE PRIME MINISTER pointed to the great military advantages that were to be gained by operations in the Aegean. If Turkey entered the war, there would be great political reactions. Bulgaria, Rumania and Hungary might all fall into our hands. We ought to make these German satellites work for us.

MR. EDEN thought that Russia would probably agree to postponing the date for the Turkish entry into the war from 31 December 1943 to about 15 February 1944. As for Rumania, the Russians had, in the first place, refused to have anything to do with the feelers put out by Maniu, except on the basis of unconditional surrender. Maniu had now said that he was prepared to send a representative to negotiate on that basis. It was true that he did not represent the Government of Rumania, but there was always the possibility of a coup d'etat.

THE PRIME MINISTER pointed to the great advantages that were to be gained by Rumania's entry into the war. If we could get a grip on the Balkans, there would be a tremendous abridgement of our difficulties. The next Conference might perhaps be held at Budapest! All this would help *OVERLORD*. He himself was not apprehensive about the landing; but the critical period would be at about the 30th day. It was therefore essential that the Germans should be held at every point, and that the whole ring should close in together.

There followed some discussion of the conduct of the political conversations with President Inonu.

THE PRESIDENT, summing up the discussion, asked whether he was correct in thinking that there was general agreement on the following points:

a. Nothing should be done to hinder *OVERLORD*.

b. Nothing should be done to hinder *ANVIL*.

c. By hook or by crook we should scrape up sufficient landing craft to operate in the Eastern Mediterranean if Turkey came into the war.

d. Admiral Mountbatten should be told to go ahead and do his best with what had already been allocated to him.

THE PRIME MINISTER suggested that it might be necessary to withdraw resources from *BUCCANEER* in order to strengthen up *OVERLORD* and *ANVIL*.

THE PRESIDENT said that he could not agree with this. We had a moral obligation to do something for China and he would not be prepared to forego the amphibious operation, except for some very great and readily apparent reason.

THE PRIME MINISTER said that this "very good reason" might be provided by *OVERLORD*. At present the assault was only on a 3½ division basis, whereas we had put 9 divisions ashore in Sicily on the first day. The operation was at present on a very narrow margin.

FIELD MARSHAL DILL thought it was impossible for us to be strong at both *OVERLORD* and *ANVIL*.

ADMIRAL LEAHY agreed that, from the military point of view, there was everything to be said for strengthening up *OVERLORD* and *ANVIL* at the expense of other theaters; but there were serious political issues at stake.

GENERAL MARSHALL agreed with Field Marshal Dill and Admiral Leahy. He pointed out, however, that the difficulties in abandoning or postponing *BUCCANEER* were not merely political. If *BUCCANEER* was cancelled, the Generalissimo would not allow Chinese forces to take part in *TARZAN*. There would be no campaign in Upper Burma, and this would have its repercussion on the operations in the Pacific. There would be a revulsion of feeling in China; the effect on Japan would be bad, and the line of communication between Indochina would be at hazard.

THE PRIME MINISTER observed that he had never committed himself to the scale or timing of the amphibious operation in the Southeast Asia Theater. Perhaps it might be advisable to revert to Akyab or Ramree.

THE PRESIDENT said that the Generalissimo was anxious that we should secure a base from which the supply line from Bangkok could be bombed.

ADMIRAL KING, in reply to a question from the Prime Minister, said that he had no fear of the Japanese being able to retake the Andamans once we had occupied them. He added that any increase in the scale of *BUCCANEER* was out of the question.

The meeting concluded with an injunction from the President and Prime Minister to their respective staffs to meet together and try to reach agreement on the points at issue in the light of the discussion which had taken place.

SEXTANT CONFERENCE

MINUTES OF THE FOURTH PLENARY MEETING, HELD AT THE VILLA KIRK, ON SUNDAY, 5 DECEMBER 1943 AT 1100

PRESENT

United States	*British*
The President (In the Chair)	The Prime Minister
Mr. Harry L. Hopkins	The Rt. Hon. Anthony Eden
Admiral W. D. Leahy, USN	General Sir Alan Brooke
General G. C. Marshall, USA	Air Chief Marshal
Admiral E. J. King, USN	Sir Charles F. A. Portal
General H. H. Arnold, USA	Admiral of the Fleet
	Sir Andrew B. Cunningham
	Field Marshal Sir John Dill
	Lt. General Sir Hastings L. Ismay

SECRETARIAT

Brigadier L. C. Hollis
Captain F. B. Royal, USN

THE PRESIDENT read out to the Conference a report by the Combined Chiefs of Staff on operations in the European Theater. The point at issue between the two staffs was Operation *BUCCANEER*, and on this agreement still remained to be reached. He would like to have had a document to which signatures could be affixed.

THE PRIME MINISTER suggested that the difficulty might be overcome if the date of *BUCCANEER* could be advanced. Would it be possible to do it, for example, in January?

GENERAL MARSHALL said that this would not be possible.

THE PRESIDENT inquired what date Admiral Mountbatten had given for the operation.

GENERAL ARNOLD said that Southeast Asia Command were working to a date in the middle of March.

ADMIRAL LEAHY remarked that if a mid-March date was adopted, the landing craft could not be returned to the European Theater till the beginning of May.

THE PRIME MINISTER said that he was disturbed at the growth in the forces required for *BUCCANEER*. If a superiority of 10 to 1 was required, this, in fact, made the conduct of war impossible. Could not *BUCCANEER* be postponed till after the monsoon and the Generalissimo be informed that, as a result of developments arising from the discussions with the Russians, we could not carry out *BUCCANEER* as originally contemplated? *TARZAN* would, of course, be carried out as arranged.

THE PRESIDENT said that the Generalissimo had left Cairo quite clearly under the impression that an amphibious operation would be carried out simultaneously with *TARZAN*. He, the President, was a little dubious about putting all our eggs in one basket. Suppose Marshal Stalin was unable to be as good as his word; we might find that we had forfeited Chinese support without obtaining commensurate help from the Russians.

THE PRIME MINISTER observed that *BUCCANEER* would not really influence Chinese continuation in the war. This would depend much more upon the supplies she received over the "hump."

MR. HOPKINS inquired whether, if *BUCCANEER* took place on 1 March, landing craft and naval forces could leave the Indian Ocean for *ANVIL*?

SIR ANDREW CUNNINGHAM did not think this would be possible. A considerable portion of the naval forces would have to remain in the vicinity of *BUCCANEER*, perhaps up to a month, after the assault.

ADMIRAL KING agreed that the follow-up for *BUCCANEER* might take up to four weeks before the ships in any numbers could be released. This would leave no margin at all for fitting them in to *OVERLORD* or *ANVIL*, even assuming that these operations took place in late May.

MR. HOPKINS inquired whether the Combined Staffs had examined the adequacy of a two-divisional assault for *ANVIL*.

SIR ALAN BROOKE said that this question had not yet been examined in detail.

THE PRIME MINISTER, reverting to *BUCCANEER*, said that there was no question of providing any additional forces. When Admiral Mountbatten was told this, he would be quite likely to say that he could not do *BUCCANEER* and revert to *BULLFROG*. This was an operation which found favor with no one. The next step would be to discuss the possibilities of an amphibious operation in the Southeast Asia Theater with the Force Commanders.

SIR JOHN DILL inquired as to the earliest date for *OVERLORD*. It was generally agreed that no specific date had been set.

A discussion followed regarding the phases of the moon in May 1944. It was finally ascertained that the full moon would be on 8 May and the new moon on 22 May.

GENERAL MARSHALL said that *ANVIL* might take place at the same time as *OVERLORD* or possibly a week later.

MR. HOPKINS said as far as he could see, the situation was about as follows:

There were probably sufficient landing craft for a two-division lift for *ANVIL;* there were also landing craft available for *BUCCANEER* and landing craft provided for *OVERLORD* on the scale now planned, although possibly inadequate in the latter case for an additional lift which might be hoped for. Unless the Chiefs of Staff have ascertained that there are sufficient landing craft for the *required* assault on Southern France, then there would definitely not be enough landing craft for these operations.

ADMIRAL LEAHY said that while it was apparent that there was sufficient lift for two divisions for *ANVIL* it was unquestionably true that a greater lift would be more likely to insure the success of the operation. He felt that if the Generalissimo could be induced to put his forces into *TARZAN* without accomplishing *BUCCANEER*, it might be a good thing.

THE PRIME MINISTER said he felt that there were a good many new, revolutionary ideas recently injected as regards the relationship between *BUCCANEER* and *TARZAN*.

MR. HOPKINS inquired as to whether it was not a question that *OVERLORD* and *ANVIL* are of such great importance that they should be augmented if possible.

MR. ANTHONY EDEN said that it was unfortunate that we cannot separate *BUCCANEER* and *TARZAN* and continually have to consider them connected.

ADMIRAL KING said that if the *BUCCANEER* operation was postponed, he believed there would be no operations in Burma after the monsoon except possibly as a part of other incidental operations.

GENERAL BROOKE said if we do *TARZAN* and then run on into the monsoon we cannot sit still; we must go on. There are two further steps. The next operation is to go down to Mandalay and the Irrawaddy. The subsequent operation is to continue on to Rangoon.

THE PRIME MINISTER observed that operations on land such as *TARZAN* would not cut into *OVERLORD* or *ANVIL*.

SIR CHARLES PORTAL inquired whether it would not be possible to substitute some form of amphibious operations in lieu of *BUCCANEER*. The Generalissimo had made a special point of naval operations. It might be possible to organize commando groups and make a descent on some part of the coast. He considered that commando raids supported by naval forces would fulfill the Generalissimo's requirements. He believed that operations of this sort would be suitable without making a definite commitment which we will have to continue further. He also believed that the Generalissimo might be told that amphibious operations on a large scale could be carried out after the monsoon.

ADMIRAL KING said that Sir Charles Portal probably meant some sort of "hit-and-run" operations.

MR. HOPKINS inquired whether or not the Chiefs of Staff would get any further if they sent Admiral Mountbatten a wire. He inquired whether the Chiefs of Staff would recommend against the whole business if Admiral Mountbatten said he could not accomplish *BUCCANEER* with the means available. Would the Chiefs of Staff still tell Admiral Mountbatten to go ahead and do what he could with what he had?

THE PRIME MINISTER observed that both *OVERLORD* and *ANVIL* were known to be of great importance and will be seriously affected by a diversion such as *BUCCANEER*.

MR. HOPKINS said he understood there was nothing in any C.C.S. paper to the effect that landing craft were not available for either *OVERLORD* or *ANVIL*. On the other hand, the Chiefs of Staff had never stipulated that there should be a six-division assault for *OVERLORD* or a three-division assault for *ANVIL*.

THE PRIME MINISTER pointed out that the Southeast Asia Command had 50,000 men against 5,000 Japs and were now asking for more.

MR. HOPKINS said it made no difference in the number of landing craft whether 30,000 men or 50,000 men were being used for *BUCCANEER* because the size of the initial assault was gauged by the number of landing craft. He asked if Lord Mountbatten's landing craft were made available in the Mediterranean, how many more men could be lifted?

ADMIRAL CUNNINGHAM replied that Admiral Mountbatten's lift is about 25,000 men. In other words, these landing craft meant an additional lift of about one division for *ANVIL*. He also believed that the landing craft from the Indian Ocean could get to *OVERLORD* in time if necessary.

ADMIRAL KING pointed out that the difficulty in lifting additional troops in the initial assault for *OVERLORD* was a function of the ports available. There was already considerable port congestion anticipated in England with a lift of the 4½ divisions contemplated. He further observed that his understanding was that the number of troops in the initial *OVERLORD* assault was predicated on what could properly be used on the available landing front in France.

SIR ALAN BROOKE said that, in his view, the landing could be extended and use made of other beaches.

SIR ANDREW CUNNINGHAM said that the LSI(L)'s could be more economically employed in the longer Mediterranean hauls than in the short cross-Channel haul.

THE PRIME MINISTER said that while he did not feel committed to an amphibious operation on any specific date in Southeast Asia, he realized the difficulty which faced the President with regard to the Generalissimo. Either Admiral Mountbatten should plan for *BUCCANEER* with the existing resources or start sending back the forces at once. He favored *TARZAN* going ahead. He had not realized that the amphibious operation was directly related to and bound up with *TARZAN*.

Continuing, *THE PRIME MINISTER* suggested that the Generalissimo should be informed that Admiral Mountbatten had now said that he wanted more forces than had been contemplated when he, the Generalissimo, had been in Cairo. It was therefore proposed to postpone *BUCCANEER* until after the monsoon. Meanwhile, *TARZAN* would go forward. The postponement of *BUC-CANEER* would not effect *TARZAN*. If the Generalissimo expressed surprise and threatened to withhold the Yunnan forces, we should say that we would go on without them. Alternatively, we could say that the inaction of the Yunnan forces would allow more supplies to go over the "hump."

SIR ALAN BROOKE said that if the Yunnan forces were to be withdrawn from *TARZAN*, the whole plan would need recasting.

ADMIRAL KING said that the two-divisional lift for *ANVIL* was already in sight and it might even be possible to improve on this. He explained, however, that the two-divisional lift entailed keeping back one month's production of landing craft output from the Pacific. Nothing at all was going to the Pacific now.

THE PRESIDENT said he would like the possibility of a series of "hit-and-run" raids to be examined.

SIR ANDREW CUNNINGHAM, in reply to a question by the Prime Minister, said that the naval force for *BUCCANEER* would include battleships, cruisers, destroyers and one or two big carriers. No great difficulty should be encountered in doing a raid or raids. He remarked that Admiral King had promised to help by providing American naval forces for *ANVIL*.

THE PRIME MINISTER said that assuming that the President and United States Chiefs of Staff were willing to extend their time at Cairo for a day or so, it would be necessary for the Combined Chiefs of Staff to get to work on the problems which had emerged from the discussion. First came *ANVIL*. A more detailed study was required of the strength to be employed in the assault and in the follow-up. Next, we ought to deal with the Turks. He had in mind a program on the following lines: At the end of January the Turkish airdromes should be fitted out with Radar and anti-aircraft defenses. At the beginning of February the U.S. and British squadrons should be ready to move in to Turkey, and medium bombers should start a softening process from air-fields in Cyrenaica. By 15 February the bombing attacks on the islands should be intensified. By this time we should expect some reactions from Germany, but as they grew progressively stronger, the Turks would have to face up to greater risks.

ADMIRAL LEAHY said that, as far as the United States Chiefs of Staff were concerned, they were quite right to leave the Turkish program to the British Chiefs of Staff to decide upon.

SIR ALAN BROOKE said that the adjustment of resources to plans, including particularly shipping, could not yet be worked out. The adjustment of resources depended on the decision about *BUCCANEER* and *ANVIL*. As regards the former operation, the right thing seemed to be to take what was required for the European Theater, and then see what could be done with what was left in Southeast Asia.

THE PRIME MINISTER suggested that Admiral Mountbatten should be asked what he could do as an alternative to *BUCCANEER* assuming that the bulk of his landing craft and assault shipping was to be withdrawn at once. We could not get away from the fact that we should be doing wrong strategically if we used vital resources such as landing craft on operations of comparatively insignificant importance, instead of using these resources to strengthen up *OVERLORD* and *ANVIL*, where it looks like we are working to a dangerously narrow margin.

GENERAL ARNOLD explained the possibilities and capabilities of the very long range aircraft which would operate from the four airfields at Calcutta.

THE PRIME MINISTER inquired how the construction of these airfields was progressing. He called for a special report, to be followed by weekly progress reports.

THE CONFERENCE:—

a. Invited the Combined Chiefs of Staff to initiate further studies concerning the scope of *OVERLORD* and *ANVIL* with a view to increasing the assaults in each case.

b. Invited the Combined Chiefs of Staff to consult with the Force Commanders of *BUCCANEER* and thereafter to ask Admiral Mountbatten what amphibious operations he could do on a smaller scale than *BUCCANEER* if the bulk of landing craft and assault shipping were withdrawn from Southeast Asia during the next few weeks.

c. Agreed that the British Chiefs of Staff should prepare a statement for presentation to the Turks showing what assistance they would receive if they entered the war.

SEXTANT CONFERENCE

MINUTES OF FIFTH PLENARY MEETING, HELD AT THE VILLA KIRK,
ON MONDAY, 6 DECEMBER 1943 AT 1930

PRESENT

United States	*British*
The President (In the Chair)	The Prime Minister
Mr. Harry L. Hopkins	The Rt. Hon. Anthony Eden
Admiral W. D. Leahy, USN	General Sir Alan Brooke
General G. C. Marshall, USA	Air Chief Marshal
Admiral E. J. King, USN	Sir Charles F. A. Portal
General H. H. Arnold, USA	Admiral of the Fleet
	Sir Andrew B. Cunningham
	Field Marshal Sir John Dill
	Field Marshal Jan C. Smuts
	Lt. Gen. Sir Hastings L. Ismay

SECRETARIAT

Brigadier H. Redman
Captain F. B. Royal, USN

405

THE PRESIDENT read out paragraph by paragraph the report of the agreed summary of conclusions reached by the Combined Chiefs of Staff at the *SEXTANT* Conference (C.C.S. 426/1).

There was some discussion over the Emergency Return to the Continent (paragraphs 17 to 20). *THE PRESIDENT* understood that objections had been raised to the United States proposals in paragraph 18 on the grounds that they would involve a move of the United States forces from the right to the left across the British lines of communication. He understood that in practice this objection should not be a serious one, as the change-over would not take place until operations had been concluded.

THE PRIME MINISTER said that he could not commit the British Government to these proposals. They would have to be put to the War Cabinet.

With regard to the Higher Direction of Operations in the Southeast Asia Command (paragraph 23), *THE PRIME MINISTER* said that this did not affect the decision taken at the *QUADRANT* Conference that the British Chiefs of Staff were to be the channel of communication with the Southeast Asia Command.

With reference to paragraph 26, *THE PRIME MINISTER* said that he thought the Supreme Allied Commander, Southeast Asia Command, should be sent a copy of the President's recent signal to the Generalissimo on the subject of operations in the Southeast Asia Command. *THE PRESIDENT* agreed and *THE PRIME MINISTER* gave instructions for the signal to be dispatched.

After reading out paragraph 28, *THE PRESIDENT* said that he had been approached by the Chinese, here at the *SEXTANT* Conference, with a request for Chinese representation on the Combined Chiefs of Staff in Washington. He had made it clear at once that such representation could not be agreed to. The Chinese had also asked if a U.S.-Chinese Committee could be appointed for the consideration of the military operations with which China was concerned.

When *THE PRESIDENT* came to the end of the report, he commended the Combined Chiefs of Staff on the report that they had produced.

THE PRIME MINISTER classified the report as a masterly survey of the whole military scene. He gave it as his opinion that when military historians came to adjudge the decisions of the *SEXTANT* Conference, they would find them fully in accordance with the classic articles of war.

THE PRIME MINISTER then expressed his deep sense of gratitude to his United States colleagues. The *ANVIL* operation had been a great contribution made by them to this Conference. He was convinced that this operation would contribute largely to the success of *OVERLORD*.

THE PRESIDENT and *PRIME MINISTER* then initialled the report (C.C.S. 426/1).

In answer to a question from the Prime Minister as to whether the draft communique on the U-boat war had been approved, *ADMIRAL KING* stated that the communique had been cleared with the President, that it had been dispatched already to Washington, and that it would be released on the 10th of the month.

THE PRIME MINISTER suggested to the President that the communique should be made out in alternate months by the United States and the British respectively, and that as the British had prepared the present communique, that for next month should be prepared by the United States. *THE PRESIDENT* agreed with this proposal.

A draft message to Marshal Stalin was then considered. It was approved with a minor modification and instructions given for it to be sent at once.

A draft telegram to the Generalissimo was then read out. It was agreed that on grounds of security it would be undesirable to put so much secret information into a dispatch of this nature. It was decided not to dispatch a telegram to the Generalissimo until his reply had been received to the recent telegram sent to him by the President on the subject of operations in the Southeast Asia Command.

COMBINED CHIEFS OF STAFF

C.C.S. 127th Meeting

SEXTANT CONFERENCE

MINUTES OF MEETING HELD IN CONFERENCE ROOM 1, THE MENA HOUSE,
ON MONDAY, 22 NOVEMBER 1943 AT 1500

PRESENT

United States	*British*
Admiral W. D. Leahy, USN	General Sir Alan Brooke
General G. C. Marshall, USA	Air Chief Marshal
Admiral E. J. King, USN	Sir Charles F. A. Portal
General H. H. Arnold, USA	Admiral of the Fleet
	Sir Andrew B. Cunningham

ALSO PRESENT

Lt. Gen. B. B. Somervell, USA	Field Marshal Sir John Dill
Vice Adm. Russell Willson, USN	Lt. Gen. Sir Hastings L. Ismay
Rear Adm. C. M. Cooke, Jr., USN	Gen. Sir Thomas Riddell-Webster
Rear Adm. O. C. Badger, USN	Captain C. E. Lambe, RN
Rear Adm. B. H. Bieri, USN	Brigadier C. S. Sugden
Maj. Gen. T. T. Handy, USA	Air Commodore W. Elliot
Maj. Gen. M. S. Fairchild, USA	Brigadier J. K. McNair
Brig. Gen. L. S. Kuter, USA	
Brig. Gen. P. H. Tansey, USA	
Brig. Gen. H. S. Hansell, USA	
Captain A. K. Doyle, USN	
Colonel F. N. Roberts, USA	

SECRETARIAT

Brigadier H. Redman
Captain F. B. Royal, USN
Colonel A. J. McFarland, USA
Commander R. D. Coleridge, RN

ADMIRAL LEAHY suggested, and the *COMBINED CHIEFS OF STAFF* agreed, that General Sir Alan Brooke should take the Chair at the meetings of the Combined Chiefs of Staff at *SEXTANT*.

1. *CONDUCT OF CONFERENCE*

THE COMBINED CHIEFS OF STAFF discussed the future work of the Conference, with particular reference to the necessity for considering operations in the Far East as early as possible.

SIR HASTINGS ISMAY said that he understood it was likely that the President and Prime Minister would hold a plenary session with Generalissimo Chiang Kai-shek at 1700 on Tuesday, 23 November, and that it had been suggested that the Combined Chiefs of Staff should meet with Generalissimo Chiang Kai-shek on Wednesday, 24 November.

GENERAL MARSHALL read out to the Combined Chiefs of Staff a brief memorandum prepared by General Stilwell giving the Generalissimo's views of future operations in the Chinese Theater. He suggested that the United States and British Chiefs of Staff should separately study this memorandum on the following morning and that the Combined Chiefs of Staff collectively should consider it at 1430 on Tuesday, 23 November. These proposals were accepted by the Combined Chiefs of Staff. It was also agreed that the Generalissimo and his principal advisers should be invited to be present at the Combined Chiefs of Staff meeting at 1530 on Tuesday, 23 November.

At the suggestion of Admiral Leahy,

THE COMBINED CHIEFS OF STAFF:—

Agreed that the procedure to be used at *SEXTANT* should follow the lines of that used at the *QUADRANT* Conference, with specific reference to the recording of decisions, the approval of minutes, and the reports to the President and Prime Minister.

2. *PROPOSED "SEXTANT" AGENDA* (C.C.S. 404 and 404/1)

SIR ALAN BROOKE explained that the British proposals set out in C.C.S. 404/1 were designed to enable the Combined Chiefs of Staff to study at the earliest possible opportunity operations affecting the Chinese Theater. They could then turn to operations in Europe in order that if possible they should have fully considered these before meeting the U.S.S.R. representatives.

ADMIRAL KING said he felt that the British agenda was acceptable as an outline into which the details suggested by the United States Chiefs of Staff could be fitted.

THE COMBINED CHIEFS OF STAFF:—

Accepted the proposals for the main subjects for discussion on the *SEXTANT* agenda as set out in paragraph 2 of C.C.S. 404/1.

3. *"EUREKA"*

THE COMBINED CHIEFS OF STAFF discussed the arrangements for *EUREKA.*

4. *RELATIONS BETWEEN COMBINED CHIEFS OF STAFF AND THE REPRESENTATIVES OF THE U.S.S.R. AND CHINA*

GENERAL MARSHALL said that he felt the Combined Chiefs of Staff should consider the question of their relationship both during the Conference and in the future, with the military representatives of the U.S.S.R. and China. This seemed particularly important in view of the recent Four-Power agreements concluded in Moscow. There had already been an intimation from Generalissimo Chiang Kai-shek that he would welcome an invitation for a Chinese military representative to sit with the Combined Chiefs of Staff. It might facilitate the development of good faith and mutual understanding with the U.S.S.R. and China if each were invited to have a representative present with the Combined Chiefs of Staff. However, he thought that this should be based on a well thought out scheme, rather than on day-to-day decisions. There might be certain advantages in having the Soviet representatives attend at least some conferences in order that they could appreciate the difficulties of a world-wide war on every front in comparison with their own and China's highly localized operations.

ADMIRAL KING said that the question raised a basic problem in that it might lead to the permanent expansion of the Combined Chiefs of Staff into a Four-Power body. It was pointed out that it would be impossible for the Chinese and the Soviet representatives to sit at the same table since they were not engaging the same enemies, nor could the Soviet representatives attend deliberations of the Combined Chiefs of Staff dealing with the war against Japan.

ADMIRAL LEAHY suggested that the Chinese and Soviets should, during the present Conference, be invited to be present only when the Combined Chiefs of Staff were discussing the problems of the particular fronts in which each was interested. With regard to the Soviets, it would of course most certainly be necessary, when a Western Front was opened, that our action should be coordinated with theirs and that the delegates attending meetings for this purpose should be able to speak with full authority.

SIR CHARLES PORTAL pointed out that this would be equally true if Turkey was brought into the war and operations in that area were undertaken.

SIR HASTINGS ISMAY said that at Moscow it had been clear that the Soviet representatives did not realize that the machinery of the Combined Chiefs of Staff was in continuous operation. They would, he thought, expect to be invited only to Conferences such as *QUADRANT* or *SEXTANT*, but not to attend all the meetings at these Conferences. There had been no signs of their suggesting permanent representation with the Combined Chiefs of Staff.

There was general agreement that, subject to further consideration, the best procedure would be for the Chinese and Soviet Representatives to be invited to attend only those meetings of the Combined Chiefs of Staff at which matters concerning the fronts in which they were interested were under discussion. At *EUREKA*, however, it would obviously be necessary for the Soviet representatives to attend all meetings held.

5. *REAFFIRMATION OF OVER-ALL STRATEGIC CONCEPT AND BASIC UNDERTAKINGS*

Without discussion,

THE COMBINED CHIEFS OF STAFF:—

Accepted the over-all strategic concept and basic undertakings as set out in C.C.S. 380/2.

COMBINED CHIEFS OF STAFF

C.C.S. 128th Meeting

SEXTANT CONFERENCE

MINUTES OF MEETING HELD IN CONFERENCE ROOM 1, THE MENA HOUSE,
ON TUESDAY, 23 NOVEMBER 1943 AT 1430

PRESENT

United States	*British*
Admiral W. D. Leahy, USN	General Sir Alan Brooke
General G. C. Marshall, USA	Air Chief Marshal
Admiral E. J. King, USN	Sir Charles F. A. Portal
General H. H. Arnold, USA	Admiral of the Fleet
	Sir Andrew B. Cunningham

ALSO PRESENT

Lt. Gen. J. W. Stilwell, USA	Field Marshal Sir John Dill
Lt. Gen. B. B. Somervell, USA	Lt. Gen. Sir Hastings L. Ismay
Vice Adm. R. Willson, USN	Admiral Lord Louis Mountbatten
Rear Adm. C. M. Cooke, Jr., USN	Gen. Sir Thomas Riddell-Webster
Rear Adm. O .C. Badger, USN	Lt. Gen. A. Carton de Wiart
Rear Adm. B. H. Bieri, USN	Captain C. E. Lambe, RN
Maj. Gen. M. S. Fairchild, USA	Brigadier C. S. Sugden
Maj. Gen. G. E. Stratemeyer, USA	Air Commodore W. Elliot, RAF
Maj. Gen. R. A. Wheeler, USA	Brigadier E. M. W. Cobb
Maj. Gen. T. T. Handy, USA	Brigadier A. Head
Maj. Gen. A. C. Wedemeyer, USA	Brigadier J. K. McNair
Brig. Gen. L. S. Kuter, USA	
Brig. Gen. P. H. Tansey, USA	
Brig. Gen. H. S. Hansell, USA	
Captain A. K. Doyle, USN	
Colonel F. N. Roberts, USA	
Colonel E. O'Donnell, USA	
Captain W. L. Freseman, USN	
Commander V. D. Long, USN	

PRESENT FOR LAST ITEM ONLY

General Shang Chen
Lt. General Lin Wei
Vice Adm. Yang Hsuan Ch'eng
Lt. General Chou Chih Jou
Lt. General Chu Shih Ming
Maj. Gen. Tsai Wen Chih
Maj. Gen. C. L. Chennault, USA

SECRETARIAT

Brigadier H. Redman
Captain F. B. Royal, USN
Colonel A. J. McFarland, USA
Commander R. D. Coleridge, RN

1. *CONCLUSIONS OF THE 127TH MEETING*

THE COMBINED CHIEFS OF STAFF:—

Accepted the conclusions of the 127th Meeting. The detailed record of the Meeting was also accepted subject to minor amendments.

2. *THE ROLE OF CHINA IN THE DEFEAT OF JAPAN*
(C.C.S. 405)

GENERAL STILWELL informed the Combined Chiefs of Staff that he had received a message from Generalissimo Chiang Kai-shek stating that he did not wish any proposals for Chinese action laid before the Combined Chiefs of Staff until he had had a further consultation with the President and General Marshall.

SIR ALAN BROOKE said that it appeared that the operations set out in subparagraphs 2 *a, b, c,* and *d* of C.C.S. 405 were acceptable. The remaining proposals appeared unrealistic, particularly in view of the logistic difficulties which General Marshall had mentioned at a previous meeting. He could not ₍ee how Formosa could be attacked from the mainland of China without any landing craft.

ADMIRAL LEAHY said that he agreed with Sir Alan Brooke's views. Subparagraphs 2 *a, b, c,* and *d* were acceptable to the United States Chiefs of Staff; the remaining proposals were matters for the future, requiring detailed examination, particularly in view of the serious logistic implications. He suggested that the Combined Chiefs of Staff should so inform the Chinese representatives.

GENERAL MARSHALL reminded the Combined Chiefs of Staff that up till now the Generalissimo's sole interest had been in the provision of a large United States Air Force in China and a large number of transport aircraft. He had taken each step in the direction of the formation of ground forces with reluctance. Months had passed before he would agree to the training of the Chinese troops at Ramgarrh. More months had passed before he had agreed to an increase in their numbers. Negotiations with the Indian government had necessitated further delay. Yet another period had passed before the Generalissimo would agree to the habilitation of the Yunnan force. Now, for the first time, the Generalissimo had shown an active interest in and an admission of the importance of the formation and employment of Chinese ground forces. He (General Marshall) personally had confidence in the value of Chinese troops

415

provided they were properly led. Their powers of endurance should prove immensely valuable in the type of warfare in which they were to be employed. He considered that the Generalissimo's new proposals should be given the most careful and sympathetic consideration. These factors and the value of China once Germany had collapsed and the flow of supplies to the East had increased, should be borne most carefully in mind when considering the Generalissimo's plan.

ADMIRAL KING pointed out that the Generalissimo's proposals must be considered in relation to the over-all plan for the defeat of Japan. He agreed with General Marshall as to the importance of the change of heart shown by the Generalissimo in his latest proposals, and felt that he should not be discouraged if it could possibly be avoided.

GENERAL ARNOLD mentioned the problem of the employment of some two thousand heavy bombers which would be available on the defeat of Germany. Available bases in the Aleutians, Maritime Provinces, and the Islands were all of limited capacity.

SIR CHARLES PORTAL suggested that this great force might be used against shipping.

GENERAL ARNOLD pointed out that the bases he had mentioned would in fact be used by heavy bombers employed against shipping. His point was that only by using them out of China could the heart of Japan itself be attacked. Attacks on Japanese oil resources and shipping, while valuable, would not produce the final result.

THE COMBINED CHIEFS OF STAFF then discussed Generalissimo Chiang Kai-shek's views with regard to the employment of naval forces in the Bay of Bengal.

GENERAL STILWELL said he believed that the Generalissimo would be satisfied if we could guarantee naval security in the Bay of Bengal.

SIR ANDREW CUNNINGHAM said that it would be right to say that we should have general control of the Bay of Bengal but he could not absolutely guarantee its complete security. He believed that the Prime Minister intended in due course to inform the Generalissimo of the British naval forces to be employed in the Bay of Bengal but felt that this information should be imparted by the Prime Minister himself and not by the Combined Chiefs of Staff.

ADMIRAL MOUNTBATTEN explained that in discussing amphibious operations with the Generalissimo in Chungking, he had pointed out that it was intended to launch an amphibious operation in the spring, probably to synchronize with the Burma land operations. From the air bases made available by the amphibious operation it was hoped to be able to interfere with seaborne supplies, both through Rangoon and Bangkok. He believed that the Generalissimo was in fact interested in this action rather than in the actual provision of naval forces in the Bay of Bengal.

THE COMBINED CHIEFS OF STAFF:—

Agreed:

a. That the operations proposed in paragraphs 2 *a* to *d* inclusive, of C.C.S. 405 are, in general, in consonance with the present concept of operations against Japan as expressed in C.C.S. 397, Specific Operations for the Defeat of Japan, 1944.

b. That the operations proposed in paragraphs 2 *e* to *h* inclusive, of C.C.S. 405 go beyond the present concept of operations in China and require detailed examination and study with particular reference to logistic difficulties.

c. That the study indicated in *b* above, together with an examination of the employment for the defeat of Japan of the heavy bombers that would become available when Germany has been eliminated from the war, should be included in the general study of the over-all plan for the defeat of Japan now being conducted by the Combined Staff Planners.

3. *ESTIMATE OF ENEMY SITUATION, 1944—PACIFIC-FAR EAST* (C.C.S. 300/2)

SIR ALAN BROOKE said that there appeared to be minor discrepancies with regard to the estimate of enemy forces available, which could be discussed by the Combined Intelligence Committee. In other respects the paper could be accepted as an estimate of the situation.

ADMIRAL LEAHY agreed with this view.

THE COMBINED CHIEFS OF STAFF:—

Accepted and noted for future information the estimate of the enemy situation, 1944—Pacific-Far East, set out in C.C.S. 300/2.

4. FUTURE OPERATIONS IN THE SOUTHEAST ASIA COMMAND (C.C.S. 390/1)

SIR ALAN BROOKE said that he noted that the United States Chiefs of Staff were not able to provide the forces necessary for *CULVERIN*. With regard to *BUCCANEER*, he would like to defer consideration of this operation until the Conference was further advanced.

ADMIRAL MOUNTBATTEN said that the Japanese forces in *CULVERIN* had increased from one to three divisions. He was, however, prepared to accept a risk and to undertake Operation *CULVERIN* with smaller forces if this should be considered necessary. His chief concern was to be in a position to cut the Japanese lines of communication into Burma and to obtain an air base from which he could attack the Malacca Straits, Rangoon, and Bangkok. *BUCCANEER*, though not providing so many airfields, was approximately the same distance from Bangkok as was *CULVERIN*, and so offered almost equal strategical advantages; it could be undertaken with the forces now available to him. He would propose to launch *BUCCANEER* probably some two to three days after the launching of the land campaign in North Burma. This would disperse the Japanese air effort. The Burma operations and *BUCCANEER* each had a considerable effect on the other and had been planned and considered together.

After further discussion,

THE COMBINED CHIEFS OF STAFF:—

Approved C.C.S. 390/1 but agreed to suspend final decision regarding Operation *BUCCANEER* until later in the *SEXTANT* Conference in order to allow the operation to be considered in relation to the other operations to be undertaken.

5. COMBINED CHIEFS OF STAFF—UNITED CHIEFS OF STAFF (C.C.S. 406)

SIR ALAN BROOKE said that he would like further time to consider the proposals put forward by the United States Chiefs of Staff.

GENERAL MARSHALL explained that the United States Chiefs of Staff had given only very brief consideration to this matter but had felt that it would be valuable to outline a possible course of action before pressure was exerted from any quarter to widen the membership of the Combined Chiefs of Staff.

ADMIRAL KING said that, as he saw it, the United Chiefs of Staff would consist of one representative of the Chiefs of Staff of each nation who would act as spokesman. This proposal would reduce the difficulties to their simplest possible terms if the issue were to be forced upon the United States and British Chiefs of Staff.

THE COMBINED CHIEFS OF STAFF:—

Agreed to defer action on this paper.

6. *THE PRESENT SITUATION IN THE SOUTHEAST ASIA COMMAND*

THE COMBINED CHIEFS OF STAFF then entered into a general discussion of the situation in the Southeast Asia Command.

ADMIRAL MOUNTBATTEN, in reply to a question, explained that the grounding of a vessel carrying spare aircraft engines would result in a deficit in air lift over the "hump" for December of some 2,100 tons. The backlog thus caused had not been included in his calculations and he suggested that the Combined Planners should look into this question. His plans were not made on wide margins of safety and did not make allowance for acts of God since he realized fully that too heavy demands from his theater would have direct repercussions on the operations in other theaters. In reply to a further question, *ADMIRAL MOUNTBATTEN* said that his Royal Air Force transports were being used to the full. They were not being employed in China since there were insufficient numbers to train his parachute troops and long range penetration groups. It had been necessary for United States aircraft to fly in supplies to the British units in Fort Hertz.

GENERAL STRATEMEYER asked if it was possible for the Royal Air Force to provide old bombers which were not operationally fit, for use as transport aircraft.

SIR CHARLES PORTAL said that he did not feel that worn-out aircraft, even if available, could be used for this task. Manpower also was short and the production of British bombers was a direct measure of the weight of attack on Germany.

In further discussion of the possibility of interrupting Japanese communications, *SIR CHARLES PORTAL* pointed out that air bombing alone could not completely stop the use of enemy ports.

ADMIRAL MOUNTBATTEN agreed with this view but explained that he had great hopes that heavy bombing of Japanese occupied ports would result in strikes of dock labor and a resulting slowing up in the flow of supplies.

GENERAL ARNOLD felt that our present calculations with regard to air transport possibilities had been wrongly based on a 100 percent figure of accomplishment. This figure was never achieved, and it would be safer to "lower our sights" with regard to target figures and accept as a bonus any increase on this lower figure.

In reply to a question by Sir Charles Portal, *ADMIRAL MOUNTBATTEN* said that the airport at Blair in *BUCCANEER* had a 1,650 yard runway and was capable of operating three squadrons.

THE COMBINED CHIEFS OF STAFF:—

Took note of the above statements.

(At this point General Shang Chen, Lieutenant General Lin Wei, Vice Admiral Yang Hsuan Ch'eng, Lieutenant General Chou Chih Jou, Lieutenant General Chu Shih Ming, Major General Tsai Wen Chih and Major General Chennault entered the meeting.)

SIR ALAN BROOKE, in welcoming the Chinese Representatives, said that the Combined Chiefs of Staff were very pleased to have this opportunity to meet with them and discuss around the table plans for future operations in China. These discussions should lead to definite conclusions. Admiral Mountbatten had that morning put forward his plans and he suggested that the Chinese Representatives should ask any further questions that they might wish and put forward their own suggestions with regard to these plans.

GENERAL CHU, on behalf of General Shang Chen, explained that the Chinese Representatives had not had sufficient time to study these plans and would prefer to discuss them on the following day.

ADMIRAL MOUNTBATTEN suggested that the Chinese Representatives should give an outline of the state of readiness of the Yunnan Force and of the detailed plans for its employment. He pointed out that the success of our efforts to open the land route to China was dependent on the successful operation of the Yunnan Force in coordination with the British attacks.

GENERAL STILWELL then outlined in detail the Chinese Forces available and their state of readiness. There were, at present, certain shortages of personnel which were being rapidly made good. The ten assault divisions would first be brought up to strength and any deficiencies in pack transport would be compensated for by the use of manpower.

With the aid of a map *GENERAL STILWELL* outlined the three coordinated attacks which would be made by the Yunnan Force. He believed that sufficient tactical air forces were available to support these operations.

GENERAL CHENNAULT and *GENERAL STRATEMEYER* explained the arrangements which had been made for the coordination of the air effort with that of the ground forces.

THE COMBINED CHIEFS OF STAFF:—

a. Took note with interest of the above statements.

b. Agreed to meet again with the Chinese Representatives at 1530 hours on 24 November.

COMBINED CHIEFS OF STAFF

C.C.S. 129th Meeting

SEXTANT CONFERENCE

Minutes of Meeting Held in Conference Room 1, The Mena House, on Wednesday, 24 November 1943 at 1430

PRESENT

United States	*British*
Admiral W. D. Leahy, USN	General Sir Alan Brooke
General G. C. Marshall, USA	Air Chief Marshal
Admiral E. J. King, USN	Sir Charles F. A. Portal
General H. H. Arnold, USA	Admiral of the Fleet
	Sir Andrew B. Cunningham

ALSO PRESENT

Lt. Gen. B. B. Somervell, USA	Field Marshal Sir John Dill
Vice Adm. R. Willson, USN	Lt. Gen. Sir Hastings L. Ismay
Rear Adm. C. M. Cooke, Jr., USN	Admiral Lord Louis Mountbatten
Rear Adm. O. C. Badger, USN	Gen. Sir Thomas Riddell-Webster
Rear Adm. B. H. Bieri, USN	Lt. Gen. A. Carton de Wiart
Maj. Gen. M. S. Fairchild, USA	Maj. Gen. R. E. Laycock
Maj. Gen. T. T. Handy, USA	Captain C. E. Lambe, RN
Brig. Gen. L. S. Kuter, USA	Brigadier C. S. Sugden
Captain A. K. Doyle, USN	Air Commodore W. Elliot, RAF
Colonel F. N. Roberts, USA	Brigadier E. M. W. Cobb
Captain W. L. Freseman, USN	Brigadier A. Head
Commander V. D. Long, USN	Brigadier J. K. McNair
	Lt. Col. W. A. C. H. Dobson

Present for the Last Item Only

General Shang Chen
Lt. Gen. Lin Wei
Vice Adm. Yang Hsuan Ch'eng
Lt. Gen. Chou Chi Jou
Lt. Gen Chu Shih Ming
Maj. Gen. Tsai Wen Chih
Lt. Gen. J. W. Stilwell
Maj. Gen. C. L. Chennault
Maj. Gen. G. E. Stratemeyer
Brig. Gen. Frank Merrill

SECRETARIAT

Brigadier H. Redman
Captain F. B. Royal, USN
Colonel A. J. McFarland, USA
Commander R. D. Coleridge, RN

1. *THANKSGIVING DAY*

SIR ALAN BROOKE said that since the following day would be Thanksgiving he had made inquiries into the possibility of holding a service in the cathedral in Cairo and had found that this would be possible at 1800 hours. The British members of the Conference would, if agreeable to their American colleagues, like to join them in attending this service.

ADMIRAL LEAHY thanked Sir Alan Brooke for this gesture. It was very much appreciated by the United States Chiefs of Staff, who would gladly attend.

2. *CONCLUSIONS OF THE 128TH MEETING*

THE COMBINED CHIEFS OF STAFF:—

Accepted the conclusions of the 128th Meeting. The detailed report of the meeting was also accepted, subject to minor amendments.

3. *COMBINED CHIEFS OF STAFF — UNITED CHIEFS OF STAFF*
(C.C.S. 406 and 406/1)

SIR ALAN BROOKE said the British Chiefs of Staff had considered the U.S. proposals and saw certain difficulties. The United Chiefs of Staff, if organized to exercise executive functions and take decisions, would in effect be superimposed on the Combined Chiefs of Staff. Only three members of the United Chiefs of Staff would be able to sit together at any one time since Russia and China were not fighting the same enemies, and the organization would be unable to take the wide global outlook which was the function of the Combined Chiefs of Staff. The Combined Chiefs of Staff now functioned day in and day out and dealt with day-to-day problems of global strategy. He felt it better that Russian and Chinese representatives should be asked to attend all future conferences, such as *SEXTANT*, to discuss matters in which they were directly concerned.

ADMIRAL KING felt it important to have ready some possible plan to meet future demands for stronger representation.

ADMIRAL LEAHY said he felt sure the Combined Chiefs of Staff would be put under pressure to alter their present machinery. He agreed that no other body could be superimposed above the Combined Chiefs of Staff, since such a body could never take major decisions.

SIR CHARLES PORTAL said that he felt that a distinction should be drawn between the day-to-day work of the Combined Chiefs of Staff in Washington and the major decisions which were taken at the special conferences. He felt that if pressure were applied for permanent representation, the demand would be withdrawn if it were suggested that the Chinese or Russian Representatives concerned would have to be able to speak with the full authority of their governments.

SIR JOHN DILL pointed out the special position of the United States and Great Britain in that they only were fighting a global war and were completely integrated and united on all fronts.

SIR ALAN BROOKE suggested that the Combined Chiefs of Staff should not go further than to agree that, for the present, the Russians and Chinese should be asked to attend those meetings at future special conferences at which their own problems were being discussed.

THE COMBINED CHIEFS OF STAFF:—

a. Took note of C.C.S. 406 and C.C.S. 406/1.

b. Agreed:

(1) That the Combined Chiefs of Staff should not take the initiative in putting forward any proposals for machinery to secure closer military cooperation with the U.S.S.R. and China.

(2) That if the U.S.S.R. and/or the Chinese should raise the question, the difficulties of and objections to any form of standing United Chiefs of Staff Committee should be frankly explained to them. It should be pointed out:

(a) That the Combined Chiefs of Staff in Washington are responsible for the day-to-day conduct of the Anglo-American forces which are closely integrated in accordance with the broad policy laid down at the formal conferences such as Casablanca, *TRIDENT, QUADRANT,* and *SEXTANT* which are convened from time to time; and

(b) That the U.S.S.R. and/or Chinese Governments will be invited to join in any formal conferences which may be convened in the future to take part in the discussion of any military problems with which they are specifically concerned.

4. AGENDA FOR "EUREKA"

SIR ALAN BROOKE said that he regarded the *EUREKA* Conference as primarily a political meeting at which certain points would probably be referred to the Combined Chiefs of Staff for their advice. He felt that it would be wise to consider at this conference the best method of coordinating Russian military effort with our own, particularly with regard to Russian action during and prior to the *OVERLORD* assault. It was essential that this attack should not take place during a lull in the fighting on the Eastern front.

ADMIRAL LEAHY agreed with this view and pointed out that there were several other items which might be raised, including the question of the provision of Russian bases for shuttle bombing. He agreed that it was wise to have in mind certain special points for discussion but that the work of the conference would be inevitably affected by the political discussions.

THE COMBINED CHIEFS OF STAFF:—

Agreed:

a. That no formal agenda need be produced at this stage because the military problems to be considered would arise from the political discussions which would be held at the start of the conference.

b. That the three main military topics for consideration would appear to be:

(1) The coordination of Russian operations with Anglo-American operations in Europe.

(2) Turkish action on entry into the war.

(3) Supplies to Russia.

(At this point Admiral Mountbatten, General Wheeler, General Wedemeyer, Brigadier Cobb, and Lt. Colonel Dobson entered the meeting, and Admiral Leahy withdrew.)

5. OPERATIONS IN SOUTHEAST ASIA COMMAND

GENERAL MARSHALL reported that he had discussed the proposed operations in the Southeast Asia Command with Generalissimo Chiang Kai-shek. The Generalissimo disapproved of the present plan, which he felt would lead to heavy losses and possibly defeat. The Generalissimo had made the following stipulations: Firstly, that there must be an amphibious operation carried out simultaneously with the land attack in Burma. In this connection the Generalissimo had suggested action against the Andaman Islands. Secondly, that the advances by the columns as now envisaged in the plan should all be aimed at a line running east and west through Mandalay, including the occupation of Mandalay by one of the columns. The Generalissimo was satisfied that the Yunnan force should not advance beyond Lashio, its present objective.

He *(GENERAL MARSHALL)* had pointed out that the plan as explained to the Generalissimo was only the first stage of the operations to recapture Burma and was a conservative one and much less dangerous than that suggested by the Generalissimo. In view of the Generalissimo's extreme interest in the naval situation in the Bay of Bengal, he suggested he be given, as soon as possible, the build-up of the British naval forces. Admiral Mountbatten should see him and explain his plan, pointing out that it was the first step only of a long campaign and that it was in the nature of a safe and conservative first step.

ADMIRAL MOUNTBATTEN explained that the plan was based on the principle that the advance should end at the time that the monsoon would break. This would prevent Japanese repercussions. He stressed the point that it would be impossible to remain stationary in the positions captured at the end of the first stage. It would be essential therefore to have collected sufficient resources by October for the next step forward.

SIR ALAN BROOKE said that in taking the first step we were committing ourselves to the recapture of all Burma. There could be no question of holding a halfway line and we should probably have finally to undertake an airborne attack on Rangoon and amphibious operations. The alternatives were to continue the Burma land campaign to a finish or to give up the campaign altogether and endeavor to open the Malacca Straits. It was probably now too late to reverse our decision. This decision would, of course, affect the final plan for the defeat of Japan, and this must be realized.

ADMIRAL KING said he felt there was one alternative — to attack Bangkok instead. This would sever the Japanese lines of communication into Burma.

In reply to a question, *GENERAL MARSHALL* confirmed that the Generalissimo did not feel that the Chinese force from Yunnan should advance further than Lashio. The Generalissimo's fear with regard to the present plan was that it would enable the Japanese to attack and defeat in detail the various columns, particularly the Chinese.

ADMIRAL MOUNTBATTEN asked for direction from the Combined Chiefs of Staff as to what he should say to the Generalissimo with regard to future operations after the monsoon. These operations were largely dependent on the amount of air transport he could obtain in order to make his columns fully mobile. It might be possible to launch an amphibious operation in the Prome area and to put in more long range penetration groups. He again emphasized that at the end of the monsoon it would be essential either to advance, in which case sufficient resources would have to be provided, or to retire. To remain stationary was impossible. He would have liked to advance as far as Mandalay in the present dry season if the resources had been available but the lines of communication to Mandalay did not permit this. Further, he had no reserve divisions. He hoped to gain his present objectives by early April when it might be expected that the monsoon would break. During the monsoon, long range penetration groups would operate. He asked that the Combined Chiefs of Staff should consider as early as possible the provision of resources to enable him to renew his advances at the end of the next monsoon.

GENERAL MARSHALL said that the Chinese fear appeared to be mainly that they might be left to carry out their Yunnan advance unsupported.

THE COMBINED CHIEFS OF STAFF:—

Took note of the above statements.

6. *BOUNDARIES OF THE SOUTHEAST ASIA COMMAND*
(C.C.S. 308/7)

THE COMBINED CHIEFS OF STAFF considered a memorandum presented by the United States Chiefs of Staff on the revision of the boundaries of the Southeast Asia Command.

ADMIRAL MOUNTBATTEN said that the proposals in the paper dealing with the boundaries themselves were acceptable to him but he did not believe that a committee sitting in Chungking should deal with political matters in Thailand and Siam. He pointed out that the Kra Isthmus was far removed from Chungking with which there was no communication. The Siamese and the French were not suspicious of the United States or Great Britain acting in concert, but rather of the Chinese themselves. His two main considerations were that preoccupational activity by such agencies as the S.O.E. and O.S.S. into Thailand and Siam must be permitted from his theater and that political questions should not be dealt with in Chungking, but either through the ordinary machinery of Government or perhaps even by the Combined Chiefs of Staff.

THE COMBINED CHIEFS OF STAFF:—

Agreed to defer action on C.C.S. 308/7.

(At this point General Shang Chen, Lieutenant General Lin Wei, Vice Admiral Yang Hsuan Ch'eng, Lieutenant General Chou Chih Jou, Lieutenant General Chu Shih Ming, Major General Tsai Wen Chih, Lieutenant General Stilwell, Major General Chennault, Major General Stratemeyer and Brigadier General Merrill entered the meeting.)

7. *DISCUSSIONS WITH REPRESENTATIVES OF CHINESE GOVERNMENT ON OPERATIONS IN SOUTHEAST ASIA COMMAND*

SIR ALAN BROOKE asked if the Chinese representatives had now had time to consider the plan for operations in the Southeast Asia Command put forward by Admiral Mountbatten.

GENERAL SHANG confirmed that he had had time to study the plan. He had certain questions and comments. Though there might be differences of opinion, these comments were offered in a spirit of helpfulness and he hoped they would be accepted in the same spirit.

With regard to enemy intelligence, there were certain points of difference but he did not propose to raise these at the meeting but rather to exchange views with the appropriate staff officers. General Shang then put the following questions:

a. How many purely British units would be used in the area?

b. Would there be any further British units other than those now in the area?

c. Were there any armored or special troops?

d. What was the fighting experience of the formations which would be engaged?

ADMIRAL MOUNTBATTEN and *BRIGADIER COBB* outlined in considerable detail the nature of the British and Indian formations which would be engaged in the coming operations. Further details which might be required would be available from the staff of the Southeast Asia Command.

GENERAL SHANG then asked for the plan for the employment of the Imphal column. *ADMIRAL MOUNTBATTEN* explained that this column would fight its way through as far as possible. Strong resistance was, however, expected in the Kalewa area. He had insufficient air transport to supply this column from the air and, therefore, its rate of advance would be limited by the line of communications which could be built up behind them. All of the columns would advance as far as possible and exploit to the full the success they achieved.

GENERAL SHANG then asked for details with regard to the Indaw column.

ADMIRAL MOUNTBATTEN said that Indaw would be captured by the 50th Indian Parachute Brigade and the 26th Indian Infantry Division would then be flown in to hold it. It was essential to hold Indaw since it would serve as an essential base for the operations of long range penetration groups against the Japanese lines of comunication. An airfield was essential for this purpose since insufficient parachutes were available to supply the column by this means. The L.R.P. groups were invaluable, not only for harrying lines of communication but also for killing Japanese.

In reply to a further question, *ADMIRAL MOUNTBATTEN* explained the operations which would take place from Fort Hertz. He pointed out that the details of the coordination of these operations with those of General Stilwell's Yunnan force had not yet worked out. Plans with regard to amphibious operations could not yet be disclosed. There would, of course, be a land advance in the direction of Akyab which would be exploited to the full. He hoped to put an L.R.P. group in by gliders west of the Salween River, commanded by an officer well known to the Chins who inhabited this area.

GENERAL SHANG then made certain comments. The Generalissimo had instructed him to emphasize his conviction that the land operations in Burma must be synchronized with naval action and a naval concentration in the Bay of Bengal. The Generalissimo would be most disappointed if he was not fully apprised, before leaving the Conference, of the intention with regard to the strength and time of the arrival of the naval forces in the Bay of Bengal. The Generalissimo also considered that in the present plan the columns did not advance far enough. He considered that the plan also should cover the recapture of all Burma with Rangoon as an objective and the Mandalay-Lashio line as the first stage. Lastly the Generalissimo was insistent that, whatever the needs of the land campaign, the air lift to China must not drop below 10,000 tons a month. Though this might be thought to hinder the land operations, it must be remembered that operations in China and in Burma were closely related and the pressure exerted from China on Japanese forces must be maintained. The Generalissimo was most insistent with regard to the maintenance of the air lift to China.

SIR ANDREW CUNNINGHAM said that he could state definitely that by the time that the land operation in Burma started, there would be adequate naval forces in the Bay of Bengal. The details of strength and date of this concentration would, he was sure, be communicated by the Prime Minister to the Generalissimo.

ADMIRAL MOUNTBATTEN said that the plan for the first stage as outlined by General Shang was very similar to the one he had originally considered but logistic difficulties made it impossible. His staff could explain these difficulties in detail to the Chinese representatives. It was illogical to demand in the same breath that this extensive plan should be carried out and a 10,000 ton air lift to China maintained. He then outlined the relatively small reductions below 10,000 tons which would be necessary over a period to enable his present operations to take place. He pointed out that the 10,000 ton lift had never, in fact, been reached and was no more than a target. In his opinion, the U.S. Air Force had achieved miracles in reaching their present capacity over the "hump." It was essential that the Chinese should make up their minds whether to insist on a 10,000 ton lift to China or whether they wished his present operations carried out. The Generalissimo had told him that he would regard with sympathy any small reductions below 10,000 tons necessary to enable the operations to be undertaken which, in fact, were designed to open the Burma Road to China. He must know where he stood. China could not have both the 10,000 tons and the land operations to open the road.

He would like an explanation with regard to the questions asked as to the numbers of British and Indian troops engaged. Did the Chinese Representatives wish to infer that the fighting qualities of the Indian troops were bad? This suggestion he most strongly refuted. The Indian divisions had fought magnificently in the North African campaigns. If, on the other hand, the Chinese Representatives wished to imply that British troops were remaining in India without playing an active part in the operations, he wished it to be clearly understood once and for all that this was not the case. There were only two British divisions not engaged; one of those was training for an amphibious role and the other was being broken up to form the long range penetration groups.

GENERAL SHANG explained that he had asked the questions referred to merely in order to have full details of the position and that, of course, he wished in no way to criticize the fighting qualities of either the Indian or British troops. With regard to tonnage over the "hump," 10,000 tons per month was an absolute minimum, essential to maintain and equip the Chinese Army. Had it been possible to obtain it, they would have asked for ten times this amount.

ADMIRAL MOUNTBATTEN pointed out that, in order to make the airline safe or to open the Burma Road, it was essential to put everything into the present battle. He considered that the Chinese, at this stage, should only equip troops which would actually take part in the present battle and that tonnage designed to equip or maintain the remainder must be foregone until the battle had been won.

GENERAL MARSHALL pointed out that the present campaign was designed to open the Burma Road, for which the Chinese had asked, and that the opening of the Road was for the purpose of equipping the Chinese Army. The Chinese must either fight the battle for opening the Road or else call for more American planes to increase the air lift over the "hump." Any further increase in those American planes, at this time, he was opposed to. There must be no misunderstanding about this. The battle was to be fought to open the Burma Road. Unless this road were opened there could be no increase in supplies to China at this time since no further aircraft or equipment could be provided from the United States due to commitments elsewhere to meet serious shortages.

GENERAL SHANG said that all were agreed that the Burma Road should be opened but in spite of that he felt that 10,000 tons per month was necessary for the China area. These supplies would not be hoarded or sold but would be used against the enemy. All the 10,000 tons was required for the Yunnan force and for the Chinese Air Force.

ADMIRAL MOUNTBATTEN said that the requirements for the campaign had been calculated in consultation with General Stilwell and General Chennault. These requirements were met by the reduced tonnages he had suggested. The figure of 10,000 tons was a purely arbitrary one whereas his own were based on exact calculations. The Generalissimo had promised him that he would regard minor reductions sympathetically, and he, Mountbatten, hoped that he would now do so.

433

GENERAL SHANG said that he was not in a position to give any decision with regard to a reduction in the tonnage over the "hump" but would report the points which had been made.

GENERAL STILWELL said that he had been instructed by the Generalissimo to put forward four points which the Generalissimo considered essential: Firstly, naval and amphibious operations to be synchronized with the land campaign; secondly, that the Indaw and Imphal advances should continue as far as Mandalay; thirdly, that the Yunnan force should advance to Lashio; and lastly, that the needs of the Chinese Air Force should be met.

GENERAL CHENNAULT outlined the present and projected strengths of the 14th Air Force and the Chinese Air Force, together with the additional monthly tonnages required to maintain these forces. The present role of the Chinese Air Force was to defend the Szechwan basin, but the Generalissimo considered it must be equipped and trained to undertake an offensive role. The tonnages required by this plan for the two air forces in China amounted to some 10,000 tons per month.

GENERAL ARNOLD asked how it was proposed to use this 10,000 tons which, if all diverted to the air, would leave no lift for the ground forces.

GENERAL CHENNAULT said that it was proposed to build up the Chinese and United States Air Forces equally. The figures he had given were the requirements to meet the plan. He was not putting forward any recommendations.

GENERAL MARSHALL suggested that the Chinese Representatives should arrange for Admiral Mountbatten to wait on the Generalissimo to explain his operations and the considerations with regard to the air lift to China.

SIR ALAN BROOKE said that he had believed that the Generalissimo earnestly desired that the Burma Road should be opened. This could only be done if the air lift to China was reduced.

GENERAL SHANG undertook to arrange a meeting between Admiral Mountbatten and the Generalissimo.

THE COMBINED CHIEFS OF STAFF:—

a. Took note with interest of the discussion between the Chinese military representatives and Admiral Mountbatten on the subject of the operations planned in Burma in the Southeast Asia Command.

b. Noted that the Chinese military representatives undertook to arrange a meeting between Admiral Mountbatten and the Generalissimo at which details of the plan, the reasons underlying it, and the considerable effort involved, could be explained to the Generalissimo as well as the implications on the air lift to China.

COMBINED CHIEFS OF STAFF

C.C.S. 130th Meeting

SEXTANT CONFERENCE

MINUTES OF MEETING HELD IN CONFERENCE ROOM 1, THE MENA HOUSE,
ON THURSDAY, 25 NOVEMBER 1943 AT 1430

PRESENT

United States	*British*
Admiral W. D. Leahy, USN	General Sir Alan Brooke
General G. C. Marshall, USA	Air Chief Marshal
Admiral E. J. King, USN	Sir Charles F. A. Portal
General H. H. Arnold, USA	Admiral of the Fleet
	Sir Andrew B. Cunningham

ALSO PRESENT

Field Marshal Sir John Dill
Admiral Lord Louis Mountbatten
(For Item 1 only)

SECRETARIAT

Brigadier H. Redman
Captain F. B. Royal, USN

437

1. *OPERATIONS IN THE SOUTHEAST ASIA COMMAND*

At the request of the Combined Chiefs of Staff, *ADMIRAL MOUNT-BATTEN* gave an account of his meeting with the Generalissimo the day before on the subject of the plan of operations in the Burma campaign. At this meeting the Generalissimo insisted that the alternative plan of campaign should be carried out, the plan for which, in fact, the resources were not available and which demanded an additional 535 transport aircraft.

When Admiral Mountbatten expressed his opinion that these aircraft could not be found and insisted that in this event it would be necessary for the Generalissimo to give his enthusiastic and personal support to the less extensive plan being put into effect, the Generalissimo acceded but said that first the Combined Chiefs of Staff must be asked formally to provide the aircraft necessary for the more extensive plan.

The Generalissimo also insisted that an amphibious operation should be carried out at the same time as the land operation in North Burma.

The Prime Minister gave the Generalissimo the details of the British Fleet to be available at which the Generalissimo expressed great pleasure.

Also, The Prime Minister informed him that the amphibious operation would not affect the land battle.

The Generalissimo made the point that it would, in that it would draw off part of the enemy air forces available.

SIR CHARLES PORTAL then made it clear that this would act both ways and that for an amphibious operation to be carried out at the same time as a land operation would mean that the whole air force would not be made available for the land operation.

GENERAL ARNOLD said that possibly 25 aircraft could be made available but that the figure of 535 might be impossible to find without taking aircraft away from other operations to which they had already been allotted.

In regard to the amphibious operation, *SIR ALAN BROOKE* said that the Generalissimo must be told that he must wait for the answer as it depends upon progress at *SEXTANT*. The question of air lift to China was then discussed.

ADMIRAL MOUNTBATTEN said that the Generalissimo had been told that the average air lift over the "hump" for a period of six months during the course of the operation would be 8,900 tons per month.

The Generalissimo had demanded that the full 10,000 tons per month should be made available.

Admiral Mountbatten had made it clear that this was only a target figure which, indeed, had not been reached hitherto.

The Generalissimo had then said that he would deal direct with General Somervell in the matter.

GENERAL ARNOLD said that he would like the Combined Chiefs of Staff to decide that support should not be given to the Chinese Air Force over and above that which had already been agreed upon.

ADMIRAL MOUNTBATTEN asked that it should be accepted as a principle that if there should be an increase in the transport available over the "hump," the right to use that additional transport should be reserved to the Southeast Asia Command.

GENERAL MARSHALL said this acceptance could not be given without reference to the President.

ADMIRAL MOUNTBATTEN said that in view of the important issues involved, it was necessary to get a written agreement from the Generalissimo regarding the Burma campaign to be carried out before the monsoon in 1944. He understood that the Generalissimo would give the campaign his enthusiastic support and had accepted the implication of reduced air lift.

After further discussion,

THE COMBINED CHIEFS OF STAFF:—

a. Agreed that it would not be possible to find the additional 535 aircraft that would be required for the more ambitious plan of campaign in North Burma to be adopted, and for the increased tonnage over the "hump."

b. Took note that Admiral Mountbatten would draw up a paper for submission to the Generalissimo with a view to getting the latter's written agreement to the Burma operations now contemplated; this paper to be submitted for approval to the Combined Chiefs of Staff as soon as possible in view of the impending departure of the General-issimo from *SEXTANT*.

c. Agreed that it would be very desirable if Admiral Mountbatten would get a clearance to this paper in view of the dealings he had already had with the Generalissimo in the matter.

2. *APPROVAL OF DECISIONS OF C.C.S. 129TH MEETING*

THE COMBINED CHIEFS OF STAFF:—

Accepted the conclusions of the 129th Meeting. The detailed report of the meeting was also accepted, subject to minor amendments.

3. *OVER-ALL PLAN FOR THE DEFEAT OF JAPAN*

THE COMBINED CHIEFS OF STAFF:—

Agreed that instructions should be issued to the Combined Staff Planners to have the Over-All Plan for the Defeat of Japan, now under study by them, completed prior to the return of the Combined Chiefs of Staff from Jerusalem. This date should be assumed to be about 1 December.

4. *"OVERLORD" AND THE MEDITERRANEAN*

THE COMBINED CHIEFS OF STAFF:—

Discussed the subject of *"OVERLORD* and the Mediterranean" in closed session.

COMBINED CHIEFS OF STAFF

C.C.S. 131st Meeting

SEXTANT CONFERENCE

MINUTES OF MEETING HELD IN CONFERENCE ROOM 1, THE MENA HOUSE, ON FRIDAY, 26 NOVEMBER 1943 AT 1430

PRESENT

United States	British
Admiral W. D. Leahy, USN	General Sir Alan Brooke
General G. C. Marshall, USA	Air Chief Marshal
Admiral E. J. King, USN	Sir Charles F. A. Portal
General H. H. Arnold, USA	Admiral of the Fleet
	Sir Andrew B. Cunningham

ALSO PRESENT

United States	British
General D. D. Eisenhower, USA	Field Marshal Sir John Dill
Lt. Gen. B. B. Somervell, USA	Lt. Gen. Sir Hastings L. Ismay
Vice Adm. R. Willson, USN	Gen. Sir Thomas Riddell-Webster
Rear Adm. C. M. Cooke, Jr., USN	Admiral Sir John Cunningham
Rear Adm. B. H. Bieri, USN	Air Chief Marshal Sir Arthur Tedder
Rear Adm. O. C. Badger, USN	General Sir H. Maitland Wilson
Maj. Gen. R. K. Sutherland, USA	Air Chief Marshal Sir Sholto Douglas
Maj. Gen. M. S. Fairchild, USA	Vice Admiral Sir A. U. Willis
Maj. Gen. G. E. Stratemeyer, USA	Major General J. F. M. Whiteley
Maj. Gen. R. A. Wheeler, USA	Major General R. H. Lewis
Maj. Gen. T. T. Handy, USA	Brigadier R. de Rhe Phillipe
Maj. Gen. A. C. Wedemeyer, USA	Captain M. L. Power, RN
Brig. Gen. L. S. Kuter, USA	Colonel J. H. Lascelles
Brig. Gen. P. H. Tansey, USA	Captain C. E. Lambe, RN
Brig. Gen. H. S. Hansell, USA	Brigadier C. S. Sugden
Captain A. K. Doyle, USN	Air Commodore W. Elliot, RAF
Colonel F. N. Roberts, USA	Brigadier A. Head
Colonel E. O'Donnell, USA	Brigadier J. K. McNair
Colonel R. E. Jenkins, USA	
Captain W. L. Freseman, USN	
Commander V. D. Long, USN	

SECRETARIAT

Brigadier H. Redman
Captain F. B. Royal, USN
Colonel A. J. McFarland, USA
Commander R. D. Coleridge, RN

OPERATIONS IN THE SOUTHEAST ASIA COMMAND
(C.C.S. 411 and 411/1)

THE COMBINED CHIEFS OF STAFF:—

Approved the amendments to C.C.S. 411 set out in C.C.S. 411/1 and directed that the amended paper, subsequently published as C.C.S. 411/2, should be forwarded to the Generalissimo via the Supreme Commander S.E.A.C. without delay.

2. *REPORTS FROM COMMANDERS IN CHIEF*

a. *Report by Commander in Chief, AFHQ*

SIR ALAN BROOKE asked General Eisenhower to give his views with particular reference, firstly, to the question of centralization of command in the Mediterranean, and secondly, to the best ways and means of prosecuting the war in the Mediterranean area.

GENERAL EISENHOWER said that with regard to the first question, he regarded centralization of command as being absolutely essential. In practice, the air and naval commands were already centralized and he considered the whole command must similarly be coordinated and controlled from one headquarters. With regard to future operations in the Mediterranean, he considered that these had to be looked at under two different assumptions. Firstly, that there would be a full-out effort in the Mediterranean throughout the winter. On this assumption, taking into consideration the Russian advances and the effect of *POINTBLANK*, Italy was, in his view, the correct place in which to deploy our main forces and the objective should be the Valley of the Po. In no other area could we so well threaten the whole German structure including France, the Balkans and the Reich itself. Here also our air would be closer to vital objectives in Germany. The seven divisions for *OVERLORD* had all left his theater so that, to implement his suggested course of action, only additional landing craft were needed. It was necessary to keep all that he now had and certain others would be required for certain phases of his operations. His build-up must go on continuously. In addition, it was essential to have enough landing craft to insure that one amphibious division can be always ready to attack. With regard to the timing of operations, it would be quite impossible to reach the Po by 15 January, a date which he believed had been suggested. The fighting was particularly bitter and it was necessary to keep fresh infantry divisions in the front line. Amphibious operations, it must be remembered, depended on weather conditions and therefore the timing of

443

the advances could not be exactly predicted. The next best method of harrying the enemy was to undertake operations in the Aegean. There are sufficient forces in the Mediterranean to take action in this area provided it is not done until after the Po line has been reached. It could then be undertaken while the forces in Italy were reorganizing for thrusts either to the east or west. When the Aegean operations were undertaken it would be necessary to bring Turkey into the war. The French High Command were most anxious to undertake operations into the south of France but these were ruled out since all available landing craft were required for the Italian campaign.

Turning to operations in the Mediterranean, based on the assumption that only limited means were available, *GENERAL EISENHOWER* considered that only the line north of Rome could be achieved and that after that he would have to maintain a strategic defensive with strong local offensive action. Lack of landing craft would prevent him from amphibious turning movements designed to cut off enemy forces. The time to turn to the Aegean would be when the line north of Rome had been achieved. German reactions to our occupation of the islands had clearly proved how strongly they resented action on our part in this area. From here the Balkans could be kept aflame; Ploesti would be threatened and the Dardanelles might be opened. Sufficient forces should be used for operations in the Aegean and no unnecessary risks run. He considered that the earlier British occupation of the islands had been right and justified, but the position was now different and strong German reactions could be expected. In either of the two assumptions it was essential to bring Turkey into the war at the moment that the operations in the Aegean were undertaken.

SIR ALAN BROOKE explained that the date of 15 January had been suggested, not for the capture of the Po line but for that of the Pisa-Rimini line. He asked for General Eisenhower's views with regard to action in Yugoslavia.

GENERAL EISENHOWER said that on the assumption that he would advance to the Po line, he would propose action to establish small garrisons in the islands on the eastern coast of the Adriatic from which thrusts as far north as possible could be made into Yugoslavia and the Patriots furnished with arms and equipment. If only the Rome line was reached, it would not be possible to thrust as far up the Adriatic as he would have liked.

GENERAL EISENHOWER then outlined the program for the build-up of his forces in Italy. He confirmed that the ground forces available to him should be sufficient to reach the Po line. His present strength was the maximum which the poor lines of communication could maintain. It must be remembered that there was no good port north of Naples until Leghorn was reached. With regard to his air force build-up, *GENERAL EISENHOWER* said he would like it clearly understood that all of this was not for use in *POINTBLANK* but much of it took an active part in assisting the land battle. This air force, based in Italy, was twice as effective as if it had remained in Tunisia. Only the initial build-up of the air force was a costly business since, once established, six groups could be maintained for the same tonnage as two divisions.

GENERAL EISENHOWER stressed the vital importance of continuing the maximum possible operations in an established theater since much time was invariably lost when the scene of action was changed, necessitating, as it did, the arduous task of building up a fresh base.

With regard to supply of equipment to the Yugoslavian guerrillas, one officer had now been placed in charge of these operations and arms captured in North Africa and Sicily were being sent in. Italian equipment captured in Italy was at present being used to equip one Italian parachute division, which was believed to be of good fighting quality, and a further division would possibly also be equipped. He believed that all possible equipment should be sent to Tito since Mikhailovitch's forces were of relatively little value.

SIR JOHN CUNNINGHAM agreed that everything in our power should be done to support Tito, who had some hundred thousand men under his control. The Germans would have great difficulties operating against the guerrillas since their lateral communications were immensely difficult and there was only one poor railway. They would have largely to supply their forces by sea. It would be impossible, therefore, for them to rapidly concentrate against Tito's forces. He believed that by air and naval action, their seaborne lines of communication could be cut and, in fact, he hoped shortly to be operating destroyers in the Venice-Trieste-Pola area. He questioned whether it would be possible or right to continue to supply Italian equipment since this was rapidly running short.

AIR MARSHAL TEDDER said that the present system of air operations into the Balkans worked reasonably well. The tactical commander in Italy was given his targets from the Middle East. He agreed with Sir Charles Portal that when the joint staff under the officer responsible for operations in the Balkans had been set up, coordination of effort would be more satisfactory.

GENERAL EISENHOWER said that he believed that given 50 percent good weather, he would, once his air forces were firmly established in Italy, be able to almost completely cut the seven German lines of communication into Italy and keep them cut.

b. Report by Commanders in Chief, Middle East

GENERAL WILSON, referring to operations in the Aegean, said that it was essential to cut the German iron ring which included Rhodes, Scarpanto, Crete, and Greece. Rhodes was the key to the situation and to capture this, additional equipment would be required from the western Mediterranean. Once Rhodes had fallen, these resources could be returned and the remainder of the operations in the Aegean carried out with the resources available in the Middle East. All of this was based on the assumption that Turkey had entered the war on our side. For Rhodes, one British division including two assault loaded brigades with previous amphibious experience would be required. These could be withdrawn after the capture of Rhodes. The additional forces required included one armored brigade and one parachute brigade, which were available from the Middle East. He considered that Turkey should be asked to take other islands of the Dodecanese. This he felt should be within their power with the possible exception of Lemnos, which the Germans were using as a base and had reinforced. The commitment to Turkey to protect them against air attack, i.e., Operation *HARDIHOOD*, could be met, with the exception of certain administrative units, without affecting Aegean operations.

AIR MARSHAL SIR SHOLTO DOUGLAS said that he would require some 17 to 20 squadrons and these could be provided with certain assistance which Air Marshal Tedder could provide. With this, Smyrna and Constantinople could be protected, Rhodes captured, and convoys to the Dardanelles given adequate cover. He considered that the capture of Rhodes was a prerequisite to running convoys since without it unacceptably heavy losses must be expected.

Most of the airports required in Turkey were already completed with the exception of two in the neighborhood of Rhodes, on which steel mats were now being laid. Negotiations were being undertaken with the Turks to enable us to put into Turkey the necessary equipment to provide R.D.F. cover and operation rooms. Only one of the airfields was situated to the west of the Bosphorus, and he believed the Turkish forces, including the two divisions in the neighborhood of airdromes opposite Rhodes were adequate to protect them even against airborne attack.

GENERAL WILSON stressed the importance of action in support of the guerrillas as far north as possible in Yugoslavia. The islands on the eastern

Adriatic would be a valuable stepping stone to the mainland and would assist in the maintenance of guerrillas. Operations in northern Yugoslavia would constitute a serious threat to the Germans' rear.

In reply to a question by Admiral Leahy, *GENERAL WILSON* said that the Turks had not got the necessary resources for a full-scale amphibious attack but that he believed that with the assistance of air attack and seaborne bombardment and by using local craft and small landing craft, some of which might have to be provided from the western Mediterranean, the Turks could stage the short shore-to-shore assault required for the capture of certain of the islands.

With regard to Rumania, *GENERAL WILSON* said that he was in touch with resistance groups and that a wireless station had been established in Bucharest. The resistance groups, however, were fearful of the Germans and were taking little action. His knowledge of resistance in Bulgaria was small but he believed this resistance to be growing. He had discussed with General Donovan the possibility of further efforts being made to establish contact with this country.

In reply to a question by General Arnold, *AIR MARSHAL SIR SHOLTO DOUGLAS* said that the airfields in Turkey would be ample for the forces he was able to deploy, and consisted of about eight fighter airdromes and six bomber airdromes. Sites had been selected at a reasonable distance back from the coast and all were equipped with hard surfaces except those in the neighborhood of Rhodes, on which work was now in hand.

THE COMBINED CHIEFS OF STAFF:—

Took note with interest of the statements of the Commanders in Chief, North African and Middle East Theaters, and of the resulting discussion.

(At this point General D. D. Eisenhower, Admiral Sir John Cunningham, Air Chief Marshal Sir Arthur Tedder, General Sir H. Maitland Wilson, Air Chief Marshal Sir Sholto Douglas, Vice Admiral Sir A. U. Willis, Major General J. F. M. Whiteley, Major General R. H. Lewis, Brigadier R. de Rhe Phillipe, Captain M. L. Power, R.N., Colonel J. H. Lascelles and Colonel R. E. Jenkins, U.S.A. withdrew from the meeting.)

3. *APPROVAL OF DECISIONS OF C.C.S. 130TH MEETING*

THE COMBINED CHIEFS OF STAFF:—

Accepted the conclusions of the 130th Meeting. The detailed record of the meeting was also accepted subject to minor amendments.

4. *"OVERLORD" AND THE MEDITERRANEAN*

    A. *ESTIMATE OF THE ENEMY SITUATION, 1944 — EUROPE (C.C.S. 300/3)*

THE COMBINED CHIEFS OF STAFF:—

Accepted the "Estimate of the Enemy Situation, 1944—Europe," presented by the United States Chiefs of Staff in C.C.S. 300/3 *(SEXTANT)*.

    B. *"OVERLORD" AND THE MEDITERRANEAN (C.C.S. 409, 410, and 387)*

ADMIRAL LEAHY said that the United States Chiefs of Staff tentatively accepted the proposals for action in the Mediterranean contained in paragraph 6 of C.C.S. 409 as a basis for discussion with the Soviet Staff.

It was the understanding of the United States Chiefs of Staff that the British proposals would include the opening of the Dardanelles and the capture of Rhodes for which the retention of landing craft in the Mediterranean was essential but that the retention of these landing craft would in no way interfere with the carrying out of Operation *BUCCANEER*.

SIR ALAN BROOKE explained that *BUCCANEER* would not be interfered with provided the date for *OVERLORD* was put back. The British Chiefs of Staff had prepared a detailed examination of the relationship of *OVERLORD*, Mediterranean and Aegean operations, and *BUCCANEER*.

GENERAL MARSHALL explained that the United States Chiefs of Staff tentatively accepted the British proposals for negotiations with the Soviets. He understood that these proposals implied the capture of the Rimini-Pisa line, the capture of Rhodes and the retention of the 68 landing craft until its capture. He understood that Operation *BUCCANEER* would not be interfered with and that further discussion would take place on these proposals when the Combined Chiefs of Staff returned to *SEXTANT*.

SIR ALAN BROOKE said that if the capture of Rhodes and Rome and Operation *BUCCANEER* were carried out, the date of *OVERLORD* must go back.

GENERAL MARSHALL said that he quite understood this point. He was of the opinion that it was essential to do Operation *BUCCANEER*, for the reasons that firstly, not only were the forces ready but the operation was acceptable to the Chinese; secondly, it was of vital importance to operations in the Pacific; and, thirdly, for political reasons it could not be interfered with.

In the course of a full discussion the following points were made:

a. SIR ALAN BROOKE said that it might be necessary to consider earnestly the possibility of putting off Operation *BUCCANEER* since by so doing the full weight of our resources could be brought to bear on Germany, thus bringing the war as a whole to an end at the earliest possible date. The matter should be looked at from a purely strategical aspect.

b. SIR CHARLES PORTAL felt that the Russians might well say that not only did they agree with the proposed course of action outlined by the British Chiefs of Staff and tentatively accepted by the United States Chiefs of Staff but also that they required Operation *OVERLORD* at the earliest possible date. In this case we must surely consider the possibility of putting off Operation *BUCCANEER*. He did not believe this operation essential to the land campaign in Burma.

c. ADMIRAL KING considered it unsound to bring back landing craft from *BUCCANEER*. In his view the land campaign in Burma was not complete without Operation *BUCCANEER*. Our object was to make use of China and her manpower and the delay of a year in achieving this object must most certainly delay the end of the war as a whole.

d. GENERAL MARSHALL stressed the U.S. contribution to the war in Europe. He believed that the suggestion that putting off the Operation *BUCCANEER* would shorten the war was an overstatement. The United States Chiefs of Staff were most anxious that *BUCCANEER* should be undertaken. They had gone far to meet the British Chiefs of Staff views but the postponement of *BUCCANEER* they could not accept.

e. ADMIRAL LEAHY said he wished it clearly understood that the United States Chiefs of Staff were not in a position to agree to the abandonment of Operation *BUCCANEER*. This could only be decided by the President and the Prime Minister.

449

(At this point the Combined Chiefs of Staff continued the meeting in closed session.)

THE COMBINED CHIEFS OF STAFF:—

a. Agreed to the unification of command in the Mediterranean as outlined in C.C.S. 387, and that this unification of command should be made effective forthwith.

b. Tentatively accepted paragraph 6 *b, c, d, e,* and *f* (modified) of C.C.S. 409 as a basis for discussion with the Soviets, subject to the following understandings and modifications:

   (1) That these proposals necessitate a delay in the target date for *OVERLORD.*

   (2) That paragraph 6 *e* includes the capture of Rhodes and the retention of certain landing craft in the Mediterranean.

   (3) That in paragraph 6 *f* the words "do everything possible to" in the second line be deleted.

   (4) That the United States Chiefs of Staff could not accept the abandonment of the *BUCCANEER* operation; also that if further discussion should show the postponement of *BUCCANEER* to be desirable, this would need to be taken up with the President and the Prime Minister.

c. Took note of the memorandum by the British Chiefs of Staff on the effect of weather on Operation *OVERLORD.* (C.C.S. 410).

5. *COLLABORATION WITH THE U.S.S.R.*
   (C.C.S. 407)

THE COMBINED CHIEFS OF STAFF:—

Accepted C.C.S. 407, with certain amendments as a basis for the agenda at the forthcoming conference with the U.S.S.R. [The amended paper, in which are incorporated the conclusions on this subject reached at C.C.S. 129th Meeting, has been published as C.C.S. 407 (Revised).]

COMBINED CHIEFS OF STAFF

C.C.S 132d Meeting

EUREKA CONFERENCE

MINUTES OF MEETING HELD IN THE BRITISH LEGATION, TEHRAN, IRAN,
ON TUESDAY, 30 NOVEMBER 1943 AT 0930

PRESENT

United States	*British*
Admiral W. D. Leahy, USN	General Sir Alan Brooke
General G. C. Marshall, USA	Air Chief Marshal
Admiral E. J. King, USN	Sir Charles F. A. Portal
General H. H. Arnold, USA	Admiral of the Fleet
	Sir Andrew B. Cunningham

ALSO PRESENT

Captain W. L. Freseman, USN	Field Marshal Sir John Dill
	Lt. Gen. Sir Hastings L. Ismay

SECRETARIAT

Brigadier H. Redman
Captain F. B. Royal, USN
Colonel A. J. McFarland, USA

SIR ALAN BROOKE began by saying that the problem was to arrive at an agreed basis for discussion with the Soviets at this afternoon's Plenary Meeting. He then went on to consider operations in the Mediterranean from west to east. It had always been agreed that some operation should take place against the South of France. In Italy he felt that it was agreed we should not stay in the position now reached and must advance farther. For political and other reasons, it was important to get Rome, and he thought it was probably generally accepted that we should advance as far as the Pisa-Rimini line. For operations in Italy it was clear that landing craft would be wanted. General Eisenhower had asked for the retention of the landing craft due to return to *OVERLORD* until 15 January. This would have a repercussion on the *OVER-LORD* date.

In Yugoslavia it was important to give all possible help to the Partisans and there was general agreement regarding this. As regards Turkey and operations in the Aegean, agreement was much more in question. If Turkey were to be brought into the war, it would be desirable to open the Dardanelles and operations in the Aegean would be necessary. If Turkey were not to come into the war, the operations in the Aegean would not be called for.

If examination showed the operation against the South of France to be feasible, sufficient landing craft might be provided for the purpose. The sequence would then be Italian campaign, Rhodes (only if Turkey comes into the war), South of France, landing craft from Rhodes returning in time for the South of France. The date for the South of France operation would therefore be affected by the undertaking of the Rhodes operation.

ADMIRAL LEAHY said that the problem seemed to be a straightforward one of the date of *OVERLORD*. The Russians wanted *OVERLORD* on a fixed date in May. They also wanted an expedition against the South of France at the same time, or perhaps a little earlier or a little later. As far as he could see, the date of *OVERLORD* was the only point confusing the issue. If this matter was settled, everything would be settled. If *OVERLORD* was to be done by the date originally fixed, other operations could not be carried out. It was entirely agreed, he felt, that the operations in Italy must be carried on. On the U.S. side it was felt that this could be done without interfering with *OVERLORD* and, indeed, the U.S. Planners were of the opinion that the operation against the . South of France could be undertaken as well, without interfering with *OVER-LORD*. If the landing craft were to be kept in Italy until 15 January, the U.S. calculation was that they could still be back in time for *OVERLORD*.

SIR ALAN BROOKE said that this was not thought by the British to be the case. Landing craft would need repair and there were also training demands. According to British calculations, even the date of 15 December for returning landing craft to *OVERLORD* was rather tight and it would be a great help if U.S. repair facilities could be made available for the British landing craft returning.

GENERAL MARSHALL then said that the paper submitted the day before by the United States Chiefs of Staff on the operation against the South of France had been produced at Cairo but was based on logistic and other data prepared in detail before *SEXTANT*. He said that four questions had been put to the U.S. Planners. Firstly, assuming that the operations against the South of France, set out in the paper in question, were undertaken, could *OVERLORD* take place on 15 May? In this connection the answer had been that, with the possible exception of transport aircraft, this date would still be possible for *OVERLORD*. There was reasonable expectation that the transport aircraft would be available from elsewhere. It was possible, moreover, that an airborne division might be brought from the U.S. by cargo ship infiltration, thus making it unnecessary to bring an airborne division from the United Kingdom.

As regards the timing of the operation against the South of France, he considered that it should not be carried out more than two to three weeks before *OVERLORD*.

The second question asked the U.S. Planners was how long the 68 LST's could remain in the Mediterranean and still arrive in time for an *OVERLORD* date of 15 May. The U.S. calculation was that the landing craft must be released 2½ months before *OVERLORD* in order both that the necessary repair of craft could be effected and that the craft might be available for training purposes. This gave a date of 1 March. The time for training might be reduced by using more fully the craft already in the United Kingdom. It was clear that all U.S. resources must be used to assist in the repair of the landing craft returning late from the Mediterranean.

The U.S. calculation was that, after allowing for losses, the landing craft remaining in the Mediterranean after the departure of the 68 LST's for *OVER-LORD* would be sufficient to lift 27,000 troops and 1,500 vehicles.

SIR ANDREW CUNNINGHAM said that the British felt that 100 days were necessary instead of the 2½ months calculated by the U.S. This put 15 February as the latest date to which the landing craft could be retained.

ADMIRAL KING agreed and said that therefore it should be safe to leave the landing craft in the Mediterranean until 1 February.

SIR ANDREW CUNNINGHAM said that this also might allow for some small refits to be carried out in the Mediterranean before returning to the United Kingdom.

GENERAL MARSHALL then went on to the third question which had been asked the U.S. Planners, which was that if the Rhodes operation had to be undertaken as well as the operation against the South of France, how would *OVERLORD* be affected? It was difficult to get an answer to this question. In the first place, the dates were quite uncertain. Rome had not yet been taken and the date of the amphibious operation in Italy must be dependent on land operations. Moreover, in an amphibious operation such as might be carried out in the Italian campaign maintenance across the beaches might be necessary, which would delay accordingly the availability of landing craft. It was understood, however, that the amphibious operation contemplated was such that the main forces would join up quickly with it. Assuming that the Rome operation would have been completed by the end of January, the landing craft required for Rhodes could be in the Middle East by 15 February; the Rhodes operation could take place then on 21 March. Allowing a month for the operation, the landing craft could return to Corsica on 21 April, arriving 30 April. A month would probably be necessary for the repair of landing craft before the operation against the South of France which could, therefore, be undertaken at an earlier stage — 15 July. Moreover, the total landing craft available would be barely sufficient for operations against the South of France, and this was not allowing for any losses that might occur.

The Planners were also asked how long *OVERLORD* would be delayed if the 68 LST's were never returned to the United Kingdom for *OVERLORD*. The answer to this was that these craft represented a three months' production and, in consequence, three months' delay to *OVERLORD*. As the landing craft could be made available alternatively only by withdrawing them from allocations to the Pacific, operations there would also be put back by three months.

SIR ALAN BROOKE said that the only landing craft that had not been mentioned were those allocated to Operation *BUCCANEER*, in which 20 LST's and 12 LSI(L)'s were involved. He then read certain extracts from NAF 492, giving General Eisenhower's views on operations against the South of France.

GENERAL MARSHALL expressed himself as being opposed to an early date for the attack against the South of France in advance of the *OVERLORD* date. He was more inclined to a simultaneous operation.

ADMIRAL KING considered that D-day should be the same for both operations and that this would provide a much better basis for planning. This met with general agreement.

SIR ALAN BROOKE then referred to the U.S. paper on the operation against the South of France and said that the paper would need careful examination as to the number of divisions that were available from Italy for such an operation, and the number that would need to be retained for the operations in Italy.

GENERAL MARSHALL explained that the figure of four British divisions represented garrison requirements in Italy outside the immediate zone of operations.

SIR ALAN BROOKE thought the figure of 10 divisions and an amphibious lift of 2 divisions, available from Italy for the South of France operation, to be too high.

ADMIRAL KING stressed the importance of insuring that landing craft were employed for the purposes for which they were designed and not diverted to other uses for convenience. This had happened in the Pacific and no doubt also in the Mediterranean and it was necessary to be firm in view of the importance of the landing craft factor.

SIR ANDREW CUNNINGHAM agreed and said that once the assault was over and ports were open, all landing craft should be withdrawn for refit for the next operation. It was true that although in the Mediterranean the Commanders were alive to the situation and had tightened up matters considerably, there was still some misuse of landing craft.

In this connection, *SIR CHARLES PORTAL* referred to the tendency to be too conservative in the build-up. He referred particularly to the large stocks that had been accumulated in Sicily as an insurance. Probably there was a tendency to over-insure.

There was general agreement on the above considerations and some discussion ensued in which two extremes were quoted, one, in which the 8th Army landing in Sicily had taken a bare minimum of transport and in consequence had been delayed in their subsequent advance; and the other, in the planning for *OVERLORD* in which so many vehicles had been put down to accompany the leading formations, that the whole operation would tend to be hampered thereby.

As regards relief work, *ADMIRAL KING* considered that it was necessary to be hard-hearted and to cut out anything that was being taken across beaches which was not absolutely necessary. There was general agreement regarding this.

SIR CHARLES PORTAL then referred to the aspect of fighter cover for the operation against the South of France. He said he was not satisfied that the range from the available air bases would allow of adequate air support and thought the matter would need to be examined carefully. In *AVALANCHE* two alternative plans had been considered and one of these had had to be turned down because fighter cover could not be insured. Salerno had been 180 miles from available fighter strips in North Sicily. Marseilles was 190 miles from the nearest part of Corsica and 225 miles from the eastern side on which the best air bases were sited. We might want to go farther than Marseilles.

ADMIRAL LEAHY questioned as to why we should need to go as far west as Marseilles. There were good beaches at various places along the coast.

GENERAL ARNOLD agreed that the whole question would have to be studied very carefully. He stated that the estimates in the U.S. draft paper on operations against Southern France had been based on the use of long-range fighter aircraft.

ADMIRAL KING then asked whether he was correct in understanding that, should all other operations be dropped, the landing craft would not be available for *OVERLORD* to take place on 1 May.

SIR ALAN BROOKE replied that this was the case and that if the landing craft due to return to *OVERLORD* did not leave the Mediterranean until 15 January, 1 June would be the earliest date possible for *OVERLORD* because of the need for repairing the landing craft and using them for training purposes.

ADMIRAL LEAHY pointed out that the U.S. figures did not agree with this and that if the landing craft were retained until 15 February, *OVERLORD* would still be possible by 15 May.

ADMIRAL KING said that any U.S. facilities available for the repair of landing craft would be placed at the disposal of the Commander of *OVERLORD* for this urgent task.

SIR CHARLES PORTAL then made the suggestion that if an amphibious lift of one division were left in Italy until the capture of Rome and one division with its amphibious lift were kept mounted in the Middle East until the middle of February, by then it would be known whether Turkey would come in. If Turkey did not come in, the division could be dismounted and the landing craft made available for *OVERLORD*.

SIR ALAN BROOKE said, in reply to this, that he felt that the landing craft that would be required for this division for the Aegean were already being used for the Italian campaign.

ADMIRAL LEAHY said that if the proposed operation were to take place after 15 February, this would surely delay *OVERLORD*.

SIR CHARLES PORTAL agreed but suggested that we might have two alternative dates for *OVERLORD* — the one if Turkey were to come into the war, and the other if Turkey were not to come in.

ADMIRAL KING made it clear that whereas the operations against Rhodes and the Dodecanese were contingent upon Turkey entering the war and were not concerned with *OVERLORD*, the operations against the South of France and in Italy were completely interlocked with *OVERLORD*. It should be possible for the Combined Chiefs of Staff to work out roughly on these bases two alternative dates for *OVERLORD*, as suggested by Sir Charles Portal.

SIR CHARLES PORTAL remarked that while he agreed with Admiral King, he could not accept that the entry of Turkey into the war would have no effect on *OVERLORD*.

GENERAL MARSHALL then said that disregarding the question of postponing the date for *OVERLORD* and considering the matter of landing craft only, it seemed to him that the suggestion of Sir Charles Portal would involve the dividing of the resources of landing craft available in the Mediterranean so that no real strength would be left anywhere. This, he thought, was serious as it would be splitting the most potent means of influencing the war. It would reduce correspondingly the effort in Italy and might have serious consequences. General Eisenhower's views were different from those expressed formerly, and he now talked of a two division amphibious lift whereas formerly he had only asked for one.

GENERAL MARSHALL felt, moreover, that there was the chance that the landing craft so withdrawn to the Aegean, to which Sir Charles Portal referred, might never be used. He said that he agreed completely with the Prime Minister as to the importance of keeping a tighter hold on supply. There was general agreement in this connection.

SIR ALAN BROOKE said that the *OVERLORD* plan should be coordinated with the plans for a Russian offensive. No Russian offensive had ever started before the end of May. Marshal Stalin clearly, and quite reasonably, would like us to draw the German strength away from the Russian front before the Russian offensive started.

A general discussion then ensued as to the answer that could be given to the Russians regarding the date on which it would be possible to undertake *OVERLORD*.

SIR ALAN BROOKE said that unless we could give the Russians a firm date for *OVERLORD*, there would be no point in proceeding with the Conference. As far as he could see, we could do *OVERLORD* in May if we did not undertake other operations. Sir Alan Brooke said that he did not think that 1 May would be possible although 1 June might be. This brought us back to the *BUCCANEER* operation to which, of course, there was a political background. He still thought that it would be better to use the landing craft allocated to *BUCCANEER* for this main effort against the Germans. In response to a question of Admiral Leahy as to whether the *BUCCANEER* landing craft would help *OVERLORD* at all, *SIR ALAN BROOKE* replied that it would, as it could be used both in the Aegean and against the South of France. Moreover, the amphibious lift for *OVERLORD* was itself all too small. It was even smaller than it had been at Salerno.

ADMIRAL LEAHY said that this affected the validity of the whole of the *OVERLORD* plan.

SIR ALAN BROOKE pointed out that if *OVERLORD* were delayed it would make more landing craft available.

SIR CHARLES PORTAL remarked that whatever operations were undertaken in the European theater, the *OVERLORD* operation would undoubtedly be helped indirectly.

SIR ANDREW CUNNINGHAM said that unless *BUCCANEER* landing craft were to be used, it would not be possible, except at the expense of *OVERLORD*, to have more than a one-division lift for the South of France operation, a lift which, in his opinion, was not sufficient.

ADMIRAL KING said that the Prime Minister had laid great stress on the importance of keeping actively employed all forces now in the Mediterranean. He agreed with this in principle but drew attention to the 2½ months' inactivity that would ensue for 35 divisions in the United Kingdom if the *OVERLORD* date was postponed from 1 May to 15 July. He had always felt that the *OVERLORD* operation was the way to break the back of Germany.

SIR ANDREW CUNNINGHAM questioned the 2½ months referred to by Admiral King, saying that the earliest date possible for *OVERLORD* would be 1 June. Both *ADMIRAL KING* and *ADMIRAL LEAHY* then said that this came to them as a complete surprise as 1 May was the date agreed upon.

ADMIRAL LEAHY asked Sir Alan Brooke whether he believed that the conditions laid down for *OVERLORD* would ever arise unless the Germans had collapsed beforehand.

SIR ALAN BROOKE said that he firmly believed that they would and that he foresaw the conditions arising in 1944, provided the enemy were engaged on other fronts as well.

SIR CHARLES PORTAL said that it was still in the balance as to whether we would overcome the German increase in fighter production. The success of the combined bomber offensive had not been as complete as had been hoped for. The Germans were making tremendous efforts and were aiming at a production of 1,600 to 1,700 fighters per month. If they succeeded, the *OVERLORD* operation might be faced by a very strong fighter force acting against it.

GENERAL ARNOLD then said how important it was to examine carefully the whole question of air strengths throughout the world in order to ensure that our great air superiority could be applied to best advantage.

SIR CHARLES PORTAL expressed his opinion that from the air point of view a June or July date for *OVERLORD* would seem to be better, as regards weather, than one in May.

ADMIRAL LEAHY suggested that the Russians would not refuse a 1 June date for *OVERLORD* but that we would have to be firm about it.

SIR ALAN BROOKE said that the date would have to be fixed earlier than 1 June because of the need to retain landing craft for Italy until 15 January. It would be possible to fix a *RANKIN* date for 1 May when probably an attack could be made across the Channel with about two-thirds the strength now envisaged for *OVERLORD*. It was generally felt that the Russians would not understand the *RANKIN* operation if it were put to them. He reminded the Combined Chiefs of Staff that 1 May had been settled at *TRIDENT* as the date for *OVERLORD* by splitting the difference between the U.S. suggestion of 1 April and the British suggestion of 1 June. It had not been based on any particular strategic consideration.

GENERAL ISMAY said that at Moscow the Russians had been told that the operation was scheduled for some time in May. They had not been told 1 May.

SIR ALAN BROOKE said that we might tell the Russians that *OVERLORD* could be undertaken not later than 1 June but that we would expect, in that case, the Russian offensive to take place also not later than 1 June.

SIR ANDREW CUNNINGHAM agreed that 1 June could be adhered to.

SIR CHARLES PORTAL said that Marshal Stalin's statement that the Russians would enter the war against Japan when Germany had been defeated, seemed to alter the whole relative importance of the war in Europe and the Pacific, and to shift the emphasis rather towards Europe for the time being.

There was some further discussion in which the dependence of the attack upon moon and tide and weather conditions was considered, and also the desirability of giving a bracket of dates instead of a fixed target date for the operation.

THE COMBINED CHIEFS OF STAFF:—

Agreed:

a. That we should continue to advance in Italy to the Pisa-Rimini line. (This means that the 68 LST's which are due to be sent from the Mediterranean to the United Kingdom for *OVERLORD* must be kept in the Mediterranean until 15 January.)

b. That an operation shall be mounted against the South of France on as big a scale as landing craft permit. For planning purposes D-day to be the same as *OVERLORD* D-day.

c. To recommend to the President and Prime Minister respectively that we should inform Marshal Stalin that we will launch *OVERLORD* during May, in conjunction with a supporting operation against the South of France on the largest scale that is permitted by the landing craft available at that time.

NOTE: The United States and British Chiefs of Staff agreed to inform each other before the Plenary Meeting this afternoon of the decisions of the President and Prime Minister respectively on the above point.

The Combined Chiefs of Staff were unable to reach agreement on the question of operations in the Aegean until they had received further instructions from the President and Prime Minister respectively.

COMBINED CHIEFS OF STAFF

C.C.S. 133d Meeting

SEXTANT CONFERENCE

MINUTES OF MEETING HELD IN CONFERENCE ROOM 1, THE MENA HOUSE,
ON FRIDAY, 3 DECEMBER 1943 AT 1430

PRESENT

United States	*British*
Admiral W. D. Leahy, USN	General Sir Alan Brooke
General G. C. Marshall, USA	Air Chief Marshal
Admiral E. J. King, USN	Sir Charles F. A. Portal
General H. H. Arnold, USA	Admiral of the Fleet
	Sir Andrew B. Cunningham

ALSO PRESENT

Lt. Gen. B. B. Somervell, USA	Field Marshal Sir John Dill
Vice Adm. R. Willson, USN	Lt. Gen. Sir Hastings L. Ismay
Rear Adm. C. M. Cooke, Jr., USN	Gen. Sir Thomas Riddell-Webster
Rear Adm. O. C. Badger, USN	Captain C. E. Lambe, RN
Rear Adm. B. H. Bieri, USN	Brigadier C. S. Sugden
Maj. Gen. R. K. Sutherland, USA	Air Commodore W. Elliot, RAF
Maj. Gen. M. S. Fairchild, USA	Brigadier J. K. McNair
Maj. Gen. T. T. Handy, USA	Colonel A. T. Cornwall-Jones
Brig. Gen. L. S. Kuter, USA	
Brig. Gen. F. N. Roberts, USA	
Captain A. K. Doyle, USN	
Captain W. L. Freseman, USN	
Commander V. D. Long, USN	

SECRETARIAT

Brigadier H. Redman
Captain F. B. Royal, USN
Colonel A. J. McFarland, USA
Commander R. D. Coleridge, RN

1. *APPROVAL OF DECISIONS OF C.C.S. 131ST AND 132D MEETINGS*

THE COMBINED CHIEFS OF STAFF:—

Accepted the conclusions of the 131st meeting and the conclusions of the 132d meeting, subject to the insertion of the words "via the Supreme Commander, S.E.A.C." after the word "Generalissimo" in the conclusion of Item 1 of C.C.S. 131st meeting. The detailed reports of the meetings were also accepted, subject to minor amendments.

2. *IMPLICATIONS OF MILITARY CONCLUSIONS OF THE "EUREKA" CONFERENCE*
(C.C.S. Memorandum for Information No. 165)

SIR ALAN BROOKE suggested that the Combined Chiefs of Staff should consider the military conclusions reached at the *EUREKA* Conference as set out in the enclosure to C.C.S. Memorandum for Information Number 165, and consider the implications of these decisions and the action necessary. The *military conclusions were then examined in turn.*

(1) *Partisans*

SIR ALAN BROOKE suggested that a directive should be issued to General Eisenhower on the lines of this conclusion. There were certain points which should be covered. He understood that General Eisenhower had set up, or was setting up, a commander with a joint staff to deal with the whole question of supplies to Yugoslavia on a regular basis. There was also the question of the supply of equipment. He understood from General Eisenhower that captured Italian equipment was running short. It might be better to give this equipment to the Partisans who already had weapons and ammunition of Italian make and would use the equipment to good advantage, and to arm Italian troops where necessary with Allied weapons.

ADMIRAL KING suggested that these points might form a part of the general directive to the Supreme Commander, Mediterranean area.

After further discussion, it was agreed that the Combined Staff Planners should, as soon as possible, produce a short directive to the Supreme Commander dealing with the question of supplies to the Partisans.

(2) *Turkey*

SIR ALAN BROOKE said that all the necessary preparations were going forward in anticipation of Turkey entering the war.

ADMIRAL KING said he felt that there were implications in this decision which should be considered. For instance, how many squadrons of aircraft and how many anti-aircraft regiments would be required to support Turkey?

SIR ALAN BROOKE explained that the details of the commitments were set out in C.C.S. 418.

ADMIRAL KING said that he considered that paper, at least in part, out of date. For instance, a target date of 15 July was regarded as a possibility for *OVERLORD*.

(C.C.S. 418, "Entry of Turkey into the War" was later considered in closed session.)

(3) *Russian Declaration of War on Bulgaria*

It was generally agreed that there were no particular implications to this conclusion.

(4) *OVERLORD and Operations Against the South of France*

SIR ALAN BROOKE felt the first step in considering the implications of this conclusion should be that the whole landing craft situation must be examined in order to discover from where the necessary landing craft for the South of France assault could be obtained. He suggested that the Combined Staff Planners should examine this at once on the basis that the *OVERLORD* operation took place during May and that a two-divisional assault took place against the South of France.

ADMIRAL KING pointed out that the decision at *EUREKA* was only that the operation against the South of France should be undertaken in as great a strength as the availability of landing craft permitted and that there was no decision as to the strength of the assaulting force.

SIR ALAN BROOKE said that he regarded a two-divisional assault as the minimum which could be accepted. The attack must be planned with sufficient strength to make it successful.

SIR CHARLES PORTAL suggested that the Combined Staff Planners must be given an agreed basis on which to consider the landing craft situation. The British Chiefs of Staff felt and hoped that the United States Chiefs of Staff agreed with them, that an assault with less than two divisions would be asking for failure. He reminded the Committee that the plan which had been considered at *EUREKA* envisaged something in the neighborhood of a two-divisional assault with an advance up the Rhone by some ten divisions. If undertaken with less strength, the operation could only be in the nature of a diversion. It appeared that in order to carry out a successful operation in the South of France, other operations would have to suffer. Unless the Planners were given an indication from the Combined Chiefs of Staff of the strength of the assault, they would probably do no more than report that this operation was impossible of successful accomplishment.

ADMIRAL LEAHY felt that the Planners should be told that this operation should be carried out without interference with Operation *OVERLORD.*

ADMIRAL KING said that the problem might be approached in two ways: The Planners could be directed to study and report on the lift possible with the landing craft available; the other method was to begin with an arbitrary number of divisions and determine whether resources could be made available for a lift of this size.

SIR ANDREW CUNNINGHAM said that in considering the availability of resources, all other operations must be taken into consideration except *OVERLORD.* He considered that if no strength was set, the Planners could not examine the availability of resources properly. He suggested that they be told, firstly, to report on the required strength for the assault and, secondly, to put forward proposals from where the landing craft resources to lift this assault force could be made available.

ADMIRAL KING said that he believed there was no record in the *EUREKA* discussions with regard to a two-division assault. As far as his recollection went, the paper, which had been hastily prepared, showed that without interfering with other operations, there was an amphibious lift for some 37,000 personnel .

GENERAL MARSHALL pointed out that the conclusion at *EUREKA* implied a definite limitation of resources. What was required was a report on the landing craft necessary for a successful operation against the South of

France without affecting Operation *OVERLORD*. This operation could not be planned on a lavish scale.

SIR CHARLES PORTAL suggested that one hypothesis might be that the necessary resources could be found by giving up the Andaman operations.

It was agreed that the Combined Staff Planners should be directed in collaboration, as necessary, with the Combined Administrative Committee, to examine the agreed operation against the South of France on the following premises:

a. That this operation should be carried out with a minimum of two assault divisions, and;

b. That the necessary resources shall not be found at the expense of *OVERLORD.*

This report to include a statement showing where the necessary resources particularly in assault shipping and landing craft might be found.

(5) *Coordination with the Russian Staff*

It was generally agreed that coordination of effort with the Russian Staff should be achieved through the U.S. and British Missions in Moscow.

It was suggested that it might be desirable that experts should be sent to Moscow from Washington and London in order to deal with the problem of deception.

3. *DRAFT AGENDA FOR THE REMAINDER OF "SEXTANT" CONFERENCE*

SIR ALAN BROOKE suggested that the future subjects for discussion might be grouped in blocks under main headings. He presented for consideration, a draft agenda set out on this principle.

ADMIRAL LEAHY then explained that he believed the United States Chiefs of Staff would have to leave Cairo on the morning of Monday, 6 December, or possibly on the morning of Sunday, 5 December.

SIR ALAN BROOKE said that he felt that it would be a calamity if the Combined Chiefs of Staff broke up without fully agreeing on all the many points still to be resolved.

ADMIRAL LEAHY said he saw no hope of postponing their departure after these dates.

GENERAL MARSHALL then suggested an agenda designed to deal only with the essential points before the Combined Chiefs of Staff.

After further discussion,

THE COMBINED CHIEFS OF STAFF:—

Agreed:

a. That all but the most essential items should be excluded from the *SEXTANT* Agenda.

b. That the following should be the order of priority in which they should be dealt with:

  (1) Entry of Turkey into the war.

  (2) Integration of the U.S. Air Command — directive to Supreme Commander, Mediterranean Theater.

  (3) Over-all Plan for the Defeat of Japan.

  (4) *RANKIN* — discussion only.

  (5) Operations against the South of France.

  (6) Relation of resources to requirements.

  (7) Final Report.

(At this point the Combined Chiefs of Staff went into closed session.)

4. *ENTRY OF TURKEY INTO THE WAR*
(C.C.S. 418)

THE COMBINED CHIEFS OF STAFF:—

Approved C.C.S. 418 as amended during the course of the discussion. (Subsequently published as C.C.S. 418/1.)

5. *PROGRESS REPORTS*

THE COMBINED CHIEFS OF STAFF:—

Agreed that all progress reports submitted for the *SEXTANT* Conference should be taken as having been noted by them. This is not to be taken as meaning that any recommendations that there may be in different progress reports have been accepted. Should such acceptance be needed, the recommendations in question must be put forward separately.

6. *COMBINED BOMBER OFFENSIVE*

THE COMBINED CHIEFS OF STAFF:—

Agreed:

a. That the present plan for the Combined Bomber Offensive should remain unchanged.

b. That General Eaker should not be urged to catch up the three months of arrears.

c. That General Eaker should be told to expand his operations to the extent possible with the aircraft and crews available.

COMBINED CHIEFS OF STAFF

C.C.S. 134th Meeting

SEXTANT CONFERENCE

MINUTES OF MEETING HELD IN CONFERENCE ROOM 1, THE MENA HOUSE,
ON SATURDAY, 4 DECEMBER 1943 AT 1430

PRESENT

United States	*British*
Admiral W. D. Leahy, USN	General Sir Alan Brooke
General G. C. Marshall, USA	Air Chief Marshal
Admiral E. J. King, USN	Sir Charles F. A. Portal
General H. H. Arnold, USA	Admiral of the Fleet
	Sir Andrew B. Cunningham

ALSO PRESENT

Field Marshal Sir John Dill
Lt. Gen. Sir Hastings L. Ismay

SECRETARIAT

Brigadier H. Redman
Captain F. B. Royal, USN
Colonel A. J. McFarland, USA
Commander R. D. Coleridge, RN

471

1. *CONCLUSIONS OF C.C.S. 133D MEETING*

THE COMBINED CHIEFS OF STAFF:—

Accepted the conclusions of the 133d Meeting. The detailed record of the meeting was also accepted, subject to minor amendments.

2. *INTEGRATED COMMAND OF U.S. STRATEGIC AIR FORCES IN THE EUROPEAN-MEDITERRANEAN AREA*
(C.C.S. 400/1 and 400/2)

SIR CHARLES PORTAL said that he had not had time to study the United States Chiefs of Staff paper thoroughly but felt from a brief consideration of it that the points put forth by the British Chiefs of Staff in their memorandum on this subject had not been fully appreciated. He would like to discuss the matter quite frankly. He would like to make three points. Firstly, he fully conceded the right of the United States Chiefs of Staff to organize their own air forces as they saw fit. Secondly, in spite of this he would like to go on record as advising most strongly against the arrangements proposed by the United States Chiefs of Staff since, in his view, they would not attain the objects desired, were unnecessary, and would prove inefficient. Finally, he would like to make it quite clear that, if in spite of his advice, the United States Chiefs of Staff made the reorganization they proposed, he, for his part, would do his utmost to ensure that it worked as smoothly as possible.

From paragraph 2 of the United States Chiefs of Staff paper, it was clear that the U.S. had sufficient personnel and equipment for each AAF group station to be organized to take care of the needs of two groups for brief periods. He had not appreciated this point.

The points which the U.S. reorganization was aimed to achieve were better coordination of the air operations based on Italy and the United Kingdom, the ability to take advantage of varying weather in the two theaters, and the ability of one man to decide on the movements of groups of aircraft from one theater to another.

He would like to point out that after two or three years of experience in the operation of bombers, he considered that it was impossible to coordinate bomber operations from two theaters or work rigidly to a given program. The technical difficulties of getting some 2,000 aircraft in the air at a time required days of planning done by a committee which brought together all the best available knowledge. The final decision to launch the operation had to be taken within four or five hours of its taking place. No amount of unity of command or drive could overcome the inherent difficulties in the operation of large bomber forces.

In his view the insertion of an over-all air commander for Europe would merely insert another link in the chain of command.

With regard to the moving of groups, a quick decision was not always the right decision, and the views not only of the bomber commander but also of the theater commanders concerned must be considered. To give the power to move groups to one man who could take his decisions without consultation with others concerned might result in faulty decisions being taken and even in the movements of groups having to be countermanded by the Combined Chiefs of Staff.

The new proposals would, he believed, tend to break up the close integration which had been achieved between the Royal Air Force and the Eighth Bomber Command. The Air Ministry had a large staff fully integrated with all the R.A.F. commands in England, and here the operations of the various U.S. and British commands were coordinated. This was done under his own direction and he exercised his functions under the Combined Chiefs of Staff. To insert another commander over the U.S. Air Forces would rupture the present relations between the 8th Air Force and the Air Ministry.

The U.S. proposals would also result in the elimination of the present system of dual responsibility of the Chief of the Air Staff to the British Government and the Combined Chiefs of Staff. It must be remembered that the United Kingdom was in the front line and the operations of the bomber forces from the U.K. were of vital moment to the life and industry of England. When the use of "Window" had been advocated, it had had to be debated in consultation with the British Government over a long period. If a supreme commander were appointed, he might take action of this nature on his own initiative since he would have no responsibility to the British Government.

From the Naval point of view the Commander of the Strategic Air Force would be divorced from that close contact now existing between the Air Ministry and the Admiralty. If, for example, the German Fleet put to sea, the quickest possible action was required and aircraft of many different forces had to be brought to bear. For quick action in a case like this, coordination by the Chief of the Air Staff was, in his view, essential.

473

The question of additional staffs must also be considered. If the supreme commander for *OVERLORD* had only one air commander under him to deal with, then he, the supreme commander, did not require an air staff. If, however, there were two air commanders under him, the supreme commander must be provided with such a staff in order to integrate the two air commands. The Commander of the Strategic Air Force would also require a large staff which would be duplicating the staff already in existence in the Air Ministry. He *(SIR CHARLES PORTAL)* could not undertake any commitment to provide additional staffs.

With regard to the power of the Strategic Air Commander to move forces from one theater to another, he considered that no theater commander would advocate a system where he might, without consultation, be bereft of a large part of his air forces. His own proposal to deal with this matter was, briefly, that his (the Chief of the Air Staff's) own operation headquarters should be used by the 15th Air Force as it was used at present by the 8th Air Force, under himself, acting for the Combined Chiefs of Staff. He would then indicate or recommend to the Combined Chiefs of Staff the targets for the 8th and 15th Air Forces and would move these forces as might be necessary after consultation with the theater commanders concerned.

He did not claim that he could vote against the U.S. proposal, but he did feel that he must most strongly advise against it. He would, however, if the United States Chiefs of Staff insisted on adhering to their proposal against his advice, move heaven and earth to make the new organization work.

In reply to a question by Admiral Leahy, *SIR CHARLES PORTAL* said that he would certainly allow General Eisenhower to use the 15th Air Force in his theater as might be necessary since he conceded the principle that a theater commander had a right in an emergency to use such forces as were in his theater provided that he informed the Combined Chiefs of Staff of his action.

With regard to coordination between the Royal Air Force and the U.S. Strategic Air Forces, he felt that only one man must have authority over both or the interest of one must be subordinated to those of the other. For his part, he could not undertake to subordinate the operations of the R.A.F. to those of the 8th Air Force.

In reply to a question by General Marshall, he said the present position with regard to operations of the 8th Air Force was as satisfactory as was possible without the full resources envisaged in the bomber plan. General Eaker had only some 75 percent of his full resources and was, as he had pointed out in his paper, therefore achieving only some 54 percent of the results expected. The program was, in fact, some three months behind. He realized the reasons which had caused this and would like to say that he felt that the 8th Air Force had done everything that was possible in the circumstances. General Eaker had done his utmost to keep the plan to schedule. In spite of his smaller resources, he had penetrated deep into Germany and had accepted the consequent losses. Air operations in Europe and in the Pacific could not be compared. In no other part of the world were our bomber forces up against some 1,600 German fighters over their own country.

GENERAL ARNOLD said that the proposals he had put forward were designed in part to overcome the lack of flexibility in the operations of the U.S. bomber forces in Europe. They had not changed their technique. He had sent a series of inspectors to the United Kingdom to try to probe into the reasons for this. In other theaters 60 or 70 percent of available aircraft were used in operations. In the U.K. only some 50 percent were used. Even on this basis some 1,900 sorties had been launched during the month of September. There were approximately 1,300 bombers supplied to the U.K. This gave 800 with the units and a 50 percent reserve. In addition, two crews were provided. In spite of this, only once in the last month had 600 aircraft taken part in operations on one day.

He could see no reason why at least 70 percent of the planes available should not be regularly employed. The failure to destroy targets was due directly to the failure to employ planes in sufficient numbers. A sufficient weight of bombs was not being dropped on the targets to destroy them, nor was the proper priority of targets being followed.

With regard to the transfer of groups in the U.K., aircraft were flying on an average some five sorties per month whereas in North Africa six sorties per month were being achieved. The question of flexibility between the two theaters was, therefore, of the utmost importance. Transfers of groups must be made as proved necessary and a decision to make the transfer must be taken in 24 to 48 hours. The appointment of a Strategic Air Commander would not break up the close integration between the 8th Air Force and the Royal Air Force. Interchange of ideas must and would continue. The commander to be appointed would be responsible mainly for operations. Administration and supply would be handled by the theater commanders. Training, technique, and operational efficiency must all be improved. Only a new commander divorced from day-to-day routine could achieve this.

At present, the necessary drive and ideas were coming from Washington. He believed that more aircraft were being sent to the U.K. than were being effectively used and that unless better results could be achieved no more planes should be sent.

SIR CHARLES PORTAL pointed out the difficulties inherent in the operation of huge numbers of aircraft. The joint U.S. and British staffs had yet to learn fully their lessons on this point. If a commander were appointed who insisted on keeping the bomber force rigidly to the program, it would undoubtedly be found that, in fact, less sorties would be flown, and he, for one, could never permit his own fighters to escort bombers on a mission which he did not believe to be sound. It was not always right nor was it possible to keep rigidly to a plan laid down in advance.

GENERAL MARSHALL said that it had always proved the case that a combat commander was loath to release any forces in his possession lest they should not return to him. As far as the air forces were concerned, there was required a commander for the strategic air both in Italy and in Europe who, by reason of his position, was not affected by this very human weakness. He realized that the U.K. was in the front line and that this entailed certain complications. He believed that the technique of precision daylight bombing was not being completely carried out in Europe. The U.S. daylight bombers were being operated from bases all over the world and in some of these places were achieving twice the results obtained in the U.K. Flexibility of thought and imagination were required. A huge force could not be allowed to collect in the U. K. unless it was employed to the maximum possible extent. Whether the 8th and 15th Air Forces were integrated or not, he still believed that a commander in England was required who could give full consideration to the many problems involved and impart the necessary drive. He suggested that action be deferred in order to afford additional time to consider the views put forward by Sir Charles Portal and General Arnold.

THE COMBINED CHIEFS OF STAFF:—

Agreed to defer consideration of C.C.S. 400/1 and 400/2.

3. *MEDITERRANEAN COMMAND ARRANGEMENTS*
(C.C.S. 387/1)

THE COMBINED CHIEFS OF STAFF:—

Agreed to defer consideration on C.C.S. 387/1 pending receipt of a memorandum on the same subject by the British Chiefs of Staff.

4. *OVER-ALL PLAN FOR THE DEFEAT OF JAPAN*
   (C.C.S. 417)

SIR ALAN BROOKE said that he felt that C.C.S. 417 would serve as a basis for further work but that it required recasting in certain respects. Paragraph 2 c would, for instance, require revision in the light of the statements made by Marshal Stalin at *EUREKA*. He (General Brooke) was in agreement with the general concept set out in paragraph 4 that the main effort against Japan should be made in the Pacific. He was frankly disturbed with regard to present ideas on operations in Southeast Asia. The Supreme Allied Commander had recently put forward his views which he had stressed while present at *SEXTANT*, that once the operations in North Burma were undertaken, either they would have to be continued to complete the capture of the whole of Burma or, alternatively, our forces would have to withdraw when the monsoon stopped. The Supreme Allied Commander had also put forward his requirements in order to continue the campaign at the end of the monsoon. He feared that Burma might become a huge vacuum and if this were the case, it would not fit in with the strategic concept set out in the plan under consideration, i.e., that the main effort should be made in the Pacific.

ADMIRAL LEAHY said that he had always regarded operations in Burma as a diversionary effort.

SIR CHARLES PORTAL said that he felt that the Combined Chiefs of Staff could not agree to an initial campaign in Burma without considering the implications of a large further effort or a retirement. It was now considered that the major effort must be made in the Pacific and large operations to recapture North Burma would not be in accordance with this concept.

ADMIRAL LEAHY said that as he understood the position, the Combined Chiefs of Staff had not yet considered the provision of the additional requirements necessary to continue the campaign.

SIR ALAN BROOKE suggested that the paper should be returned to the Combined Staff Planners for further study in the light of a further assumption with regard to the necessity of continuing the reconquest of Burma if once the campaign were launched.

ADMIRAL KING agreed with this suggestion.

SIR ANDREW CUNNINGHAM said that it would obviously help the Combined Staff Planners in their further study if it could be agreed to accept paragraph 4 of the report. There were many logistic implications which would have to be taken into consideration.

SIR CHARLES PORTAL said that he felt that paragraph 6 *b*, of Annex III, was politically unacceptable since British heavy bombers must, to a large extent, be employed to fight the enemy rather than being used as transport aircraft.

GENERAL ARNOLD said that he quite appreciated this point.

THE COMBINED CHIEFS OF STAFF:—

Agreed:

a. That the following additional subparagraph 2 *d* should be inserted in the enclosure to C.C.S. 417:

> "The possibility that a full campaign in Burma may have to be carried out following on the *TARZAN* operation."

b. That the Combined Staff Planners should be instructed to reexamine and amend C.C.S. 417 in the light of the above, before resubmission to the Combined Chiefs of Staff.

5. *OPERATION "RANKIN"*
   (C.C.S. 320/4)

ADMIRAL LEAHY said that he understood that the proposal in C.C.S. 320/4 had been mentioned by the President to the Prime Minister. He considered that it would have to be examined by the political agencies concerned in both countries.

SIR ALAN BROOKE pointed out that the proposals would entail a crossing of the lines of communication. This did not appear acceptable from the military point of view.

GENERAL MARSHALL said the logistic implications had been briefly examined and found to be difficult but possible. They were most serious when the forces were most deeply committed, i.e., in *RANKIN* Case "A" and least serious in *RANKIN* Case "C." It had been felt necessary to put forward this paper since at present *COSSAC* was planning on a different basis and an early decision was required in order to be prepared when the need arose.

SIR CHARLES PORTAL suggested that paragraph 3 should be amended to read, "That *COSSAC* be at once directed to examine and report on the implications of revising his planning on the basis of the new allocation of spheres of occupation." This amendment was accepted.

After further discussion,

THE COMBINED CHIEFS OF STAFF:—

Agreed to accept C.C.S. 320/4 as modified (subsequently circulated as C.C.S. 320/4 (Revised)).

6. *REVIEW OF CONDITIONS IN EUROPE*

SIR ALAN BROOKE said that Sir John Dill had suggested, and he himself fully agreed, that since some six weeks were required to prepare for Operation *RANKIN*, the Combined Chiefs of Staff should either fix a date for planning for this operation or review at monthly intervals the state of Europe in order that they could decide the date on which the operation might have to be mounted. Plans were kept up to date by *COSSAC* but six weeks were required to take up the necessary shipping.

After a brief discussion,

THE COMBINED CHIEFS OF STAFF:—

Agreed to instruct the Combined Intelligence Committee to keep the situation in Europe under constant review in relation to *RANKIN* and to report on the first of each month regarding this to the Combined Chiefs of Staff.

7. *OCCUPATION OF EUROPE*

The Combined Chiefs of Staff briefly discussed the occupation and administration of Europe after the defeat of Germany.

SIR ALAN BROOKE said that he felt that each occupying power would be responsible for an area and that broad directives would be given by a centralized body. Occupation forces should be kept to a minimum and the maximum use made of the threat of air power and action by armored and mobile forces.

SIR CHARLES PORTAL said that the administration must, wherever possible, be undertaken by the Germans with the necessary degree of military control by ourselves. A European Advisory Commission had already been set up in London.

GENERAL MARSHALL said that there might be difficulties due to the different methods adopted, for example, by ourselves and the Russians in administering adjacent territories.

8. *RESULTS OF THE PLENARY SESSION HELD AT* 1100, *3 DECEMBER* 1943

The Combined Chiefs of Staff discussed the conclusions of the plenary session held that morning.

GENERAL ISMAY presented a brief note setting out the general sense of the meeting on the main points considered.

The Combined Chiefs of Staff then discussed the relationship of *BUCCANEER* to Operations *OVERLORD* and *ANVIL* and the naval, shipping, and landing craft requirements for these operations.

ADMIRAL KING pointed out that since Operations *OVERLORD* and *BUCCANEER* had been planned for some time, the requirements for these were presumably available. The deficiency would lie in the resources necessary for Operation *ANVIL*. If necessary, he would do his utmost to provide the resources required for this operation, particularly in aircraft carriers.

After further discussion,

THE COMBINED CHIEFS OF STAFF:—

Agreed that the United States and British Chiefs of Staff, respectively, should draw up a paper setting out a draft of matters of high policy regarding the European Theater and the Southeast Asia Command; these papers to be exchanged this evening and considered at the meeting of the Combined Chiefs of Staff tomorrow at 1100.

COMBINED CHIEFS OF STAFF

C.C.S. 135th Meeting

SEXTANT CONFERENCE

MINUTES OF MEETING HELD IN CONFERENCE ROOM 1, THE MENA HOUSE,
ON SUNDAY, 5 DECEMBER 1943 AT 1030

PRESENT

United States	British
Admiral W. D. Leahy, USN	General Sir Alan Brooke
General G. C. Marshall, USA	Air Chief Marshal
Admiral E. J. King, USN	Sir Charles F. A. Portal
General H. H. Arnold, USA	Admiral of the Fleet
	Sir Andrew B. Cunningham

ALSO PRESENT

Field Marshal Sir John Dill
Lt. Gen. Sir Hastings L. Ismay

SECRETARIAT

Brigadier H. Redman
Captain F. B. Royal, USN
Colonel A. J. McFarland, USA
Commander R. D. Coleridge, RN

481

1. *APPROVAL OF CONCLUSIONS OF C.C.S. 134TH MEETING*

THE COMBINED CHIEFS OF STAFF:—

Accepted the conclusions of the 134th Meeting. The detailed report of the meeting was also accepted, subject to minor amendments.

2. *DRAFT AGREEMENT BY THE COMBINED CHIEFS OF STAFF*
(C.C.S. 423 and 423/1)

THE COMBINED CHIEFS OF STAFF had before them draft agreements prepared by the United States and British Chiefs of Staff, respectively.

ADMIRAL LEAHY said he felt that the United States Chiefs of Staff paper expressed better the views put forward at the Plenary Session of the Combined Chiefs of Staff with the President and the Prime Minister. The United States Chiefs of Staff believed that Operation *TARZAN* and a simultaneous amphibious operation were essential. The Supreme Commander must be told to do his best with the amphibious forces available to him. The British Chiefs of Staff paper, on the other hand, visualized the abandonment of the amphibious operation. If no agreement could be reached by the Combined Chiefs of Staff it would be necessary for the United States and British Chiefs of Staff to submit their different views to the President and Prime Minister.

SIR ALAN BROOKE suggested that the Combined Chiefs of Staff were in agreement militarily and only in disagreement on the political aspects of the operations in Southeast Asia.

ADMIRAL LEAHY said he did not think this was the case. The United States Chiefs of Staff believed that the abandonment of the amphibious operation would mean either the failure or the abandonment of *TARZAN*. In the latter case, there would be serious military repercussions throughout the Pacific. In his opinion, the military implications of the abandonment of the amphibious operation were therefore equally as important as the political implications. He considered that the enemy must be engaged in Burma, since unless this were done, they would be able to stop the supply route to China.

SIR CHARLES PORTAL said he did not believe this would be the case, since if there was no land battle, the whole Allied air force could be directed against the Japanese air instead of supporting the troops.

GENERAL ARNOLD said that if there were no land operations the Japanese could put more air forces into their many fields out of range of our fighters.

SIR CHARLES PORTAL reminded General Arnold that the ferry route was now being flown at night. Though our fighters might not be able to reach the Japanese airfields, our bombers could, and this form of attack would prove increasingly effective with the good weather now prevailing. In Sicily it had been possible completely to defeat the German air effort by intensified bombing.

GENERAL ARNOLD said he agreed that more could be done with better weather, but it must be remembered that the Japanese were on interior lines and had a very large number of airfields available.

GENERAL MARSHALL said that he considered that it was not only a question of cutting the air line; there was also the Japanese ground effort to be considered. The appointment of Admiral Mountbatten with its consequent publicity had resulted in large Japanese reinforcements to the area. If Operation *TARZAN* were not carried out, this large Japanese force would take the initiative and could not be stopped by the use of long range penetration groups only. The Japanese could carry out a ground campaign against our lines of communication to China. The Chinese might well be better in defensive operations than in the offensive, but their task would be a difficult one. We had provoked an increased Japanese garrison, and to take no action against it would have serious results in relation to our supply line to China. Further, extraordinary efforts had been made to increase our forces in the area, and these increased forces would now remain immobile. All this was based on the assumption that if no amphibious operation took place, Operation *TARZAN* would also not take place. This in turn was based on the assumption that the Chinese would not advance unless the amphibious operation took place. There were therefore strong military reasons why the amphibious operation should take place, and there would be serious military implications if it did not take place, particularly in the Southwest Pacific. If it were possible to abandon the amphibious operation and still to do the North Burma campaign, he personally would not be seriously disturbed. He did not believe, however, that without the amphibious operation, there would be any Burma campaign.

SIR CHARLES PORTAL asked if it was considered that the amphibious operation was essential on purely military grounds.

GENERAL MARSHALL expressed the personal view that it would be of assistance but was not vital.

SIR CHARLES PORTAL then drew attention to paragraph 7 of the United States Chiefs of Staff paper. Had the implications of the proposal that the Supreme Commander should be told that he must do his best with the resources already allocated to him been fully considered? He had now put forward his requirements, which were in excess of the resources he now had. There seemed two courses open to him; either to carry out the operation with these smaller resources and risk a reverse, or to ask to be relieved of the task.

GENERAL MARSHALL pointed out that there was no insistence on Operation *BUCCANEER*. He could, for example, undertake the amphibious operation against Ramree instead. He recalled that prior to Guadalcanal, the commanders had felt that the operation was impossible of achievement without additional resources, yet it had been undertaken and had been successful.

SIR ANDREW CUNNINGHAM said that there were admittedly advantages in the taking of the Andaman Islands. They would form a base not only for reconnaissance, but to some extent for bombing Bangkok and the Japanese lines of communication. They would also form a good stepping-off place for a further advance on Sumatra. Their seizure would, however, produce for ourselves a very heavy commitment in maintenance. They were a thousand miles away from our nearest base. They were surrounded by Japanese air and it would be difficult to supply them to an extent which would make their use possible. In his opinion, the capture of the Andamans was not worth the candle, except as a stepping-stone to a southward advance. In this connection, however, it had been agreed that the main effort should be made in the Pacific, and therefore neither amphibious operations against the Andamans nor against Ramree were worthwhile.

ADMIRAL KING said that all were agreed that the capture of Ramree would not give us much. He realized that the abandonment of *BUCCANEER* might fit in with the British view that it would be best to withdraw the Eastern Fleet to the Mediterranean.

SIR ANDREW CUNNINGHAM denied this suggestion.

ADMIRAL KING, continuing, said that he felt that the commander of the Eastern Fleet would feel more secure if he had an air base in the Andamans. He (Admiral King) was much concerned over the success of *TARZAN*. He had always felt that the Andaman operation was the most useful one with the means available, far better, for instance, than *CULVERIN*. On purely military grounds he considered that Operation *BUCCANEER* was as much a part of *TARZAN* as *ANVIL* was of *OVERLORD*.

SIR ALAN BROOKE said he felt that the military implications had been overstated. If Operation *BUCCANEER* were not undertaken, the Chinese forces might withdraw from *TARZAN*, but they were, even at present, an unknown factor, and reports suggested that their troops now in action were not too promising. With regard to the security of the air route to China, he did not believe that this would be seriously threatened. The Assam airfields could be protected and Japanese air bases bombed. An offensive-defensive should hold the Japanese forces, coupled as it would be by a serious threat. We had, in fact, by our preparations in the Southeast Asia Command, built up an ideal cover plan which would hold the Japanese forces away from the Pacific front. He did not regard Operation *BUCCANEER* as a justifiable diversion from our main object.

GENERAL ARNOLD said that the 14th Air Force was operating "on a shoestring." They were operating at only 50% of their strength, through lack of supplies. Transport aircraft were being shot down, and for each one of these lost, 3 aircraft must stay on the ground. If our aircraft were grounded, the Japanese could then attack Kunming, and knock out our aircraft on the ground.

SIR CHARLES PORTAL pointed out that if the Chinese troops refused to advance from Yunnan, then we should be relieved from the need to supply them with 3,000 tons per month by air, and this tonnage could be diverted to the use of the 14th Air Force.

ADMIRAL KING felt that it would, on the other hand, be necessary to give more to the Chinese in order to assist them to defend the Kunming base.

GENERAL ARNOLD said that as he saw it, there were three threats: firstly, the air threat against our bases in Assam; secondly, the air threat to the transport line itself, which was difficult to contend with, since the Japanese airfields were numerous and well scattered, and full use was made of dispersal; thirdly, the threat to Kunming both by ground and more particularly air action.

SIR CHARLES PORTAL asked if it was agreed that if *BUCCANEER* was abandoned and the amphibious lift of 35,000 men was transferred to Europe, it would be of the greatest assistance to *OVERLORD* and *ANVIL*.

ADMIRAL KING said that on this basis it might be suggested that resources should be given up from the Pacific to *OVERLORD* and *ANVIL*.

SIR CHARLES PORTAL said that this consideration too, ought not to be ruled out. The British Chiefs of Staff felt no doubt that the abandonment of *BUCCANEER* must increase the chances of success of *OVERLORD* and *ANVIL* and must therefore be accepted. We could not afford to take chances with either of these two operations. The abandonment of *BUCCANEER* would give far greater military advantages to the war as a whole than the disadvantages entailed in its postponement.

After further discussion,

THE COMBINED CHIEFS OF STAFF:—

Agreed to put forward a memorandum to the President and Prime Minister setting out the various points of agreement and disagreement (subsequently circulated as C.C.S. 423/2).

3. *INTEGRATED COMMAND OF U.S. STRATEGIC AIR FORCES IN THE EUROPEAN-MEDITERRANEAN AREA*
(C.C.S. 400, 400/1 and 400/2)

THE COMBINED CHIEFS OF STAFF:—

a. Took note of the alterations proposed by the U.S. Chiefs of Staff to the draft directive proposed by them in C.C.S. 400/2.

b. Agreed to defer action on these papers.

4. *DIRECTIVE FOR UNIFICATION OF COMMAND IN THE MEDITERRANEAN*
(C.C.S. 387/1 and 387/2)

THE COMBINED CHIEFS OF STAFF discussed the directive for unification of command in the Mediterranean on the basis of C.C.S. 387/2. Certain amendments were suggested and agreed to in this paper.

THE COMBINED CHIEFS OF STAFF:—

Accepted C.C.S. 387/2 as amended in the course of the discussion (subsequently circulated as 387/3).

5. *AMPHIBIOUS OPERATION AGAINST THE SOUTH OF FRANCE*
(C.C.S. 424)

THE COMBINED CHIEFS OF STAFF:—

Agreed to consider C.C.S. 424 at their meeting to be held at 1500 that afternoon.

6. *DIRECTIVE FOR INTENSIFICATION OF SUPPORT OF PARTISAN FORCES IN YUGOSLAVIA* (C.C.S. 425)

THE COMBINED CHIEFS OF STAFF:—

a. Approved the draft directive to Commander in Chief, Allied Forces in North Africa with regard to Balkan support, and

b. Instructed the Secretaries to include this directive in the main directive to the Supreme Commander, Mediterranean, now being issued.

COMBINED CHIEFS OF STAFF

C.C.S. 136th Meeting

SEXTANT CONFERENCE

MINUTES OF MEETING HELD IN CONFERENCE ROOM 1, THE MENA HOUSE,
ON SUNDAY, 5 DECEMBER 1943 AT 1500

PRESENT

United States	British
Admiral W. D. Leahy, USN	General Sir Alan Brooke
General G. C. Marshall, USA	Air Chief Marshal
Admiral E. J. King, USN	Sir Charles F. A. Portal
General H. H. Arnold, USA	Admiral of the Fleet
	Sir Andrew B. Cunningham

ALSO PRESENT

Lt. Gen. B. B. Somervell, USA	Field Marshal Sir John Dill
Vice Adm. R. Willson, USN	Lt. Gen. Sir Hastings L. Ismay
Rear Adm. C. M. Cooke, Jr., USN	Gen. Sir Thomas Riddell-Webster
Rear Adm. O. C. Badger, USN	Lt. Gen. J. Stopford
Rear Adm. B. H. Bieri, USN	Rear Adm. T. Troubridge, RN
Maj. Gen. M. S. Fairchild, USA	Air Vice Marshal
Maj. Gen. G. E. Stratemeyer, USA	J. W. Baker, RAF
Maj. Gen. R. K. Sutherland, USA	Maj. Gen. R. E. Laycock
Maj. Gen. T. T. Handy, USA	Captain C. E. Lambe, RN
Maj. Gen. A. C. Wedemeyer, USA	Brigadier C. S. Sugden
Brig. Gen. L. S. Kuter, USA	Air Commodore W. Elliot, RAF
Brig. Gen. H. S. Hansell, USA	Brigadier J. K. McNair
Brig. Gen. F. N. Roberts, USA	Colonel A. T. Cornwall-Jones
Captain W. L. Freseman, USN	
Commander V. D. Long, USN	

SECRETARIAT

Brigadier H. Redman
Captain F. B. Royal, USN
Colonel A. J. McFarland, USA
Commander R. D. Coleridge, RN

1. OPERATIONS IN SOUTHEAST ASIA

THE COMBINED CHIEFS OF STAFF discussed future operations in Southeast Asia with Lt. Gen. Stopford, Rear Admiral Troubridge and Air Vice Marshal Baker.

GENERAL STOPFORD said that a plan had been made for the capture of the Andamans, based on a troop lift of 58,000. It was now felt that the operation to capture Port Blair could be undertaken with a troop lift of 50,000 men. However, the latest intelligence on Japanese dispositions, particularly their air dispositions, had led to the conclusion that it would be necessary to capture Kar Nicobar and retain it for use by ourselves.

In reply to a question by Sir Andrew Cunningham, *ADMIRAL TROU-BRIDGE* said that shipping was available for the required assault lift of 24,700 for Port Blair. The remainder of the shipping required could be procured. The estimate of the potential strength of Japanese air forces in the area had recently risen from some 300 aircraft to 600. It had originally been intended to knock out the air strip on Kar Nicobar with a commando raid, but now it was felt that a brigade was required and the Air Commander in Chief considered that the 120 carrier-borne aircraft provided in the plan were insufficient and should be raised to 240 carrier-borne aircraft. Virtually all the assault shipping required was now available.

AIR VICE MARSHAL BAKER explained that the estimate of 600 enemy aircraft was the total force the enemy could assemble within striking distance of the Andamans. This would include those based on an arc from South Burma to the north tip of Sumatra. Some 80 to 100 enemy aircraft could be based in the Andamans and Kar Nicobar.

GENERAL STOPFORD said that no plan had yet been completed for the capture of Kar Nicobar. It was estimated that there were 5,000 Japanese troops in the Port Blair area and that they could build up to a total of 3,000 in Kar Nicobar.

ADMIRAL LEAHY said that an estimate of 50,000 Allied troops against some 5,000 Japanese appeared excessive.

GENERAL STOPFORD explained that the figure of 50,000 included troops required for the development of facilities in the island, the building of airfields and strips, and for work in the docks. It was estimated that of the total of 50,000 some 34,000 would be fighting troops, inculding headquarters, engineers, and anti-aircraft units; some 16,000 would be non-fighting troops.

In reply to a question by General Arnold, *ADMIRAL TROUBRIDGE* explained that the present date fixed for Operation *BUCCANEER* was 23 March. This date was dependent on tide and moon conditions and could not be advanced since the necessary naval covering force would not be available in the area before 15 March.

SIR ALAN BROOKE then asked what operations of a hit-and-run nature might be undertaken, assuming that the bulk of the *BUCCANEER* landing craft and shipping was returned to the European Theater. This operation might take place either against the islands or on the mainland.

GENERAL STOPFORD said that he would like to consider this possibility further before giving a definite reply.

ADMIRAL KING said that he would like to repeat a statement he had made at the Plenary Meeting earlier that day to the effect that if additional carriers were found necessary for *BUCCANEER*, he believed, though he could not guarantee, that he could find some four to six additional CVE's.

(The Combined Chiefs of Staff considered the remainder of the agenda in closed session.)

THE COMBINED CHIEFS OF STAFF then discussed the relationship of Operation *BUCCANEER* to Operation *ANVIL*.

SIR ALAN BROOKE said that as regards *ANVIL*, the critical part of the operation would be the seizure of a bridgehead, including a port through which the build-up could take place. The assault must be in sufficient strength to tide us over this dangerous period, otherwise we were in danger of being thrown into the sea.

GENERAL MARSHALL, in discussing the timing of Operation *ANVIL,* said that he felt that it should take place after rather than before *OVERLORD* and suggested that a period of approximately one week should lapse between the launching of the two operations.

SIR ALAN BROOKE said that he agreed with this view. *COSSAC* had been of the same opinion. He did not wish France to rise before the launching of Operation *OVERLORD*, nor could the timing of Operation *OVERLORD* itself be exact in view of weather conditions in the Channel.

THE COMBINED CHIEFS OF STAFF then discussed the wording of a telegram to Admiral Mountbatten with regard to possible operations in his theater on the assumption that certain of his resources were removed to the European Theater.

(At this point General Wedemeyer entered the meeting.)

SIR ALAN BROOKE said that, had he realized General Wedemeyer was still here, he would of course have asked him to be present during the discussion with the Force Commanders. He asked General Wedemeyer if he would give his views on possible alternative amphibious operations of a hit-and-run nature capable of accomplishment with less forces than *BUCCANEER*.

GENERAL WEDEMEYER said that he considered that some operation commensurate with these lesser resources could be undertaken. The Supreme Commander had been given the objective of opening the land route to China through Upper Burma. It was considered that an amphibious operation would contribute in the military sense to the success of this task, and Operation *BUCCANEER* had been decided on as the operation most likely, with the means available, to assist this task. It would deceive the enemy and split his air forces. Amphibious operations along the coast had also been considered but were rendered difficult by weather, tides, and the lack of ports through which they could be maintained.

GENERAL WEDEMEYER considered that a hit-and-run operation could be undertaken but would not be so effective as *BUCCANEER*. For *BUCCANEER* it was now considered that some 120 more carrier-borne aircraft were required. This would mean 4 or 5 additional CVE's or 2 fleet carriers. He considered that both the Andamans and Kar Nicobar could be captured with an amphibious lift of 50,000. It was strongly felt that the first large operation undertaken in the Southeast Asia Command must be a success. The morale of certain of the Indian troops was low, and a smashing victory would restore it. Operation *ANAKIM* might be undertaken with only slightly less resources than those required for the Andamans, but it would be against a strong defensive position and would not, he considered, contain as many Japanese forces as would *BUCCANEER*. Hit-and-run operations would not, in his opinion, divert strong enemy forces, and their cost might well prove incommensurate with the results achieved.

After further discussion,

THE COMBINED CHIEFS OF STAFF:—

a. Took note:

  (1) That the assault forces for *BUCCANEER* have not been increased.

(2) That the resources necessary for the operation were either already available in the theater, or in sight, excepting for an increased demand of some 120 carrier-borne fighter aircraft.

(3) Of a statement by Admiral King that there was a possibility of making from 4 to 6 CVE's available from U.S. sources for this operation.

b. Agreed:

(1) That the representatives of the Supreme Allied Commanders, S.E.A.C. and the *BUCCANEER* force Commanders now at *SEXTANT*, in consultation with the Combined Staff Planners should examine and report on the morning of 6 December 1943 what operations of a hit-and-run nature might be carried out in the S.E. Asia Theater in 1944, assuming that the bulk of landing craft is returned to the European Theater, the report to indicate the scale, nature, and objectives of the operations proposed.

(2) To dispatch a signal to Admiral Mountbatten asking for a flash estimate on the above. (Annex)

(At this point General Wedemeyer left the meeting.)

2. *OPERATION "ANVIL"*
(C.C.S. 424)

THE COMBINED CHIEFS OF STAFF considered a report by the Combined Staff Planners (C.C.S. 424) on Operation *ANVIL*.

ADMIRAL LEAHY said that he considered that forces should be taken from *BUCCANEER* only if they were essential to the success of *ANVIL*. They should not be taken for diversionary operations, such as Rhodes.

SIR ANDREW CUNNINGHAM pointed out that an early decision would have to be taken with regard to Operation *BUCCANEER*, since otherwise we were in danger of "falling between two stools" and the necessary time for the training of any craft which might be withdrawn would not be available.

THE COMBINED CHIEFS OF STAFF then agreed to amend paragraph 4 C on page 3 of C.C.S. 424 by striking from the first sentence the words "from the United States" and by deleting the second sentence.

GENERAL ARNOLD discussed the air transport requirements for both *ANVIL* and operations in the Burma-China area. The additional transport aircraft required for *ANVIL* could only be found by cutting out the provision of these aircraft to all countries other than the United States, and to the domestic air lines in America. This he was quite prepared to do.

It was also agreed to amend paragraph 4 of Appendix "B" on page 8 by inserting the words "at least" between the words "for" and "two."

THE COMBINED CHIEFS OF STAFF:—

a. Approved C.C.S. 424 as amended, and directed that the directive contained in Appendix "B" be forwarded to General Eisenhower.

b. Agreed that the detailed planning for this operation should be left entirely to General Eisenhower's planning staff.

3. *DIRECTIONS TO COMBINED STAFF PLANNERS AND THE U.S. AND BRITISH SHIPPING AUTHORITIES*

THE COMBINED CHIEFS OF STAFF discussed what instructions or directions could usefully be given to the Combined Staff Planners or to the United States and British shipping authorities.

THE COMBINED CHIEFS OF STAFF:—

a. Agreed that the Combined Staff Planners should be instructed to keep the shipping authorities closely in touch with the progress of the discussions by the Combined Chiefs of Staff; and that both the Combined Staff Planners and the shipping authorities should do all possible preliminary work on their estimates of the resources required. This to be undertaken both on the basis of the decisions already taken, and on the basis of the various possible assumptions with regard to operations on which final decisions had not yet been reached.

b. Instructed the Secretaries to inform the Combined Staff Planners and the U.S. and British shipping authorities of the above decision.

4. *FUTURE WORK*

THE COMBINED CHIEFS OF STAFF agreed to meet at 1100 on 6 December to consider the draft report to the President and Prime Minister (C.C.S.

426), the report by the Combined Staff Planners on the over-all plan for the defeat of Japan (C.C.S. 417), and the study of alternative amphibious operations being undertaken by the Force Commanders in consultation with General Wedemeyer and the Combined Staff Planners. *THE COMBINED CHIEFS OF STAFF* further agreed to meet on the following afternoon, if necessary, and on the following evening on receipt of the report called for from the Supreme Commander, Southeast Asia Command.

ANNEX

To: SACSEA

From: Mideast

*MOST
IMMEDIATE*

CLEAR THE LINE

Following for Admiral Mountbatten from Combined Chiefs of Staff.

1. If, as a result of *EUREKA* Conference overriding priority were to be given to European operations, this would make it necessary to withdraw bulk of your landing craft and assault shipping during the next few weeks.

2. This would rule out *BUCCANEER* as at present planned before the monsoon, but the necessity would remain to stage, in conjunction with *TARZAN*, amphibious operations on a smaller scale, possibly of a hit-and-run nature involving carrier raids and landings of commandos.

3. Do you consider operations of this kind feasible? If so, telegraph urgently flash estimate of resources you would require.

4. Your reply must be received by 1600 G.M.T. 6th December.

COMBINED CHIEFS OF STAFF

C.C.S. 137th Meeting

SEXTANT CONFERENCE

MINUTES OF MEETING HELD IN CONFERENCE ROOM 1, THE MENA HOUSE,
ON MONDAY, 6 DECEMBER 1943 AT 1100

PRESENT

United States	*British*
Admiral W. D. Leahy, USN	General Sir Alan Brooke
General G. C. Marshall, USA	Air Chief Marshal
Admiral E. J. King, USN	Sir Charles F. A. Portal
General H. H. Arnold, USA	Admiral of the Fleet
	Sir Andrew B. Cunningham

ALSO PRESENT

Lt. Gen. B. B. Somervell, USA	Field Marshal Sir John Dill
Vice Adm. R. Willson, USN	Lt. Gen. Sir Hastings L. Ismay
Rear Adm. C. M. Cooke, Jr., USN	Gen. Sir Thomas Riddell-Webster
Rear Adm. O. C. Badger, USN	Maj. Gen. R. E. Laycock
Rear Adm. B. H. Bieri, USN	Captain C. E. Lambe, RN
Maj. Gen. M. S. Fairchild, USA	Brigadier C. S. Sugden
Maj. Gen. R. K. Sutherland, USA	Air Commodore W. Elliot, RAF
Maj. Gen. T. T. Handy, USA	Brigadier J. K. McNair
Brig. Gen. H. S. Hansell, USA	Colonel A. T. Cornwall-Jones
Brig. Gen. F. N. Roberts, USA	
Captain W. L. Freseman, USA	
Commander V. D. Long, USN	

SECRETARIAT

Brigadier H. Redman
Captain F. B. Royal, USN
Colonel A. J. McFarland, USA
Commander R. D. Coleridge, RN

1. *APPROVAL OF CONCLUSIONS OF C.C.S. 135TH AND 136TH MEETINGS*

   THE COMBINED CHIEFS OF STAFF:—

   Accepted the conclusions of the 135th and 136th C.C.S. meetings and also the minutes of the 4th Plenary Session held at the Kirk Villa. The detailed records of the meetings were also accepted, subject to minor amendments.

2. *AMPHIBIOUS OPERATIONS IN SOUTHEAST ASIA COMMAND ALTERNATIVE TO "BUCCANEER"*
   (C.C.S. 427)

   ADMIRAL LEAHY suggested that the report by the Combined Staff Planners (C.C.S. 427) should be noted by the Combined Chiefs of Staff.

   SIR ALAN BROOKE pointed out that the Appendix would require revision in the light of the decisions taken.

   ADMIRAL LEAHY agreed with this view.

   THE COMBINED CHIEFS OF STAFF:—

   a. Took note of C.C.S. 427.

   b. Agreed that the forces to be left in the Indian Ocean or to be withdrawn for the European Theater should be decided later.

3. *CONTROL OF STRATEGIC AIR FORCES IN N.W. EUROPE AND IN THE MEDITERRANEAN*
   (C.C.S. 400, 400/1 and 400/2)

   At the request of General Arnold,

   THE COMBINED CHIEFS OF STAFF:—

   Agreed to defer consideration of C.C.S. 400, 400/1 and 400/2 until their meeting on Tuesday, 7 December.

4. *OVER-ALL PLAN FOR THE DEFEAT OF JAPAN*
   (C.C.S. 417 and 417/1)

ADMIRAL LEAHY said that he felt no final decision could be taken on these papers pending decisions on operations to be undertaken in Burma and the Bay of Bengal.

SIR ALAN BROOKE suggested that it would assist the Combined Staff Planners in their further studies if the *over-all plan for the defeat of Japan* could be accepted in principle as a basis for further work.

GENERAL MARSHALL said that he considered that in their further study, the Combined Staff Planners should be instructed to prepare a plan of campaign for the China Theater proper, together with an estimate of forces required. He did not agree with the amendment suggested in paragraph 4 of the Enclosure to C.C.S. 417/1 and preferred the original wording of paragraph 14 of C.C.S. 417.

SIR ANDREW CUNNINGHAM asked if the Combined Chiefs of Staff were prepared to approve the general concept that the main effort against Japan should be made in the Pacific.

ADMIRAL KING said that he agreed with this concept in principle.

After further discussion,

THE COMBINED CHIEFS OF STAFF:—

a. Approved in principle C.C.S. 417 and 417/1 (less paragraph 4 of the enclosure to 417/1) as a basis for further investigation and preparation, subject to final approval by the Combined Chiefs of Staff.

b. Directed the Combined Staff Planners to prepare a plan of campaign for the Chinese Theater proper, together with an estimate of the forces involved.

5. *SPECIFIC OPERATIONS FOR THE DEFEAT OF JAPAN, 1944*
   (C.C.S. 397 (Revised))

ADMIRAL KING said that he considered that this paper should be approved by the Combined Chiefs of Staff less any references contained therein to Operation *BUCCANEER*.

THE COMBINED CHIEFS OF STAFF:—

Approved the specific operations against Japan, 1944 set out in C.C.S. 397 (Revised) with the exception of the references contained therein to Operation *BUCCANEER*.

6. *OPERATIONS IN THE SOUTHEAST ASIA COMMAND*
(C.C.S. 427)

THE COMBINED CHIEFS OF STAFF:—

Approved the proposals of the United States Chiefs of Staff with regard to decisions covering operations in the Southeast Asia Command, as follows:

a. Delay major amphibious operations in the Bay of Bengal until after the next monsoon and divert the landing craft now assigned to *BUCCANEER* to Operations *ANVIL* and *OVERLORD*.

b. Make all preparations to conduct *TARZAN* as planned, less *BUCCANEER*, for which will be substituted naval carrier and amphibious raiding operations simultaneous with the launching of *TARZAN;* and carry out air bombardment of the Bangkok-Burma railroad and the harbor of Bangkok, in the meantime maintaining naval control of the Bay of Bengal, or, alternatively,

c. Postpone *TARZAN*, increase to a maximum with planes available the air lift to China across the "hump," and intensify the measures which will enable the B-29's to be brought to bear on the enemy.

d. The choice between alternatives b and c above will be made at a later date by the Combined Chiefs of Staff after obtaining an expression of opinion by the Generalissimo and the Supreme Allied Commander, Southeast Asia Command.

7. *DRAFT REPORT TO THE PRESIDENT AND PRIME MINISTER*
(C.C.S. 426)

THE COMBINED CHIEFS OF STAFF had before them a draft report to the President and Prime Minister (C.C.S. 426). Certain additions and amendments were considered and agreed.

THE COMBINED CHIEFS OF STAFF:—

Approved the draft report to the President and the Prime Minister as amended in the course of discussion (amended paper subsequently circulated as C.C.S. 426/1).

8. *RELATION OF RESOURCES TO PLANS*

It was pointed out that though no final decision could be taken on operations in Burma pending replies to the messages sent to the Generalissimo and the Supreme Allied Commander, Southeast Asia Command, the Combined Staff Planners, in consultation with the shipping authorities, might well proceed with their examination of the extent to which the resources of the United Nations would meet the requirements in the light of decisions already taken. In this examination they should take into account the fact that the amphibious resources previously allocated to *BUCCANEER* would now be available for operations in Europe.

THE COMBINED CHIEFS OF STAFF:—

Agreed to instruct the Combined Staff Planners to proceed as proposed above.

9. *MESSAGES TO MARSHAL STALIN AND THE GENERALISSIMO*

GENERAL MARSHALL read out draft messages which he had prepared which might be sent by the President and Prime Minister to Marshal Stalin and the Generalissimo. *General Marshall undertook to circulate copies of these messages to the Combined Chiefs of Staff.*

10. *FUTURE BUSINESS*

THE COMBINED CHIEFS OF STAFF:—

Agreed to meet on Tuesday, 7 December 1943, and to include on their agenda the discussion of the Control of Strategic Air Forces in Northwest Europe and the Mediterranean, and Facilities for U.S. Forces in the Azores.

COMBINED CHIEFS OF STAFF

C.C.S. 138th Meeting

SEXTANT CONFERENCE

MINUTES OF MEETING HELD IN CONFERENCE ROOM 1, THE MENA HOUSE,
ON TUESDAY, 7 DECEMBER 1943 AT 1100

PRESENT

United States	*British*
General G. C. Marshall, USA	General Sir Alan Brooke
Admiral E. J. King, USN	Air Chief Marshal
General H. H. Arnold, USA	Sir Charles F. A. Portal
	Admiral of the Fleet
	Sir Andrew B. Cunningham

ALSO PRESENT

Lt. Gen. B. B. Somervell, USA	Field Marshal Sir John Dill
Rear Adm. C. M. Cooke, Jr., USN	Lt. Gen. Sir Hastings L. Ismay
Rear Adm. O. C. Badger, USN	Gen. Sir Thomas Riddell-Webster
Maj. Gen. R. K. Sutherland, USA	Maj. Gen. R. E. Laycock
Maj. Gen. M. S. Fairchild, USA	Captain C. E. Lambe, RN
Brig. Gen. H. S. Hansell, Jr., USA	Brigadier C. S. Sugden
Brig. Gen. F. N. Roberts, USA	Air Commodore W. Elliot
Commander V. D. Long, USN	Brigadier J. K. McNair
	Brigadier A. Head
	Colonel A. T. Cornwall-Jones
	Lt. Colonel G. Mallaby

SECRETARIAT

Brigadier H. Redman
Captain F. B. Royal, USN
Colonel A. J. McFarland, USA
Commander R. D. Coleridge, RN

1. *APPROVAL OF CONCLUSIONS OF C.C.S. 137TH MEETING*

THE COMBINED CHIEFS OF STAFF:—

Accepted the conclusions of the 137th Meeting of the Combined Chiefs of Staff. The detailed record of the Meeting was also accepted, subject to minor amendments.

2. *INTEGRATED COMMAND OF U.S. STRATEGIC AIR FORCES IN THE EUROPEAN-MEDITERRANEAN AREA*
(C.C.S. 400, 400/1 and 400/2)

THE COMBINED CHIEFS OF STAFF had before them C.C.S. 400/2 as amended by the corrigendum issued on 7 December.

SIR CHARLES PORTAL said that the attitude of the British Chiefs of Staff to the proposals had already been stated and to these views he had nothing to add. He recognized, however, that the new directive proposed by the United States Chiefs of Staff was designed to meet some of the objections which had been put forward. The British Chiefs of Staff could not signify their approval of the proposals, but recognized the right of the United States Chiefs of Staff to issue such directives to their own air forces as they might see fit. If the new directive were issued, he, for his part, was prepared to assume the responsibility laid on him by this directive, and to carry it out to the best of his ability. He would suggest, however, that before implementing the new policy, General Arnold should, if possible, hear the views of General Eisenhower, General Wilson, and Air Chief Marshal Tedder.

GENERAL ARNOLD said he was anxious to implement the proposals as soon as possible. He would, however, discuss the matter as suggested by Sir Charles Portal before taking final action.

THE COMBINED CHIEFS OF STAFF:—

a. Accepted C.C.S. 400/2.

b. Took note:

   (1) that although the British Chiefs of Staff do not agree in principle with C.C.S. 400/2, the United States Chiefs of Staff have decided to issue the directive giving effect to their proposals;

   (2) that before issue of the directive, the Commanding General, U.S.

Army Air Forces would consult General Eisenhower, Air Marshal Tedder and General Wilson;

(3) that the Chief of the Air Staff undertook to carry out the duties laid upon him by the directive contained in C.C.S. 400/2 (as corrected by corrigendum of 7 December).

3. *AMPHIBIOUS OPERATIONS IN SOUTHEAST ASIA ALTERNATIVE TO "BUCCANEER"*
(C.C.S. 427 and 427/1)

THE COMBINED CHIEFS OF STAFF had before them a telegram from Admiral Mountbatten (C.C.S. 427/1).

SIR ALAN BROOKE said that he felt that no decisions should be taken until the views of the Generalissimo were known.

GENERAL MARSHALL said that the United States Chiefs of Staff had given brief consideration to the subject that morning. In general, their views were that since *BUCCANEER* had been postponed, the trained forces earmarked for this operation would be available for use elsewhere. Some might be required for commando operations, if these were decided upon. The service troops might be used to assist in overcoming the logistic difficulties in Calcutta and Assam. The combat troops might be used as a reliable reserve in the rear of the Chinese forces operating on the Ledo Road. He was most anxious to ensure that our Assam bases and the pipeline should not be lost. The report received with regard to the bad morale of the Chinese forces had, he felt, been given too much weight. It was a report from one officer only, who was not in contact with the troops. The reactions of the Generalissimo could not be foretold, but if Operation *TARZAN* was called off he felt that the operations outlined by Admiral Mountbatten might well be undertaken with an additional advance by the Chinese forces on the Ledo Road with the United States long range penetration group of 2,500 to 3,000 men operating ahead of them, and with some of the British forces released from *BUCCANEER* forming a reserve.

SIR ALAN BROOKE said he was in general agreement with the views which had been expressed. If the Generalissimo did not agree to the undertaking of Operation *TARZAN*, but preferred an additional air lift over the "hump," then a new directive might be given to Admiral Mountbatten, giving him as his objective the assurance of the Assam lines of communication and instructing him that the combat forces released from *BUCCANEER* should be used in active offensive operations to achieve the object while the non-fighting

505

troops released should be used to assist in overcoming logistics difficulties and in the construction of the facilities required for the operations of the B-29's. He suggested that the British Chiefs of Staff should inform General Wedemeyer of these views, telling him that they should form a basis for future planning, but could not be taken as a firm instruction until a reply from the Generalissimo had been received. In the meantime, a draft directive could be prepared for Admiral Mountbatten on the assumption that the Generalissimo would prefer the postponement of *TARZAN*.

THE COMBINED CHIEFS OF STAFF:—

Agreed:

a. That a new directive along the lines indicated in the above discussion should be issued to the Supreme Commander, Southeast Asia Command regarding the campaign to be carried out in North Burma in 1944; and

b. That this directive should not be dispatched until the receipt of the Generalissimo's reply to the President's dispatch of 5 December on the subject of operations in the Southeast Asia Command.

4. *PROVISION OF MERCHANT SHIPPING TYPES FOR THE WAR AGAINST JAPAN*
(C.C.S. 415/3)

Without discussion,

THE COMBINED CHIEFS OF STAFF:—

Approved that the Ministry of War Transport and the War Shipping Administration should take into consideration the need for Fleet Auxiliaries for the British Fleet for operations in the war against Japan, and that they should take steps to provide the requisite ships after agreement in detail between the Commander in Chief, United States Fleet and the First Sea Lord, as set out in C.C.S. 415/3.

5. *RELATION OF AVAILABLE RESOURCES TO THE OPERATIONS DECIDED UPON*
(C.C.S. 428)

SIR ALAN BROOKE said that the paper under consideration had been prepared in great haste as an interim report, and as such it could be accepted.

Further work would have to be done in the light of the final decisions yet to be taken.

GENERAL MARSHALL agreed with this view. He suggested certain amendments to the report, which were agreed.

THE COMBINED CHIEFS OF STAFF:—

Accepted in principle the relation of available resources to agreed operations outlined in C.C.S. 428 with the modifications approved in the course of discussion. (Amended paper subsequently circulated as C.C.S. 428 (Rev.))

6. *DEVELOPMENT OF FACILITIES IN THE AZORES*
   (C.C.S. 270/13 and 270/14)

SIR CHARLES PORTAL said that there were two sides to this problem. Firstly, with regard to the political position, the latest information from Lisbon showed that Dr. Salazar was ready to allow the operation of United States anti-submarine forces and the ferrying of United States aircraft through the Azores on condition that acceptable formulae to cover these operations could be found. The British Chiefs of Staff memorandum (C.C.S. 270/14) suggested certain formulae. These were contained in paragraphs 2, 3, and 4 of the paper. He would like to know if these were acceptable to the United States Chiefs of Staff.

GENERAL MARSHALL said that the United States Chiefs of Staff had already put forward a draft memorandum for the President to send to the State Department with regard to the changing of the insignia on the United States aircraft to be used in the Azores.

SIR CHARLES PORTAL said that he did not believe that this would now be necessary. It seemed to him that provided Dr. Salazar could be satisfied that the United States anti-submarine forces were operating on loan to His Majesty's Government under command of a British officer from a British base, and that the American transit aircraft were controlled by the British Air Transport Command, he, Dr. Salazar, would be satisfied.

With regard to the military aspects, it had been found necessary to obtain additional facilities; for instance, more land was required, and it was desired to run a pipeline to take the place of the long haul for gasoline by road. In this connection, it was proposed that the British Government should make a further approach to the Portuguese Government, asking for these additional facilities, on the ground that these were a natural development on the agreement already in force.

GENERAL ARNOLD said that the formulae suggested by Sir Charles Portal were entirely acceptable to him, except for the proposal in the second half of paragraph 4 of C.C.S. 270/14 with regard to the second airfield. He suggested, therefore, that the British proposals with this exception should be accepted and that he and Sir Charles Portal should work out the necessary details.

THE COMBINED CHIEFS OF STAFF:—

a. Approved C.C.S. 270/14 with the elimination of the last sentence of paragraph 4.

b. Agreed that details regarding the use of the Azores facilities by United States Army air forces should be settled directly between General Arnold and Air Chief Marshal Portal.

7. *NEW COMMAND ARRANGEMENTS*

THE COMBINED CHIEFS OF STAFF discussed the date on which the new Mediterranean Command should be set up, and the most suitable time for General Eisenhower to leave this theater and assume command of the Allied Expeditionary Force.

It was generally agreed that it was undesirable to publish the fact that unification of command in the Mediterranean had been set up, or to announce General Eisenhower's new appointment. In this latter case, however, it was accepted that for political reasons the announcement of this appointment would be necessary.

SIR HASTINGS ISMAY put forward a draft memorandum covering these points. The Combined Chiefs of Staff accepted this memorandum for submission to the President and Prime Minister.

THE COMBINED CHIEFS OF STAFF:—

a. Agreed that the unification of Command in the Mediterranean shall take effect from 10 December. There should be no public announcement of this change of organization.

b. Agreed to recommend that General Eisenhower should hand over Command of the Mediterranean Theater on 1 January, or as soon after that date as General Eisenhower himself thinks desirable, having regard to the progress of the operations to capture Rome.

c. Agreed to recommend, that, if there is to be a public announcement of General Eisenhower's move from the Mediterranean to the U.K., his new appointment should be described as Supreme Commander, Allied Expeditionary Force.

d. Recommend that concurrently with the above, the announcement should be made of the new Allied Commander in Chief, Mediterranean Theater.

e. Took note that the approval of the President and Prime Minister would be sought to the above before transmission of the necessary instructions.

8. *OPERATIONS IN SOUTHEAST ASIA COMMAND*
(C.C.S. 411/5)

The United States Chiefs of Staff presented a memorandum (C.C.S. 411/5) setting out certain proposals with regard to the air lift to China.

After a brief discussion,

THE COMBINED CHIEFS OF STAFF:—

Approved C.C.S. 411/5.

9. *EMPLOYMENT OF FRENCH FORCES*

SIR ALAN BROOKE reminded the Combined Chiefs of Staff that General Giraud had put forward a proposal for employing at least one French armored division from the United Kingdom. He felt that in view of shipping limitations and the fact that Operation *ANVIL* had now been decided on, it would be better to maintain the principle that the main French effort should be made in the South of France.

GENERAL MARSHALL agreed with this view. The training of a French armored division in the United Kingdom would prove difficult. It would be better that the French armored division and other French forces should if possible be given a period of active service in Italy, and then used for Operation *ANVIL*. It must be remembered of course that General Giraud did not know that this operation had been decided on. As he saw, it would probably be best for the *ANVIL* forces to be principally United States and the remainder French. The majority of the forces in Italy would then be British. It was most important that the French forces for *ANVIL* should have had experience in battle before this operation. There would, of course, have to be a token French force for Operation *OVERLORD*.

THE COMBINED CHIEFS OF STAFF:—

Agreed:

    a. That for shipping and other reasons it was undesirable that a French armored division should be sent to take part in Operation *OVERLORD*.

    b. That as a general policy:

        (1) A French force should participate in *ANVIL* and only a token force in *OVERLORD*.

        (2) It will probably be best to undertake the *ANVIL* operation with U.S. forces with French participation, and to continue the campaign in Italy with British forces.

    c. That all French formations should be given battle experience in Italy.

10. *FINAL REMARKS*

    SIR ALAN BROOKE said he would like to express on behalf of the British Chiefs of Staff their deep gratitude for the way in which the United States Chiefs had met their views.

    There was one other point he would like to mention. The British Chiefs of Staff would like to express their appreciation of the unstinting help given to the British and other Allies from American production. This aspect of United States assistance was not mentioned in the consideration of strategy, but nevertheless had the widest repercussions on all our plans, and was playing a great part in the successful development of the war. The British Chiefs of Staff would like to express their deep admiration of the stupendous efforts which the United States had made in the field of production.

    GENERAL MARSHALL said that he very much appreciated Sir Alan Brooke's gracious tributes. He felt that it was most important that during the next month or so the British and United States Chiefs of Staff should both study how best the magnitude of future conferences could be reduced. They would undoubtedly in future have to take place at shorter intervals.

ADMIRAL KING, in agreeing with this view, said that every effort should also be made to cut down the number of subjects discussed at these important conferences.

THE COMBINED CHIEFS OF STAFF:—

Agreed:

a. That it was desirable to cut down as much as possible the attendance at future U.S.-British Conferences.

b. That a study with this in view should be carried out within the next month.

EUREKA CONFERENCE

EUREKA CONFERENCE

MINUTES OF PLENARY SESSION
BETWEEN THE U.S.A., GREAT BRITAIN AND THE U.S.S.R.,

HELD IN THE RUSSIAN LEGATION, TEHRAN, IRAN,
ON SUNDAY, 28 NOVEMBER 1943 AT 1600

PRESENT

United States	*British*
President Roosevelt (In the Chair)	Prime Minister Churchill
Mr. Harry L. Hopkins	Mr. Anthony Eden
Admiral W. D. Leahy, USN	Field Marshal Sir John Dill
Admiral E. J. King, USN	General Sir Alan Brooke
Maj. General J. R. Deane, USA	Admiral Sir Andrew B. Cunningham
	Air Chief Marshal Sir Charles F. A. Portal
Capt. F. B. Royal, USN, Secretary	Lt. Gen. Sir Hastings L. Ismay, Secretary
Mr. C. E. Bohlen (Interpreter)	Major Birse (Interpreter)

U.S.S.R.

Marshal Stalin

Mr. Molotov
Marshal Voroshiloff

One Secretary

Mr. Pavlov (Interpreter)

THE PRESIDENT said, as the youngest of the three Chiefs of State present, he had the privilege of welcoming Marshal Stalin and Prime Minister Churchill to this auspicious conference. We are sitting around this table for the first time as a family, with the one object of winning the war. Regarding the conduct of naval and military meetings, it has been our habit, between the British and the United States, to publish nothing but to speak our minds very freely. In such a large family circle we hope that we will be very successful and achieve constructive accord in order that we may maintain close touch throughout the war and after the war. The General Staffs of the three countries should look after military matters. Marshal Stalin, the Prime Minister and I have many things to discuss regarding matters pertaining to conditions after the war. If anyone of us does not want to talk about any particular subject brought up we do not have to. *THE PRESIDENT* added that before he came to the discussion of military problems he felt that perhaps the Prime Minister would like to say something about matters pertaining to the years to come.

THE PRIME MINISTER said that we represent here a concentration of great worldly power. In our hands we have perhaps the responsibility for the shortening of this war. In our hands we have, too, the future of mankind. I pray that we may be worthy of this God-given opportunity.

THE PRESIDENT then turned to Marshal Stalin and said, "Perhaps our host would like to say a few words."

MARSHAL STALIN said, "I take pleasure in welcoming those present. I think that history will show that this opportunity has been of tremendous import. I think the great opportunity which we have and the power which our people have invested in us can be used to take full advantage within the frame of our potential collaboration. Now let us get down to business."

THE PRESIDENT said he would like to start with a general survey of the war and of the meaning of the war. This survey will be from the American point of view. We earnestly hope that the completion of the war will come just as soon as possible. Let us begin with a subject that affects the United States more than either Great Britain or the U.S.S.R., the subject of the Pacific. It is most important to us to bring back to the United States those forces which are now in the Pacific. We are bearing a major part of the Pacific war. The United States has the greatest part of its naval power in the Pacific, plus about one million men. We are proceeding on the principle of attrition as regards Japan. At the present that policy is being accepted in our country. We believe we are sinking many Jap ships, both naval and merchant — more than they can

514

possibly replace. We have been moving forward toward Japan from the south and now we are moving toward Japan through the islands from the east. There is very little more that we can do as regards operations from the north. On the west of Japan it is necessary for us to keep China in the war. Hence, we have arranged plans for operations through North Burma and into the Yunnan Province. That operation will advance us far enough so that China herself can strike into the Yunnan Province. In addition, we are still discussing an amphibious operation in order to strike at the supply lines from the Jap base at Bangkok. This base is a veritable storehouse for Japan. The whole operation covers a huge territory, and large numbers of ships and men and planes are necessary to carry it out. We must definitely keep China actively in the war.

THE PRESIDENT said, in the second place, we hope, by opening the Burma Road and increasing the transportation of supplies by plane into China, we will be in a position to attack Tokyo from China by air this summer. All this is regarding the Southeast Asia operations. But we want to express to you the very great importance not only of keeping China in the war but of being able to get at Japan with the greatest possible speed.

Now to come down to the more important operations which are of immediate concern to the U.S.S.R. and Great Britain. In the last two or three conferences at Casablanca, Washington and Quebec, we have made many plans. As a matter of fact, about a year and a half ago the major part of our plans were involved in consideration of an expedition against the Axis across the English Channel. Largely because of transportation difficulties we were not able to set a definite date. Not only do we want to get across the English Channel but once we are across, we intend to proceed inland into Germany. It would be impossible to launch such an operation before about 1 May 1944 — it was decided at Quebec. The Channel is such a disagreeable body of water. No matter how unpleasant that body of water might be, however, we still want to get across it. *(MR. CHURCHILL* interpolated that we were very glad it was an unpleasant body of water at one time.) We can not do everything we would like to do in the Mediterranean and also from the United Kingdom, as there is a definite "bottleneck" in the matter of war called landing craft. If we were to conduct any large expedition in the Mediterranean, it would be necessary to give up this important cross-Channel operation, and certain contemplated operations in the Mediterranean might result in a delay in *OVERLORD* for one month or two or three. Therefore, I pray in this military Conference to have the benefit of the opinion of the two Soviet Marshals and that they will inform us how in their opinion we can be of most help to the U.S.S.R.

515

THE PRESIDENT said that he felt that even though *OVERLORD* should be delayed, we can draw more German divisions from the Soviet front by means of that operation than any other. We have the troops in the Mediterranean but there is a shortage of landing craft. We might help the U.S.S.R. by doing certain immediate operations in the Mediterranean, but we must avoid, if possible, delaying *OVERLORD* beyond May or June. There were several things we could do: (a) increase the drive into Italy; (b) undertake an operation from the Northeast Adriatic; (c) operations in the Aegean; (d) operations from Turkey. That is what this military conference is concerned with and we want to create a withdrawal of German divisions from the Western Front. (*THE PRIME MINISTER* interpolated "as soon as possible.")

THE PRIME MINISTER said we would like to know what we can do that would most gratefully help that which the Soviets are doing on their Western Front. He added that we have tried to outline matters in the simplest terms. There are no differences between Great Britain and the United States in point of view except as regards "ways and means." We would like to reserve any further comments until after we have heard from Marshal Stalin.

MARSHAL STALIN said, as regards the first part of the President's remarks, we Soviets welcome your successes in the Pacific. Unfortunately we have not so far been able to help because we require too much of our forces on the Western Front and are unable to launch any operations against Japan at this time. Our forces now in the East are more or less satisfactory for defense. However, they must be increased about three-fold for purposes of offensive operations. This condition will not take place until Germany has been forced to capitulate. *Then* by our common front we shall win.

Regarding the second part of the President's remarks concerning Europe, *MARSHAL STALIN* said he had certain comments to make. Firstly, in a few words, he would like to tell how the Soviets are conducting their own operations, especially since they started their advance last July. (Here *THE MARSHAL* inquired whether he would be taking too much time to discuss the operations on the Soviet front, and *THE PRESIDENT* and *PRIME MINISTER* both replied emphatically in the negative and requested him to proceed.)

MARSHAL STALIN said that after the German defense had collapsed, they were prepared to start their offensive, i.e., they had accumulated sufficient munitions, supplies and reserves, etc. They passed easily from the defensive into the offensive. As a matter of fact, they did not expect the successes they achieved in July, August, and September. Contrary to the Soviet expectations, the Germans are considerably weakened. At the present time the Germans have on the Soviet front 210 divisions, plus 6 German divisions that are in the process of being furnished for this front. In addition, there are 50 non-German divisions, which include 10 Bulgarian, 20 Finnish, and 16 to 18 Rumanian.

THE PRESIDENT asked what the present strength of these divisions was.

MARSHAL STALIN replied that the Germans considered a normal division to be eight to nine thousand men, not counting the corps troops, anti-aircraft artillery, and so forth. Including these special troops, the divisions totaled about twelve thousand. He said that last year the Germans had 240 divisions on the Soviet front, 179 of which were German. However, this year they have 260 divisions on the Soviet front, 210 of which are German, plus the six that are now moving from the West. The Red Army has 330 divisions opposing the Germans. This Soviet excess of 70 divisions is used for offensive operations. If the excess did not exist, no offensive operations would be possible. However, as time goes on the difference between the German and Soviet strength decreases, particularly as to the result of demolitions which the Germans construct during their withdrawals, which makes supply difficult. As a result, the operations have slowed down, but the Red Army still maintains the initiative. In some sectors the operations have come to a standstill.

MARSHAL STALIN said that as to the Ukraine, west and south of Kiev, the Germans have taken the initiative. In this sector they have three old and five new tank divisions, plus 22 or 23 infantry or motorized divisions. These are for the purpose of capturing Kiev. Some difficulties may, therefore, be foreseen. All of these factors make it necessary that the Soviets continue operations in the West and remain silent as far as the Far Eastern front is concerned. The above is a description of the Soviet operations during this past summer.

Now a few words as to how the U.S.S.R. believes the forces of the United States and Great Britain could be best used to help the Soviet front. Possibly this is a mistake, but the U.S.S.R. has considered the operations in Italy as of great value in order to permit ships to pass through the Mediterranean. As to other large operations against Germany from the Italian front, it is not considered that operations in Italy are of great value to further the war against the Axis. Thus, it is believed that the Italian operations were of great importance in order to produce freedom of navigation, but that now they are of no further great importance as regards the defeat of Germany. There was once a time when the Soviets tried to invade the Alps, but they found it a very difficult operation.

In the U.S.S.R. it is believed that the most suitable sector for a blow at Germany would be from some place in France — Northwestern France or Southern France. It is thought that Hitler is trying hard now to contain as many Allied divisions in Italy as possible because he knows things cannot be settled here, and Germany is defended by the Alps. It would be a good thing if Turkey could open the way to Germany, and it would then be unnecessary to launch a cross-Channel operation. However, despite the fact that the heart of Germany is far from the Balkans, it would be a better area from which to launch an attack than from Italy. Soviet military authorities believe it would be better to use Northern France for invasion purposes, but it must be expected that the Germans will fight like devils to prevent such an attack.

THE PRIME MINISTER then said that the British had long agreed with the United States that an invasion of North and Northwestern France across the Channel should be undertaken. At the present time preparations for such an operation are absorbing the major part of our energies and resources. He said it would take a long statement to explain why the U.S. and U.K. have not been able to strike against France in 1943, but that they are resolved to do so in 1944. In 1943 operations in Africa and across the Mediterranean were the best that could be accomplished in view of the limitations imposed by the lack of shipping and landing craft. He said that the United States and Great Britain had set before themselves the object of carrying an army into France in the late spring or early summer of 1944. The forces set up for this operation amount to 16 British divisions and 19 U.S. divisions, a total of 35. It must be remembered, however, that these divisions are almost twice as strong as the German divisions. The enterprise will involve a force of a million men being placed into France in 1944.

At this point *MARSHAL STALIN* stated that he had not wished to imply that the Mediterranean operations had been unimportant.

THE PRIME MINISTER said he was very grateful for the Marshal's courtesy, but both he and the President had never regarded the Mediterranean operations as more than a stepping stone to the main offensive against Germany. He said that after the British 16 divisions had been committed, there would be no more British divisions available for the operations. The entire British manpower would be necessary to maintain the divisions thus committed in France and elsewhere throughout the world. The remaining build-up for the offensive against Germany would rest with the United States. *THE PRIME MINISTER* said, however, that the summer of 1944 is far away. This particular operation is six months away. It is asked now what can be done in the mean-

518

while that will be of more use and take more weight off the U.S.S.R., possibly without delaying *OVERLORD* more than a month or two. Already seven of the best divisions have been withdrawn from the Mediterranean for *OVERLORD* and many landing craft have already gone or are being collected together. These withdrawals, plus bad weather, have resulted in our great disappointment at not now being in Rome. However, it is hoped to be there in January. General Alexander, who is commanding these operations under the direction of General Eisenhower, feels that that offensive might result in completely cutting off the 10 or 12 divisions now opposing the Anglo-American forces. This would result from amphibious operations, flanking movements, which would cut off their lines of withdrawal.

The United States and the British have not come to any decision regarding plans for going into the Valley of the Po or for trying to invade Germany from Northern Italy. It was felt that when the Pisa-Rimini line should be reached we could then look toward Southern France or the Adriatic. It would be possible to use sea power in order to open the way.

THE PRIME MINISTER said, however, that the operations referred to above were not enough. Ways of doing much more were now being talked of. Splendid things had been accomplished in Yugoslavia by Tito, who is doing much more than Mihailovich had accomplished. There were no plans to put a large army into Yugoslavia, but a blow could be struck at the Germans by means of assisting the Tito forces through increased supplies.

THE PRIME MINISTER said that one of the greatest things under consideration was the matter of bringing Turkey into the war, persuading her in, and opening the communications into the Dardanelles, Bosphorus and the Black Sea. Such operation would make possible an attack on Rhodes and other islands in the Aegean. The above would have a very important effect in that it would be possible for convoys to supply the U.S.S.R. through that route and these convoys could be maintained continuously. At the present time four convoys are scheduled via the northern routes, but it will not be possible to send more because of the necessity of utilizing the escorts for the *OVERLORD* build-up.

THE PRIME MINISTER said one of the most important questions is how Turkey can be persuaded to come into the war. What should be done about this matter? If Turkey should enter the war, should she be asked to attack Bulgaria or should her forces stop on the Thrace front? What would be the effect of Turkey's action on Bulgaria? What do the Soviets think Bulgaria would do in the event of Turkey's coming into the war? How would Turkey's entry into the war affect Rumania and Hungary? Would not Turkey's entry into the war and consequent operations in the Aegean bring about a political "turnover" and force a German evacuation of Greece? It would be appreciated if the Soviets would let us know their opinion, political as well as military, on the above questions.

MARSHAL STALIN said with regard to the remark of the Prime Minister as to whether it was thought Bulgaria would remember the Soviet action in freeing her from the Turks — the liberation of Bulgaria has not been forgotten.

THE PRIME MINISTER continued that the objective of operations which were contemplated in the Eastern Mediterranean was to support the Soviets provided the U.S.S.R. considered the matter of sufficient interest for these operations to be undertaken — even if it meant as much as about two months' delay in *OVERLORD*. Until it is known how the Soviets feel about Turkish and Aegean operations, the matter can not be definitely decided. The U.S. and U.K. can only decide this point after consulting with the U.S.S.R.

THE PRESIDENT said that possibly an entry through the Northeastern Adriatic for offensive operations against Germany in the direction of the Danube would be of value. Such operations were being considered together with a movement into Southern France. Plans for these operations had not been worked out in detail. Such plans would be based, of course, on the assumption that the Red Army would at the same time be approaching Odessa. It was thought, however, that it would be desirable to have a subcommittee go into the details of this matter.

THE PRIME MINISTER said that if the Anglo-American forces take Rome and break up the German formation south of the Apennines they would then have the choice of proceeding to Southern France or eastward across the Adriatic.

MARSHAL STALIN said that he understood it would require 35 divisions to invade France. Did these include the forces to be used in the Mediterranean?

THE PRIME MINISTER indicated that the Mediterranean forces were entirely separate from those included in the *OVERLORD* build-up. He added that after the Italians had been defeated in Italy there remained the possibility of an attack against Southern France or across the Adriatic in the direction of Hungary and the Danube. Entirely separate from the *OVERLORD* build-up there would be 22 divisions available in the Mediterranean; these should all be used. However, it was not possible to move more than seven of them to the *OVERLORD* build-up because of a lack of shipping. He explained again that

520

the *OVERLORD* build-up was to include 16 British and 19 American divisions; that once the 16 British divisions had been committed there would be no more British divisions available. However, the United States would continue to pour divisions into France as fast as they could be shipped across the Atlantic until a total force of 50 to 60 divisions had been reached. He pointed out, incidentally, the British and American divisions with their necessary supporting troops could be roughly estimated at 40,000 men each.

THE PRIME MINISTER also spoke of the large air forces being assembled in England. The present R.A.F. has about reached its maximum strength and be maintained at this strength in the future. However, it is contemplated that the American Air Forces in England will be doubled or tripled in the next six months. The U.S. has already shipped a million tons of stores to the United Kingdom in preparation for the *OVERLORD* operation. *MR. CHURCHILL* said that the President and he would be delighted to have the whole schedule of the *OVERLORD* build-up, both as to personnel and supply, presented to the Soviet authorities and answer any questions which they might have on this subject. He added that the schedule so prepared is being carried out.

MARSHAL STALIN said it seemed to him that in addition to the operations to capture Rome and in addition to those envisaged for the Adriatic, an operation in Southern France was contemplated.

THE PRIME MINISTER replied it was hoped that an operation against Southern France might be carried out as a diversion for *OVERLORD* but that detailed plans for such an operaton had not been worked out.

MARSHAL STALIN asked if Turkey enters the war will Anglo-American forces be allocated to assist them?

THE PRIME MINISTER said that speaking for himself, two or three divisions would be required to take the islands in the Aegean that control communications to Turkey, that 20 squadrons of fighter aircraft and several regiments of anti-aircraft artillery could also be supplied by the British without seriously affecting other operations in the Mediterranean.

MARSHAL STALIN then said that the Anglo-American presentation was clear to him and indicated that he would like to make some comments. He said that it was not worthwhile to scatter the British and American forces. The plans presented seemed to indicate that part would be sent to Turkey, part to be utilized in Southern France, part in Northern France and part for operations across the Adriatic. He suggested that *OVERLORD* be accepted as a basis for operations in 1944 and other operations should be considered as diversionary. He thought that after Rome had been captured there might be a chance for an operation against Southern France from Corsica, in which event the *OVER-LORD* forces plus the Southern France invasion force could establish contact in France. This, he thought, would be a much better operation than to scatter forces in several areas distant from each other. He considered that France was the weakest of all German-occupied areas. He added that he had no hopes of Turkey entering the war and in fact was convinced that she would not, in spite of all pressure that might be exerted.

THE PRIME MINISTER said that he and the President had understood that the Soviet authorities wanted Turkey to come into the war. They were prepared to make every effort to persuade or force her to do so.

MARSHAL STALIN said the Soviets do want Turkey to enter the war but he felt that she could not be taken in by "the scruff of the neck."

THE PRIME MINISTER said that he agreed that the Anglo-American forces should not be scattered but that the operations he had outlined in the Eastern Mediterranean would require only three or four of a total of 25 divisions that might be available. He thought that this could be accomplished without seriously affecting the main operations of *OVERLORD*. Most of the operations would be done by divisions from the Middle East. The air power necessary to assist Turkey would be taken from that now protecting Egypt and thus they would be brought into a better position to strike at the enemy.

THE PRIME MINISTER said he dreaded the six months' idleness between the capture of Rome and the mounting of *OVERLORD*. Hence, he believed that secondary operations should be considered in order to deploy forces available.

MARSHAL STALIN said he would like to express another opinion, i.e., that he believed *OVERLORD* has the greatest possibilities. This would particularly be the case if *OVERLORD* operations were supported by another offensive movement from Southern France. He believed that the Allies should be prepared to remain on the defensive in Italy and thus release 10 divisions for operations in Southern France. Within two or three months after operations commenced in Southern France and the German forces had thus been diverted, the time would be propitious to start an operation in the North of France such as *OVER-LORD*. Under these conditions the success of *OVERLORD* would be assured. Rome might then be captured at a later date.

THE PRIME MINISTER observed that we should be no stronger if we did not capture Rome. If the airfields north of Rome are not secured it would be impracticable to place adequate aircraft for an attack on Southern France. He said it would be difficult for him to agree not to take Rome this January. He added that failure to do so would be considered as a crushing defeat, and that the House of Commons would feel that he was failing to use his British forces in full support of the Soviet ally. He said that in this event he felt it would be no longer possible for him to represent his government.

MARSHAL STALIN suggested that an operation against Southern France might be undertaken and given air cover from bases on Corsica.

THE PRIME MINISTER said that it would take considerable time to construct the necessary airfields on the Island of Corsica.

THE PRESIDENT said that Marshal Stalin's proposals concerning Southern France were of considerable interest to him. He would like to have the Planners make make a study of the possibilities of this operation. The question of relative timing in the Eastern Mediterranean with reference to these operations posed a very serious question. The point was whether it would be better to go into the Eastern Mediterranean and delay *OVERLORD* for one or two months or to attack France one or two months before the first of May and then conduct *OVERLORD* on the original date. He was particularly desirous that this operation not be delayed if it were possible to avoid it.

MARSHAL STALIN said as the result of the Soviet experience in the past two years they have come to the conclusion that a large offensive from one direction is unwise. The Red Army usually attacks from two directions, forcing the enemy to move his reserves from one front to the other. As the two offensives converge the power of the whole offensive increases. Such would be the case in simultaneous operations from Southern and Northern France.

THE PRIME MINISTER said he agreed with the views expressed by Marshal Stalin but did not feel that his proposals concerning Turkey and Yugoslavia were inconsistent with them. He wished to go on record as saying that it would be difficult and impossible to sacrifice all activity in the Mediterranean in order to keep an exact date for *OVERLORD*. There would be 20 divisions which could not be moved out of the Mediterranean because of a lack of shipping. These should be used to stretch Germany to the utmost. He expressed the hope that careful and earnest consideration should be given to making certain that operations in the Mediterranean were not injured solely for the purpose of keeping the May date for *OVERLORD*. He added that agreement between the three powers was necessary and would be reached but he hoped that all factors would be given careful and patient consideration before decisions were reached. He suggested meditating on the discussions of the first meeting and reviewing them at the meeting of the next day.

THE PRESIDENT said he thought it would be a good idea for the staff to immediately conduct a study on the operations against Southern France.

THE PRIME MINISTER agreed that the staff should investigate plans for operations against Southern France but added that they should also work on Turkey.

MARSHAL STALIN agreed that it would be well to continue consideration of these matters the next day. He had not expected that the conference would deal with purely military questions and therefore they had not brought a large military staff. He added, however, that Marshal Voroshiloff was present and would be available for military discussions.

THE PRIME MINISTER asked how the question of Turkish entry into the war should be considered. He asked if she could be brought in, what she should be expected to do in the event that she did come in and what the cost of her entry would be to the three powers concerned.

MARSHAL STALIN said that the entry of Turkey into the war was both a political and a military question. Turkey must take pride in the policy of entry from the point of view of friendship. The British and the United States should use their influence to persuade Turkey to help. In this way it would be impossible for Turkey to maintain her position as a neutral and continue to play fast and loose between our side and the Axis. It was his opinion that if it were not possible to induce Turkey to enter the war as a matter of friendship, she should not enter. *MARSHAL STALIN* added that all neutral states, including Turkey, look upon belligerents as fools. We must prove to them that if they do not enter this war they will not reap the benefits of the victory.

THE PRIME MINISTER observed that Christmas time would be a dangerous season for Turkey. He added that he proposed submitting a paper which he would present before the conference, containing six or seven questions which should be answered in order to clarify the Turkish situation.

THE PRESIDENT said that he would do all he could to persuade the President of Turkey to enter the war. However, he felt personally that Turkey would ask such a high price for her entry as a belligerent that *OVERLORD* would be jeopardized.

MARSHAL STALIN said that the Turks have not yet answered the proposals already made to them but that he expected their reply would be in the negative.

THE PRIME MINISTER said that Turkey would be mad not to accept the Soviet invitation to join the winning side. If she failed to align herself with us she would certainly loose the sympathy of the British people and almost certainly of the American people.

MARSHAL STALIN observed that "a bird in the hand is worth two in the bush." The Turks are now inactive and they should help us.

THE CONFEREES then agreed that the plenary session should be held at 1600 the following day.

THE PRESIDENT observed that it would be desirable to have a military conference first.

It was agreed that a military conference should be held at 1030 the following day, that Marshal Voroshiloff should represent the U.S.S.R., Admiral Leahy and General Marshal should represent the U.S.A and General Brooke and Air Marshal Portal should represent Great Britain.

EUREKA CONFERENCE

MINUTES OF MILITARY CONFERENCE
BETWEEN THE U.S.A., GREAT BRITAIN AND THE U.S.S.R.,

HELD IN THE RUSSIAN LEGATION, TEHRAN, IRAN,

ON MONDAY, 29 NOVEMBER 1943 AT 1030

PRESENT

United States	*British*
Admiral W. D. Leahy, USN	General Sir Alan Brooke
General G. C. Marshall, USA	Air Chief Marshal
	Sir Charles F. A. Portal
Colonel A. J. McFarland, USA	
Secretary	Brigadier H. Redman, Secretary
Captain H. Ware, USA (Interpreter)	Captain Lunghi (Interpreter)

U. S. S. R.

Marshal Voroshiloff

Mr. Pavlov (Interpreter)

GENERAL SIR ALAN BROOKE expressed his pleasure at being able to sit down at a table around which were gathered the military representatives of the U.S., the U.K., and the U.S.S.R. He said that he would run through a brief account of the war as seen by the British representatives at the present moment and then examine the relation of the *OVERLORD* operation to the other parts of the war effort.

He thought that one of the most important things at the present time was to keep the German divisions actively engaged. For this reason, the British were interested in stopping the movement to the Russian front of all the German divisions which it was possible to hold. *OVERLORD* would engage a large number of German divisions, but it could not possibly be mounted until 1 May at the very earliest date. Therefore, there would ensue, between the present time and the launching of *OVERLORD*, a period of some five or six months during which something must be done to keep the German divisions engaged. It was therefore desired to take full advantage of the forces now established in the Mediterranean area.

At this point *GENERAL BROOKE* expressed the hope that General Marshall would interrupt his statement if anything was said with which General Marshall did not agree or on which he wished to offer any comment.

Continuing his account of the war, *GENERAL BROOKE* said that for the reasons already stated, all the plans on which we have been working have been designed to deploy the maximum forces on all fronts. Pointing out on a map the present location of the Italian Front, he said that on that line we are assembling the forces in Italy necessary to drive the Germans to the north. There are some 23 German divisions now in Italy, part of them in the south and a part of them in the north. The present conception is to assemble sufficient forces to drive the Germans from their present line to a line north of Rome. To do this it would be necessary to employ amphibious forces around the German flanks (pointing to the west flank), and by these operations it was hoped to engage the 11 or 12 German divisions in the south, render them inoperative, and force the Germans to relieve them. By these means we should be able to contain the German divisions now present in Italy and to reduce their efficiency.

Turning to Yugoslavia, *GENERAL BROOKE* said that since the withdrawal of Italian forces there, the Germans have found it difficult to maintain their communications in that country. Therefore, full advantage must be taken of all opportunities to increase the German difficulties in Yugoslavia by assisting the Partisans. It is desired to organize a system by which arms can be supplied to them and air assistance rendered as well.

528

GENERAL BROOKE said that there were now some 21 German divisions deployed in Yugoslavia as far down as the Grecian border. Replying to an indication from Marshal Voroshiloff that he did not quite agree with these figures, he stated that this was his information and that he would ask the British Intelligence to check the accuracy of his figures. He said that there were also 8 Bulgarian divisions in addition to the German divisions in the Yugoslav area.

With reference to Turkey, *GENERAL BROOKE* said that, looking at Turkey from a military point of view and omitting all political considerations, we see a great military advantage in getting Turkey into the war. By this we shall have an opportunity of opening the sea communications through the Dardanelles. By doing this, the position of Bulgaria and Rumania will become more difficult and the chances of getting them out of the war will be greatly increased. There will also be opened up the possibility of establishing a supply line to Russia through the Dardanelles.

By establishing airdromes in Turkey, it will be possible to launch bombing attacks on German oil establishments in eastern Europe. The shortening of the sea route to Russia will save shipping and thereby assist greatly in the general shipping shortage. In order to open sea communications through the Dardanelles, it is considered that it will be necessary to capture some of the Dodecanese Islands, beginning with Rhodes. With airdromes established in Turkey and with Turkish help, it was not believed that this would be a difficult task nor that it would detract from other operations.

GENERAL BROOKE said that we have in the Mediterranean now a certain number of landing craft for special operations. These landing craft would be required for the operations he had outlined, and their retention for these operations would require the retarding of the date set for *OVERLORD*. The landing craft are being used to maintain and build up the forces now in Italy. By the operations he had outlined we should be able to hold and destroy the German forces now in the Mediterranean area while awaiting the date for *OVERLORD*.

He considered it also of great importance to establish airdromes to the north of Rome in order to bring bombing to bear on German installations. He said that this air operation in conjunction with the operations now being carried on from England would play a great part in the conduct of the whole war.

He pointed out that air attacks were now containing about a million men now held in Germany solely by reason of the bomber offensive. He said that if we adopt defensive operations in Italy now, as had been suggested at yesterday's conference, we should still have to maintain strong forces in Italy in order to contain the German forces there. Therefore, there would be left over only very limited forces for the operation against the coast of Southern France. In addition, the landing craft available for that operation would be limited to a very small assault force.

GENERAL BROOKE said that he agreed with Marshal Stalin's pincer strategy of two cooperating forces whenever such a strategy was possible but he thought that this strategy was better when based on land instead of on long sea communications. In the latter case, the two forces are not sufficiently self-supporting. It is not easy to reinforce one from the other or to keep a reserve from which to reinforce either from a central point. The building up of land forces by sea is a lengthy business.

GENERAL BROOKE said that if the attack against Southern France were launched two months prior to *OVERLORD*, that it was certain to be defeated before *OVERLORD* starts. He said that a more nearly simultaneous execution of these operations would be required and also that large numbers of landing craft would be necessary. However, it had been considered that during *OVERLORD* a small landing might be made in Southern France to draw German forces away from the larger operation.

He said that the difficulties and dangers for *OVERLORD* would develop during the building up of the forces. It was possible to assault the French coast only with some three or four divisions and the process of building up to 35 divisions would be long and difficult. During this period it was imperative that the Germans should not be able to concentrate large forces against the operation .

GENERAL BROOKE said that this concluded a rough outline of the projected land operations and that Air Marshal Sir Charles Portal would explain the air aspects of the operations.

AIR MARSHAL PORTAL inquired as to whether he should, in his comments, cover the U.S. air operations or whether General Marshall would do this.

In reply, *GENERAL MARSHALL* requested Air Marshal Portal to cover the entire operations and said that he would elaborate as necessary.

In response to Marshal Voroshiloff's request that the U.S. representatives give their comments on the land operations before the taking up of the air aspects, *ADMIRAL LEAHY* requested General Marshall to state the U.S. views.

GENERAL MARSHALL said that he should first explain the purely American point of view of this stage of the war. He pointed out that the U.S. now has a going war on two fronts, the Pacific and the Atlantic, and this fact of two major operations at one time presents a dilemma. In contrast to the usual difficulties of war, there is no lack of troops and no lack of supplies. There are now more than fifty divisions in the United States which we wish to deploy as soon as possible in addition to those already overseas. The military problem, therefore, resolves itself almost entirely into a question of shipping and landing craft. While this is, of course, an exaggeration, it might almost be said that we have reached the point of having to ignore strategy in order to advance communications. Our great desire is to bring these troops into action as soon as possible.

When we speak of landing craft we mean, most of all, special craft for *the transport of motor vehicles and tanks.* As the Chief of the Imperial General Staff has already stated, our problem in the Mediterranean is largely one of landing craft, and of those landing craft, we are particularly concerned with the special craft for transporting motor vehicles.

GENERAL MARSHALL said that he wished to repeat and emphasize that there was no lack of troops or of supplies. He said we are deeply interested in the length of voyages, the length of time required in ports, and the over-all time for the turn-around. Our air forces had been sent overseas just as soon as they had been trained and hence, the air battle was far more advanced than the situation on land. One of the delays in the build-up of land forces in Italy had been the getting in of air support and the necessary ground troops to maintain it.

GENERAL MARSHALL said that one reason for favoring *OVERLORD* from the start is that it is the shortest oversea transport route. After the initial success, transports will be sent directly from the United States to the French ports because there are about sixty divisions in the United States to be put into *OVERLORD.*

As to the Mediterranean factors in the situation, *GENERAL MARSHALL* said that no definite conclusions have been reached up to the present as to further operations, pending the results of this conference. The question now before us is: What do we do in the next three months, and then in the next six months? He pointed out that what was done in the second period would necessarily depend on the decisions made in the first period.

GENERAL MARSHALL said he would like to repeat the statement made by General Brooke that it is considered dangerous to launch an operation against the coast of Southern France a long time (that is, what we consider a long time) prior to *OVERLORD*. On the other hand, action in Southern France has been considered and planned on as very important for the support of the operation in Northwestern France. He said that at the present moment he and his U.S. colleagues feel that from two to three weeks should be the maximum limit for launching this operation in advance of *OVERLORD*.

GENERAL MARSHALL said he wished to point out, in addition to what General Brooke had said, that the destruction of ports imposes an initial and serious delay in getting heavy equipment and ammunition ashore, and it is necessary that we assume in our planning that the ports will be destroyed. Our engineers have accomplished marvels in restoring the damaged ports but despite this, a considerable period of dangerous delay inevitably follows the initial assault. He illustrated this by reference to the U.S. experience in Salerno, a comparatively small landing. In the first 18 days there had been landed over the beaches a total of 108,000 tons of supplies, 30,000 motor vehicles and 189,000 troops. He wished to emphasize that all of this had to be done over the beaches and that none of it came through a port. The U.S. was fortunate, of course, to have had during this period a very slight enemy air reaction.

GENERAL MARSHALL said that the difficulty in such an operation is to get sufficient fighter air cover. In almost every case it had been found, therefore, that an additional operation was necessary in order to get the airfields for this fighter cover.

In answer to a question from Marshal Voroshiloff as to how long it had taken to land the men and material just enumerated, *GENERAL MARSHALL* said it had required 18 days; thereafter a port had been secured. Then, beginning with an initial entry of 2,000 tons of supplies, the intake through the port was increased more and more as the demolished equipment was rehabilitated until it was possible to take care of all requirements in this manner.

In summarizing, *GENERAL MARSHALL* said that he wished to emphasize that shipping and landing craft, with the provision of fighter air cover, are the problems for which we have to find solutions in order to decide the question of Mediterranean operations. He added that over Salerno fighter aircraft had had only 15 or 20 minutes of actual combat flying time.

MARSHAL VOROSHILOFF remarked that for *OVERLORD* this would be a very short time.

GENERAL MARSHALL replied that a total combat time of 30 minutes had been planned for *OVERLORD*.

In reply to Marshal Voroshiloff's statement that he did not think this was sufficient time, *AIR MARSHAL PORTAL* explained that the 30 minutes was not measured from take-off to landing but was the actual time in which the fighter planes were actually engaged over the battle area.

In reply to Marshal Voroshiloff's question as to what fighters were envisaged as being in this area, *AIR MARSHAL PORTAL* said that these would be the high-performance fighters, like the British Spitfires and American P-51's and P-38's. He explained that the long-range fighters were not so suitable against the German defenses as the short-range.

GENERAL MARSHALL said that in the Mediterranean we face the problem of where to employ our available landing craft. If we undertake certain operations, *OVERLORD* will inevitably be delayed. If we confine ourselves to reduced operations in the Mediterranean for the next three or four months, this course entails the least interference with *OVERLORD*. He repeated that the problem is not a lack of troops or of equipment. He would like Marshal Voroshiloff to understand that at the present time the U.S. has landing operations going on at five different places in the Pacific, all of which involve landing craft, and that four more similar operations were due to be launched in January.

ADMIRAL LEAHY said that he thought the best procedure now would be to have *AIR MARSHAL PORTAL* discuss the air aspects of operations and then to ask Marshal Voroshiloff to present any comments or advice he may have.

AIR MARSHAL PORTAL said that he would speak only of the air war in Europe other than on the battle fronts. He said that the air offensive against Germany was being waged on an ever-increasing scale from the U.K.; from the Mediterranean it was just beginning. As to the scale of attack, the British and Americans together were launching from 15,000 to 20,000 tons of bombs per month on German communications, installations, and battle industry. Our immediate objective is the destruction of the plants and factories on which German battle industry depends. If we can do this and inflict heavy casualties

533

on German fighters, we hope to be able to range over all Germany and destroy one by one every important installation on which the German war effort depends.

The battle is heavy, with heavy losses on both sides. The Germans clearly realize their danger if our plans succeed. This is assured by the disposition of their forces in order to counter our attacks. For instance, for the defense of central and southern Germany the Germans now have deployed between 1,650 and 1,700 fighters. On all other fronts together they have only 750 fighters. These figures cover fighters only; bombers are not included. German sensitiveness to the bombing of their industrial area was recently illustrated when, in response to the comparatively light attacks made from the Mediterranean on this area, the Germans immediately transferred 200 fighters to the area.

AIR MARSHAL PORTAL said that it was recognized that the bulk of the Soviet planes were now employed in support of the land battle, but when it became possible to spare air forces from the land battle, this would help enormously on all other fronts by causing the Germans to withdraw forces to protect the area threatened by the Soviets.

In response to a suggestion from Admiral Leahy, it was now agreed that it would be helpful if Marshal Voroshiloff would express his opinion on the matters under discussion.

MARSHAL VOROSHILOFF said that before making a statement, he would like to ask some questions. He said that he knew from the statements made by the British and American military representatives in Moscow that *OVERLORD* is being prepared for next spring, with a target date about 1 May. He had just heard that morning that fifty or sixty divisions would be available from the U.S. for this operation and that the only problem was one of shipping and landing craft. He hoped that it might be possible to have a report on what is being done now to solve the problem of shipping and landing craft and to launch Operation *OVERLORD* on time. This constituted his first question.

As to his second question, he said that he had attached great importance to the remarks made by General Marshall from which he understood that the U.S. considers Operation *OVERLORD* of the first importance. He wished to know if General Brooke also considered the operation of the first importance. He wished to ask both Allies whether they think that *OVERLORD* must be carried out or whether they consider that it may be possible to replace it by some other suitable operation when Turkey has entered the war.

GENERAL MARSHALL said that in answer to Marshal Voroshiloff's question as to progress from the U.S. side on the build-up for *OVERLORD*, all preparations are now under way and have been for some time, for a target date of 1 May 1944, and that the troops are now in motion. As an example he pointed out that we now have in England, well ahead of the troops, a million tons of supplies and equipment, including munitions and heavy supplies of all kinds. It remains now only to bring the troops up to the supplies.

He pointed out that the U.S. had only one division in England in August. There are nine divisions there now with a constant flow of additional troops. There had been a tremendous flow of air personnel for the bomber offensive.

He said that in speaking of divisions, he was including the necessary corps and army troops as well as service troops. He reiterated that the problem is landing craft for *OVERLORD*. The question now is: Shall we take any landing craft from *OVERLORD* for other operations and thereby delay *OVERLORD?* The troops are in motion for *OVERLORD*. The air forces are already there and proceeding with their expansion. The problem is landing craft.

MARSHAL VOROSHILOFF said that he had an additional question. He said that General Deane and General Ismay, in explaining the *OVERLORD* build-up at the Moscow Conference, had said that both in the U.S. and U.K. there were now being built special landing craft and special vessels for the construction of temporary harbors. He would like to know the present status of these construction programs.

GENERAL MARSHALL said that he would leave the answer as to the special port construction and as to part of the landing craft construction to General Brooke. He said that in the struggle with the landing craft problem, the object of the U.S. is to get more craft in order to be able to undertake some operations in the Mediterranean that could easily be done if more landing craft were available. He wished to make clear that the landing craft program for *OVERLORD* is well in hand. General Marshall repeated and emphasized this statement.

MARSHAL VOROSHILOFF said that he understood that some ship-building yards both in England and America had been taken over for the building of landing craft. He wished to know whether the construction was actually under way or whether it was still only a program.

GENERAL MARSHALL said that General Brooke could answer for the U.K. There was no secret about the matter. He feared that he himself had misled Marshal Voroshiloff in view of the fact that he was answering the Marshal's question wholly with respect to landing craft for *OVERLORD*. For example, it had recently been decided to delay the movement from the Mediterranean to *OVERLORD* of sixty landing craft, capable of carrying 40 tanks each, in order to permit General Eisenhower not only to advance more rapidly in Italy but to force the Germans to reinforce their line from the Po Valley. In other words, the object was to absorb more German divisions in view of the fact that General Eisenhower was unable to conduct a turning movement through the mountains during the winter. For this reason it had been decided to delay the movement of these landing craft from the Mediterranean to the U.K. but it was hoped that it would be possible *to complete the operations for* which they were being retained in the Mediterranean and still get them through on time for *OVERLORD*. In the meantime, a tremendous effort was being made both in the U.S. and U.K. to increase the output of landing craft so that *OVERLORD* might be made more powerful and more certain of success, and so that it might be possible to undertake the operations in the Mediterranean that additional landing craft would permit. He pointed out that the problem in the Mediterranean involves at present more troops than can be put into action.

MARSHAL VOROSHILOFF said that this answered his question.

GENERAL BROOKE said, in answer to Marshal Voroshiloff's first question as to the importance in British eyes of operation *OVERLORD*, that the British had always considered the operation as an essential part of this war. However, they had stipulated that the operation must be mounted at a time when it would have the best chances of success. He pointed out that the fortifications in Northern France are of a very serious character, that the communications are excellent, and therefore the Germans would have an excellent opportunity of holding up the landings until they could bring their reserves into play. This is the reason for the British stipulations as to the conditions prerequisite for launching the operation. They consider that in 1944 these conditions will exist. They have reorganized all *their forces for* this purpose. These forces were originally organized for the defense of the U.K. but they are now organized as an expeditionary force for employment on the Continent. Amphibious divisions are now undergoing training for Operation *OVERLORD*. Four battle-tried divisions have been brought back from Italy to the U.K. for the operation and, in addition, there have been brought back some of the landing craft which will be required. All details and plans for the operation have been made as far as it has been possible to do so up to the present moment.

It followed, therefore, that the British attach the greatest importance to the execution of this operation in 1944 but, as General Marshall had said and as he (General Brooke) wished to say again, landing craft constituted our tactical necessity. In order to maintain the 1 May 1944 date for *OVERLORD* it will be necessary to withdraw landing craft from the Mediterranean *now*. If this were done, it would bring the Italian operations almost to a standstill. The British wished, during the preparations for *OVERLORD*, to keep fighting the Germans in the Mediterranean to the maximum degree possible. In their view, such operations are necessary not only to hold the Germans in Italy but to create the situation in Northern France which will make *OVERLORD* possible.

GENERAL BROOKE said that Marshal Voroshiloff had heard correctly as to the construction of landing craft in England at the present time. The Prime Minister has stopped certain ordinary construction in order to make additional landing craft possible. By these means it was hoped to make sixty or seventy more craft available in time for *OVERLORD*. These are being built now and are in addition to the original program.

With reference to the provision for temporary harbors, he said that the necessary gear was being built for this purpose now. In this connection many experiments have been made, and while some of them had not been as successful as it had been hoped, others had offered considerable promise and it was hoped would give fruitful results. This was a matter of the greatest importance as the success or failure of the operation may depend on these ports. He hoped that these statements would provide a satisfactory answer to Marshal Voroshiloff's question.

MARSHAL VOROSHILOFF said he wished to apologize for his failure to understand clearly but he was interested to know whether General Brooke, as Chief of the Imperial General Staff, considered *OVERLORD* as important an operation as General Marshall had indicated that he did. He would like General Brooke's personal opinion.

GENERAL BROOKE replied that as Chief of the Imperial General Staff he considered Operation *OVERLORD* as of vital importance, but there was one stipulation that he should like to make. He knew the defenses of Northern France and did not wish to see the operation fail. In his opinion, under certain circumstances it was bound to fail.

MARSHAL VOROSHILOFF said that Marshal Stalin and the Soviet General Staff attach great importance to *OVERLORD* and felt that the other operations in the Mediterranean can be regarded only as auxiliary operations.

GENERAL BROOKE said that that was exactly the way he looked at the matter but, unless the auxiliary operations are carried out, in his opinion *OVERLORD* can not be successful.

MARSHAL VOROSHILOFF said that he would now express his own point of view. He recalled that Marshall Stalin had said yesterday that he and the Soviet General Staff considered that *OVERLORD* was a very serious operation and would prove a difficult one. He said that the accomplishments of the U.S. and U.K. in the war to date, especially the brilliant operations of their air forces over Germany, served to indicate the might of these two nations and the superiority of the Allies in the Mediterranean area. If there is added to this the firm will and desire of the U.S. and British staffs, he (Marshal Voroshiloff) felt sure that *OVERLORD* would be successful and that it would go down in history as one of our greatest victories. He repeated that this view was supported by what all have seen in the fighting in North Africa and the operations of the Allied air forces over Germany.

MARSHAL VOROSHILOFF said that he had absolutely no doubt that the necessary shipping and landing craft for *OVERLORD* can be found either by construction of new craft or conversion from merchant craft. He was sure these problems can be solved successfully. He understood from the statements made by General Marshall that the U.S. now has nine divisions in the U.K. He pointed out that there are yet six months to 1 May 1944, the target date for *OVERLORD*. This will permit the U.S. forces in the U.K. to be doubled or tripled and, in addition, make possible the bringing over of tanks and other supplies.

GENERAL MARSHALL said that the nine divisions now in the U.K. consisted of seven infantry divisions and two armored divisions.

MARSHAL VOROSHILOFF said that in his opinion this force can be doubled in the next six months, to which *GENERAL MARSHALL* replied that this is already scheduled.

MARSHAL VOROSHILOFF said that he would now discuss the operation itself. He entirely agreed with General Brooke that some small operations in the Mediterranean are necessary as diversions in order to draw German troops away from the Eastern Front and from Northwestern France, but he thought as a military man, and as probably all other military men would think also, that *OVERLORD* is the most important operation and that all the other auxiliary operations, such as Rome, Rhodes and what not, must be planned to assist OVERLORD and certainly not to hinder it. He pointed out that it was possible now to plan additional operations that may hurt *OVERLORD* and emphasized that this must not be so. These operations must be planned so as to *secure OVERLORD,* which is the most important operation, and not to hurt it. The suggestion made yesterday by Marshal Stalin that simultaneous operations should be undertaken from Northern France and Southern France is based on the idea that the Mediterranean operations are secondary to *OVERLORD*. Germany can not be attacked directly from Italy because of the Alps. However, Italy does offer the possibility of successful defense with a small number of troops. The troops saved by defensive operations in Italy would be available for launching an amphibious operation against Southern France. Marshal Stalin does not insist on this but does insist on the execution of *OVERLORD* on the date already planned.

MARSHAL VOROSHILOFF said, with respect to the action of the air forces and Air Marshal Portal's suggestion of the bombing of eastern Germany by the Russian Air Force, that it must be known to the U.S. and the U.K. staffs that the Germans are still strong on the Russian front. He wished to repeat that, as Marshal Stalin had said yesterday, there are now 210 German divisions on this front and 50 satellite divisions, making a total of 260 in all. The Soviets will, of course, utilize every opportunity of attacking eastern Germany by air, but these opportunities are not very frequent. No such possibility exists at present because all air forces are employed in support of the land battle.

With respect to the difficulties of the cross-Channel operation, he said that it was understood, of course, that crossing the Channel was more difficult than crossing a large river. He pointed out, however, that during the recent Soviet advances to the west they had crossed several large rivers, the most recent of which was the Dnieper. In the latter case the ordinary difficulties of a river crossing were greatly increased by the high, steep western bank and the low eastern bank, but with the help of machine gun, mortar and artillery fire and the employment of mine throwers it had been found possible to lay down a fire so intense that the Germans could not endure it. It was so in the vicinity of Kiev, Gomel, and other points. He believed, therefore, that with similar aids it will be possible for the Allies to land in Northern France.

GENERAL BROOKE said that he would like to point out that the question as to whether or not Operation *OVERLORD* is to be executed in

1944 has not been under discussion. It has been definitely decided to carry out the operation, and it is recognized that the Mediterranean operations are definitely of a secondary nature. There are certain forces, however, now deployed in the Mediterranean from whose employment a direct benefit can and should be derived. In addition, all operations planned in the Mediterranean area are coordinated in the over-all plan for the war and are projected with a view to their eventual influence on the Eastern Front and on *OVERLORD*. He said that he had been studying the Soviet river crossings with the greatest of interest. In his opinion the Soviets had been accomplishing technical marvels.

MARSHAL VOROSHILOFF said that the crossings were the result of the efforts of all of their people. They had the will to do it.

GENERAL BROOKE said that the Channel crossing was a technical matter, the minutest details of which had been under study for several years. It must not be forgotten that the fire support for the operation must come from the sea. With reference to Marshal Voroshiloff's remarks as to artillery and mortar support, he said that the British have equipped landing craft with mortars and have studied every detail of the fire support of the cross-Channel operation from air and sea. He wished to point out the special difficulties existing in connection with this coast because of the long shelving beaches, where the tide goes out a long way. On many parts of the coast this characteristic makes landing operations very difficult and in some places, as at Calais, where the situation most favors air support, the beaches are the worst. He said the British are still engaged in experiments as to the best means of forcing a landing and are adding to the results of these experiments the best experience of the U.S. and British forces in the war to date.

MARSHAL VOROSHILOFF referred to newspaper accounts which he had read with reference to large maneuvers held in England and wished to know if these had resulted in any new developments.

GENERAL BROOKE replied that these maneuvers have been carried out mainly for the purpose of bringing about battles in the air. He said that they had carried out all preparations for the cross-Channel operation as a matter of training, and this had proved of great value to the staffs. The landing craft had been launched toward the French coast in the hope that the German air forces would be induced thereby to come out and fight. The German response had not been in keeping with the British hopes. The maneuvers referred to did not include an exercise in the actual landings. These exercises, however, are continually being carried out in certain areas on the English coasts from which the population has been cleared in order to permit the necessary supporting fire.

MARSHAL VOROSHILOFF said he wished to inquire of Air Marshal Portal what his opinion was as to the sufficiency of the air forces available for *OVERLORD*.

AIR MARSHAL PORTAL replied that there were enough air forces available to insure the success of the landing itself. The Allies would probably be superior to the Germans in the air by five or six to one. It was not, however, in the assault period that the air need would be the greatest, but during the build-up of the invading forces across the beaches. This would constitute the critical period, and it was during this period that the Germans would try to bring to bear their maximum available air power. At the same time a considerable portion of the Allied air forces would have to be used in order to interrupt communications leading from the interior of France to the front.

MARSHAL VOROSHILOFF said he considered an air superiority of five or six to one as satisfactory.

AIR MARSHAL PORTAL pointed out that all these figures must be judged in the light of distance. He said that the Germans have many airfields located close to the front on their side.

MARSHAL VOROSHILOFF said that these German airfields must be destroyed before the operation is launched. In his opinion it was impossible to begin it without air superiority.

AIR MARSHAL PORTAL replied that this initial destruction of German airfields was a part of the *OVERLORD* plan.

GENERAL MARSHALL said that he wished to offer one comment. The difference between a river crossing, however wide, and a landing from the ocean is that the failure of a river crossing is a reverse while the failure of a landing operation from the sea is a catastrophe, because failure in the latter case means the almost utter destruction of the landing craft and personnel involved.

MARSHAL VOROSHILOFF said that he appreciated the frankness of these statements.

GENERAL MARSHALL went on to say that his military education had been based on roads, rivers, and railroads and that his war experience in

France had been concerned with the same. During the last two years, however, he had been acquiring an education based on oceans and he had had to learn all over again.

GENERAL MARSHALL said that prior to the present war he had never heard of any landing craft except a rubber boat. Now he thinks about little else.

MARSHAL VOROSHILOFF replied, "If you think about it, you will do it."

To this *GENERAL MARSHALL* replied, "That is a very good reply. I understand thoroughly."

MARSHAL VOROSHILOFF said that he wished to emphasize that if in Operation *OVERLORD* our forces were launched against the hostile coast without previously destroying the enemy positions, there could, of course, be no success. He thought that the procedure must be similar to that followed on land. First the enemy positions must be destroyed with artillery fire and bombing from the air; then light forces, including reconnaissance groups, would land and take the first ground; when this had been done, the large forces would come in later. Therefore, if the advance forces were unable to land and were destroyed in the attempt, the larger forces would not be destroyed also. He felt that if the operation were conducted in this way, it would prove to be a brilliant success and not result in catastrophe.

GENERAL MARSHALL emphasized that no catastrophe was expected, but that everyone was planning for success.

ADMIRAL LEAHY suggested, in view of the lateness of the hour, that the meeting adjourn and reconvene later.

GENERAL BROOKE suggested the possibility of convening again Tuesday morning at 1030. He said that he had some questions he would like to ask Marshal Voroshiloff.

MARSHAL VOROSHILOFF thought it desirable to reach some conclusions as a result of the discussion.

GENERAL BROOKE suggested that the conclusions would properly follow the second meeting, to which *MARSHAL VOROSHILOFF* agreed.

The meeting accordingly adjourned, to reconvene at the Russian Legation, Tehran, Iran, on Tuesday, 30 November at 1030.

EUREKA CONFERENCE

MINUTES OF PLENARY SESSION
Between the U.S.A., Great Britain and the U.S.S.R.,

Held in the Russian Legation, Tehran, Iran,
on Monday, 29 November 1943 at 1600

PRESENT

United States	*British*
President Roosevelt	Prime Minister Churchill
Mr. Harry L. Hopkins	Mr. Anthony Eden
Mr. Averill Harriman	Field Marshal Sir John Dill
Admiral W. D. Leahy, USN	General Sir Alan Brooke
General G. C. Marshall, USA	Admiral Sir Andrew B. Cunningham
Admiral E. J. King, USN	Air Chief Marshal
General H. H. Arnold, USA	Sir Charles F. A. Portal
Lt. Gen. B. B. Somervell, USA	Lt. Gen. Hastings L. Ismay
Maj. Gen. J. R. Deane, USA	Lt. General Martel
Captain F. B. Royal, USN, Secretary	Brigadier L. C. Hollis, Secretary
Mr. C. E. Bohlen (Interpreter)	Sir Archibald Kerr
Capt. H. H. Ware, USA (Interpreter)	Major Birse (Interpreter)

U.S.S.R.

Marshal Stalin

Mr. Molotov
Marshal Voroshiloff

One Secretary

Mr. Pavlov (Interpreter)

543

THE PRESIDENT said he had no formal agenda for today's meeting. He thought it would be a good idea if Marshal Stalin, the Prime Minister, and possibly Marshal Voroshiloff, would give the meeting their ideas.

MARSHAL STALIN asked whether the military committee had completed its work.

GENERAL BROOKE gave an outline of the proceedings of the conference this morning. (See Minutes of Military Conference, 29 November 1943 at 1030.)

GENERAL MARSHALL stated that he had little to add to the statement of General Brooke but that the problems concerning the United States are not those of troops nor equipment but rather problems of ships, landing craft and airfields in sufficient proximity to the scene of immediate operations under consideration. Furthermore he said, in speaking of landing craft, he was speaking particularly of a special type which carries about 40 tanks or motor vehicles. He said he desired to make clear, as far as the United States forces for *OVERLORD* are concerned, that the build-up has proceeded according to schedule. Especially should it be noted that the supplies and equipment have now been assembled to the extent of one million tons in the United Kingdom, in advance of the arrival of the troops anticipated. All supplies and equipment have been set up according to schedule. The variable or questionable factor is the subject of landing craft. He said there was a schedule of landing craft construction which had been accelerated both in the United Kingdom and the United States. The purpose of this acceleration is involved with two considerations, (a) the matter of the initial assault for *OVERLORD*, and (b) operations in the Mediterranean, which could be done if additional landing craft could be made available. In brief, the *OVERLORD* build-up is going ahead according to schedule as regards ground troops, air forces and equipment. Discussions and problems regarding *OVERLORD* were related almost entirely to the employment and movement of available landing craft. Transfer of certain United States and British divisions from the Mediterranean to the United Kingdom for the *OVERLORD* build-up had virtually been completed at the present time.

MARSHAL VOROSHILOFF said that the information given by General Brooke and General Marshall corresponded to the talks which had been held this morning on the questions concerning *OVERLORD*—specifically, technical questions. Continuing, *MARSHAL VOROSHILOFF* said as far as the matters discussed by General Brooke concerning Italy, Yugoslavia, Turkey and Southern France, it was hoped that these matters would be the subject of the next meeting of the ad hoc committee. The committee also had under discussion the date of *OVERLORD* and the details of that operation, with the thought that they would be able to discuss these matters further at the next meeting.

MARSHAL STALIN asked who will be the commander in this Operation *OVERLORD*. *(THE PRESIDENT* and *PRIME MINISTER* interpolated this was not yet decided.) *MARSHAL STALIN* continued, "Then nothing will come out of these operations." He further inquired as to who carries the moral and technical responsibility for this operation. He was informed by the President and Prime Minister that the British General Morgan, who is Chief of Staff to the Supreme Allied Commander (Designate), is charged with the plans and preparations which have been and are continually being made and carried out by a Combined U.S.-British Staff.

In reply to a question from Marshal Stalin as to who has the executive responsibility for *OVERLORD* preparations, *THE PRESIDENT* replied that we have already decided the names of all the commanders except that of the Supreme Commander.

MARSHAL STALIN said that it could happen that General Morgan might say that all matters were ready; however, when the Supreme Commander reports, he, the Supreme Commander, might not think that everything necessary had been accomplished by the Chief of Staff. He felt that there must be one person in charge.

THE PRIME MINISTER informed Marshal Stalin that General Morgan had been charged with the preparation and carrying out of plans in the preliminary stages for *OVERLORD*. His Majesty's Government had expressed willingness to have Operation *OVERLORD* undertaken under the command of a United States commander. The United States will be concerned with the greatest part of the build-up, and this United States commander will have command in the field.

MR. CHURCHILL added that in the Mediterranean the British have large naval and air forces which are under direct British command under the Allied Commander in Chief. A decision had not yet been reached between the President and Prime Minister regarding the specific matter of high command. Decisions here at this conference will have a bearing on the choice. Therefore the President can name the Supreme Allied Commander for *OVERLORD* if he desires to accept the British offers to serve under a United States commander. *THE PRIME MINISTER* further suggested that Marshal Stalin be given an answer in confidence between the three Chiefs of State regarding who the Supreme Allied Commander would be.

MARSHAL STALIN said he desired it to be understood that he did not presume to take part in the selection of a commander for *OVERLORD* but merely wanted to know who this officer would be and felt strongly that he should be appointed as soon as possible and be given the responsibility for preparations for *OVERLORD* as well as the executive command of the operation.

THE PRIME MINISTER agreed it was essential that a commander be appointed for the *OVERLORD* operation without delay and indicated that such an appointment would be made within a fortnight. He hoped that it might be accomplished during his current meeting with the President.

THE PRIME MINISTER then went on to say that he was concerned with the number and complexity of problems which presented themselves before the conference. He said that the meeting was unique in that the thoughts of more than 140,000,000 people were centered upon it. He felt that the principals should not separate until agreements on political, moral, and military problems had been reached. He said that he wished to present a few points which would require study by a subcommittee. Both he and the British Staff had given long study to the Mediterranean position, in which area Great Britain has a large army. He was anxious that the British Mediterranean army should fight throughout 1944 and not be quiescent. From that point of view he asked the Soviets to survey the field and examine the different alternatives put before them and submit their recommendations.

THE PRIME MINISTER said that the first point which required study was what assistance could be given to the *OVERLORD* operation by the large force which will be in the Mediterranean. He asked in particular what the possibilities of this force might be and what should be the scale of an operation that might be launched from Northern Italy into Southern France. He did not feel that such an operation had been studied in sufficient detail but he welcomed the opportunity to give it close examination. He thought it might be well for the U.S. and U.K. staffs to consider this matter together in the light of their special knowledge concerning resources available. He pointed out that Marshal Stalin had stressed the value of pincer operations. He said that for such operations timing is of great importance. A weak attack several months in advance might result in it being defeated and permit the enemy to turn his whole strength to meet the main attack.

THE PRIME MINISTER said he wanted landing craft to carry at least two divisions. With such an amphibious force it would be possible to do operations seriatim, that is, first, up the leg of Italy by amphibious turning movements, thus offering the possibility of cutting off the enemy's withdrawal and capturing the entire German force now in Central Italy; second, to take Rhodes in conjunction with Turkey's entry into the war; and, third, to use the entire force for operations six months hence against the southern coast of France in order to assist *OVERLORD*. He said that none of these operations would be excluded but that the timing would require careful study. This force of two divisions cannot be supplied in the Mediterranean without either setting back the date of *OVERLORD* for six or eight weeks or without drawing back from the Indian Ocean landing craft which were now intended to be used against the Japanese. He said that this is one of the dilemmas which the Anglo-American staffs are balancing in their minds. In reaching their conclusions they would be greatly assisted by the views of Marshal Stalin and his officers. He welcomed these views because of his admiration for the military record of the Red Army. He therefore suggested that the military staffs continue to study these subjects.

THE PRIME MINISTER then said that the second matter which must be settled was political rather than military because of the small military forces involved. He referred to the question of Yugoslavia and the Dalmatian Coast. He said that in the Balkans there were 21 German divisions plus garrison troops, of which 54,000 troops are spread about among the Aegean Islands. There were also about 21 Bulgarian divisions or a total of 42 divisions in all. *(THE PRIME MINISTER* later corrected these figures to indicate that there were 42 divisions in all, 12 of which were Bulgarian divisions in Bulgaria.) He said that if Turkey came into the war the Bulgarian divisions would be used to face the Turks on the Thrace front. This withdrawal of Bulgarian divisions as garrison troops in the Balkans would endanger the remaining German divisions left on that duty by operations of the guerrillas. He said that he did not suggest that the Anglo-American forces put divisions into the Balkans, but he did propose that there be a continuous flow of supplies, frequent commando raids and air support furnished as and when needed. He felt it was short-sighted to let the Germans crush Yugoslavia without giving those brave people now fighting under Tito weapons for which they might ask. He emphasized that the Balkan operations would be a great factor in stretching the Germans and thus giving relief to the Russian front. He added that the British had no interests in the Balkans that were exceptional or ambitious in nature and all they wanted to do was to nail the 21 German divisions in that area and destroy them. He suggested that the Foreign Secretaries of the U.K. and the U.S.S.R. and a representative of the United States whom the President might designate should hold discussions to see if the proposed activities in the Balkans presented any political difficulties.

THE PRIME MINISTER then came to his last point, which was in reference to Turkey. He said that the British are allies of Turkey and that the British have accepted the responsibility of endeavoring to persuade or force Turkey into the war before Christmas. He said that if the President would come in with the British or take the lead, it would be agreeable to him, but he should certainly want all possible help from the U.S. and U.S.S.R. in accordance with the agreements made at the Moscow Conference.

THE PRIME MINISTER said that the British would go far in warning Turkey that her failure to enter the war would jeopardize her political and territorial aspirations, particularly with reference to the Dardanelles, when these matters were being discussed at the peace table.

THE PRIME MINISTER indicated that the military staffs had already discussed the military aspects of Turkey's entry into the war. He said, however, that the question was largely political since only two or three divisions of soldiers were involved. He again posed the question as to how the U.S.S.R. would feel about Bulgaria. Would they be inclined to tell Bulgaria that if Turkey did enter the war against Germany and Bulgaria helped Germany, the U.S.S.R. would regard Bulgaria as a foe? He felt that such a statement might have a great influence on Bulgaria's attitude because of her relationship with the Soviets. He suggested that the Foreign Secretaries study this matter, also particularly as to the methods to be used and the results which might be expected. He said that he personally felt that the results might well be decisive, particularly in their moral effect. He said that Turkey, being an ally of Germany in the last war and now turning against her, would have a profound effect on the remainder of the Balkans. He pointed to Rumania's desire to present an unconditional surrender at this time and to other indications of unrest in the Balkans, as evidence of the fact that Turkey's entry into the war would have a great effect.

THE PRIME MINISTER concluded by saying he felt that the whole Mediterranean situation should be carefully examined to see what could be done to take weight off the Soviet front.

MARSHAL STALIN said, as far as the question of the U.S.S.R. versus Bulgaria is concerned, as soon as Turkey comes into the war we can consider that the matter is closed. The U.S.S.R. will take care of Bulgaria. If Turkey declares war on Bulgaria, the U.S.S.R. will declare war on Bulgaria. Even under these circumstances Turkey will not enter the war.

As far as military matters are concerned, *MARSHAL STALIN* said he understood that two or three divisions would be made available to help Turkey should she come into the war or to help in the Partisan movement in Yugoslavia. There is no difference of opinion on this point. We feel it desirable to help in Yugoslavia and to give two or three divisions if it would be necessary to do so. The Soviets do not think, however, that this is an important matter. Even the event of the entry of Turkey into the war or the occupation of Rhodes is not the most important thing. If we are here in order to discuss military questions, among all the military questions for discussion we, the U.S.S.R., find *OVERLORD* the most important and decisive. *MARSHAL STALIN* said he would like to call the attention of those present to the importance of not creating diversions from the most important operation in order to carry out secondary operations. He suggested that the ad hoc committee, which was created yesterday, should be given a definite task as to what they were to discuss. He said if a committee is created in the U.S.S.R., we always give that committee a specific directive or instructions. *MARSHAL STALIN* suggested that the military ad hoc committee be given a specific directive. He said it was, of course, true that the U.S.S.R. needed help and that is why the representatives of the Soviet are here at this conference. He said the Soviets expect help from those who are willing to fulfill Operation *OVERLORD*. The question now was what shall be the directive to the ad hoc committee? What shall be the instructions that should be given to the committee under the guidance of General Brooke? First of all, this directive must be specific with regard to the fact that *OVERLORD* should not be postponed and must be carried out by the limiting date. Secondly, the directive to the committee should state that Operation *OVERLORD* must be reinforced by a landing in the South of France a month or two before undertaking the *OVERLORD* assault. If not possible two or three months earlier, then the landing in the South of France should be at the same time. If a landing can not be effected in the South of France at the same time as *OVERLORD*, possibly this operation could be mounted a little later than *OVERLORD*.

MARSHAL STALIN thought this operation in the South of France would be an auxiliary or supporting operation and would help and be considerably effective in contributing toward *OVERLORD*. On the other hand, operations against Rhodes and other operations in the Mediterranean would be diversions. Operations in the South of France would influence and contribute directly to *OVERLORD*. He said that the directive to the ad hoc committee must also state that the appointment of the Supreme Commander for *OVERLORD* should be made forthwith. The decision regarding the *OVERLORD* commander should be made here in Tehran. If it can not be done here, it should be done within a week at the latest. The Soviets believe that until such a commander has been appointed, no success from *OVERLORD* can be expected in the matter of organization for this operation. He added that it is the task of the British and the United States representatives to agree on the commander for *OVERLORD*. The U.S.S.R. does not enter into the matter of this selection but the Soviets definitely want to know who he will be. The above are the points of the directive which should be given to the ad hoc committee, and the work of this committee should be completed immediately.

MARSHAL STALIN asked the conference to seriously consider the points which he had just outlined. He added that he felt if the three points he had made were carried out, they would result in the successful and rapid accomplishment of *OVERLORD*.

THE PRESIDENT said he was tremendously interested in hearing all angles of the subject from *OVERLORD* to Turkey. He said that if we are all agreed on *OVERLORD*, the next question would be regarding the timing of *OVERLORD*. Therefore, if we come down to a matter of questions, the point is either to carry out *OVERLORD* at the appointed time or to agree to the postponement of that operation to some time in June or July. There are only one or two other operations in the Mediterranean which might use landing craft and air forces from some other theater. *THE PRESIDENT* said there are two dangers in creating a delay in *OVERLORD*. One of them is that the use of two or three divisions in the Eastern Mediterranean would cause a delay to *OVERLORD* and would necesitate the sending of certain landing craft for those operations which in turn could not be withdrawn from the Eastern Mediterranean in time to return for the *OVERLORD* date. He said it was believed that once we are committed to specific operations in the Eastern Mediterranean, we would have to make it a supreme operation and we probably could not then pull out of it.

MARSHAL STALIN observed that maybe it would be necessary to utilize some of the means for *OVERLORD* in order to carry out operations in the Eastern Mediterranean.

THE PRESIDENT continued that in the Balkans and Yugoslavia he believed all aid should be given which could be possibly sent to Tito without making any particular commitment which would interfere with *OVERLORD*. He said he thought that we should consider the value of the 40 divisions the Germans have in the Balkans and if we can do certain operations with a minimum effort, these divisions might be placed in a position where they could no longer be of any value.

THE PRESIDENT said he felt that commando raids should be undertaken in the Balkans and that we should send all possible supplies to Tito in order to require Germany to keep their divisions there.

MARSHAL STALIN said that in Yugoslavia the Germans have eight divisions; they have five divisions in Greece, and three or four divisions in Bulgaria. He stated that the figures given by the Prime Minister regarding German divisions in the Balkans were wrong.

In reply to a question, *MARSHAL STALIN* said there were 25 German divisions now in France.

THE PRESIDENT said we should therefore work out plans to contain these German divisions. This should be done on such a scale as not to divert means from doing *OVERLORD* at the agreed time.

MARSHAL STALIN observed, regarding the President's statement, "You are right"—"You are right."

THE PRESIDENT said we again come back to the problem of the timing for *OVERLORD*. It was believed that it would be good for *OVERLORD* to take place about 1 May, or certainly not later than 15 May or 20 May, if possible.

THE PRIME MINISTER said that he could not agree to that.

MARSHAL STALIN said he observed at yesterdays conference that nothing will come out of these proposed diversions. In his opinion *OVERLORD* should be done in May. He added that there would be suitable weather in May.

THE PRIME MINISTER said he did not believe that the attitudes of those present on this matter were very far apart. He said he (the Prime Minister) was going to do everything in the power of His Majesty's Government to begin *OVERLORD* at the earliest possible moment. However, he did not think that the many great possibilities in the Mediterranean should be ruthlessly cast aside as valueless merely on the question of a month's delay in *OVERLORD*.

MARSHAL STALIN said all the Mediterranean operations are diversions, aside from that into Southern France, and that he had no interest in any other operations other than those into Southern France. He accepted the importance of these other operations but definitely considered that they are diversions.

THE PRIME MINISTER continued that in the British view their large armies in the Mediterranean should not be idle for some six months but should be, together with the United States Allies, working toward the defeat of Germany in Italy, and at the same time be active elsewhere. He said for the British to be inert for nearly six months would be a wrong use of forces, and in his opinion would lay the British open to reproach from the Soviets for having the Soviets bear nearly all the burden of land fighting.

MARSHAL STALIN said that he did not wish the British to think that the Soviets wished them to do nothing.

THE PRIME MINISTER said if all the landing craft were taken away from the Mediterranean they will not affect the battle. Marshal Stalin must remember that at Moscow it was stated under what conditions *OVERLORD* could be mounted and that under those conditions alone could it be launched. Operation *OVERLORD* was predicated on the assumption that not more than 12 German mobile dvisions would be located behind the coastal troops, and furthermore, that not more than 15 reinforcement divisions could enter the fray within 60 days. He said that that was the basis on which he (Mr. Churchill) had stated the British would do *OVERLORD*. On those conditions, the Allies will have to utilize as many divisions in the Balkans and so forth as are necessary to contain German troops. If Turkey comes into the war, this will be particularly necessary. The German divisions now in Italy have largely come from France. Consequently, if there should be a slackening off in Italy, it would mean that the German divisions would withdraw and appear in the South of France to meet us there. On the other hand, if we do the Eastern Mediterranean, we will contain more German divisions and will create conditions indispensable to the success of *OVERLORD*.

MARSHAL STALIN inquired, "What if there are 13 divisions, not 12?"

THE PRIME MINISTER replied, "Naturally." He continued by saying there was one more word about Turkey. All are agreed here that she should enter the war. If Turkey does not enter the war, then that ends that. If she does enter, the only necessary thing to do would be to use an air attack from the Turkish bases in Anatolia and an operation to take the Island of Rhodes. For the purpose of the Rhodes operation, one assault division would be ready in the near future and that would be sufficient. Having gotten Rhodes and Turkish air bases, a course could be steered north and operations undertaken to drive and starve all German divisions out of the Aegean and then open the Dardanelles. Essentially, these specific operations were limited operations, and therefore they could not be considered as military commitments of an indefinite

552

character. If Turkey comes into the war and we get the air bases, it would be a simple matter to open the Straits. If Turkey does not come in, we do not pay any further attention to the matter. If Turkey comes into the war and we hold Rhodes and the Aegean, we will be able to use the air squadrons now in Egypt. All could move forward and help the Soviets. They now play no part except in the defense of Egypt. We can use the same troops which are now guarding Egypt to drive the Germans back. This is a big matter and should not be lightly considered.

THE PRIME MINISTER said he felt that our future will suffer great misfortune if we do not get Turkey into the war, for in such case troops and planes will stand idle.

THE PRIME MINISTER added that he agreed with General Marshall in his statement that the chief problem is one of transportation across the water and that that matter is largely a question of landing craft. He said that the British were prepared to go into the matter in great detail, and a very small number of landing craft could make the subsidiary operations feasible. If these landing craft cannot be kept in the Mediterranean because of *OVERLORD* or cannot possibly be found from some other arrangement such as the Indian Ocean, then this matter should be resolved by the technical committee. A landing in Southern France will require a great number of landing craft. He begged that this important point should be carefully weighed.

THE PRIME MINISTER said in conclusion that he accepted the proposal that a directive should be drawn up for this technical committee. He further suggested that the Soviet Government draw up terms of reference, that the United States draw up terms of reference, that Great Britain draw up terms of reference and then he felt sure that all three nations would not be far apart.

THE PRESIDENT inquired how long will the conference be in session until the staff comes to a conclusion on these matters.

THE PRIME MINISTER in this connection said he can give his own opinion on behalf of the British Government tonight.

In reply to a question from Marshal Stalin as to how many French divisions were in the Allied Armies and how many troops there were in French divisions, *THE PRESIDENT* replied he understood there were now five combat divisions and four more will soon be ready, making a total of nine. Some of these divisions are now engaged in Sardinia and Corsica.

GENERAL MARSHALL said that the French Corps is to become a part of the U.S. 5th Army in Italy and will occupy the left flank. He said that one division was now en route to the Front and will get a trial of battle. As a result of this it would be possible to judge better regarding the employment of other French divisions. All equipment for the French divisions is now in North Africa. There was some delay in four or five divisions being brought up to strength and completing their training. He said the French divisions were training with United States equipment and under the instruction of United States officers and non-commissioned officers.

In reply to a question from Marshal Stalin as to how many men there were in these French divisions, *GENERAL MARSHALL* replied, French divisions have the same number of men as the United States—15,000 men per division. The men are mostly native troops with French officers and some non-coms. In the armored command only one quarter are native troops.

MARSHAL STALIN said, with regard to the remarks of the Prime Minister, if Turkey does not enter the war it cannot be helped.

THE PRIME MINISTER replied if Turkey does not come into the war, he had no intention of asking for any troops for operations in Rhodes or Asia Minor.

In reply to a question from Marshal Stalin as to how many more days this conference would continue, *THE PRESIDENT* said that he was willing to stay here until the conference is finished.

THE PRIME MINISTER said he would stay here forever, if necessary.

THE PRESIDENT suggested that if the three Chiefs of State were in agreement, the committee need not have any written directive because they have been confronted with every suggestion made at this afternoon's meeting. He said if the Chiefs of State could agree on the proceedings of the afternoon conference as a directive, then the staff would definitely have only one directive.

MARSHAL STALIN said he considered that the ad hoc committee was unnecessary. It could not raise any new questions for the military conference. He believed that all that was necessary to be solved was the selection of the commander for *OVERLORD*, the date for *OVERLORD* and the matter of supporting operations to be undertaken in Southern France in connection with *OVERLORD*. He furthermore believed that the committee of Foreign Secretaries proposed by the Prime Minister was unnecessary. He considered that all matters could be solved here and that committees were unnecessary. He said he must leave on the first, anyway, but that he might stay over until the second of December if it had to be—then he must go away. He said that he must know when he can get away. There are two days remaining, the 30th of November and the first of December. He said the President would remember that he had said he could come to the conference for three or four days.

THE PRESIDENT then read a proposed directive for the Ad Hoc Committee of the Chiefs of Staff:

"1. The Committee of the Chiefs of Staff will assume that *OVERLORD* is the dominating operation.

"2. The Committee recommends that subsidiary operation(s) be included in the Mediterranean, taking into consideration that any delay should not affect *OVERLORD*."

MARSHAL STALIN observed that there was no mention regarding the date of *OVERLORD* in the proposed directive. He said for the U.S.S.R. it is important to know the date *OVERLORD* will be mounted in order that the Soviets could prepare the blow on their side. He said he insisted on knowing the date.

THE PRESIDENT remarked that the date for *OVERLORD* had been fixed at Quebec and that only some much more important matter could possibly affect that date, that is to say, this was the President's view.

THE PRIME MINISTER said he would like to have an opportunity to reply to the President's remarks. He said there was no decisive difference in principle. He would be very glad to stay until the first of December and make a decision. It was not clear to him what the President's plans were, however. He said he was in favor of the continuance of the ad hoc committee if that could be done. With regard to the political subcommittee, Marshal Stalin has clarified matters with regard to Bulgaria and help to Yugoslavia. Therefore, the meeting between the two Foreign Secretaries and Mr. Hopkins would be of great advantage. It would throw light on the problems and would be particularly important on the political questions. He would be grateful for Marshal Stalin's prompt answers to his questions. If it were decided to do so, *THE PRIME MINISTER* thought that on the whole this procedure would be of advantage. He considered that the timing of the supreme Operation *OVERLORD* as regards any subsidiary operations would be most necessary as a condition for the success of *OVERLORD*. Furthermore, he believed that the ad hoc staff committee should recommend what subsidiary operations should be carried out. *THE PRIME MINISTER* believed that we should take more time in drawing up a proper directive to the ad hoc committee.

THE PRESIDENT said he found that his staff places emphasis on *OVERLORD*. While on the other hand the Prime Minister and his staff also emphasize *OVERLORD*, nevertheless the United States does not feel that *OVERLORD* should be put off.

THE PRESIDENT questioned whether it would not be possible for the ad hoc committee to go ahead with their deliberations without any further directive and to produce an answer by tomorrow morning.

MARSHAL STALIN questioned, "What can such a committee do?" He said, "We Chiefs of State have more power and more authority than a committee. General Brooke cannot force our opinions and there are many questions which can be decided only by us." He said he would like to ask if the British are thinking seriously of *OVERLORD* only in order to satisfy the U.S.S.R.

THE PRIME MINISTER replied that if the conditions specified at Moscow regarding *OVERLORD* should exist, he firmly believed it would be England's duty to hurl every ounce of strength she had across the Channel at the Germans.

THE PRESIDENT observed that in an hour a very good dinner would be awaiting all and people would be very hungry. He suggested that the staffs should meet tomorrow morning and discuss the matter.

MARSHAL STALIN said that he believed that that was unnecessary. The staffs will not in any way speed our work; they will only delay matters. It is proper to decide matters more quickly.

THE PRIME MINISTER said he thought the talks of the foreign officers would be most profitable.

THE PRESIDENT observed that a few political problems might be discussed during luncheon together by the Foreign Secretaries and Mr. Hopkins in a *different* place from that where the Chiefs of State had their luncheon.

MARSHAL STALIN commented, "Then at four o'clock tomorrow afternoon we will have our conference again."

THE PRESIDENT suggested that the Chiefs of State have luncheon together tomorrow about one thirty.

EUREKA CONFERENCE

MINUTES OF PLENARY SESSION
BETWEEN THE U.S.A., GREAT BRITAIN AND THE U.S.S.R.,

HELD IN THE RUSSIAN LEGATION, TEHRAN, IRAN,
ON TUESDAY, 30 NOVEMBER 1943 AT 1600

PRESENT

United States	*British*
President Roosevelt	Prime Minister Churchill
Mr. Harry L. Hopkins	Mr. Anthony Eden
Mr. Averill Harriman	Field Marshal Sir John Dill
Admiral W. D. Leahy, USN	General Sir Alan Brooke
General G. C. Marshall, USA	Admiral Sir Andrew B. Cunningham
Admiral E. J. King, USN	Air Chief Marshal
General H. H. Arnold, USA	Sir Charles F. A. Portal
Lt. Gen. B. B. Somervell, USA	Lt. General Hastings L. Ismay
Maj. Gen. J. R. Deane, USA	Lt. General Martel
Capt. F. B. Royal, USN, Secretary	Brigadier L. C. Hollis, Secretary
Mr. C. E. Bohlen (Interpreter)	Sir Archibald Kerr
Capt. H. H. Ware, USA (Interpreter)	Major Birse (Interpreter)

U.S.S.R.

Marshal Stalin

Mr. Molotov
Marshal Voroshiloff

One Secretary

Mr. Pavlov (Interpreter)

In opening the meeting, *THE PRESIDENT* said he assumed that most of those present were familiar with what had transpired at the meeting of the British and American staffs earlier in the day, but he suggested that General Brooke be asked to read the conclusions which were reached at that meeting.

MARSHAL STALIN and *THE PRIME MINISTER* agreed.

GENERAL BROOKE said that at the meeting of the British and American staffs they had agreed to recommend to the President and Prime Minister that they should inform Marshal Stalin that the Anglo-American forces would launch *OVERLORD* during the month of May, in conjunction with a supporting operation against the South of France, on the largest scale that would be permitted by the landing craft available at that time.

THE PRIME MINISTER said it is of course understood that we shall keep in close touch with Marshal Stalin and the Soviet military authorities in order that all operations may be coordinated with each other. He said that the Anglo-American-Soviet forces would be closing in on Germany from all parts of a circle and it was essential that the pressure be exerted by all forces at the same moment. For this purpose he proposed to keep the Soviet authorities informed of the Anglo-American plans. He added that it would be possible to hold 8 to 10 German divisions on the Italian front, and he expressed the hope that the Yugoslavs could continue their good work in holding German divisions in that country. He said that if Turkey could be brought into the war, so much the better, and emphasized again the necessity for the three great Powers to work together as one team.

MARSHAL STALIN said that he understood the importance of the decision that had been reached by the Anglo-American staffs. He emphasized that there would be difficulties in the beginning and possibly dangers. The greatest danger would be that at the time of the attack the Germans might endeavor to transfer divisions from the Eastern Front to meet it and attempt to prevent its success. In order to deny the Germans freedom of action and permit them to move their forces to the West he stated that the Soviets would undertake to organize a large-scale offensive against the Germans in May in order to contain the maximum number of German divisions on the Eastern Front and thus remove the difficulties for *OVERLORD*. He added that he had already made such a statement to the President and Prime Minister but felt it necessary to repeat it at the Plenary Session of the conference.

THE PRESIDENT said that the Marshal's statement concerning the timing and coordination of operations was extremely satisfactory and it forestalled a question on that subject he was about to ask. He suggested that now that the staffs of the three nations had gotten together it was essential they should maintain close contact with each other, with particular emphasis on making certain that all future operations were timed with relation to each other.

THE PRESIDENT then said he had told Marshal Stalin that the next step was the appointment of the Supreme Commander for the *OVERLORD* operation. He said that he and the Prime Minister would take up this matter with their staffs and make the decision within three or four days, certainly soon after their arrival in Cairo.

THE PRESIDENT said that the only military matters remaining for consideration were details of the *OVERLORD* operation which would have to be worked out between the combined British and American staffs, and suggested it might be more convenient for them to return to Cairo at once for this purpose.

After ascertaining from Marshal Stalin that he had no more matters which he wished presented to the Combined British and American Staffs, *THE PRESIDENT* and *PRIME MINISTER* agreed that the staffs should return to Cairo on the following day.

THE PRIME MINISTER said there are many details about the *OVERLORD* operation which remain to be settled. He said that the necessary landing craft would have to be found, but he could not believe that the two nations, with their great volume of production, could not make the necessary landing craft available. He said also that he would like to add weight to the operation as it is now planned, especially in the initial assault. In all events, he wished to make sure that the armed forces of the three nations would be in heavy action on the Continent of Europe during the month of June. If this were so, he added, it would make it very difficult for "that man." If Hitler attempts to meet the Soviet attack from the east, the Anglo-American forces will move in on him. On the other hand, if he attempts to stop the Anglo-American forces, the Soviet forces will be able to advance into Germany.

MARSHAL STALIN said that he understood the necessity for the detailed staff planning and concurred that it would be a good idea for the staffs to return to Cairo at once.

THE PRIME MINISTER then indicated that since the military business of the conference was concluded, there were some political matters of extreme importance which remained to be decided. He hoped it would be possible for the three Heads of State to meet on the first and second of December and not to leave Tehran until December 3. He said it would be well if they remained until all questions of importance had been decided. He indicated that he was prepared to delay his departure, and *THE PRESIDENT* and *MARSHAL STALIN* agreed to stay the extra day.

THE PRESIDENT brought up the subject of the communique, particularly as it referred to the military decisions. He suggested that the military staffs draft something for the President and Prime Minister's approval.

MARSHAL STALIN agreed that this should be done insofar as military matters taken up at the conference were concerned.

THE PRIME MINISTER said he thought the communique should strike the note that all future military operations were to be concerted between the three great Powers.

MARSHAL STALIN added, certainly those in Europe from both the east and west.

THE PRIME MINISTER said that the preparations for *OVERLORD* are bound to be known to the enemy. Numerous depots are being constructed in Southern England, the entire appearance of the coast is changing and photographs indicate these changes in detail.

MARSHAL STALIN said that it was difficult, if not impossible, to hide such a large operation from the enemy.

THE PRIME MINISTER then asked if any arrangements had been made to provide a combined cover plan for the operations in May as between the three great Powers.

MARSHAL STALIN said that on such occasions the Soviets had achieved success by the construction of false tanks, airplanes and airfields. They move these items to sectors in which no operations are planned, and such movements are immediately picked up by the German intelligence. In sectors from which blows are to be launched, all movements are made quietly and mostly under cover of darkness. In this manner they had often succeeded in deceiving the Germans. He noted that at times up to 5,000 false tanks and

2,000 false airplanes had been used, as well as the construction of a number of airfields which were not actually intended to be used. Another method of deception practiced by the Red Army was by the use of radio. Unit commanders communicate freely by radio giving the Germans false information and evoke immediate attacks from the German air forces in areas where such attacks can do no harm.

THE PRIME MINISTER observed that truth deserves a bodyguard of lies.

MARSHAL STALIN said, "This is what we call military cunning."

THE PRIME MINISTER said that he considered it rather military diplomacy. He suggested that arrangements be made for liaison to be established between the three great Powers as regards the deception and propaganda methods to be adopted.

It was agreed that the Chiefs of State and their Foreign Ministers should meet on the following day at 1600.

INDEX

A

AEGEAN (*See also* Mediterranean)

Assault shipping for, 347
Opening the Aegean, 271
Operations in, *385, 395*

AGENDA FOR "SEXTANT"

See SEXTANT Conference

AIRFIELDS

Calcutta, *403*
Japanese, in Southeast Asia, *483, 485*
Statement of the Prime Minister on Corsican, *523*
Turkish, *446*
V.L.R. airfields in the China-Burma-India, 109, 112, 113

AIR FORCES (AXIS) (*See also* Germany)

German fighter production, 121, *459*

AIR FORCES (U.N.)

At Calcutta, *403*
Command of U.S. Strategic, *504*
In Italy, *445*
Long range fighters, *456*
OVERLORD, *540, 541*
Resources to implement agreed operations, 317
Technical supplies and equipment for, 353
U.S. daylight bombers, *388*

AIR INTELLIGENCE

Air Ministry Intelligence report on Allied air attack and German morale, 181
Report on bomber offensive, 171

AIR ROUTES

Over the "hump," 244, *379*
Russian:
  ALSIB, 223
  Tehran-Moscow, 224
  U.S.-U.K.-Moscow, 224
Southeast Asia, *483*

AMPHIBIOUS OPERATIONS

(*See also* Operations)

Naval Forces, 287
Southeast Asia, 64, 67, 243, 257, *391, 483*
  Commitment to the Generalissimo, *394, 398*
Southeast Asia alternative to *BUCCANEER*, 307, 311, *399, 498, 505*
South of France, 287
  Air forces supporting, 288
  Assault shipping and craft, 289, *466*
  MT Stores and shipping, 289
  Personnel shipping, 288
  Land forces, 288

ANDAMAN ISLANDS, *396, 484*

Value of, *392*

ANTI-U-BOAT WARFARE

Aircraft, 81, 84
Intercept Receivers, 84
Rocket projectiles, 84
Sono-radio buoys, 84
Surface craft, 81, 83

"ANVIL"

Assumed conditions for, 286
Assault shipping for, 346, 366, *393, 399, 402*
EUREKA Military Conference discussion, *530*
Naval forces for, 330
Planning for Operation, *393, 466, 493, 522*
Statement by Marshal Stalin re, *521*
Statement by Prime Minister re, *520*
Target date for, 321, *390*

ARNOLD, GENERAL H. H.

Statements in reference to:
  Aircraft supplies in Southeast Asia, *485*
  Air operations in Southeast Asia, *482*
  Air superiority, *459*
  Air transport requirements for *ANVIL*, *494*
  Command of U.S. Strategic Air Forces in the European-Mediterranean area, *504*
  Date for *BUCCANEER*, *398*
  Facilities in the Azores, *508*
  Japanese Airfields in Southeast Asia, *483*

Note: Italic numerals refer to pages in minutes of meeting.
Plain type numerals refer to pages in C. C. S. Papers.

INDEX

Note: Italic numerals refer to pages in minutes of meeting.
Plain type numerals refer to pages in C. C. S. Papers.

INDEX

Note: *Italic numerals refer to pages in minutes of meeting.*
Plain type numerals refer to pages in C. C. S. Papers.

INDEX

Note: Italic numerals refer to pages in minutes of meeting.
Plain type numerals refer to pages in C. C. S. Papers.

INDEX

Note: Italic numerals refer to pages in minutes of meeting.
Plain type numerals refer to pages in C.C.S. Papers.

INDEX

INDEX

Note: Italic numerals refer to pages in minutes of meeting.
Plain type numerals refer to pages in C. C. S. Papers.

INDEX

Note: Italic numerals refer to pages in minutes of meeting.
Plain type numerals refer to pages in C. C. S. Papers.

INDEX

Note: Italic numerals refer to pages in minutes of meeting.
Plain type numerals refer to pages in C. C. S. Papers.

INDEX

J

JAPAN

American and British forces available for deployment against Japan after the defeat of Germany, 265
Basic factors in Japanese situation, 9
CCS decisions re:
  Defeat of Japan, 65, 211, *417*
  Plan for defeat of, 253, *478, 498*
  Specific operations for defeat of, 65, 304, *499*
Defeat of:
  Air forces, 263
  Assault shipping and landing craft, 259
  Disposition of forces, 257
  DRAKE plan, 266
Existing local situation in the Pacific and Far East, 14
General intentions in the Pacific and Far East, 6
"Inner Zone," V.L.R. bombing of, 323
Limitations on Japanese power, 12
MATTTERHORN operation, 67, 263
Military strength, 11
Note on preparations that should be made for possible Russian entry into the war, 261
Over-all plan for defeat of 253, *440, 477 498*
Positional strength, 12
Prospective developments through 1944, 15
Provision of merchant shipping types for the war against Japan, 251, *506*
Psychology and morale, 10
Relationship to the Axis, 9
Relations with subject peoples, 9
Relations with the U.S.S.R., 9
Role of China in defeat of, 212
Schedule of operations for obtaining specific objectives in 1944 (against Japan), 70
Soviet entry of war against, statement by Marshal Stalin, *516*
Specific operations against, in 1944, 256
Specific operations for defeat of, 1944, 66, 69, 99
  Advance along the New Guinea-N.E.I.-Philippine axis, 67
  Carrier-borne raids, 67
  Central, South and Southwest Pacific, 67
  China, 67

Massed carried task forces, 67
North Pacific, 67
Southeast Asia, 67
Strategic and economic position, 10
Strategic reserves, air, ground, naval, 15
Target date.
  V.L.R. bombing of Japan, 71
U.S.S.R. in the war against Japan, 66, 261, *516*
War against, 327

JAPANESE AIRFIELDS IN SOUTHEAST ASIA, *483*

JAPANESE PROPAGANDA, 11

JAPANESE PUPPET TROOPS, 12

JOINT INTELLIGENCE

Subcommittee report on effects of bombing offensive on German war effort, 175, 178

K

KAVIENG

Seizure of, 323
Target date, 70

KING, ADMIRAL E. J.

Statements in reference to:
  Aircraft for Turkey, *465*
  Alternative dates for *OVERLORD*, *457*
  Amphibious lift for *ANVIL*, *455*
  Amphibious operations in the spring, *394*
  Andamans, *396*
  ANVIL, *465*
  Attack on Rabaul, *393*
  BUCCANEER, *396, 399, 400, 491*
  Capture of Ramree, *484*
  Communique on U-boat war, *407*
  Conversion of merchant ships, *393*
  Defeat of Japan, *499*
  Directive to the Supreme Commander, Mediterranean, *464*
  Future conferences, *511*
  Hit-and-run operations, *400*

Note: Italic numerals refer to pages in minutes of meeting.
Plain type numerals refer to pages in C. C. S. Papers.

INDEX

Note: Italic numerals refer to pages in minutes of meeting.
Plain type numerals refer to pages in C. C. S. Papers.

INDEX

Note: Italic numerals refer to pages in minutes of meeting.
Plain type numerals refer to pages in C. C. S. Papers.

INDEX

Note: Italic numerals refer to pages in minutes of meeting. Plain type numerals refer to pages in C. C. S. Papers.

INDEX

Note: Italic numerals refer to pages in minutes of meeting.
Plain type numerals refer to pages in C. C. S. Papers.

INDEX

Note: Italic numerals refer to pages in minutes of meeting.
Plain type numerals refer to pages in C. C. S. Papers.

INDEX

Note: Italic numerals refer to pages in minutes of meeting.
Plain type numerals refer to pages in C. C. S. Papers.

INDEX

Note: Italic numerals refer to pages in minutes of meeting.
Plain type numerals refer to pages in C. C. S. Papers.

INDEX

Note: Italic numerals refer to pages in minutes of meeting.
Plain type numerals refer to pages in C. C. S. Papers.

INDEX

Note: Italic numerals refer to pages in minutes of meeting.
Plain type numerals refer to pages in C. C. S. Papers.

INDEX

Note: Italic numerals refer to pages in minutes of meeting.
Plain type numerals refer to pages in C. C. S. Papers.

INDEX

UNITED CHIEFS OF STAFF

U.S. memorandum on, 216, 305, *411*, *418*, *425*

UNITED KINGDOM

Forces operationally available on 1 May 1944, 325
Training maneuvers, *540*

UNITED STATES CHIEFS OF STAFF

Agenda for *SEXTANT*, 206
Boundaries of the Southeast Asia Command, 42
Command of British and U.S. forces operating against Germany, 226
Control of Strategic Air Forces in Northwest Europe and in the Mediterranean, 105
Estimate of the enemy situation, 1944-Europe, 7
Estimate of the enemy situation, Pacific-Far East, 7
Future operations in the Southeast Asia Command, 64
General progress report on recent operations and future plans in the Pacific, 274
Integrated command of U.S. Strategic Air Forces in the European-Mediterranean area, 94
Operation *RANKIN*, 46
Operations in Southeast Asia Command, 244
Specific operations for the defeat of Germany and her Satellites, 1943-44, 74
Specific operations for the defeat of Japan, 1944, 68
United Chiefs of Staff, 216
Use of facilities in the Azores by U.S. aircraft, 2
V.L.R. airfields (B-29) in the China-Burma-India area, 110

UNITED STATES CONSTRUCTION PROGRAMS, *535*

UNITED STATES STRATEGIC AIR FORCES

(*See also* Combined Bomber Offensive)

Advantages of unity of command in Northwest Europe and the Mediterranean, 105, 108
Control of, in the European-Mediterranean area, 94
Control of Strategic Air Forces in Northwest Europe and the Mediterranean, 100
Coordination of operations, 96
Exploitation of heavy bomber capabilities, 100
Headquarters, 95
Influence of weather on, 100
Necessity for command direction, 97
Responsibility for base service and administrative control, 94

V

VERY LONG RANGE AIRCRAFT

Airfields in the China-Burma-India area, 110, 112, 113
Bombing, 341

VOGELKOP

Seizure of, 323
Target date, 71

VOROSHILOFF, MARSHAL

Statements in reference to:
Air forces for *OVERLORD*, *541*
Cross-Channel operations, *539*
German strength on the Russian front, *539*
Importance of *OVERLORD*, *538*, *539*
Maneuvers in England, *540*
Marshal Stalin's statement concerning his availability for military discussions, *524*
Matters discussed by ad hoc committee, *544*
OVERLORD, *533*, *534*, *542*
U.S. construction programs, *535*

W

WEDEMEYER, MAJ. GENERAL A. C.

Statement in reference to:
Hit-and-run operations in Southeast Asia, *492*

Note: *Italic numerals refer to pages in minutes of meeting.*
Plain type numerals refer to pages in C. C. S. Papers.

INDEX

WILSON, GENERAL SIR H. M.

Y

YUGOSLAVIA (*See also* Balkans)

Note: Italic numerals refer to pages in minutes of meeting.
Plain type numerals refer to pages in C. C. S. Papers.

Lightning Source UK Ltd.
Milton Keynes UK
UKOW011107221012

200893UK00004BA/1/P

9 781780 394862